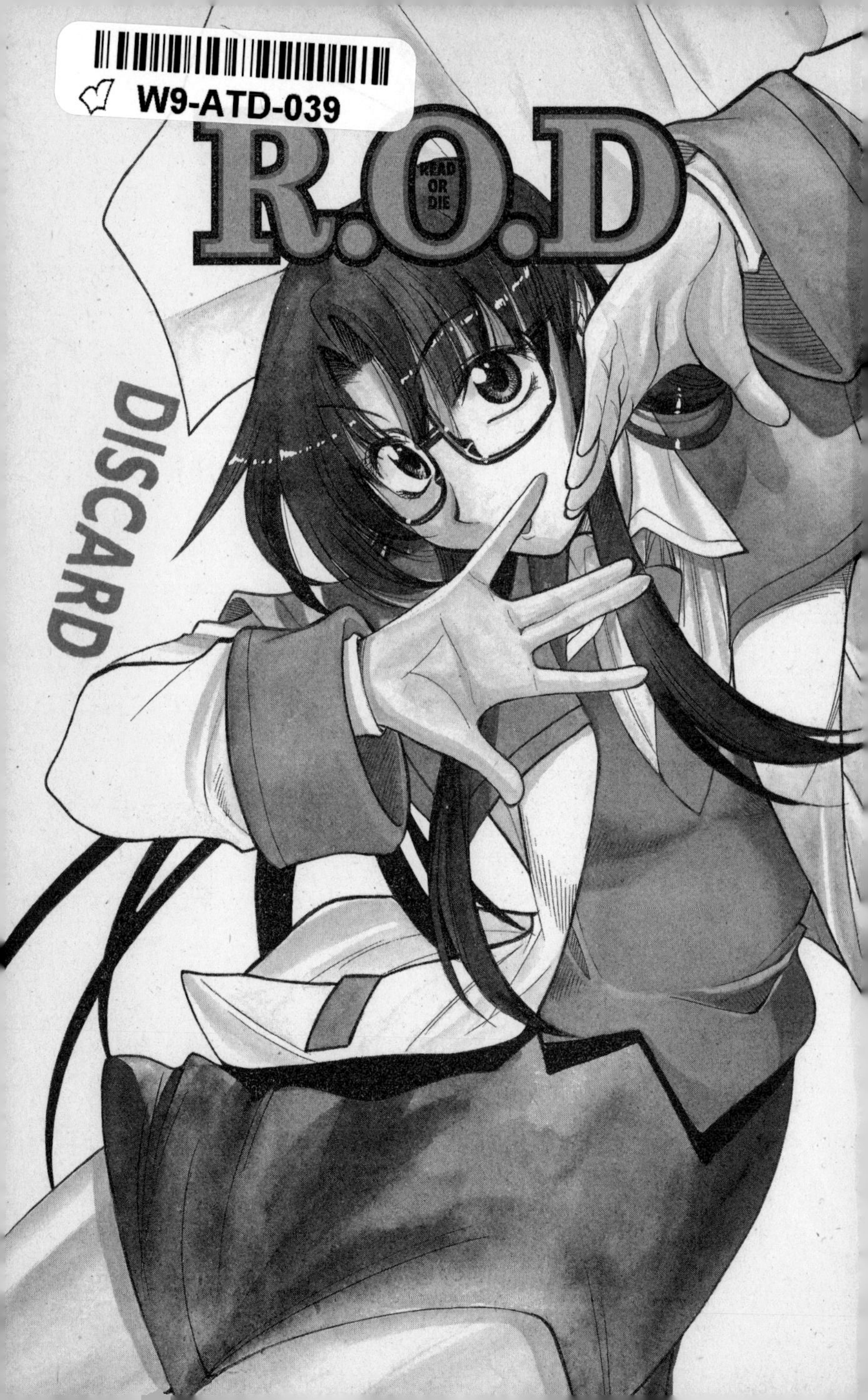
R.O.D
READ OR DIE

CONTENTS

THE LAST LITERATURE D-LINE OF U.K. AGENT YOMIKO READMAN "THE PAPER"

EPISODE ONE

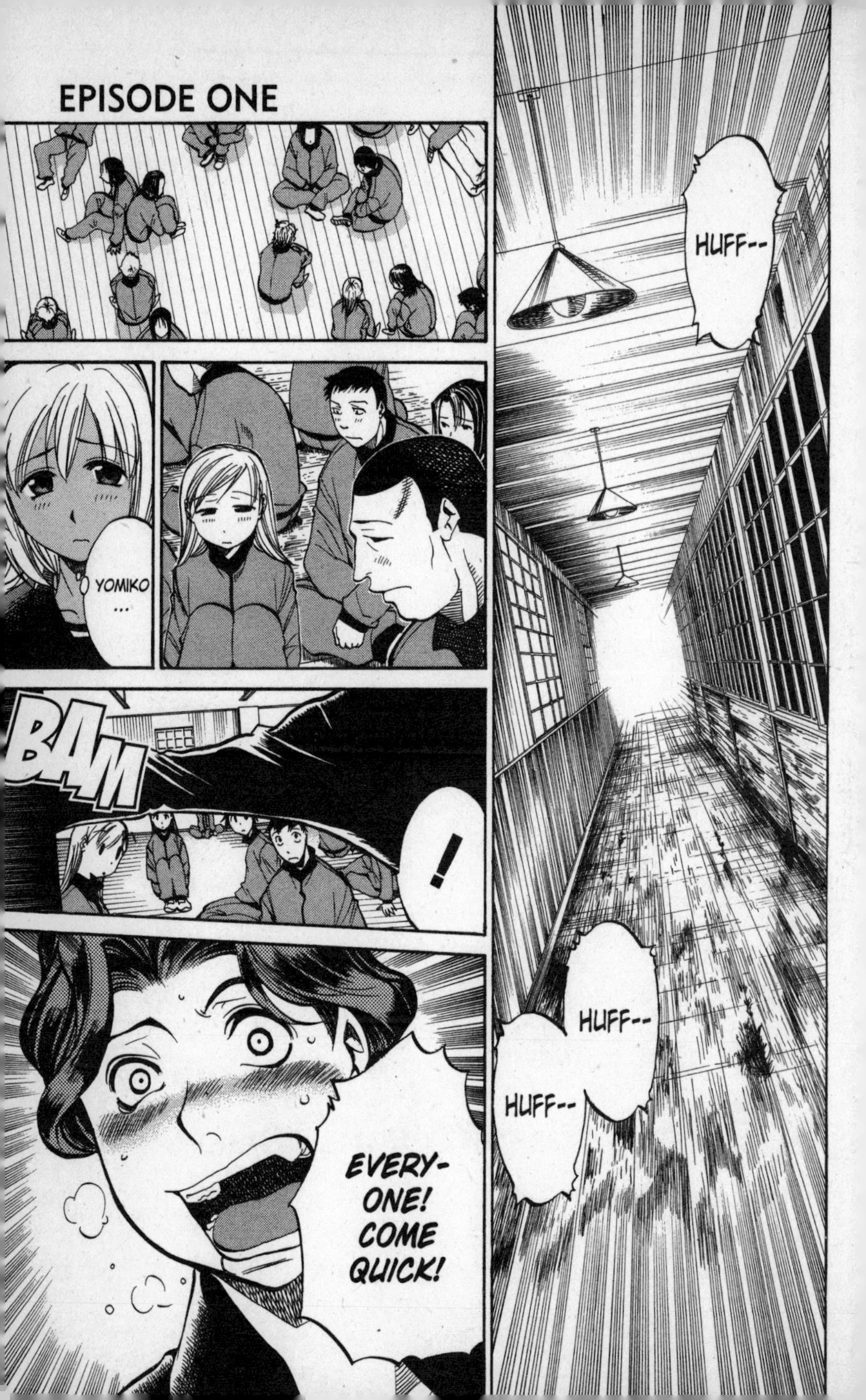
HUFF--
HUFF--
HUFF--
YOMIKO ...
BAM
!
EVERY-ONE! COME QUICK!

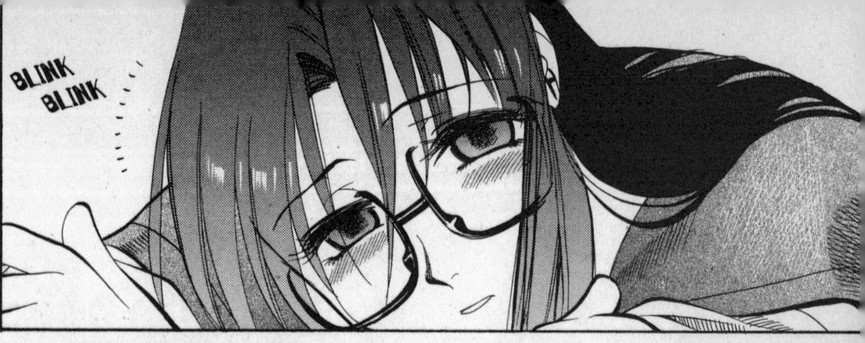
BLINK
BLINK

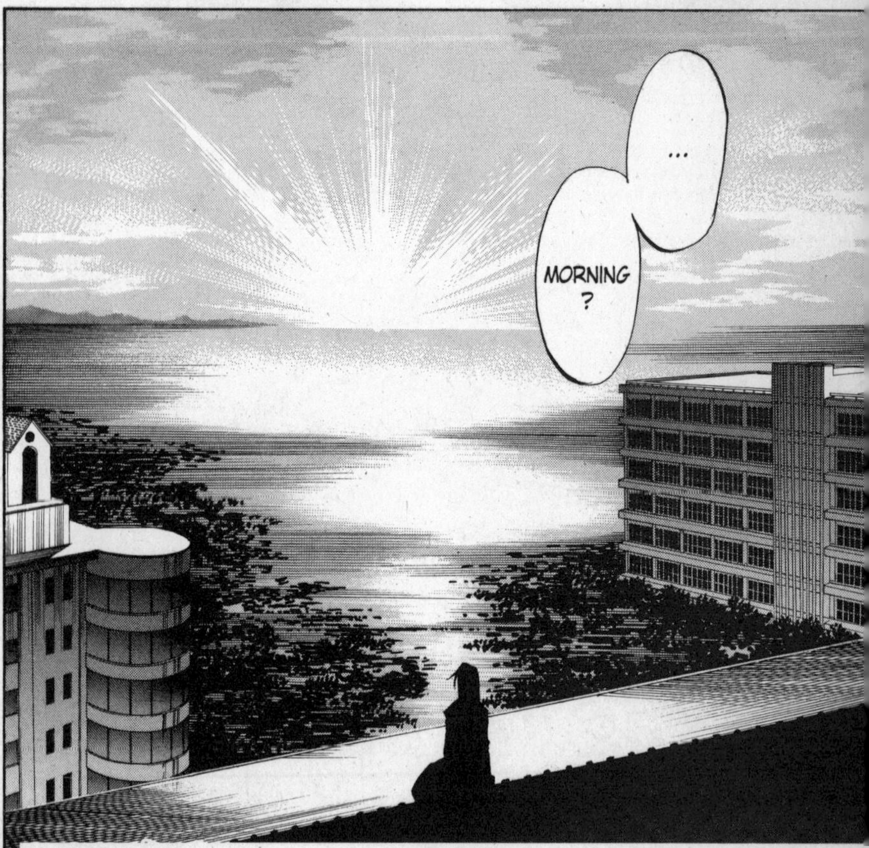
...
MORNING ?

EPISODE ONE

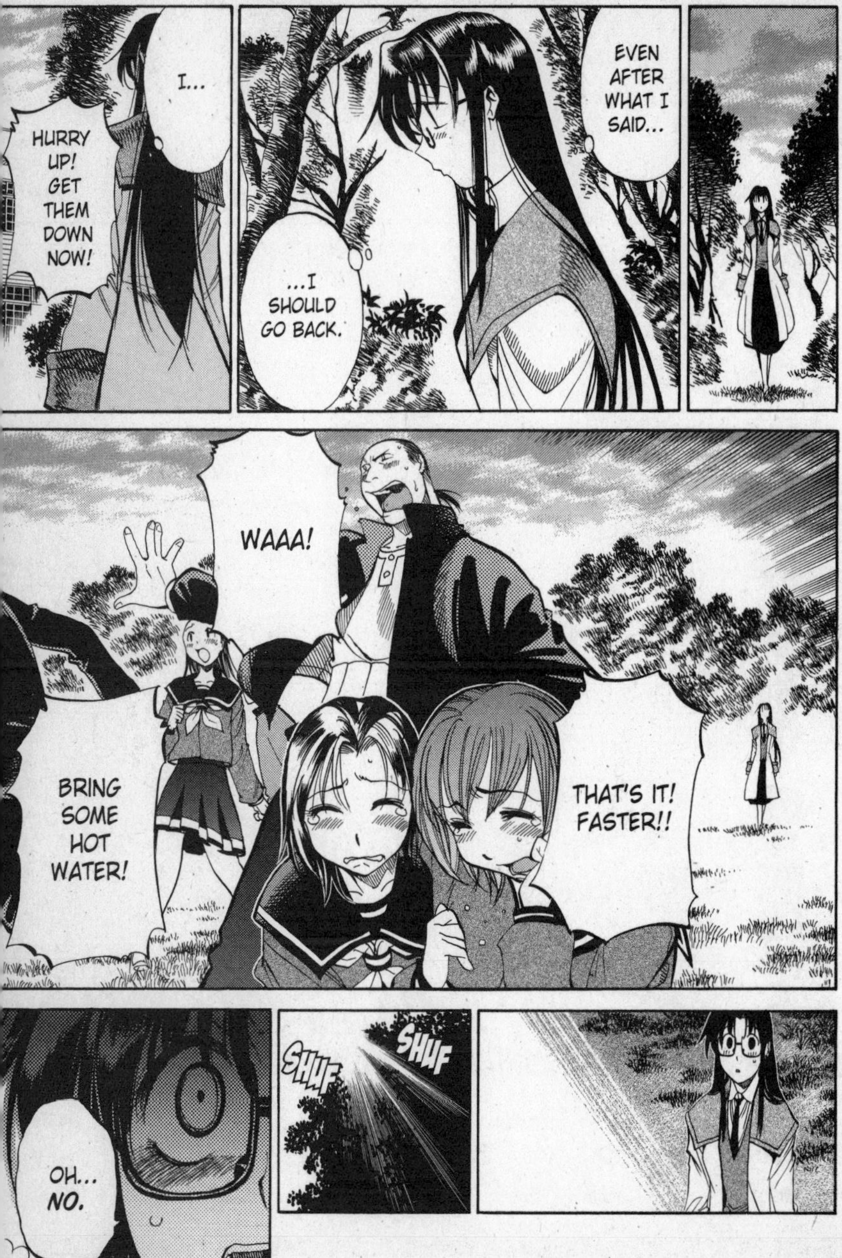
EVEN AFTER WHAT I SAID...
...I SHOULD GO BACK.
I...
HURRY UP! GET THEM DOWN NOW!
WAAA!
THAT'S IT! FASTER!!
BRING SOME HOT WATER!
SHUF
SHUF
OH... NO.

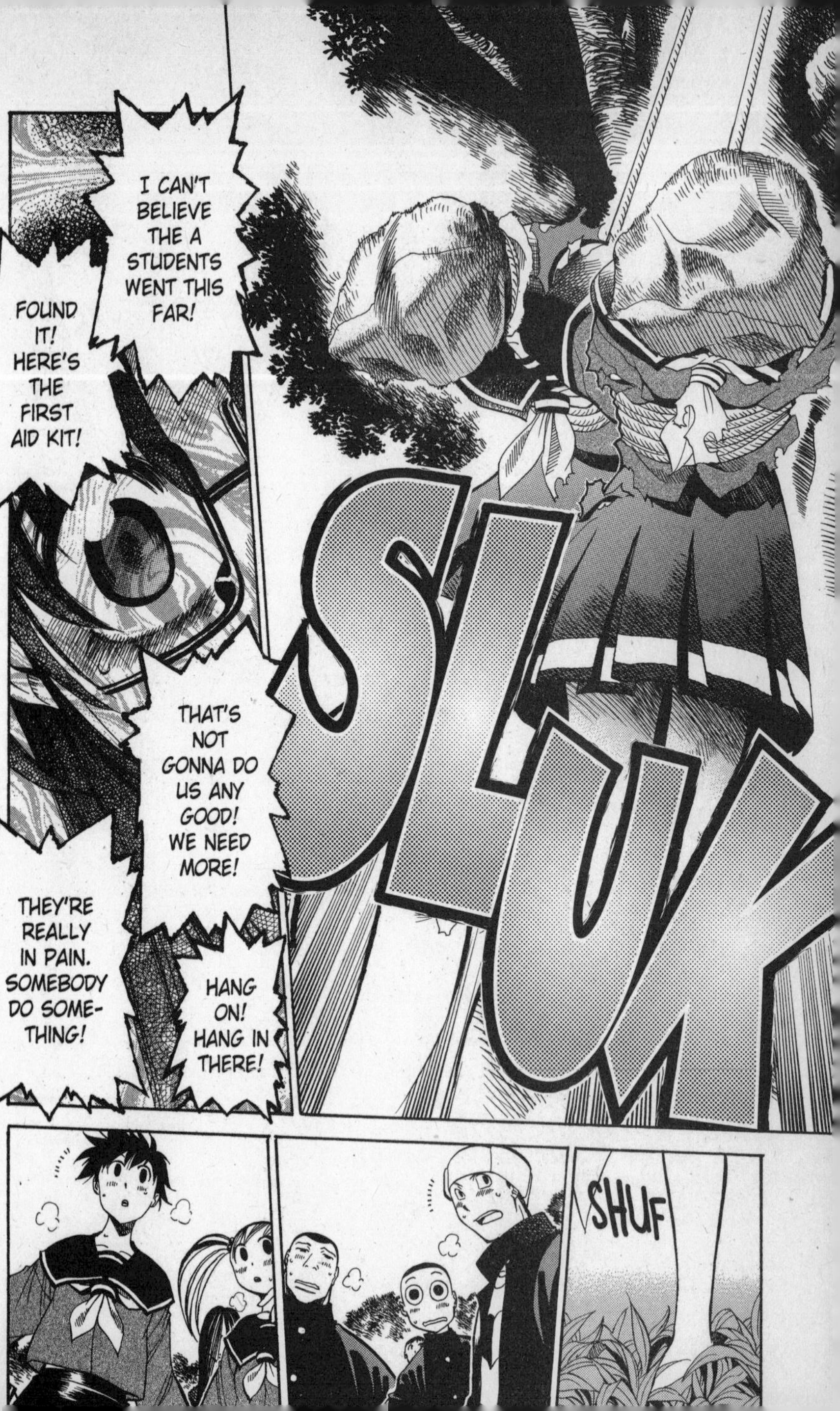
SHUK
I CAN'T BELIEVE THE A STUDENTS WENT THIS FAR!
FOUND IT! HERE'S THE FIRST AID KIT!
THAT'S NOT GONNA DO US ANY GOOD! WE NEED MORE!
HANG ON! HANG IN THERE!
THEY'RE REALLY IN PAIN. SOMEBODY DO SOME-THING!
SHUF

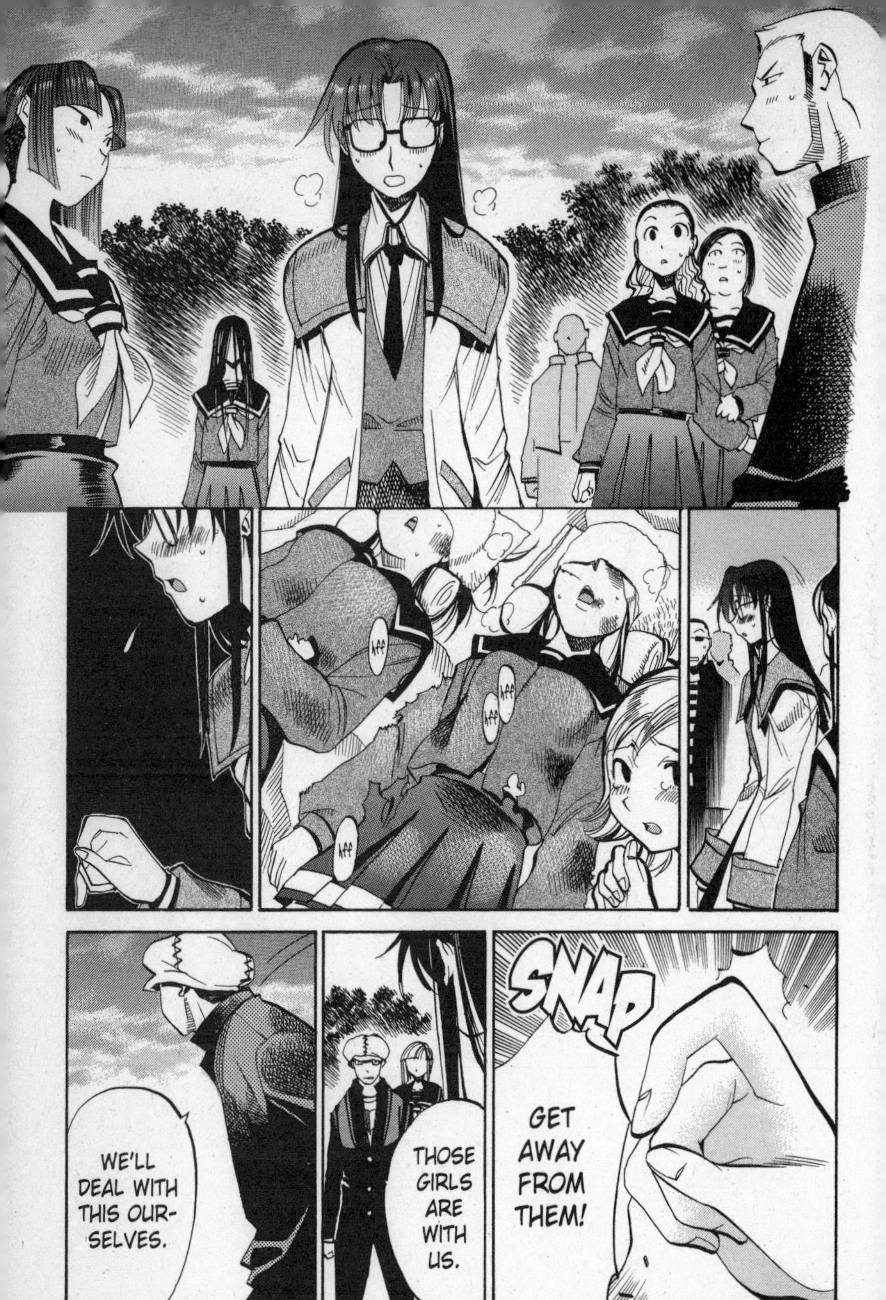
hff
hff
hff
hff
SNAP
GET AWAY FROM THEM!
THOSE GIRLS ARE WITH US.
WE'LL DEAL WITH THIS OUR-SELVES.

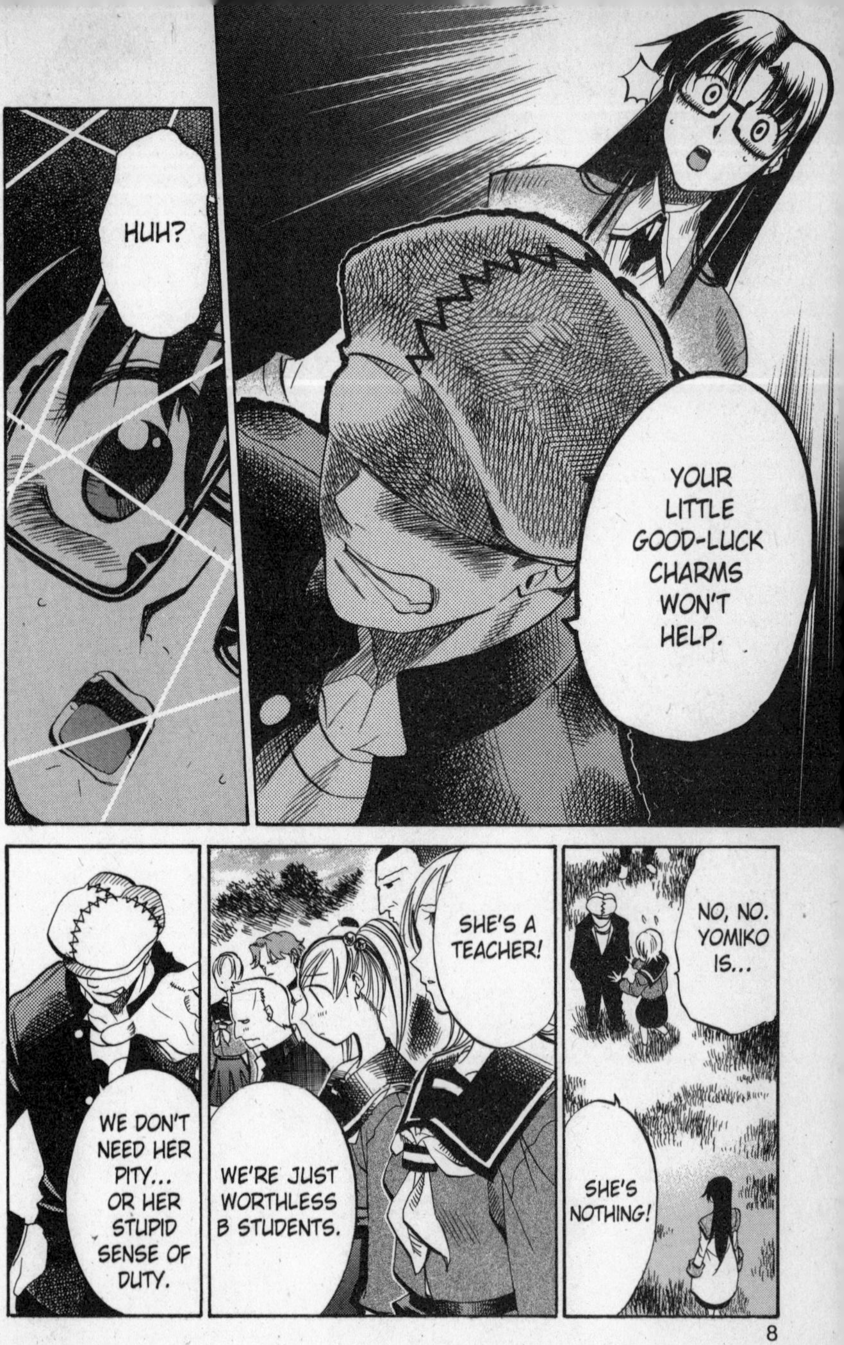
YOUR LITTLE GOOD-LUCK CHARMS WON'T HELP.
HUH?
NO, NO. YOMIKO IS...
SHE'S NOTHING!
SHE'S A TEACHER!
WE'RE JUST WORTHLESS B STUDENTS.
WE DON'T NEED HER PITY... OR HER STUPID SENSE OF DUTY.

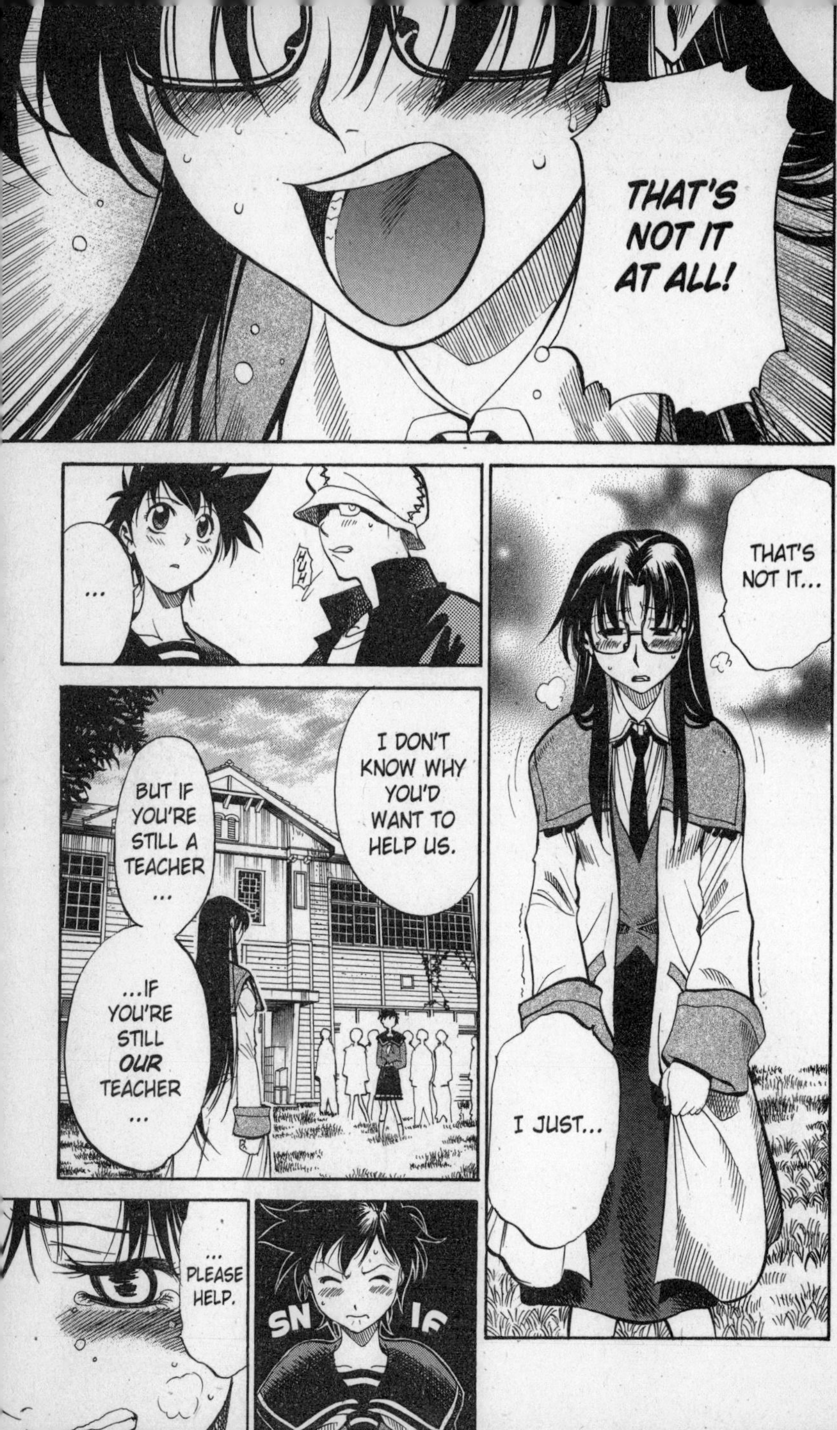
THAT'S NOT IT AT ALL!
THAT'S NOT IT...
I JUST...
...
HUH
I DON'T KNOW WHY YOU'D WANT TO HELP US.
BUT IF YOU'RE STILL A TEACHER...
...IF YOU'RE STILL OUR TEACHER...
SN IF
...PLEASE HELP.

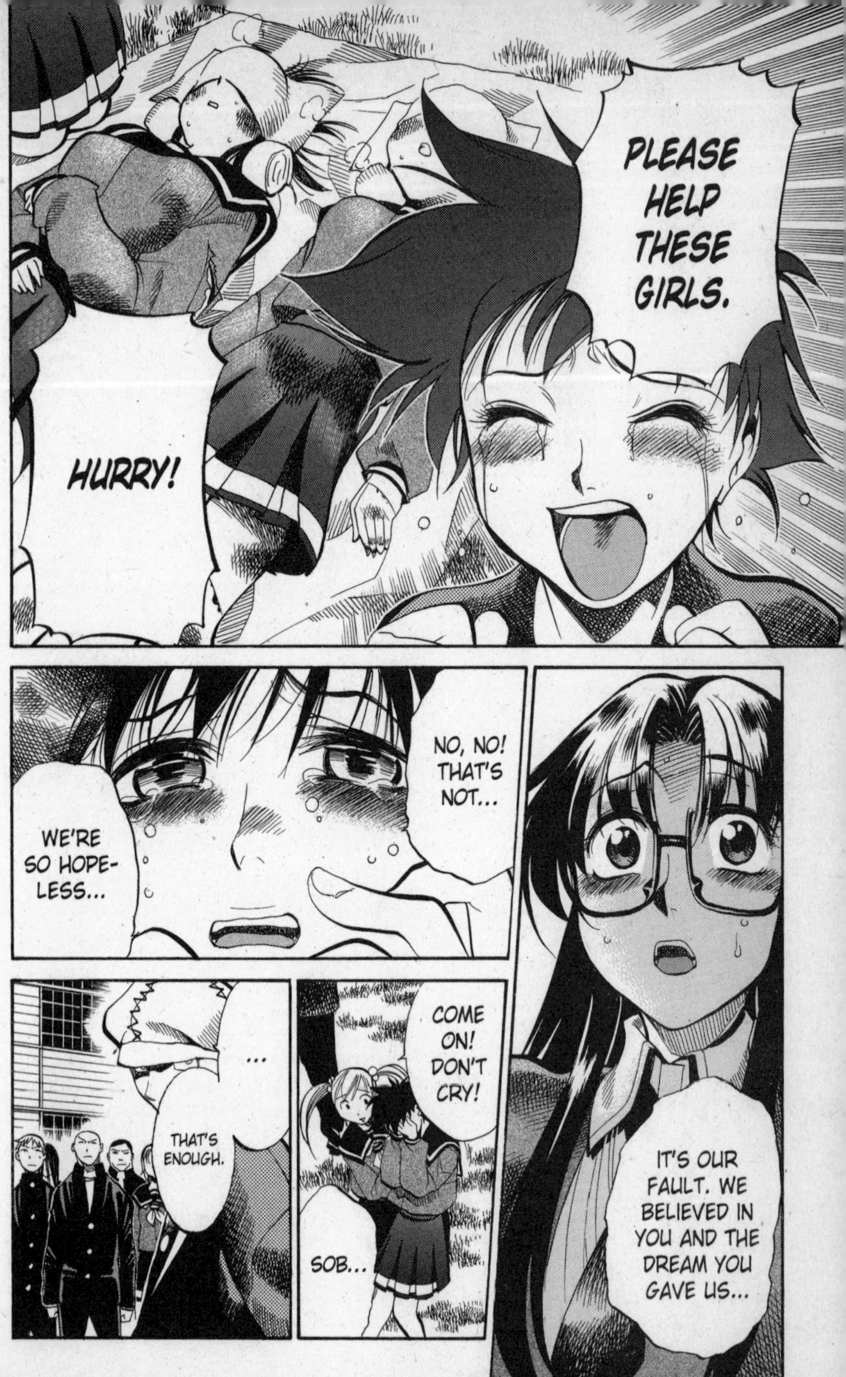
PLEASE HELP THESE GIRLS.
HURRY!
IT'S OUR FAULT. WE BELIEVED IN YOU AND THE DREAM YOU GAVE US...
NO, NO! THAT'S NOT...
WE'RE SO HOPE-LESS...
COME ON! DON'T CRY!
SOB...
...
THAT'S ENOUGH.

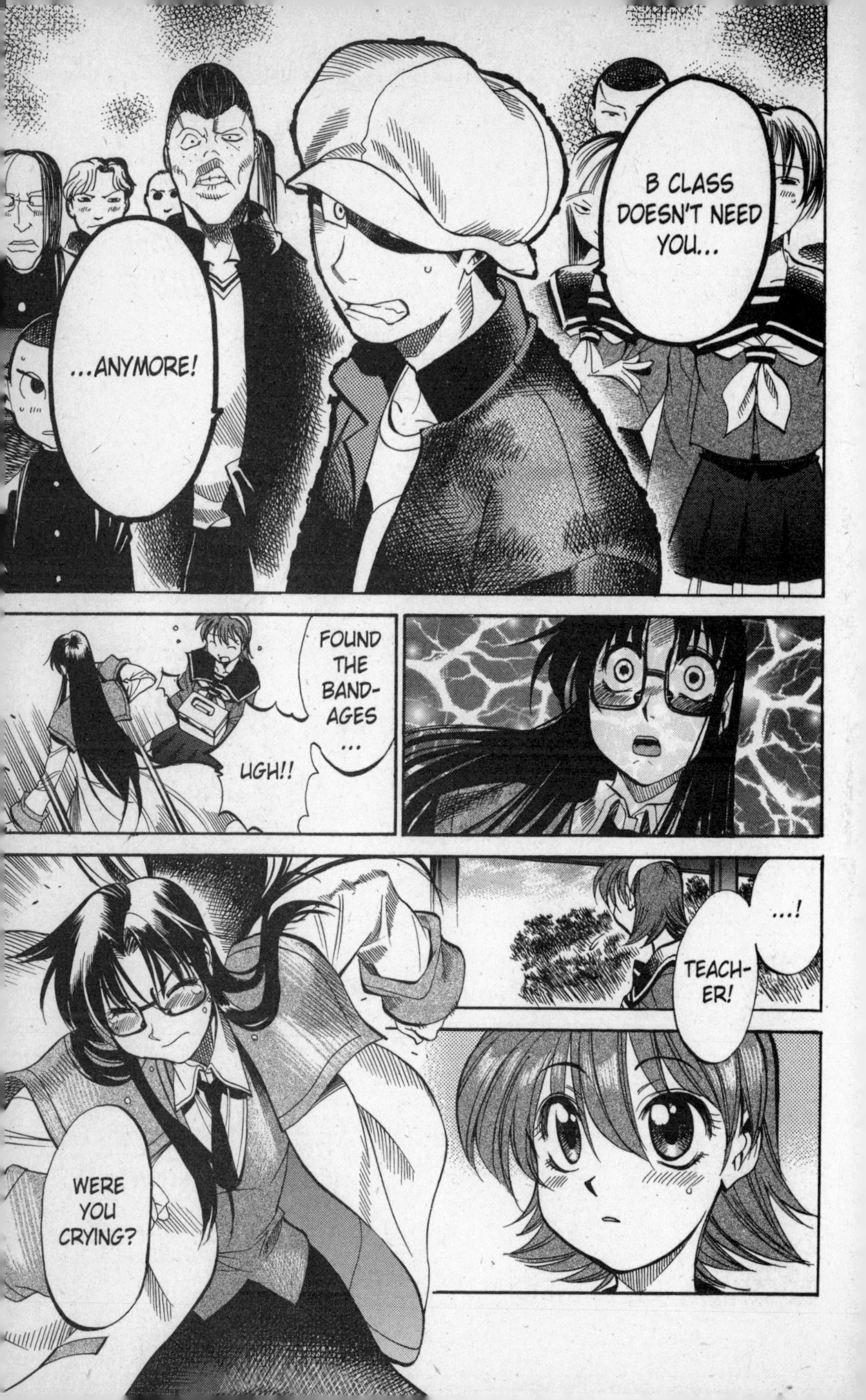
B CLASS DOESN'T NEED YOU...
...ANYMORE!
FOUND THE BAND-AGES ...
UGH!!
...!
TEACHER!
WERE YOU CRYING?

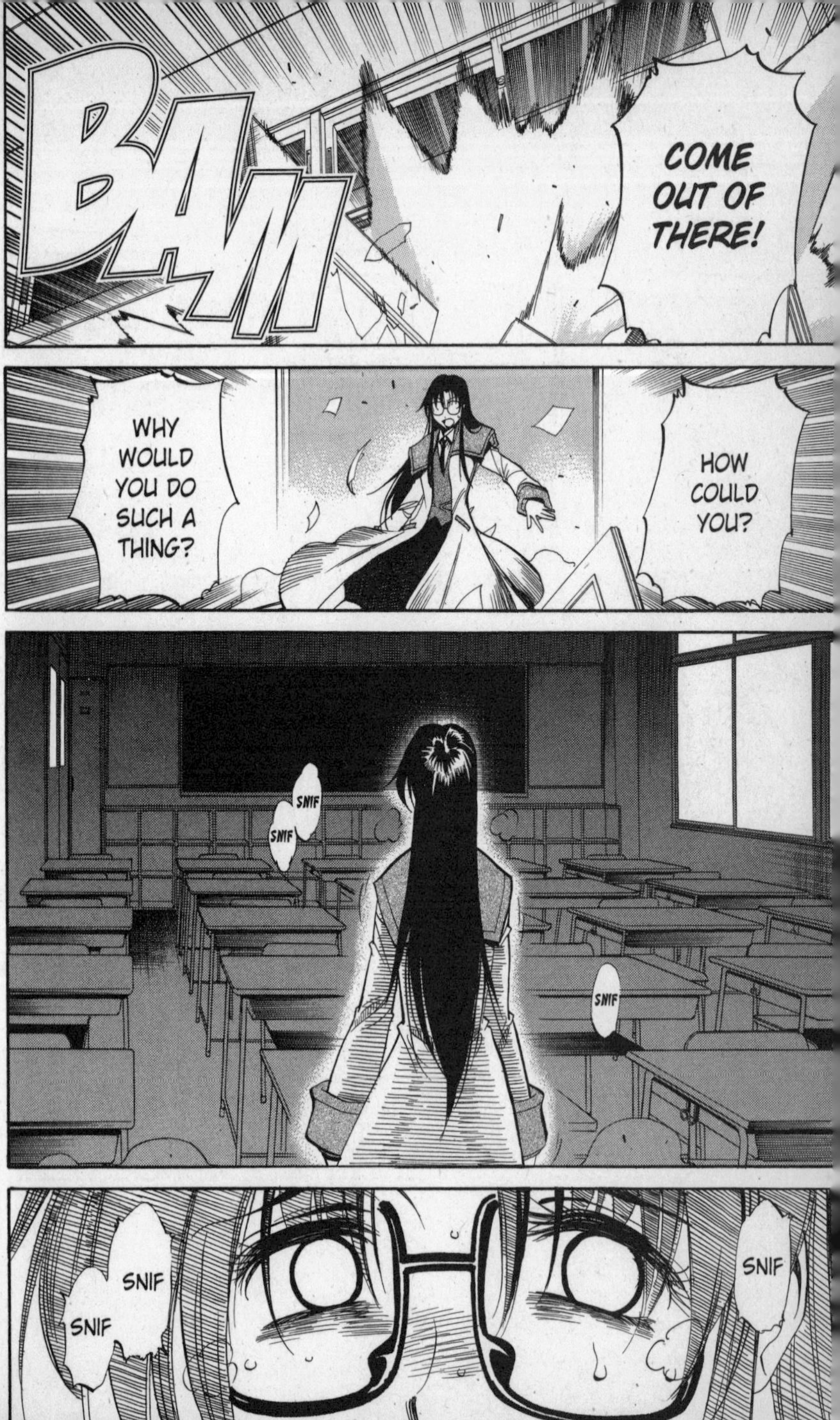
COME OUT OF THERE!
BAM
HOW COULD YOU?
WHY WOULD YOU DO SUCH A THING?
SNIF
SNIF
SNIF
SNIF
SNIF
SNIF

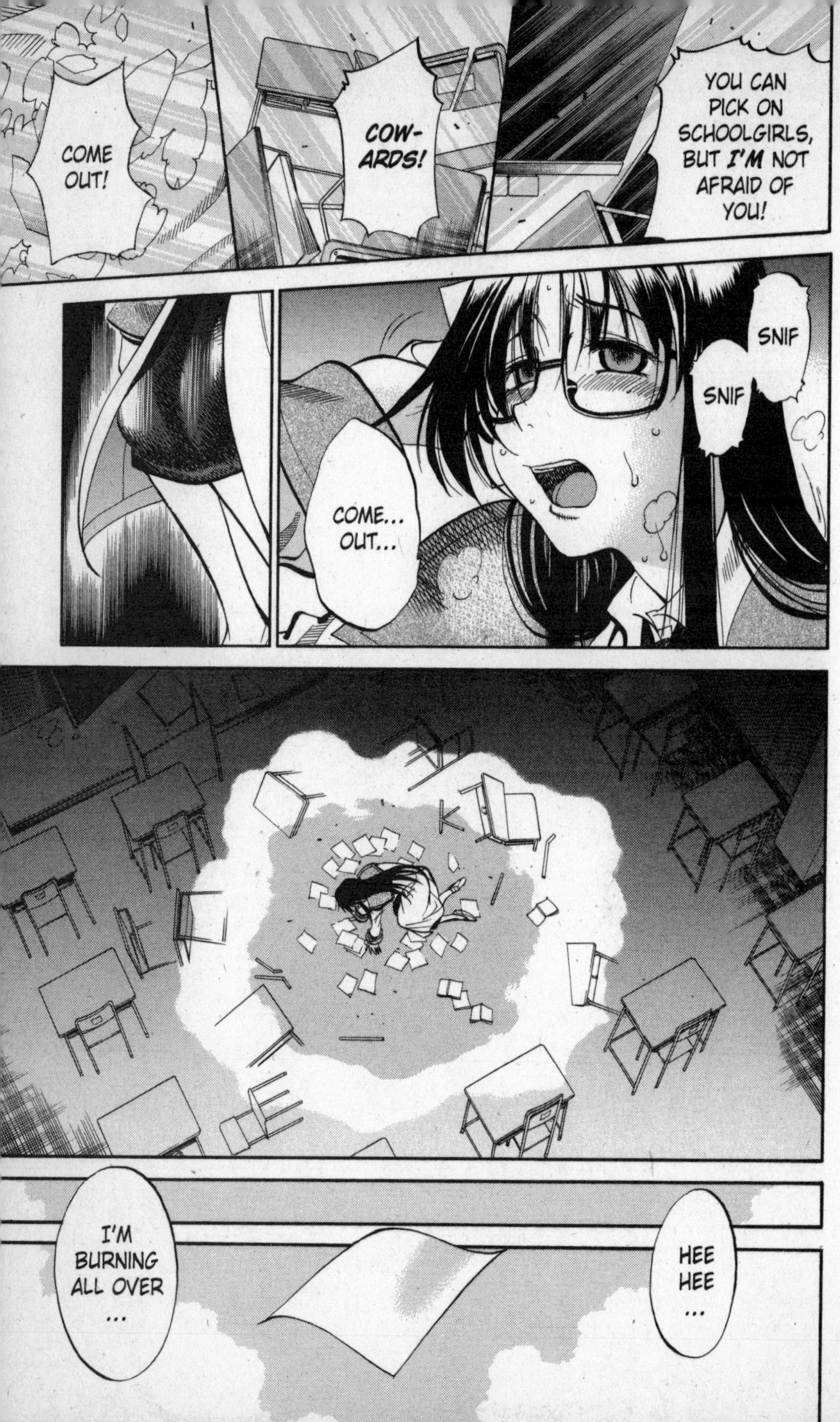
YOU CAN PICK ON SCHOOLGIRLS, BUT I'M NOT AFRAID OF YOU!
COW-ARDS!
COME OUT!
SNIF
SNIF
COME... OUT...
HEE HEE ...
I'M BURNING ALL OVER ...

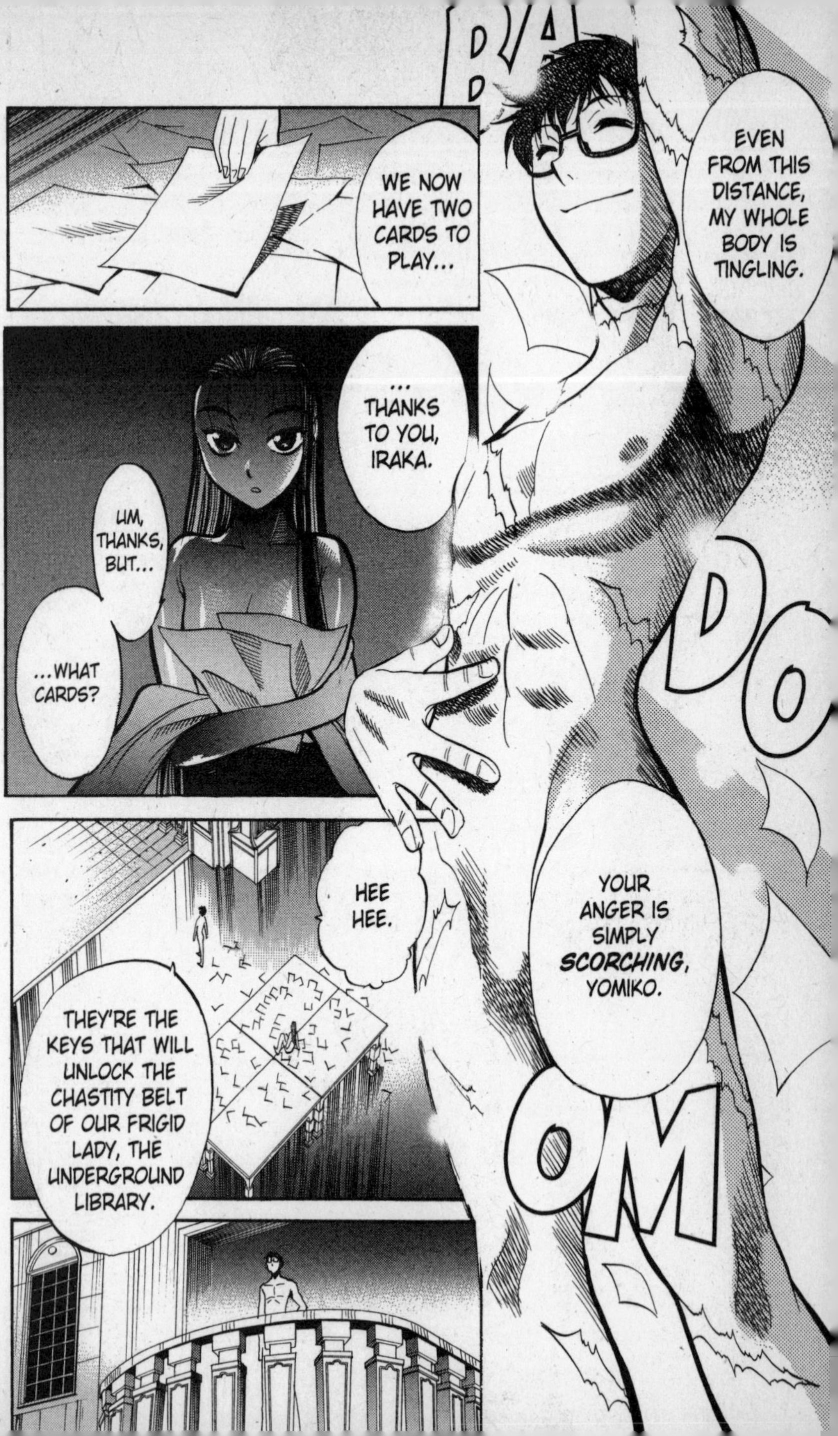
EVEN FROM THIS DISTANCE, MY WHOLE BODY IS TINGLING.
DO
YOUR ANGER IS SIMPLY *SCORCHING*, YOMIKO.
OM
WE NOW HAVE TWO CARDS TO PLAY...
... THANKS TO YOU, IRAKA.
UM, THANKS, BUT...
...WHAT CARDS?
HEE HEE.
THEY'RE THE KEYS THAT WILL UNLOCK THE CHASTITY BELT OF OUR FRIGID LADY, THE UNDERGROUND LIBRARY.

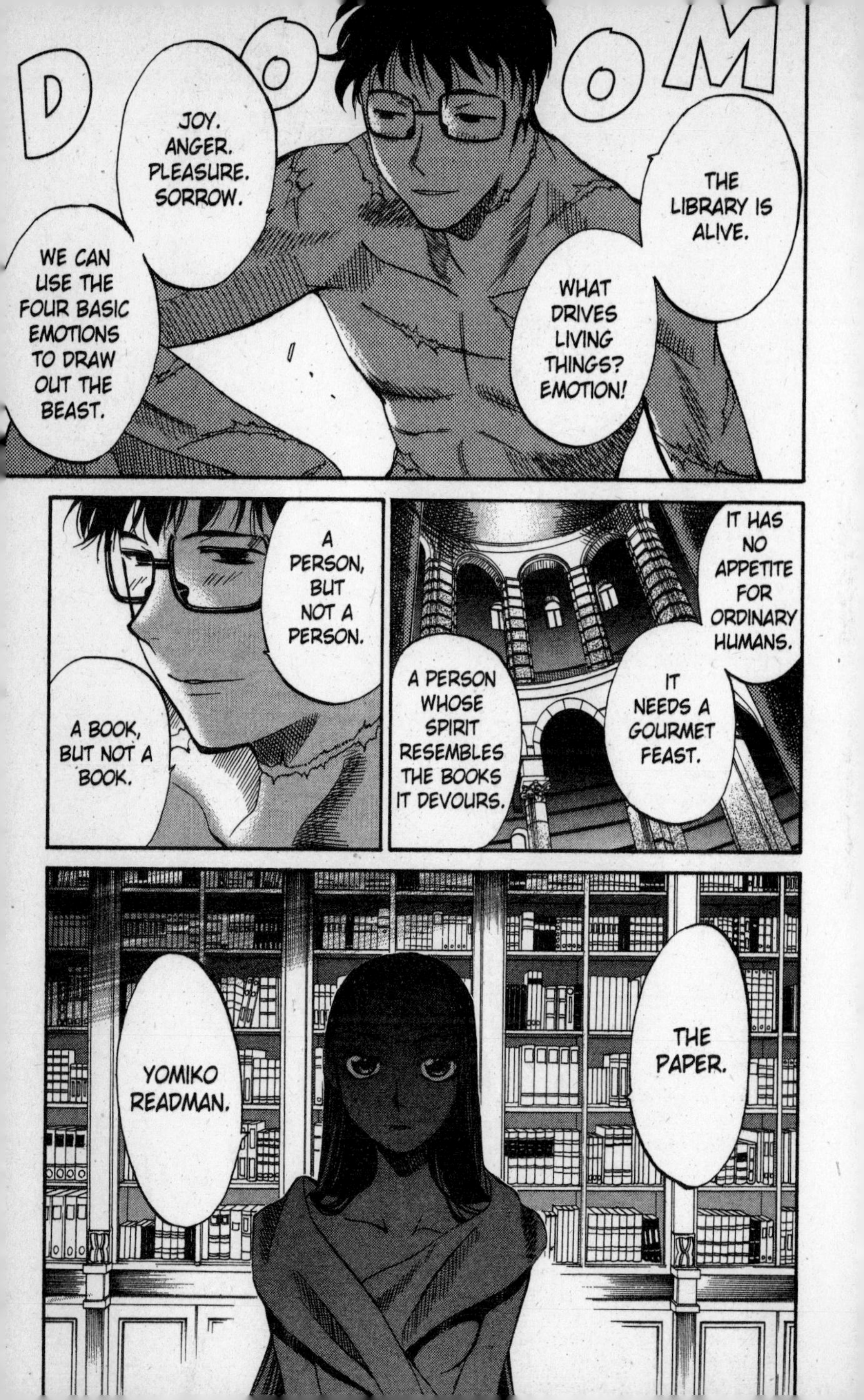
DOOOM
THE LIBRARY IS ALIVE.
WHAT DRIVES LIVING THINGS? EMOTION!
JOY. ANGER. PLEASURE. SORROW.
WE CAN USE THE FOUR BASIC EMOTIONS TO DRAW OUT THE BEAST.
IT HAS NO APPETITE FOR ORDINARY HUMANS.
IT NEEDS A GOURMET FEAST.
A PERSON WHOSE SPIRIT RESEMBLES THE BOOKS IT DEVOURS.
A PERSON, BUT NOT A PERSON.
A BOOK, BUT NOT A BOOK.
THE PAPER.
YOMIKO READMAN.

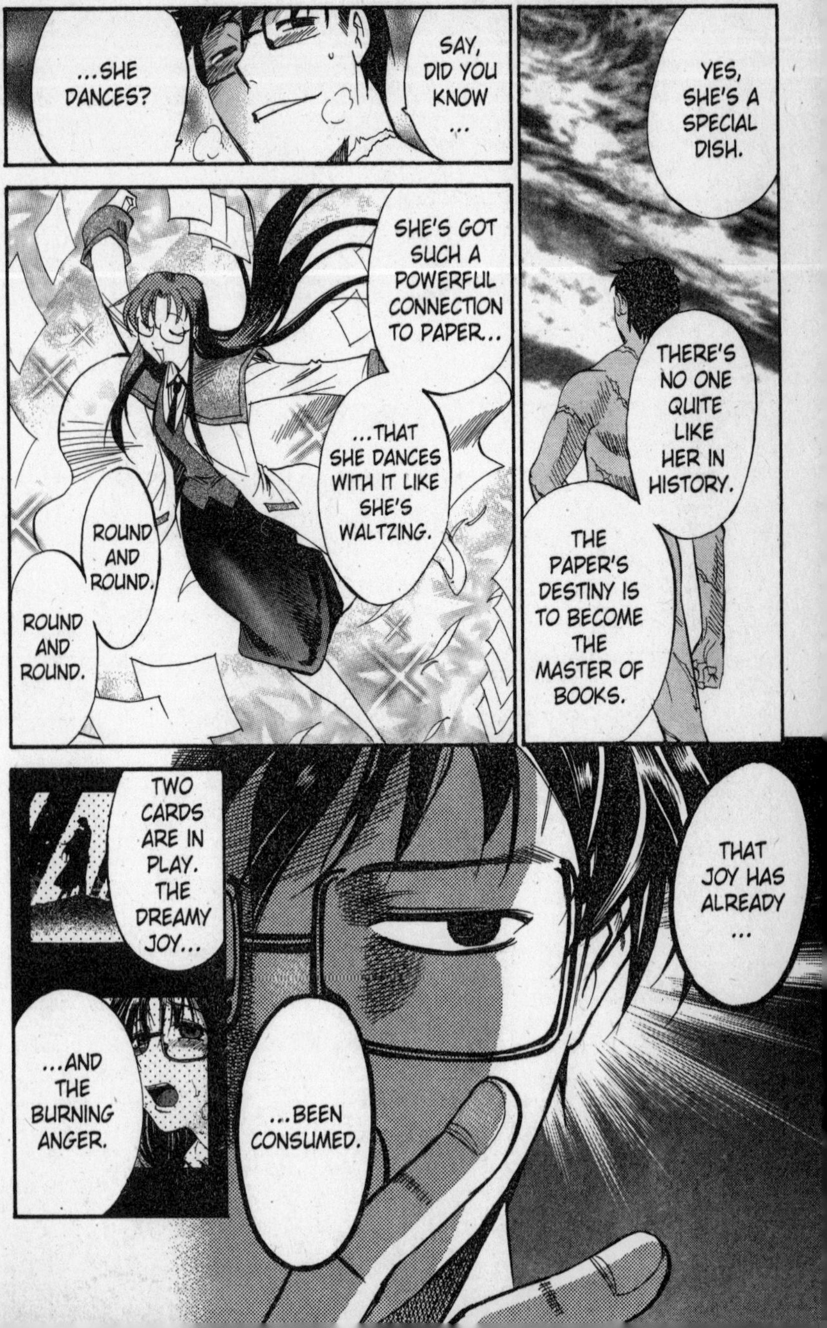
YES, SHE'S A SPECIAL DISH.
THERE'S NO ONE QUITE LIKE HER IN HISTORY.
THE PAPER'S DESTINY IS TO BECOME THE MASTER OF BOOKS.
SAY, DID YOU KNOW ...
...SHE DANCES?
SHE'S GOT SUCH A POWERFUL CONNECTION TO PAPER...
...THAT SHE DANCES WITH IT LIKE SHE'S WALTZING.
ROUND AND ROUND.
ROUND AND ROUND.
TWO CARDS ARE IN PLAY. THE DREAMY JOY...
...AND THE BURNING ANGER.
THAT JOY HAS ALREADY ...
...BEEN CONSUMED.

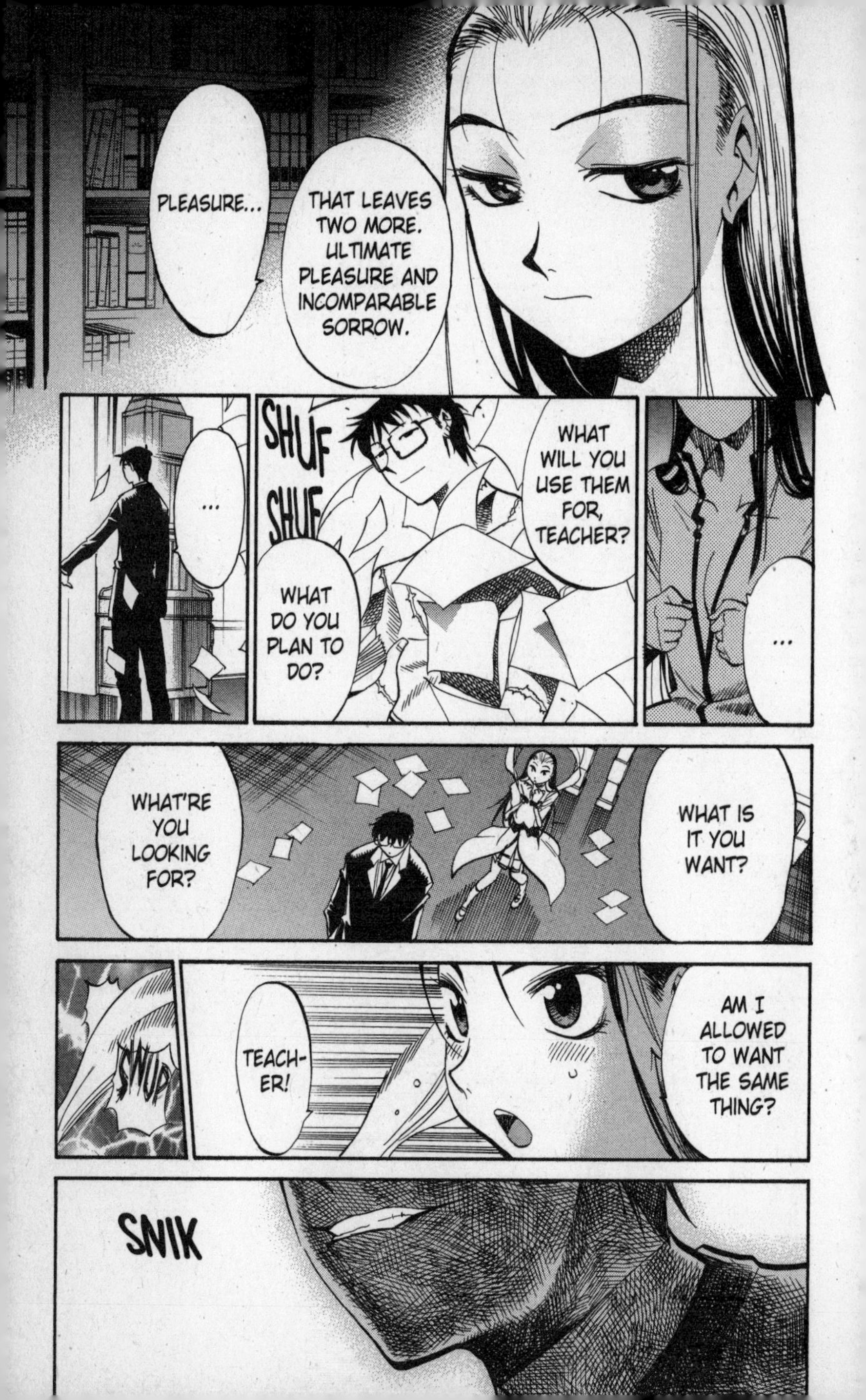
THAT LEAVES TWO MORE. ULTIMATE PLEASURE AND INCOMPARABLE SORROW.
PLEASURE...
...
WHAT WILL YOU USE THEM FOR, TEACHER?
SHUF SHUF
WHAT DO YOU PLAN TO DO?
...
WHAT IS IT YOU WANT?
WHAT'RE YOU LOOKING FOR?
AM I ALLOWED TO WANT THE SAME THING?
TEACH- ER!
SNUP
SNIK

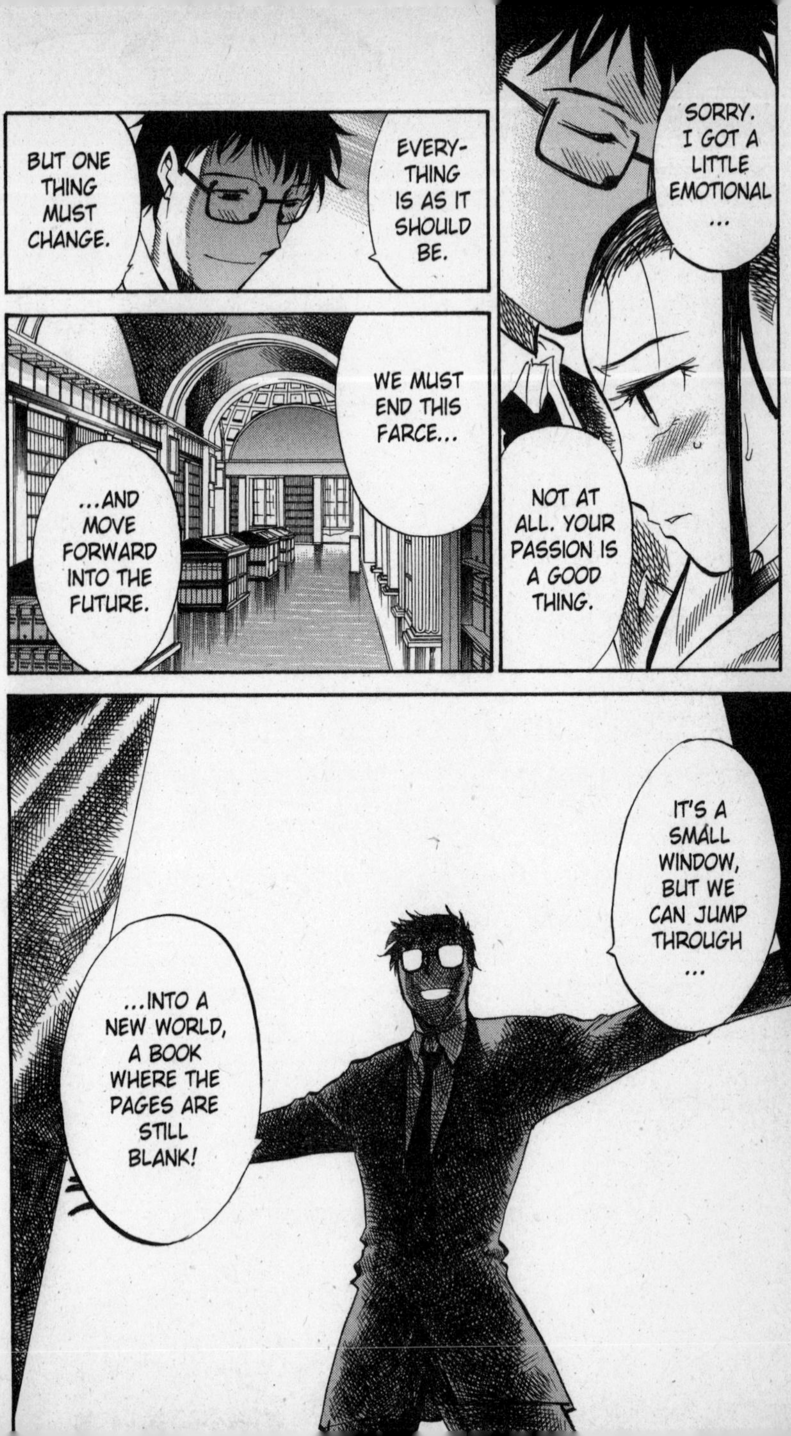
SORRY. I GOT A LITTLE EMOTIONAL...
NOT AT ALL. YOUR PASSION IS A GOOD THING.
EVERYTHING IS AS IT SHOULD BE.
BUT ONE THING MUST CHANGE.
WE MUST END THIS FARCE...
...AND MOVE FORWARD INTO THE FUTURE.
IT'S A SMALL WINDOW, BUT WE CAN JUMP THROUGH...
...INTO A NEW WORLD, A BOOK WHERE THE PAGES ARE STILL BLANK!

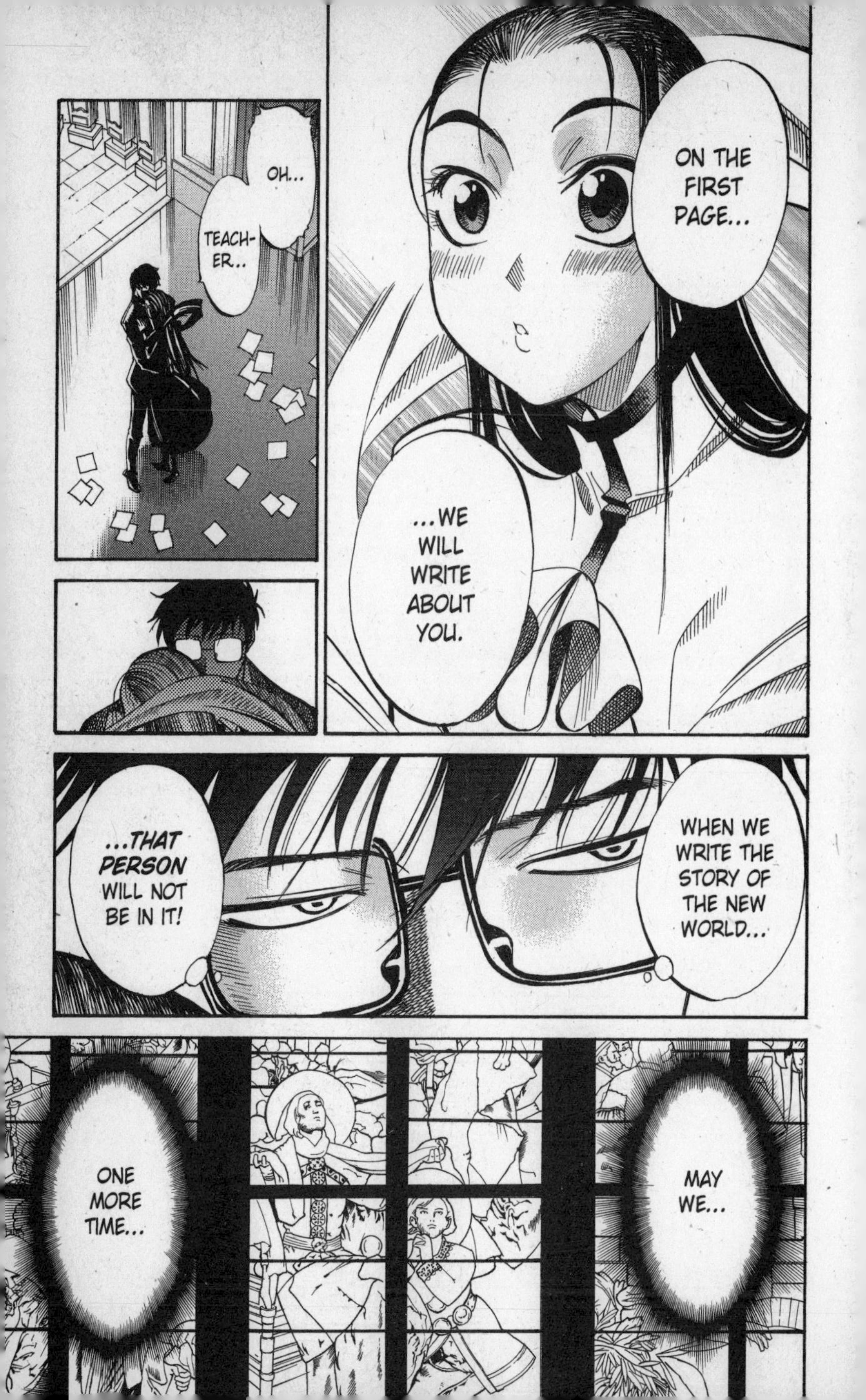
ON THE FIRST PAGE...
...WE WILL WRITE ABOUT YOU.
OH...
TEACHER-ER...
WHEN WE WRITE THE STORY OF THE NEW WORLD...
...THAT PERSON WILL NOT BE IN IT!
MAY WE...
ONE MORE TIME...

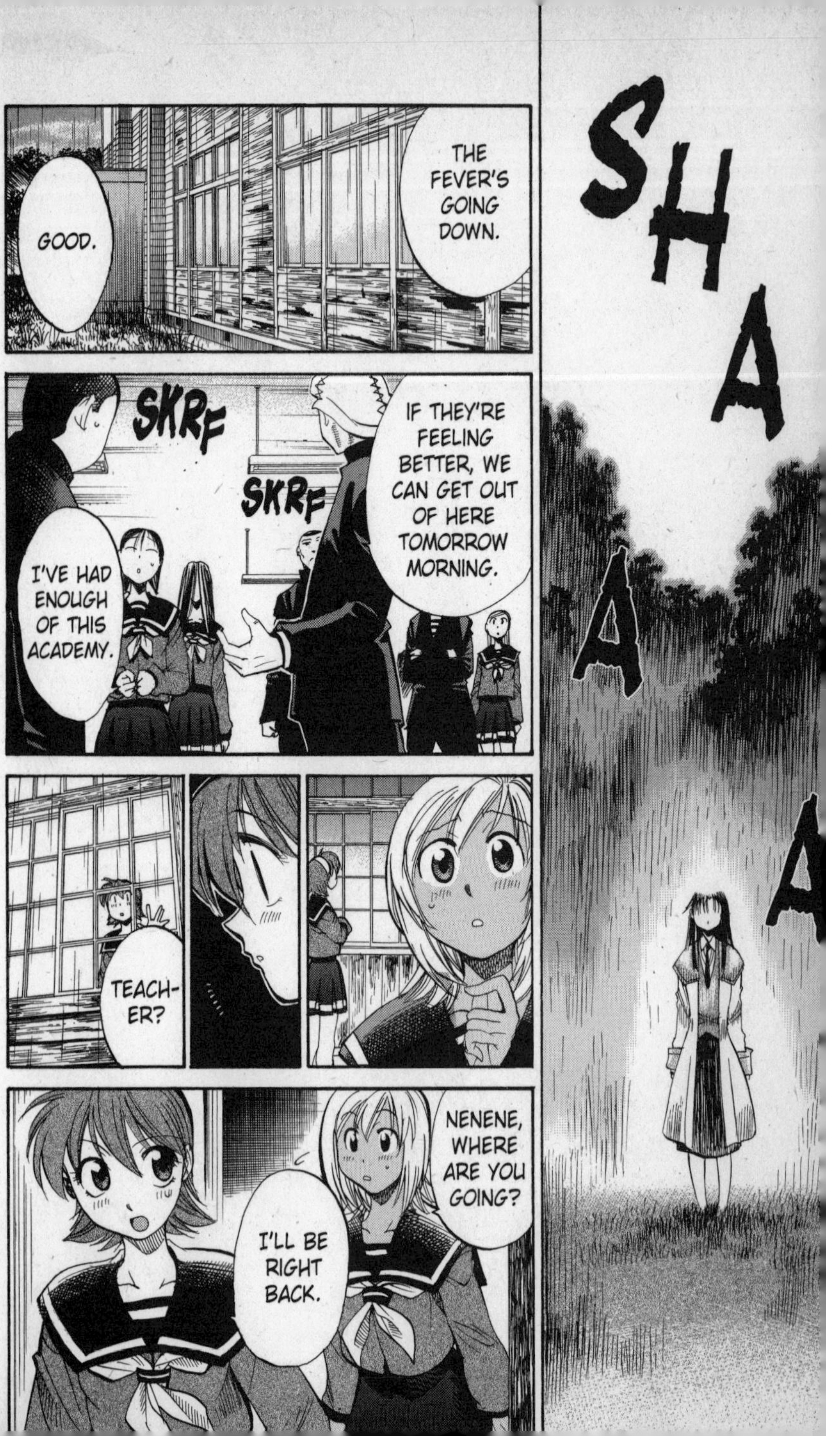
SHAAA
THE FEVER'S GOING DOWN.
GOOD.
IF THEY'RE FEELING BETTER, WE CAN GET OUT OF HERE TOMORROW MORNING.
SKRF
SKRF
I'VE HAD ENOUGH OF THIS ACADEMY.
TEACH-ER?
NENENE, WHERE ARE YOU GOING?
I'LL BE RIGHT BACK.

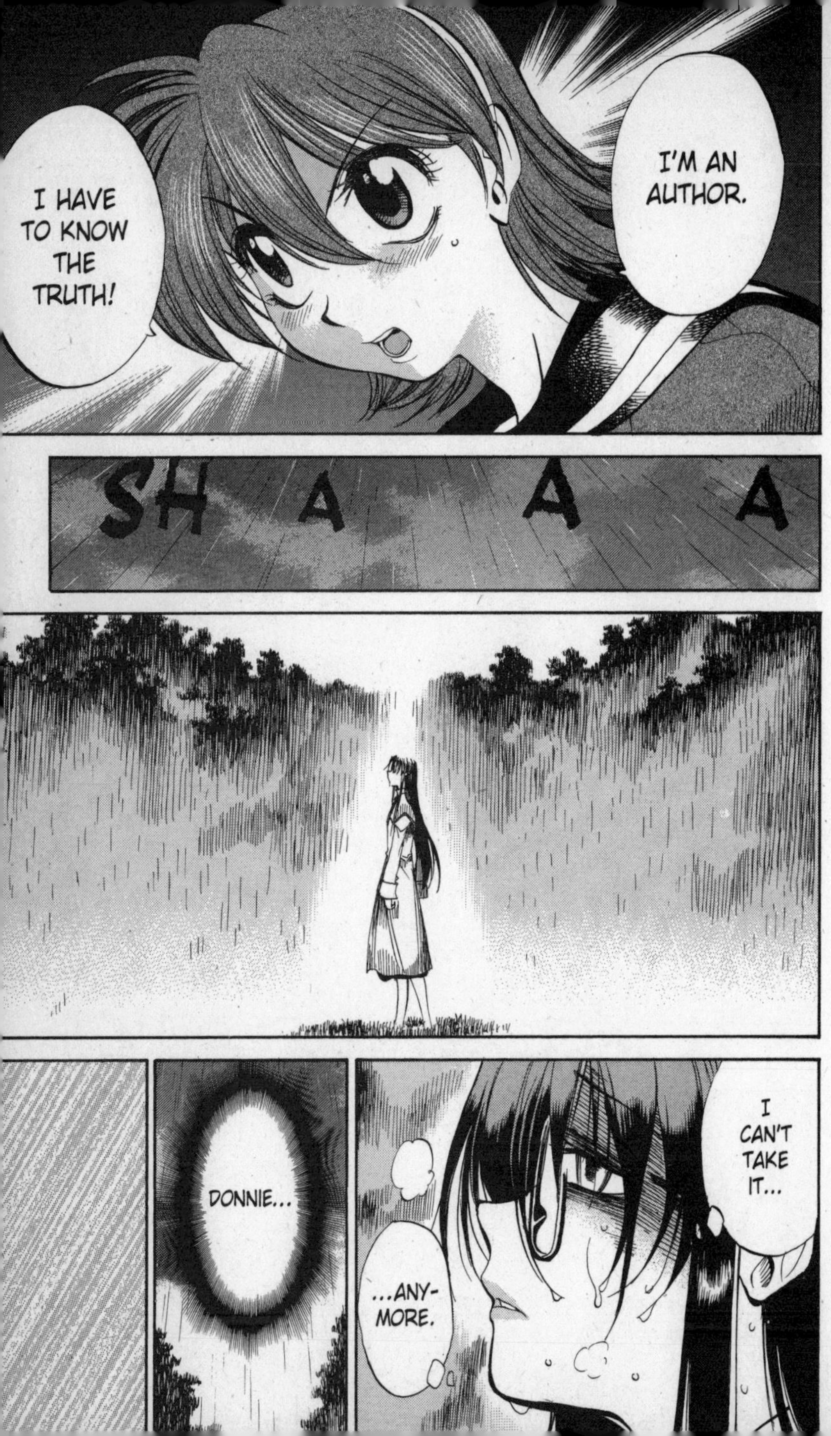
I'M AN AUTHOR.
I HAVE TO KNOW THE TRUTH!
SHAAA
I CAN'T TAKE IT...
...ANY-MORE.
DONNIE...

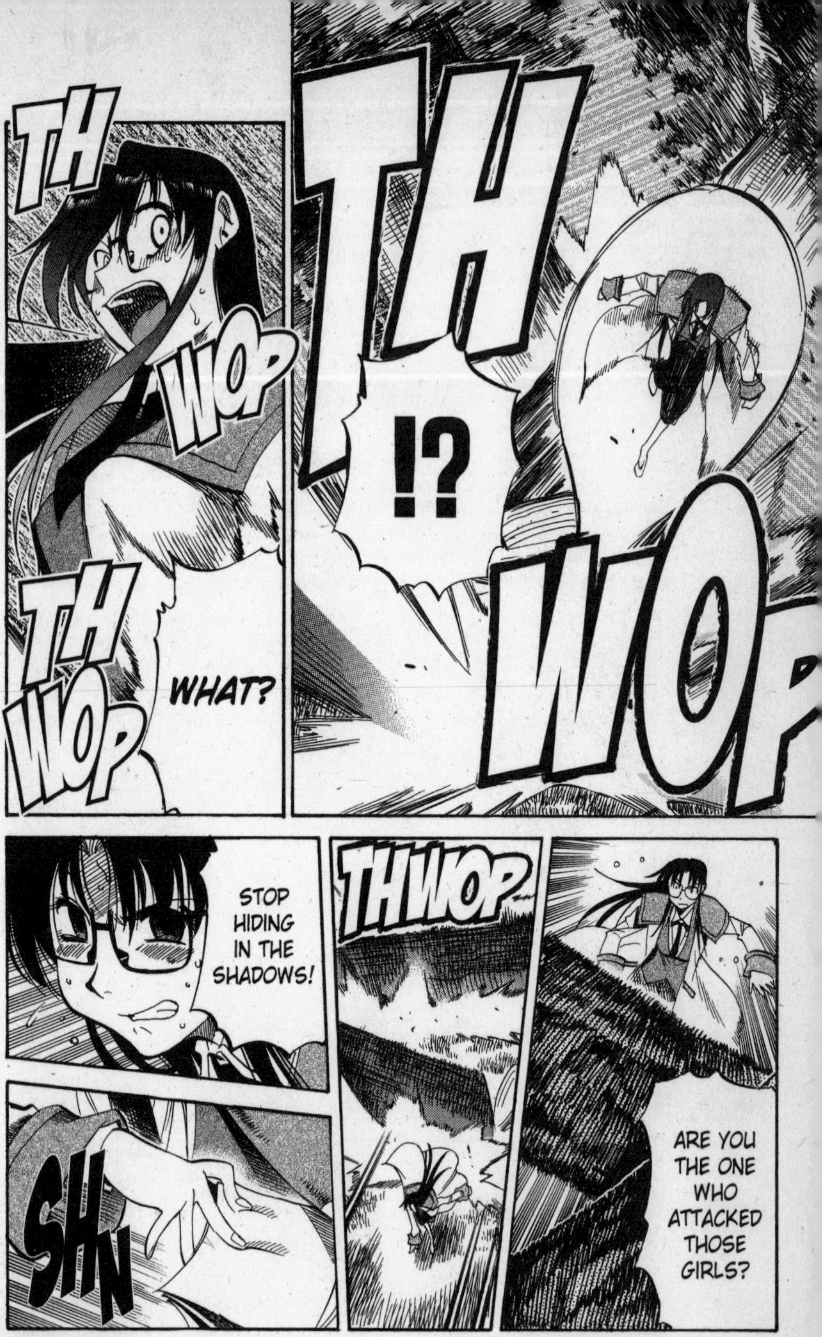
THWOP
!?
THWOP
WHAT?
THWOP
ARE YOU THE ONE WHO ATTACKED THOSE GIRLS?
THWOP
STOP HIDING IN THE SHADOWS!
SHN

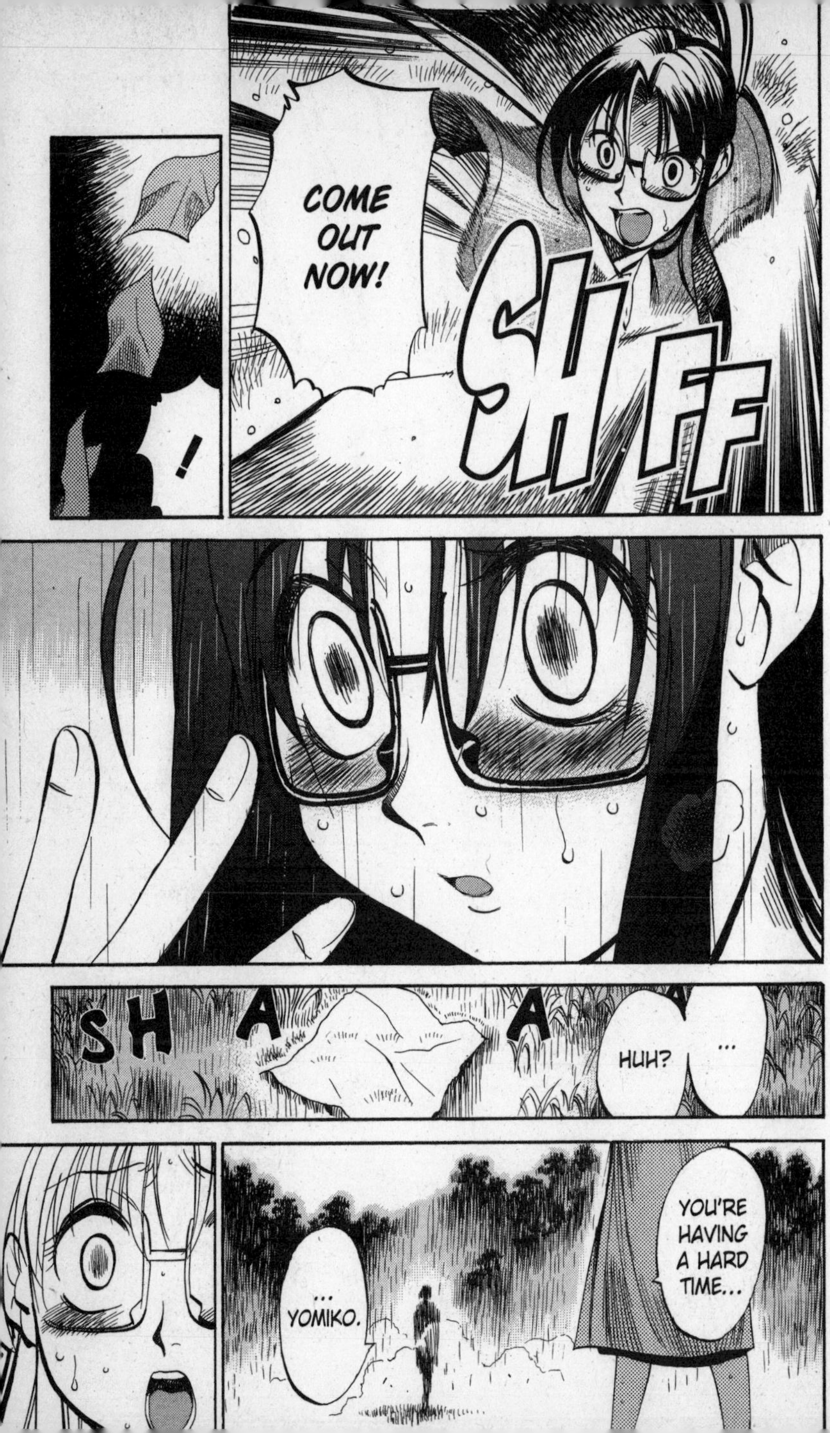
COME OUT NOW!
SHFF
!
SH A A
...
HUH?
YOU'RE HAVING A HARD TIME...
... YOMIKO.

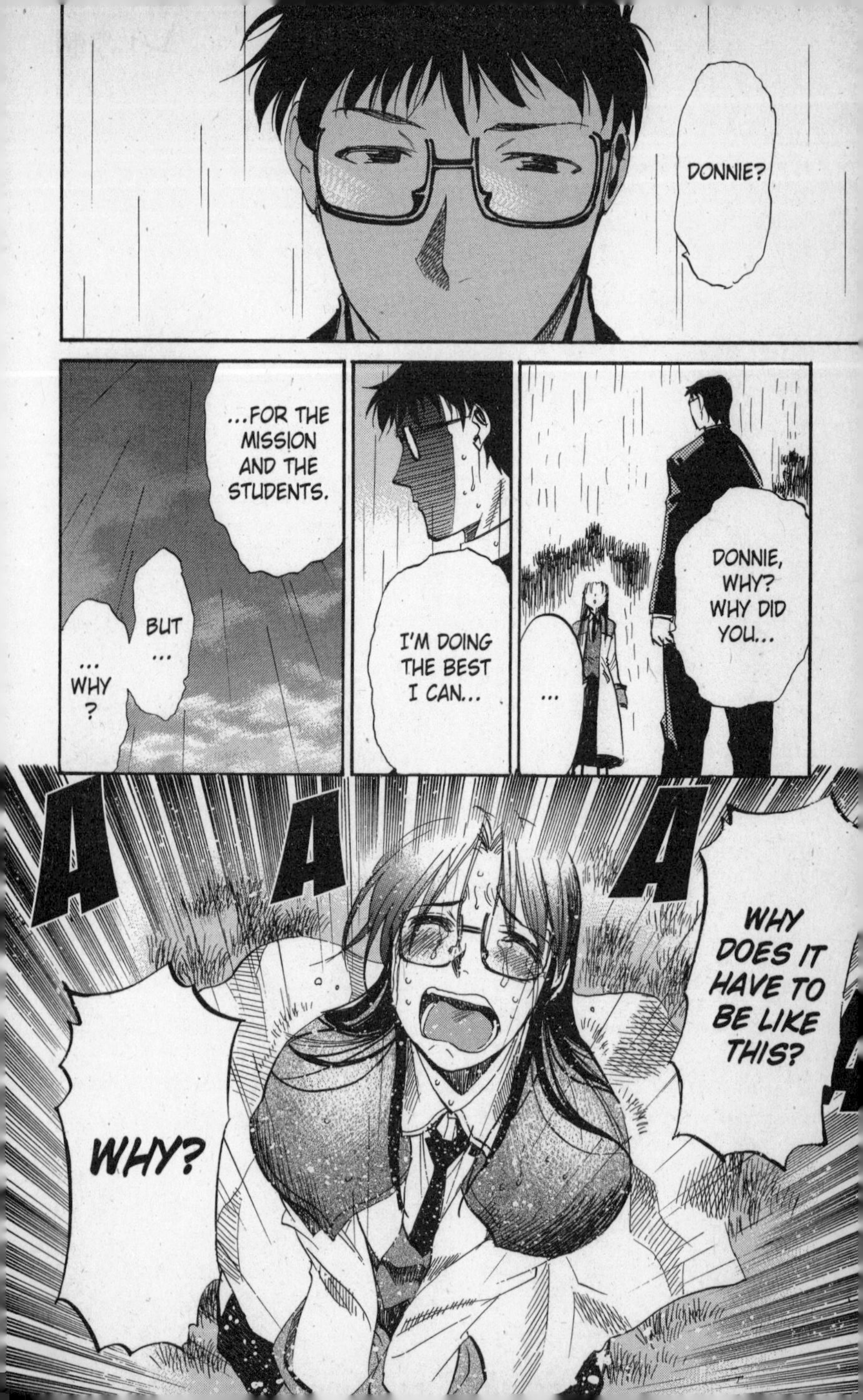
DONNIE?
DONNIE, WHY? WHY DID YOU...
...
I'M DOING THE BEST I CAN...
...FOR THE MISSION AND THE STUDENTS.
BUT ...
... WHY ?
A A A
WHY DOES IT HAVE TO BE LIKE THIS?
WHY?

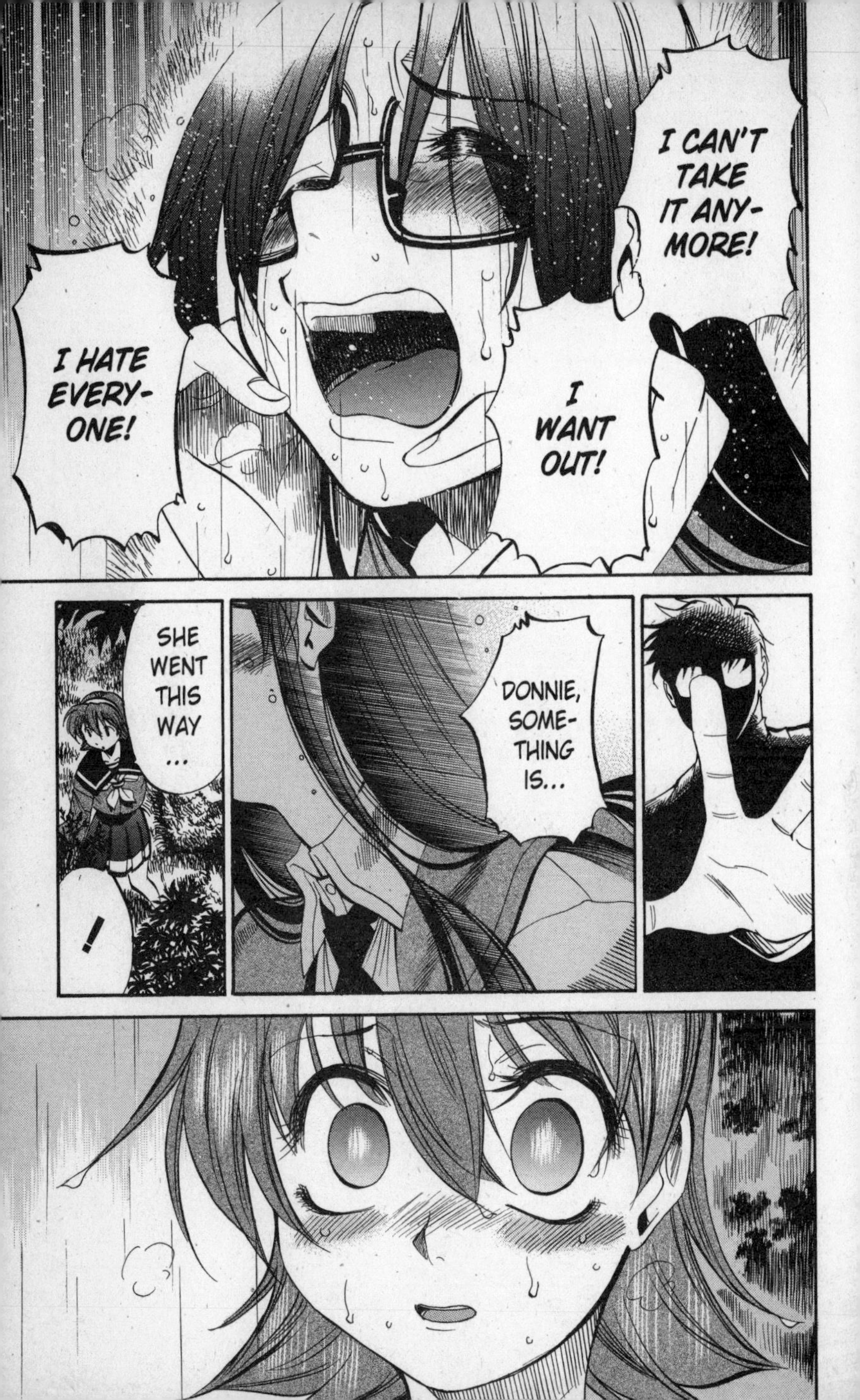
I CAN'T TAKE IT ANY-MORE!
I WANT OUT!
I HATE EVERY-ONE!
DONNIE, SOME-THING IS...
SHE WENT THIS WAY ...
!

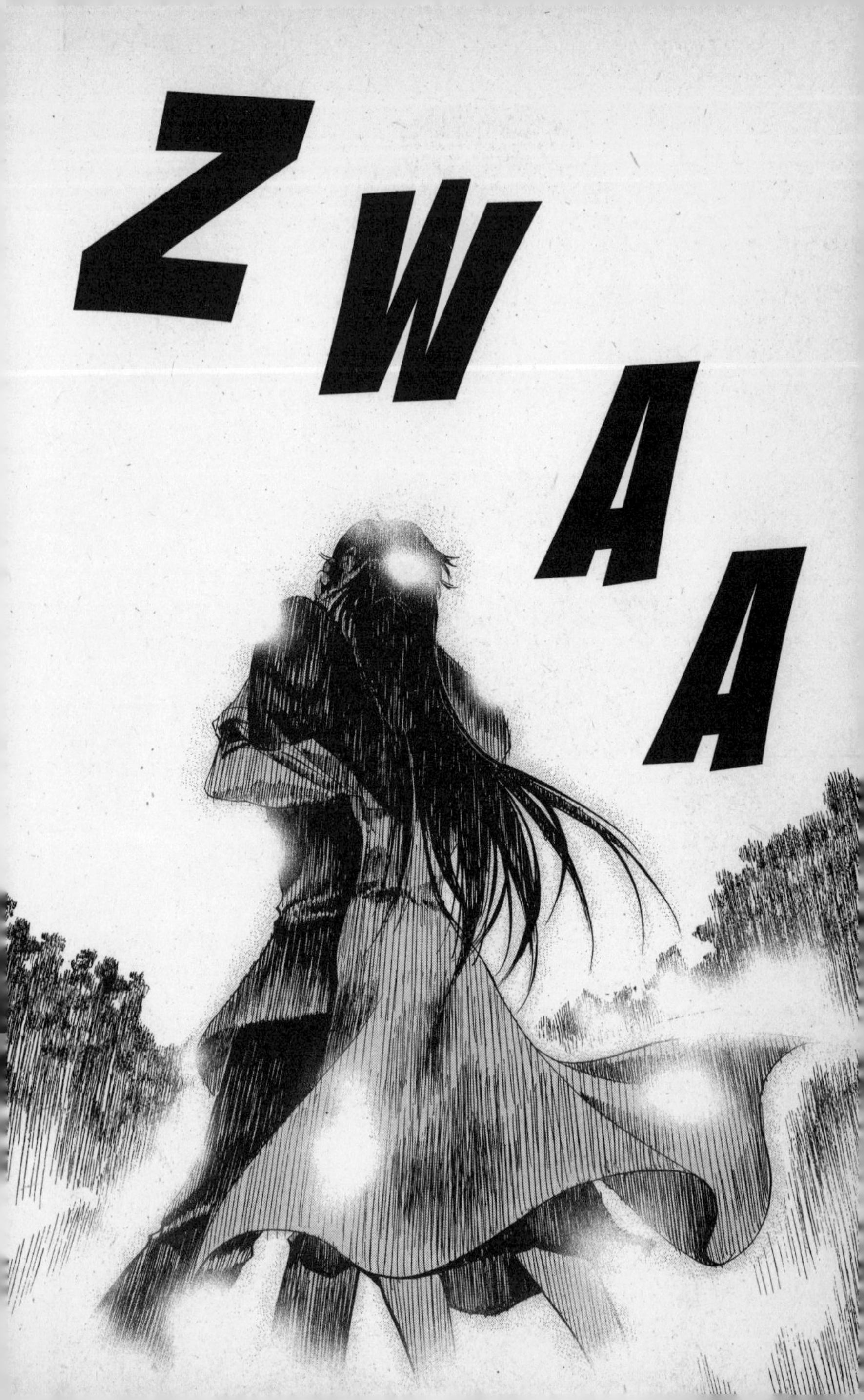
ZWAAA

EPISODE TWO

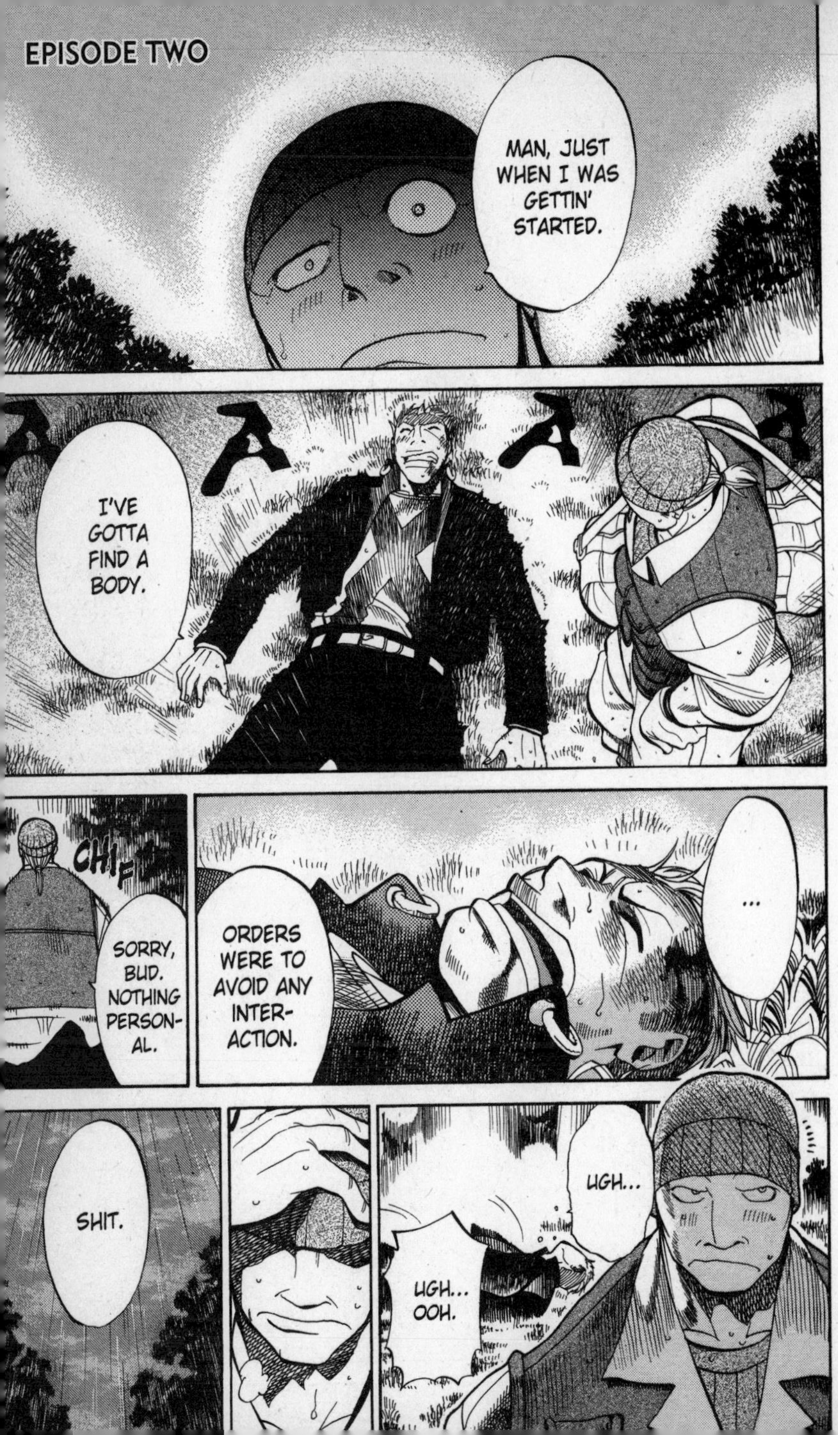
MAN, JUST WHEN I WAS GETTIN' STARTED.
I'VE GOTTA FIND A BODY.
...
ORDERS WERE TO AVOID ANY INTER-ACTION.
CHI
SORRY, BUD. NOTHING PERSON-AL.
UGH...
UGH... OOH.
SHIT.

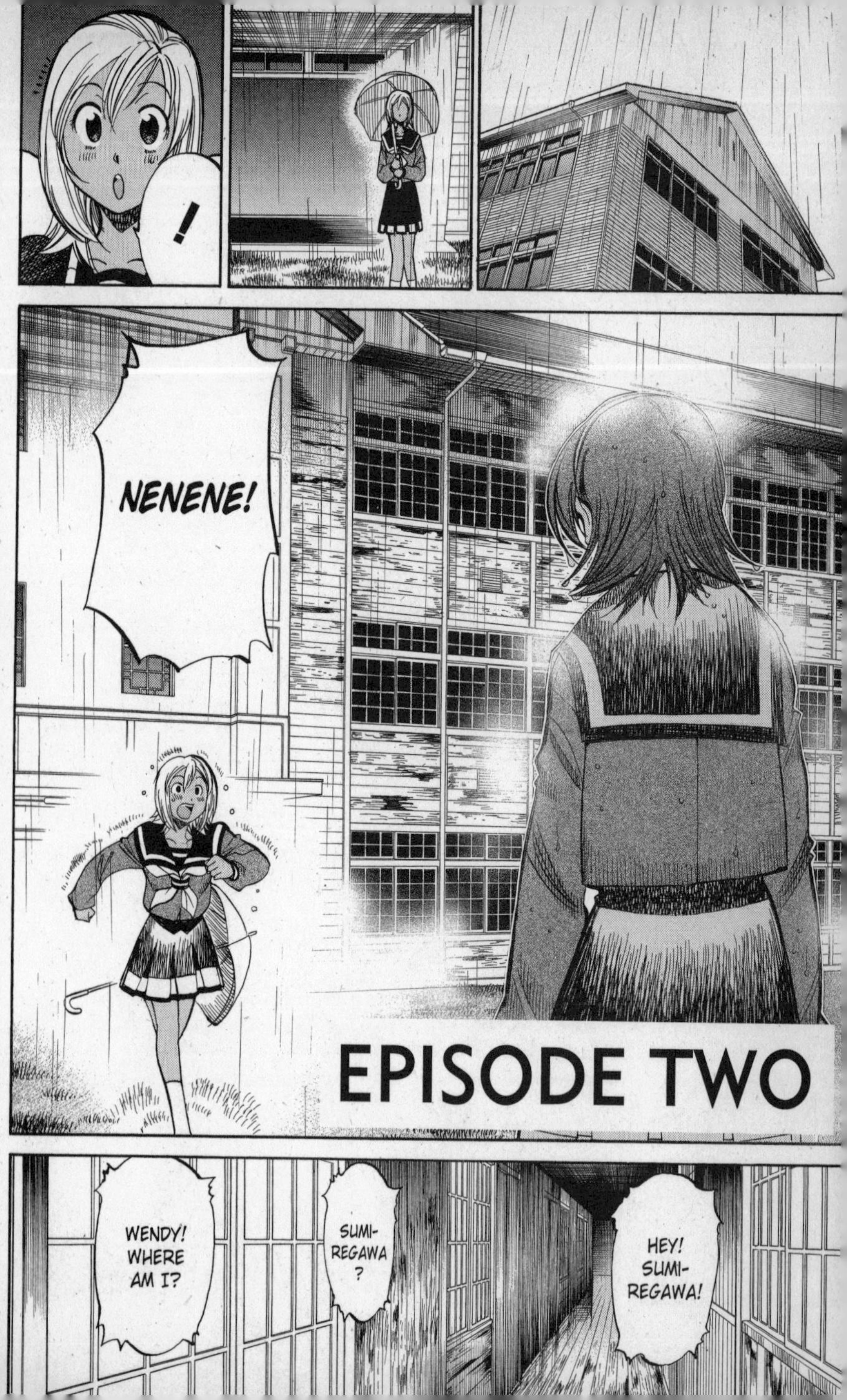
!
NENENE!
EPISODE TWO
HEY! SUMI-REGAWA!
SUMI-REGAWA ?
WENDY! WHERE AM I?

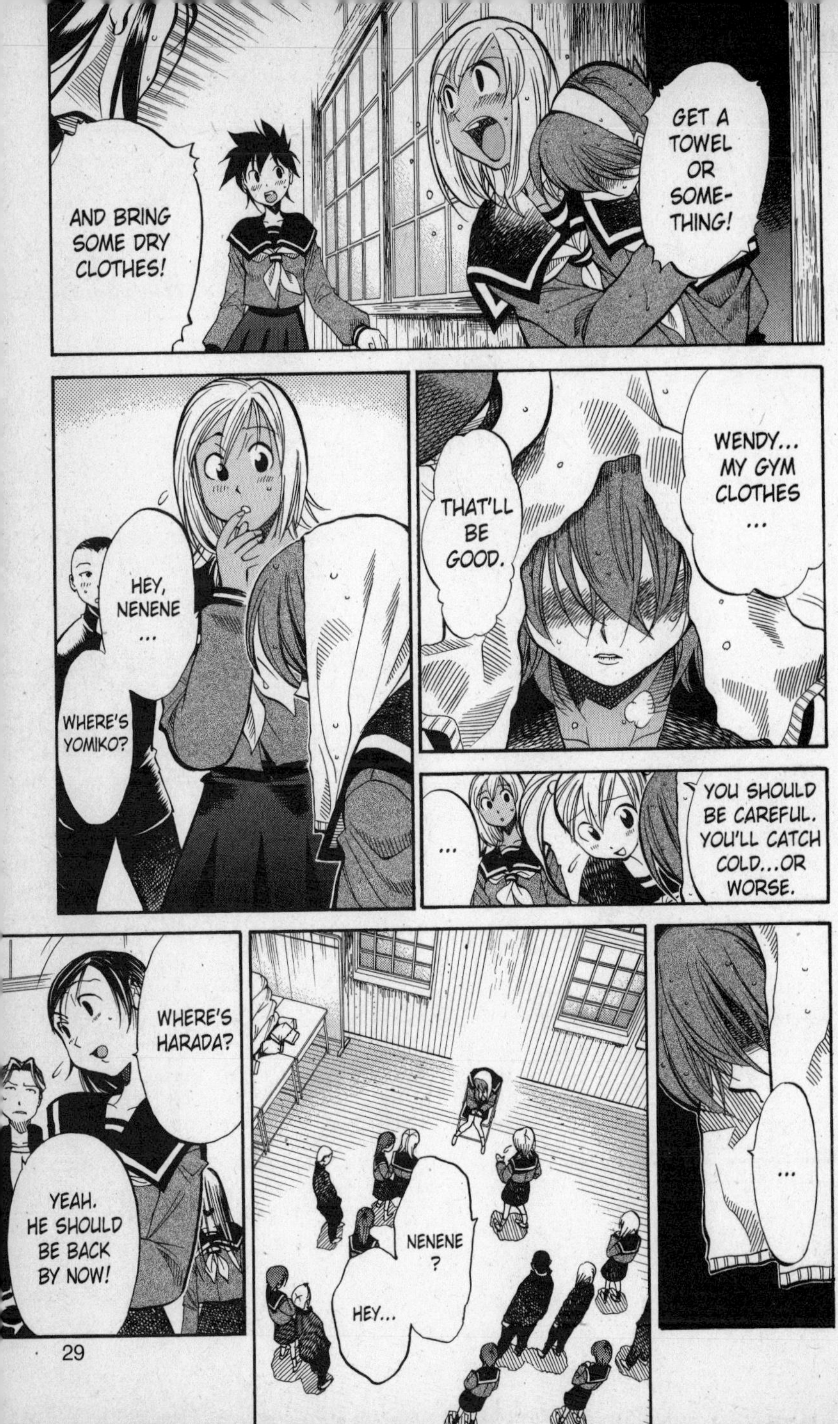
GET A TOWEL OR SOME-THING!
AND BRING SOME DRY CLOTHES!
WENDY... MY GYM CLOTHES ...
THAT'LL BE GOOD.
YOU SHOULD BE CAREFUL. YOU'LL CATCH COLD...OR WORSE.
...
HEY, NENENE ...
WHERE'S YOMIKO?
...
NENENE ?
HEY...
WHERE'S HARADA?
YEAH. HE SHOULD BE BACK BY NOW!

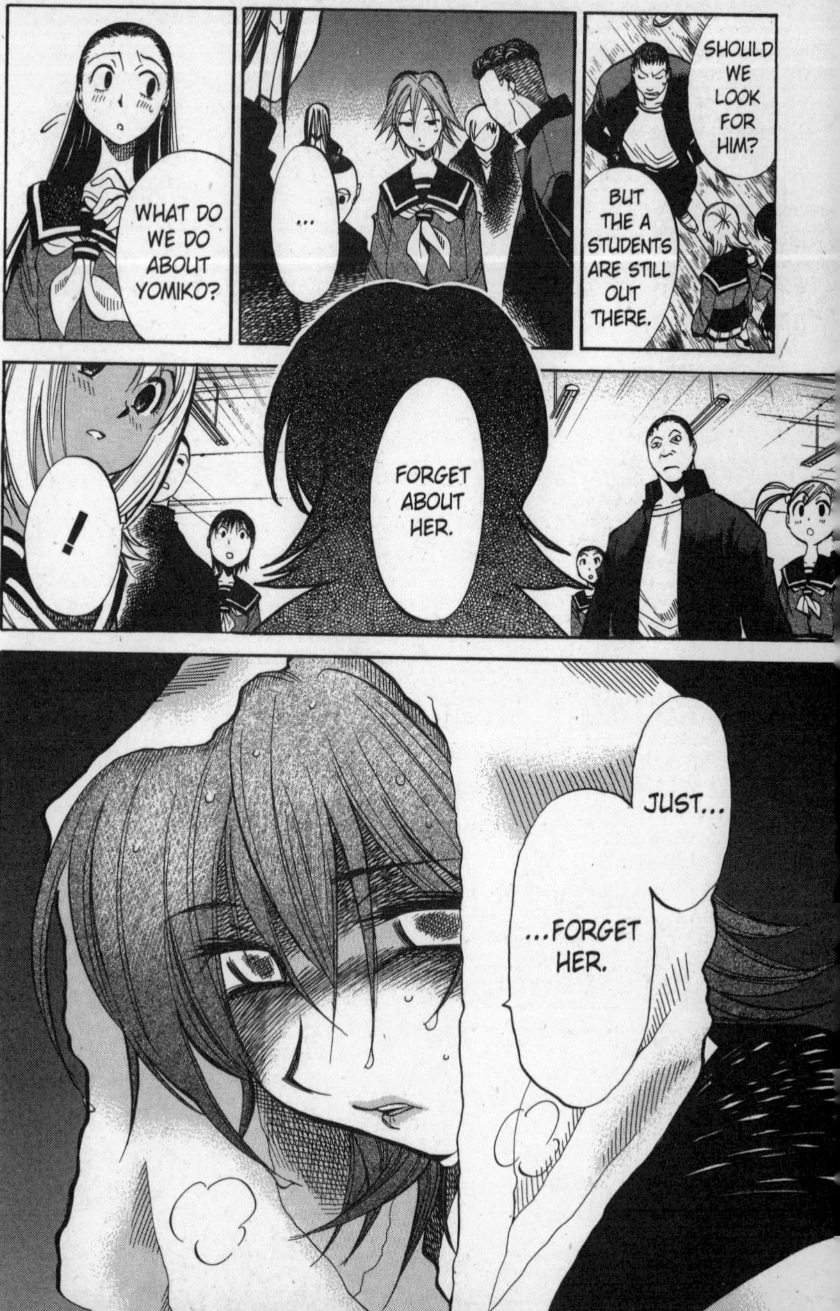
SHOULD WE LOOK FOR HIM?
BUT THE A STUDENTS ARE STILL OUT THERE.
...
WHAT DO WE DO ABOUT YOMIKO?
FORGET ABOUT HER.
!
JUST...
...FORGET HER.

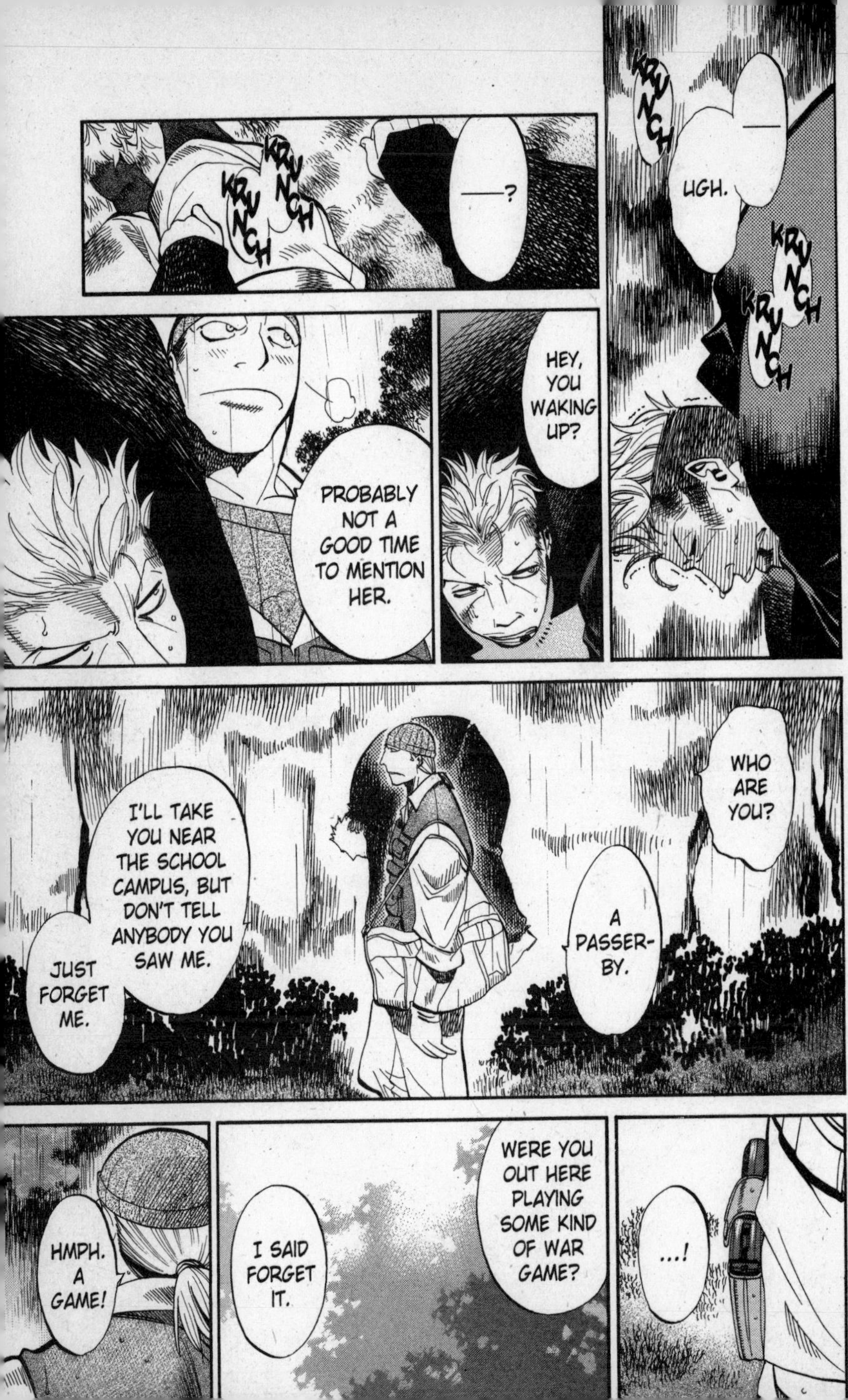

KRUNCH
——
UGH.
KRUNCH
KRUNCH
KRUNCH
KRUNCH
——?
HEY, YOU WAKING UP?
PROBABLY NOT A GOOD TIME TO MENTION HER.
WHO ARE YOU?
A PASSER-BY.
I'LL TAKE YOU NEAR THE SCHOOL CAMPUS, BUT DON'T TELL ANYBODY YOU SAW ME.
JUST FORGET ME.
...!
WERE YOU OUT HERE PLAYING SOME KIND OF WAR GAME?
I SAID FORGET IT.
HMPH. A GAME!

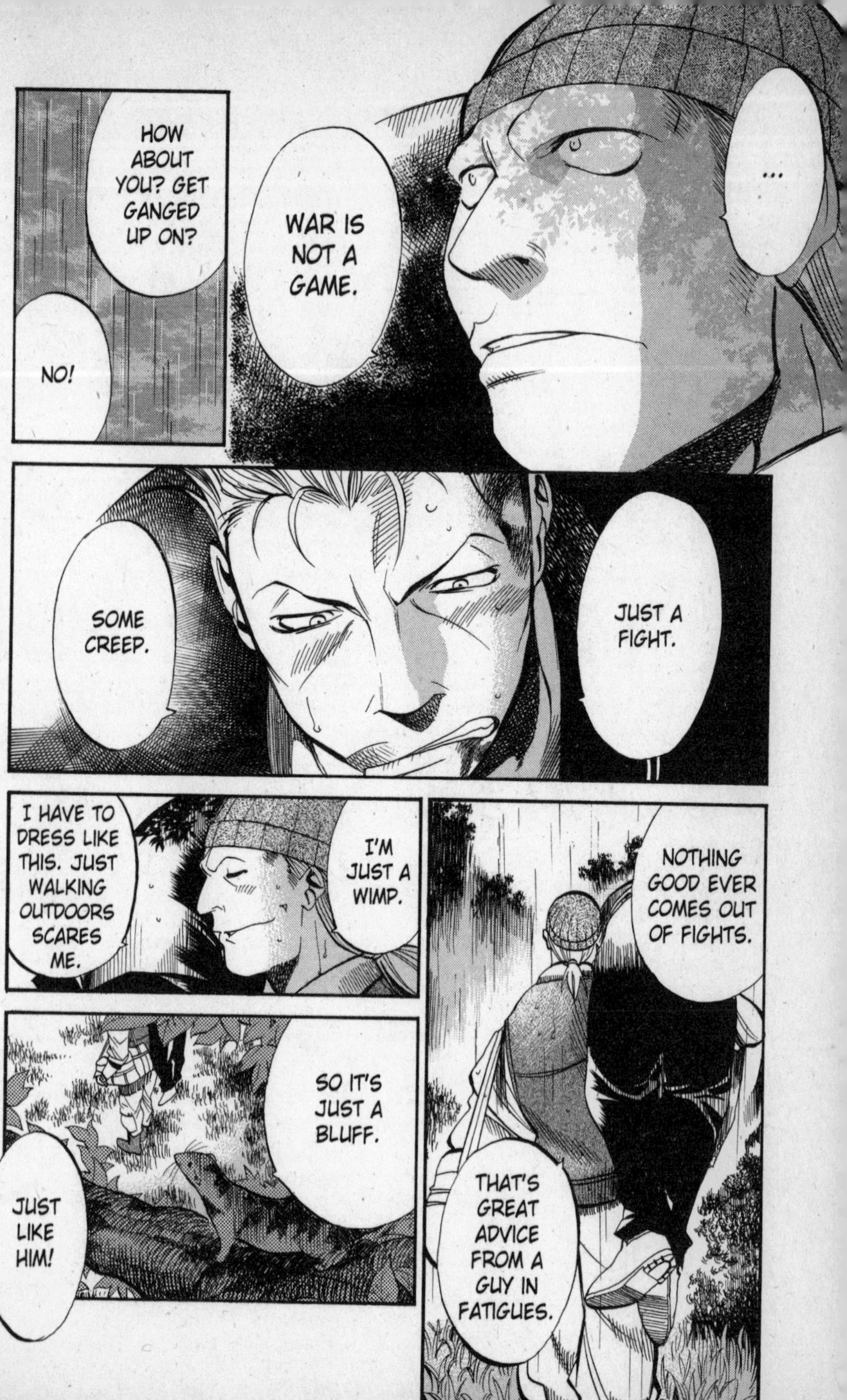
...
WAR IS NOT A GAME.
HOW ABOUT YOU? GET GANGED UP ON?
NO!
JUST A FIGHT.
SOME CREEP.
NOTHING GOOD EVER COMES OUT OF FIGHTS.
THAT'S GREAT ADVICE FROM A GUY IN FATIGUES.
I'M JUST A WIMP.
I HAVE TO DRESS LIKE THIS. JUST WALKING OUTDOORS SCARES ME.
SO IT'S JUST A BLUFF.
JUST LIKE HIM!

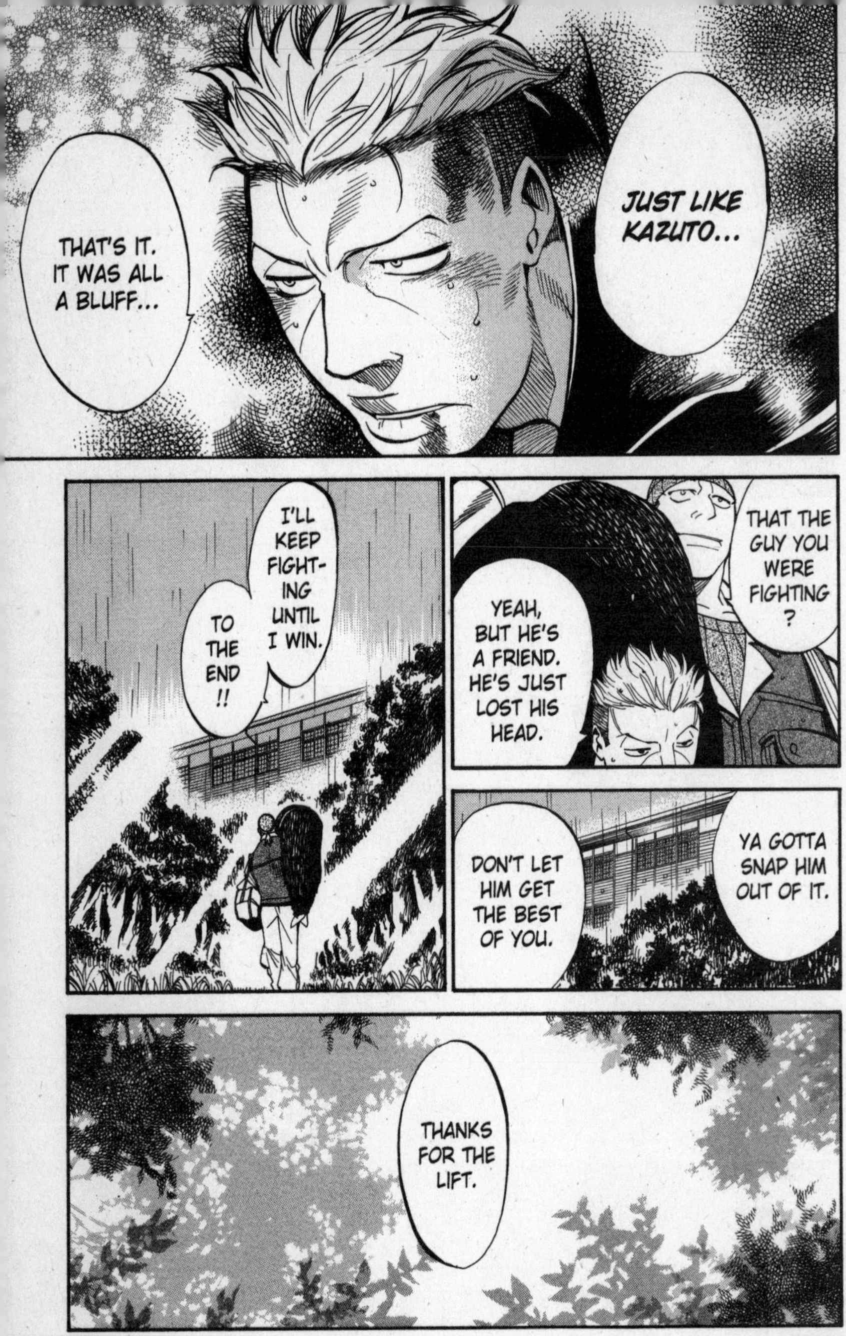
JUST LIKE KAZUTO...
THAT'S IT. IT WAS ALL A BLUFF...
THAT THE GUY YOU WERE FIGHTING ?
YEAH, BUT HE'S A FRIEND. HE'S JUST LOST HIS HEAD.
YA GOTTA SNAP HIM OUT OF IT.
DON'T LET HIM GET THE BEST OF YOU.
I'LL KEEP FIGHTING UNTIL I WIN.
TO THE END !!
THANKS FOR THE LIFT.

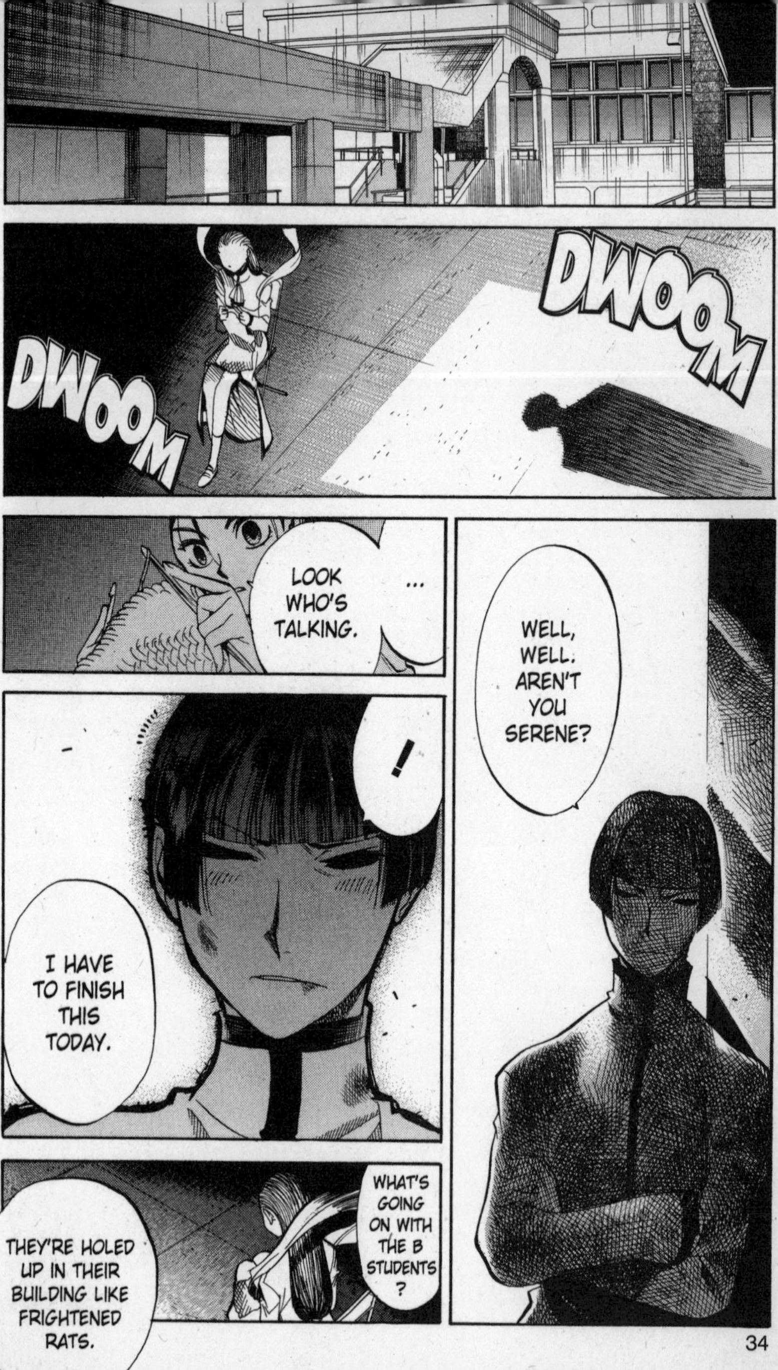
DWOOM
DWOOM
WELL, WELL. AREN'T YOU SERENE?
...
LOOK WHO'S TALKING.
!
I HAVE TO FINISH THIS TODAY.
WHAT'S GOING ON WITH THE B STUDENTS?
THEY'RE HOLED UP IN THEIR BUILDING LIKE FRIGHTENED RATS.

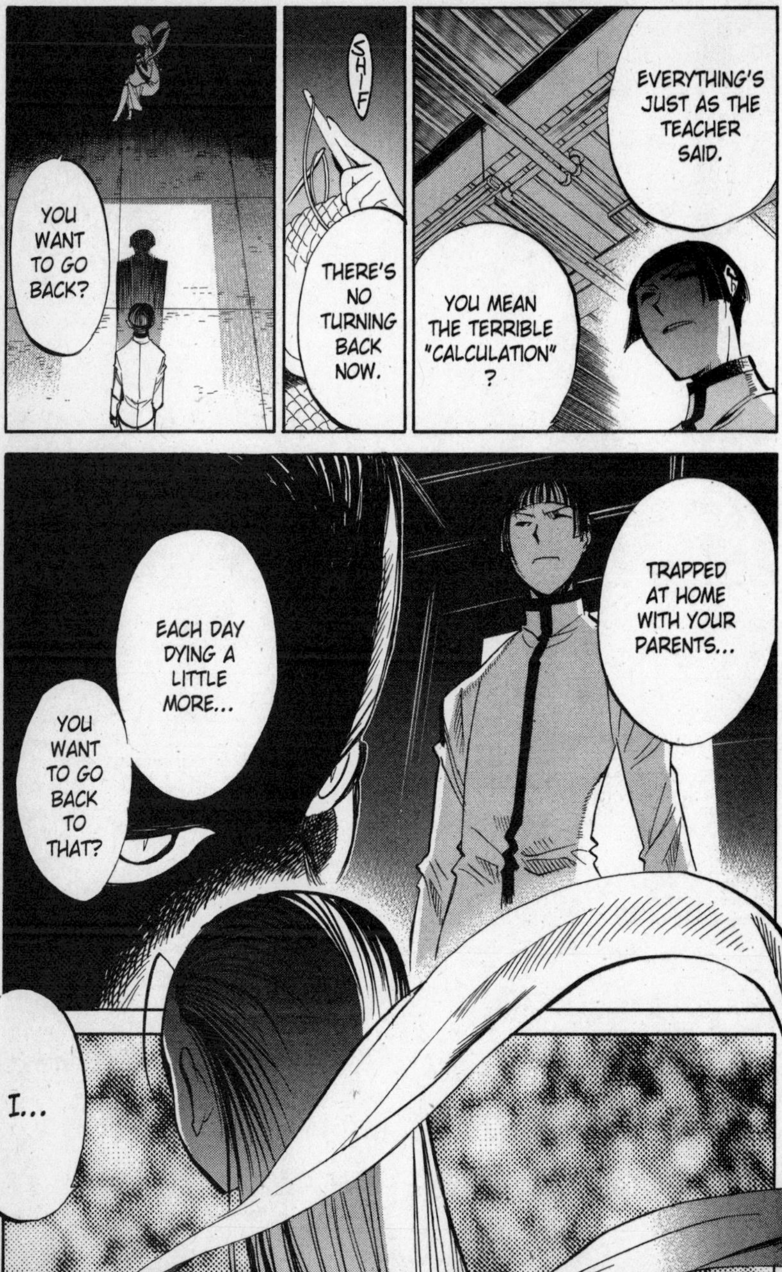
EVERYTHING'S JUST AS THE TEACHER SAID.
YOU MEAN THE TERRIBLE "CALCULATION" ?
SHIF
THERE'S NO TURNING BACK NOW.
YOU WANT TO GO BACK?
TRAPPED AT HOME WITH YOUR PARENTS...
EACH DAY DYING A LITTLE MORE...
YOU WANT TO GO BACK TO THAT?
I...

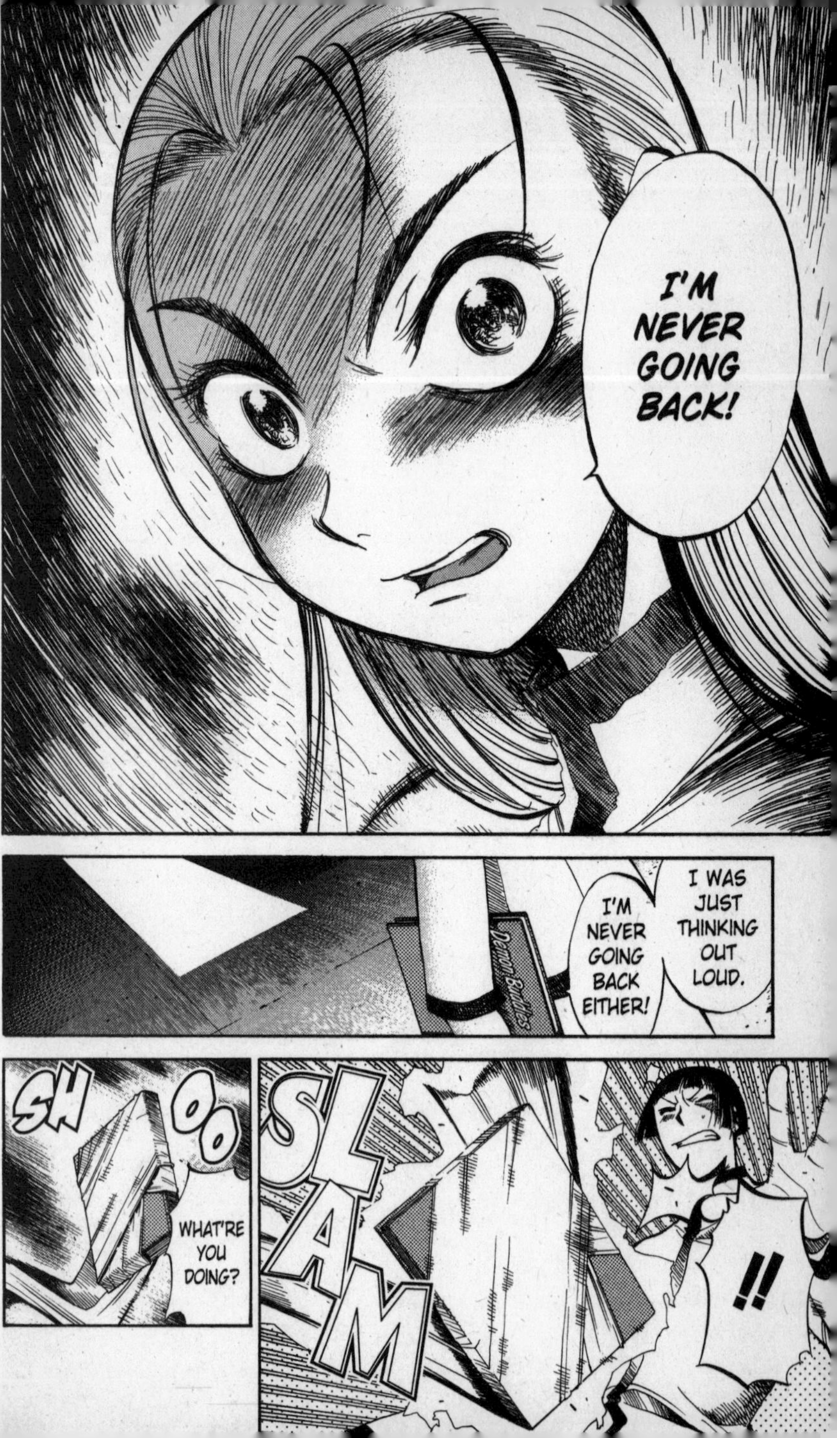
I'M NEVER GOING BACK!
I WAS JUST THINKING OUT LOUD.
I'M NEVER GOING BACK EITHER!
Demon Buddies
SLAM
!!
SHOO
WHAT'RE YOU DOING?

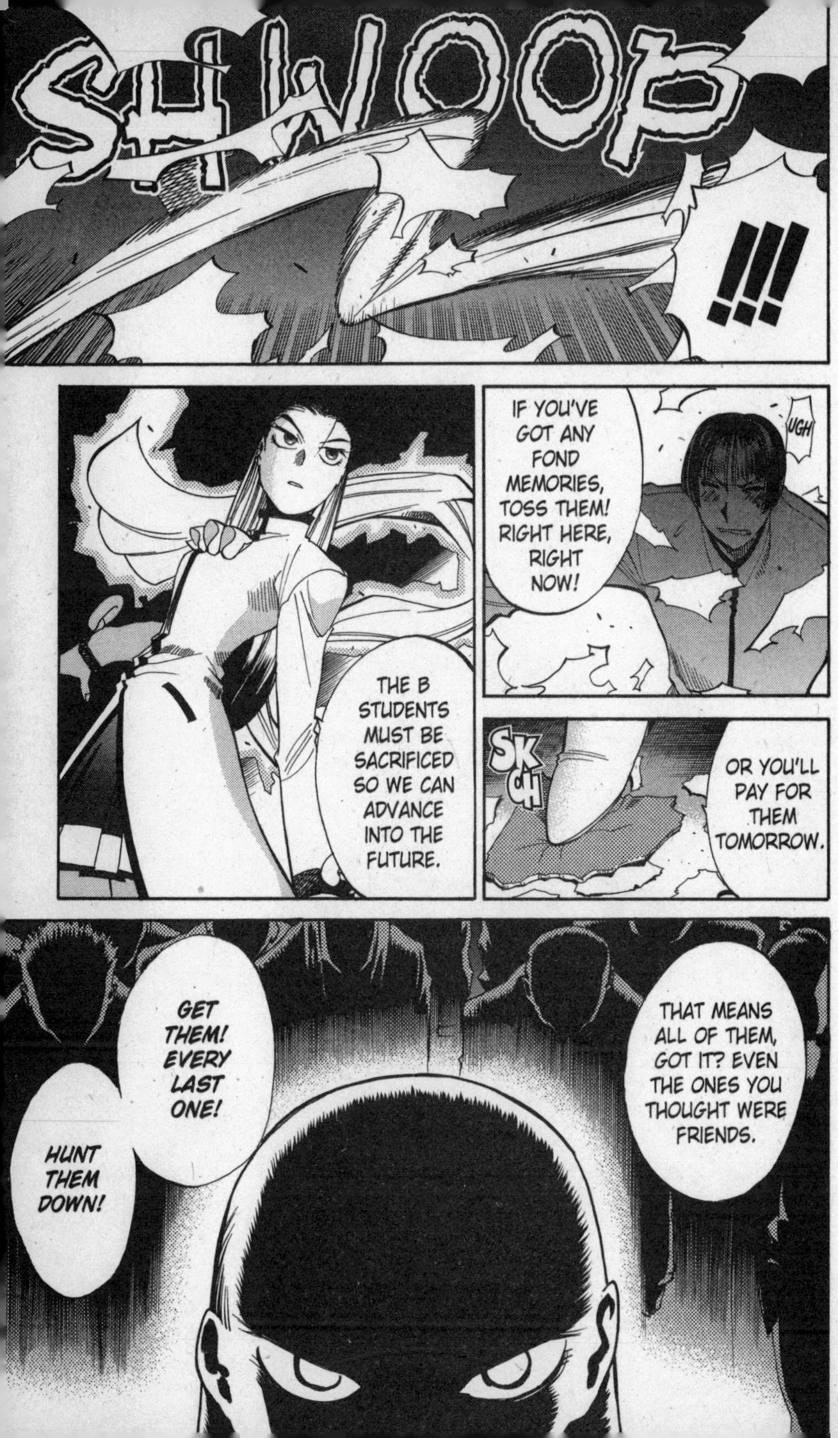
SHWOOP
!!!
UGH
IF YOU'VE GOT ANY FOND MEMORIES, TOSS THEM! RIGHT HERE, RIGHT NOW!
SKCH
OR YOU'LL PAY FOR THEM TOMORROW.
THE B STUDENTS MUST BE SACRIFICED SO WE CAN ADVANCE INTO THE FUTURE.
THAT MEANS ALL OF THEM, GOT IT? EVEN THE ONES YOU THOUGHT WERE FRIENDS.
GET THEM! EVERY LAST ONE!
HUNT THEM DOWN!

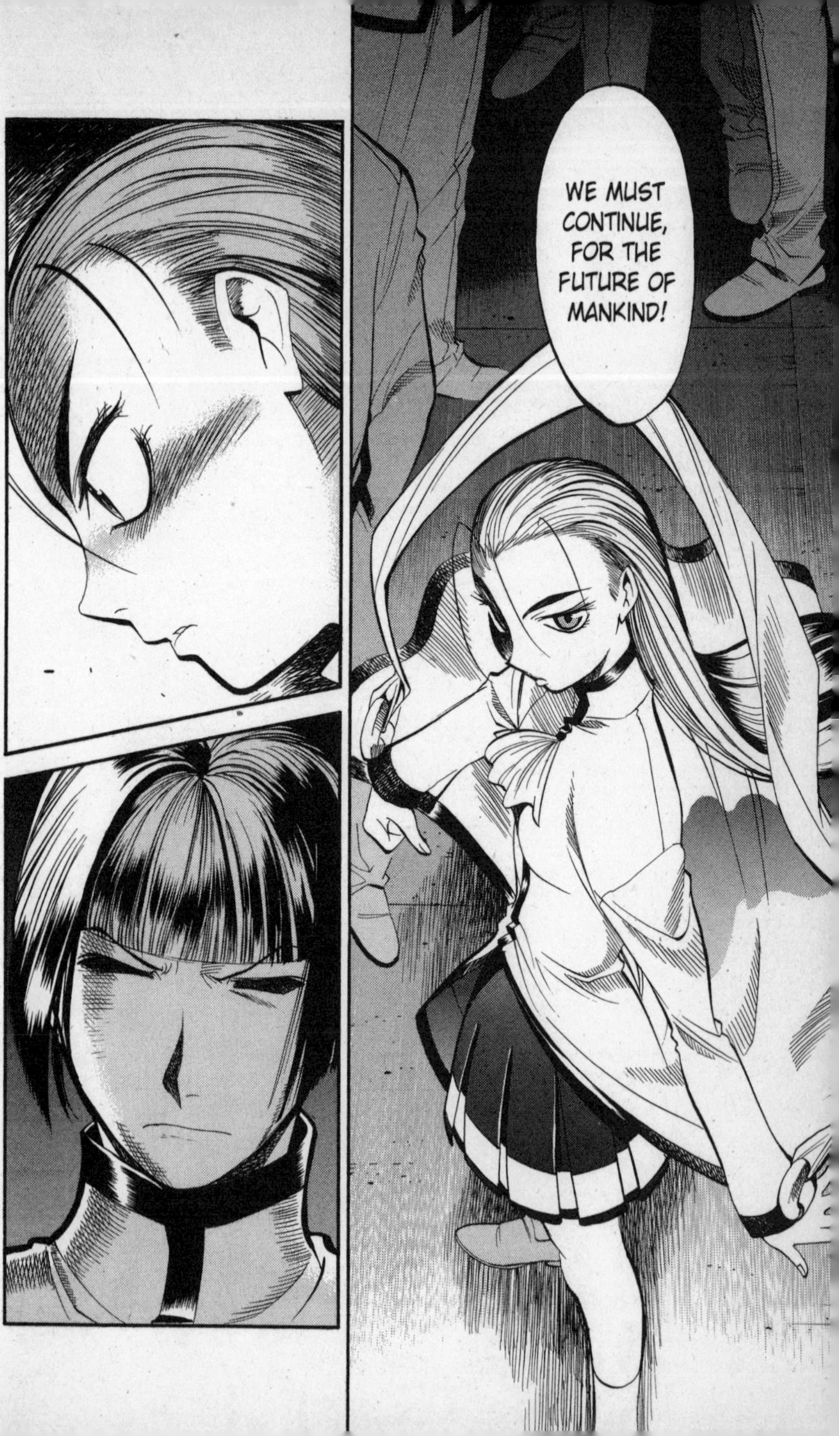
WE MUST CONTINUE, FOR THE FUTURE OF MANKIND!

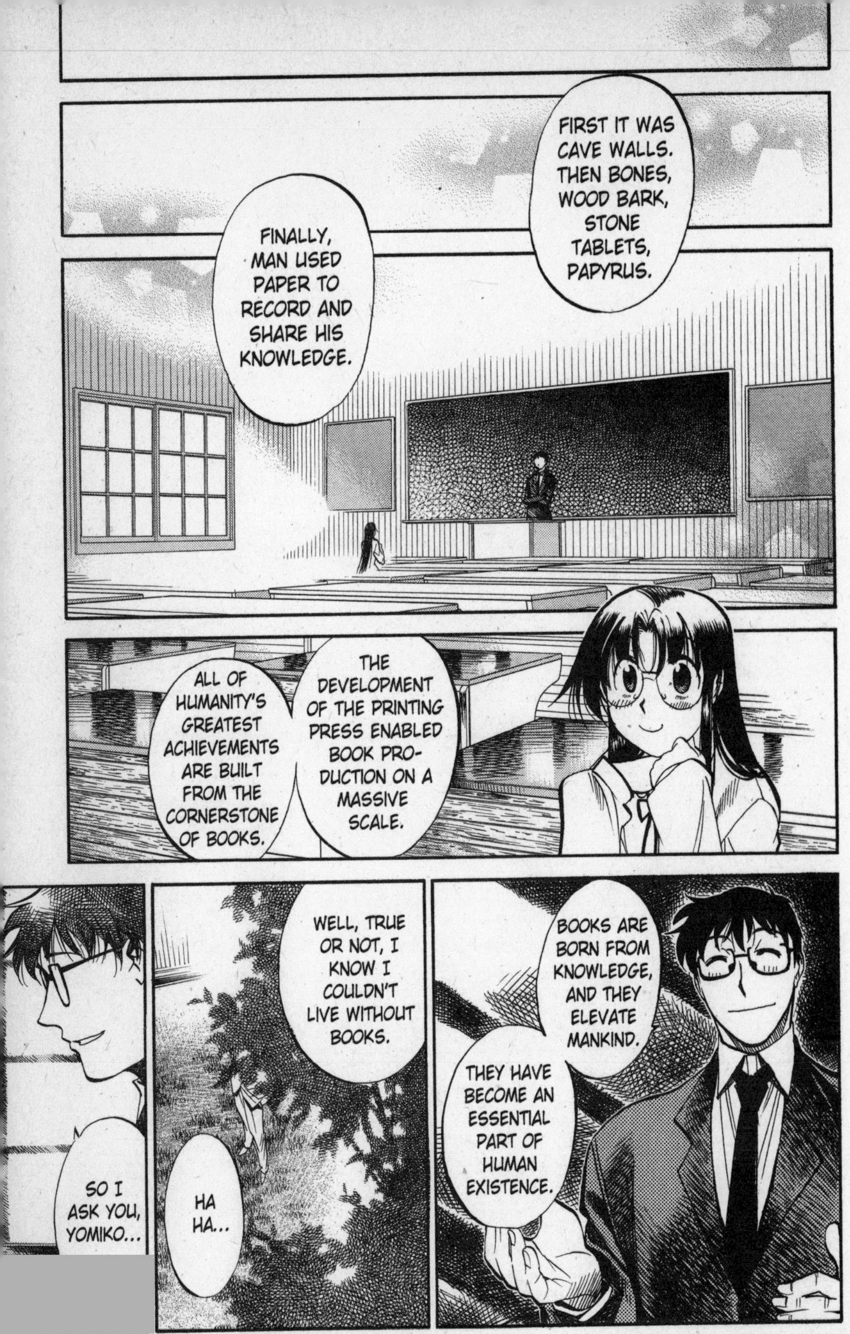
FIRST IT WAS CAVE WALLS. THEN BONES, WOOD BARK, STONE TABLETS, PAPYRUS.
FINALLY, MAN USED PAPER TO RECORD AND SHARE HIS KNOWLEDGE.
THE DEVELOPMENT OF THE PRINTING PRESS ENABLED BOOK PRO-DUCTION ON A MASSIVE SCALE.
ALL OF HUMANITY'S GREATEST ACHIEVEMENTS ARE BUILT FROM THE CORNERSTONE OF BOOKS.
BOOKS ARE BORN FROM KNOWLEDGE, AND THEY ELEVATE MANKIND.
THEY HAVE BECOME AN ESSENTIAL PART OF HUMAN EXISTENCE.
WELL, TRUE OR NOT, I KNOW I COULDN'T LIVE WITHOUT BOOKS.
HA HA...
SO I ASK YOU, YOMIKO...

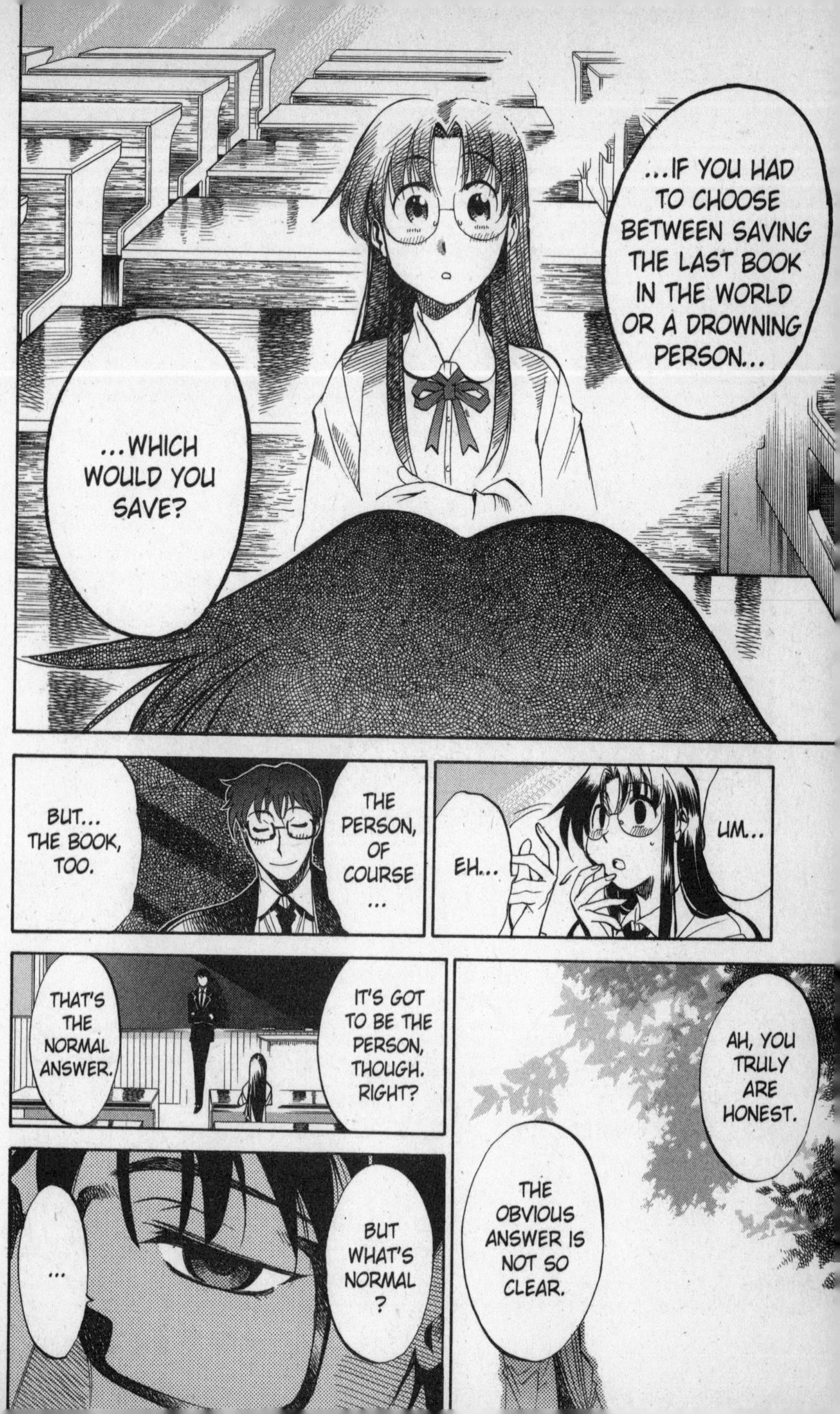
...IF YOU HAD TO CHOOSE BETWEEN SAVING THE LAST BOOK IN THE WORLD OR A DROWNING PERSON...
...WHICH WOULD YOU SAVE?
UM...
EH...
THE PERSON, OF COURSE...
BUT... THE BOOK, TOO.
AH, YOU TRULY ARE HONEST.
THE OBVIOUS ANSWER IS NOT SO CLEAR.
IT'S GOT TO BE THE PERSON, THOUGH. RIGHT?
THAT'S THE NORMAL ANSWER.
BUT WHAT'S NORMAL?
...

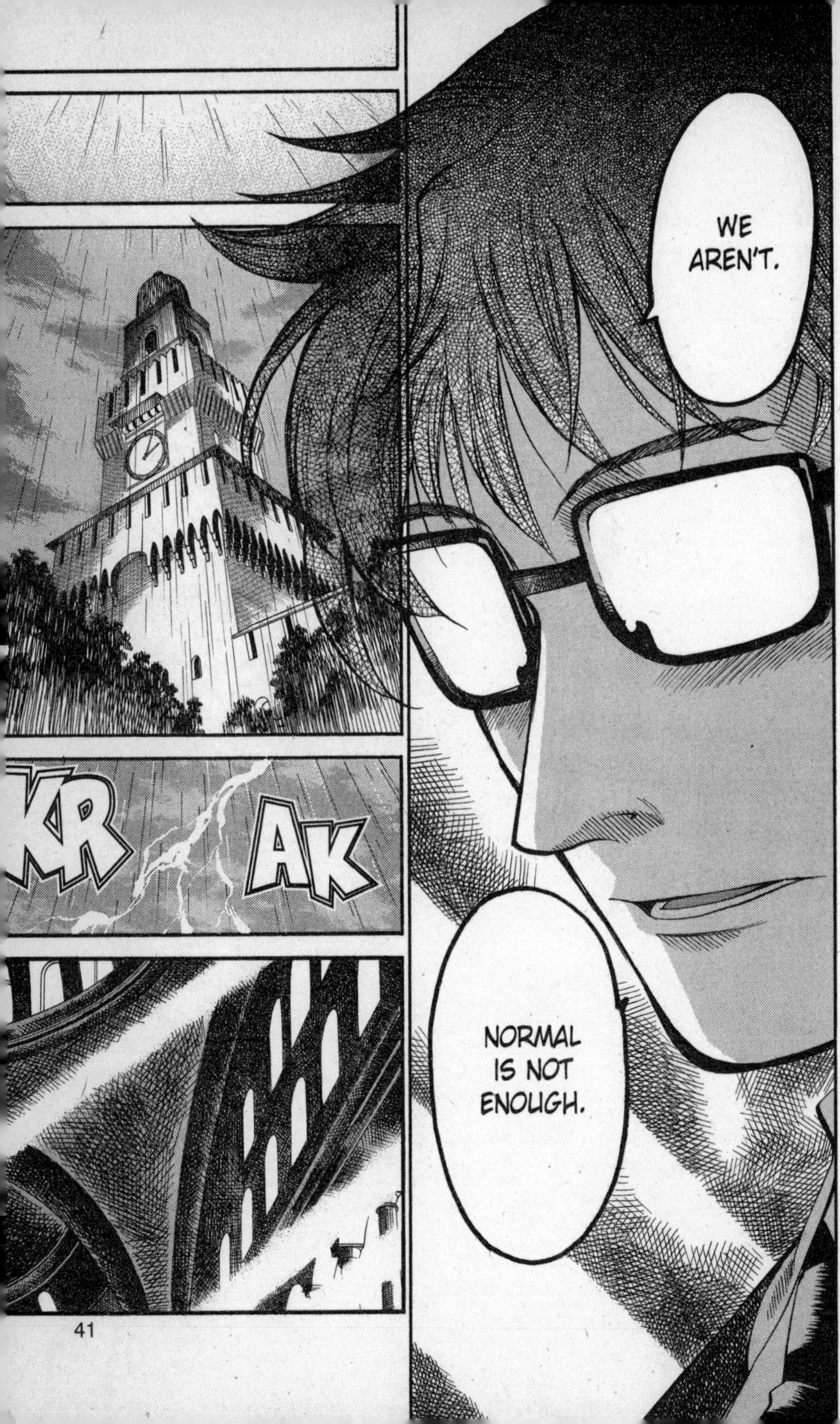
WE AREN'T.
NORMAL IS NOT ENOUGH.
KR
AK

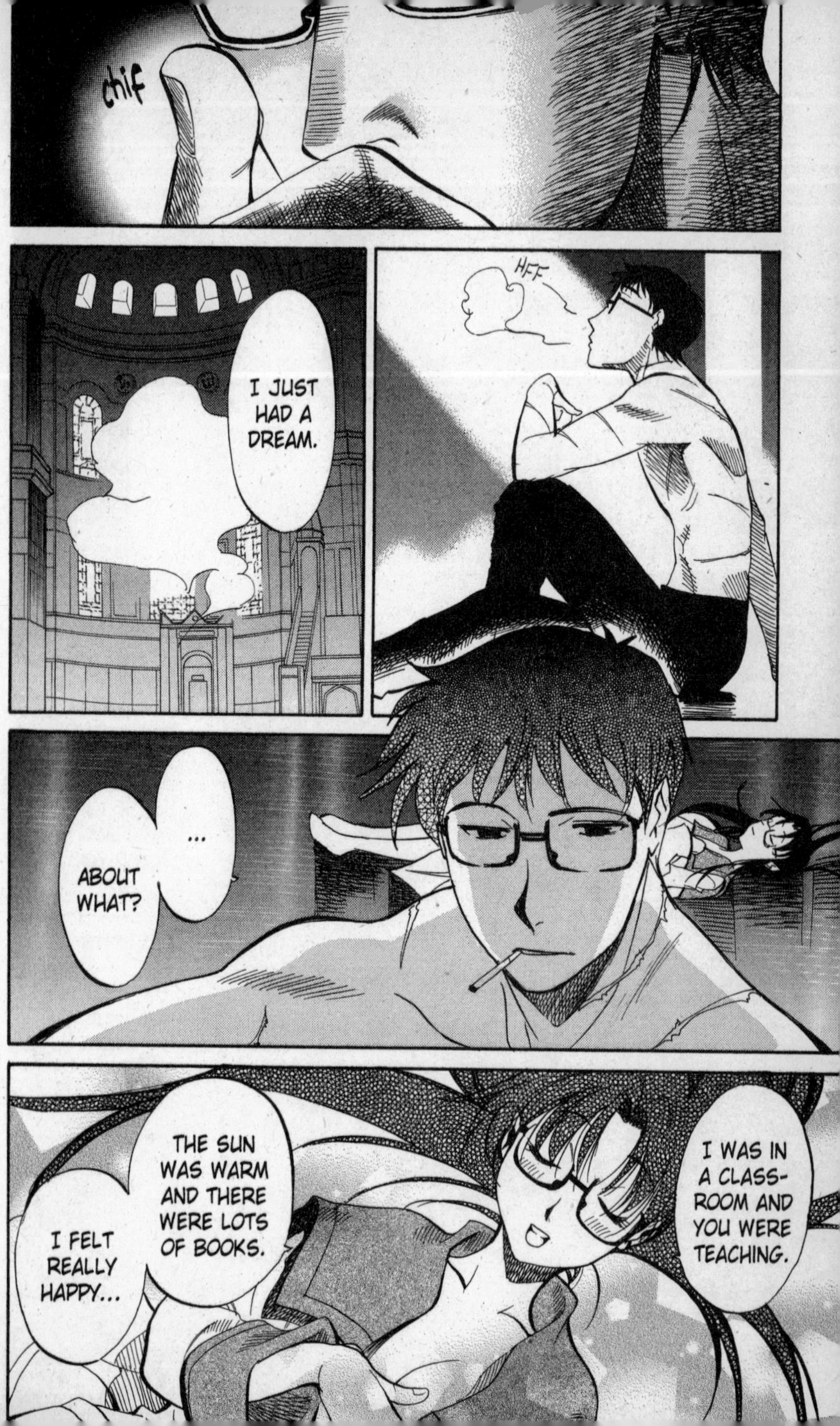
chif
HFF
I JUST HAD A DREAM.
...
ABOUT WHAT?
I WAS IN A CLASS-ROOM AND YOU WERE TEACHING.
THE SUN WAS WARM AND THERE WERE LOTS OF BOOKS.
I FELT REALLY HAPPY...

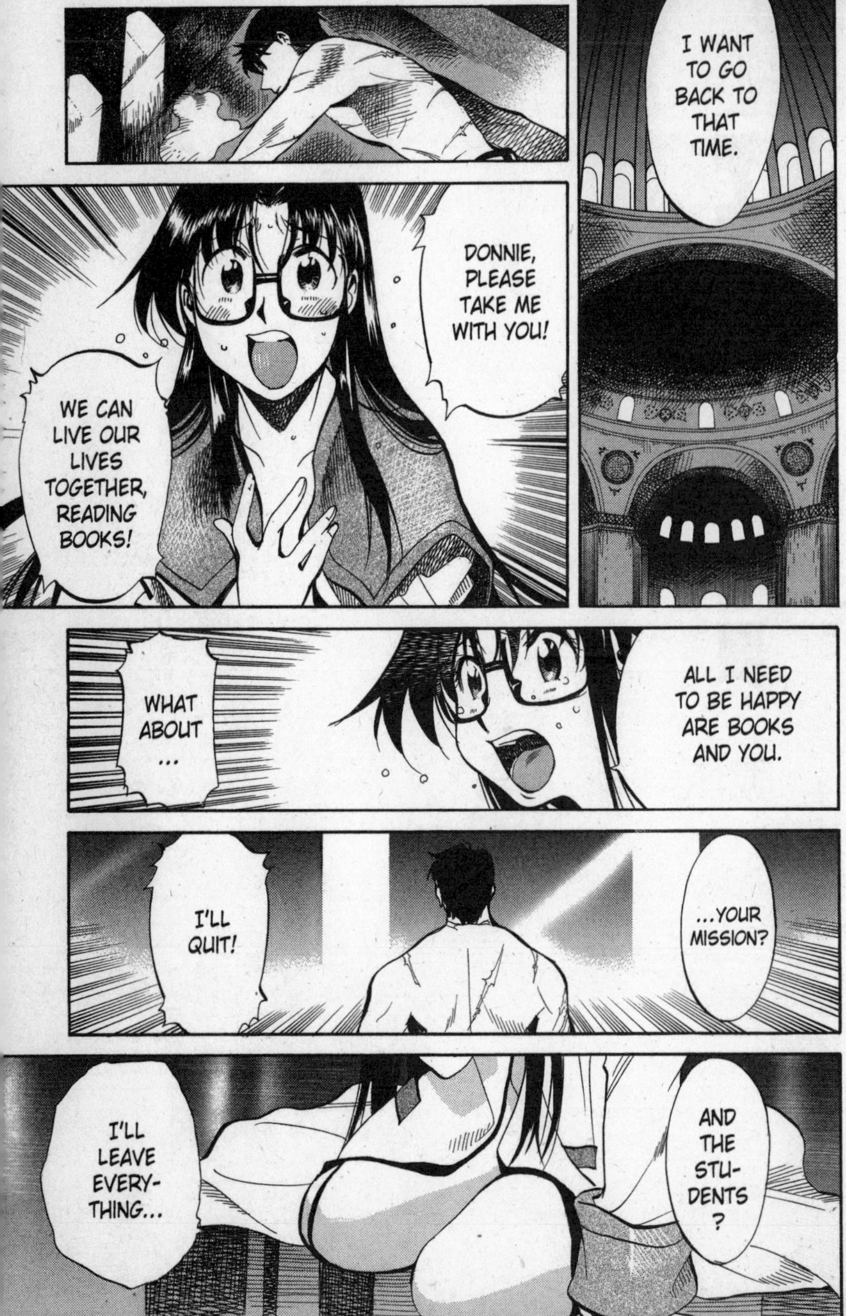
I WANT TO GO BACK TO THAT TIME.
DONNIE, PLEASE TAKE ME WITH YOU!
WE CAN LIVE OUR LIVES TOGETHER, READING BOOKS!
ALL I NEED TO BE HAPPY ARE BOOKS AND YOU.
WHAT ABOUT ...
...YOUR MISSION?
I'LL QUIT!
AND THE STU-DENTS ?
I'LL LEAVE EVERY-THING...

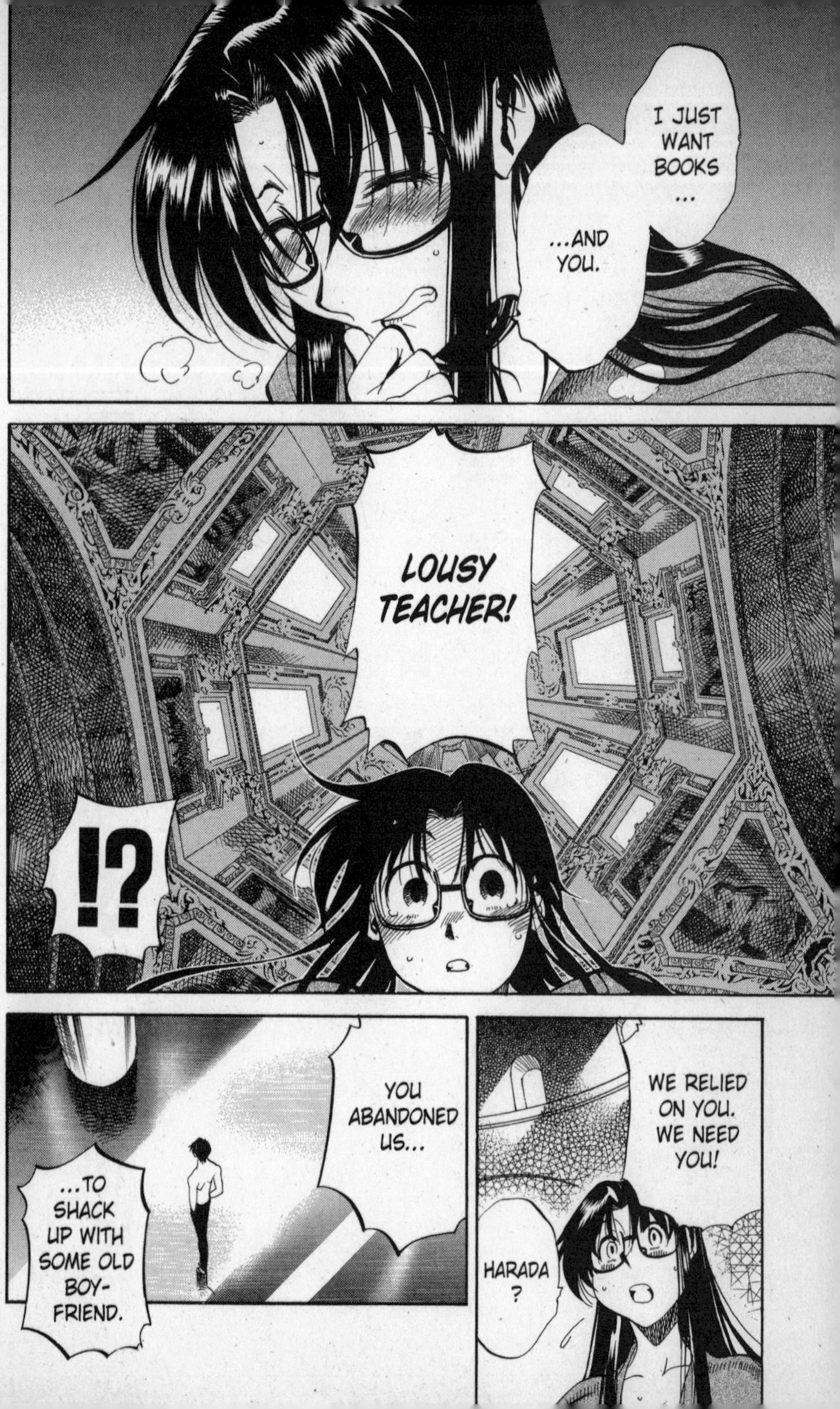
I JUST WANT BOOKS ...
...AND YOU.
LOUSY TEACHER!
!?
WE RELIED ON YOU. WE NEED YOU!
HARADA ?
YOU ABANDONED US...
...TO SHACK UP WITH SOME OLD BOY-FRIEND.

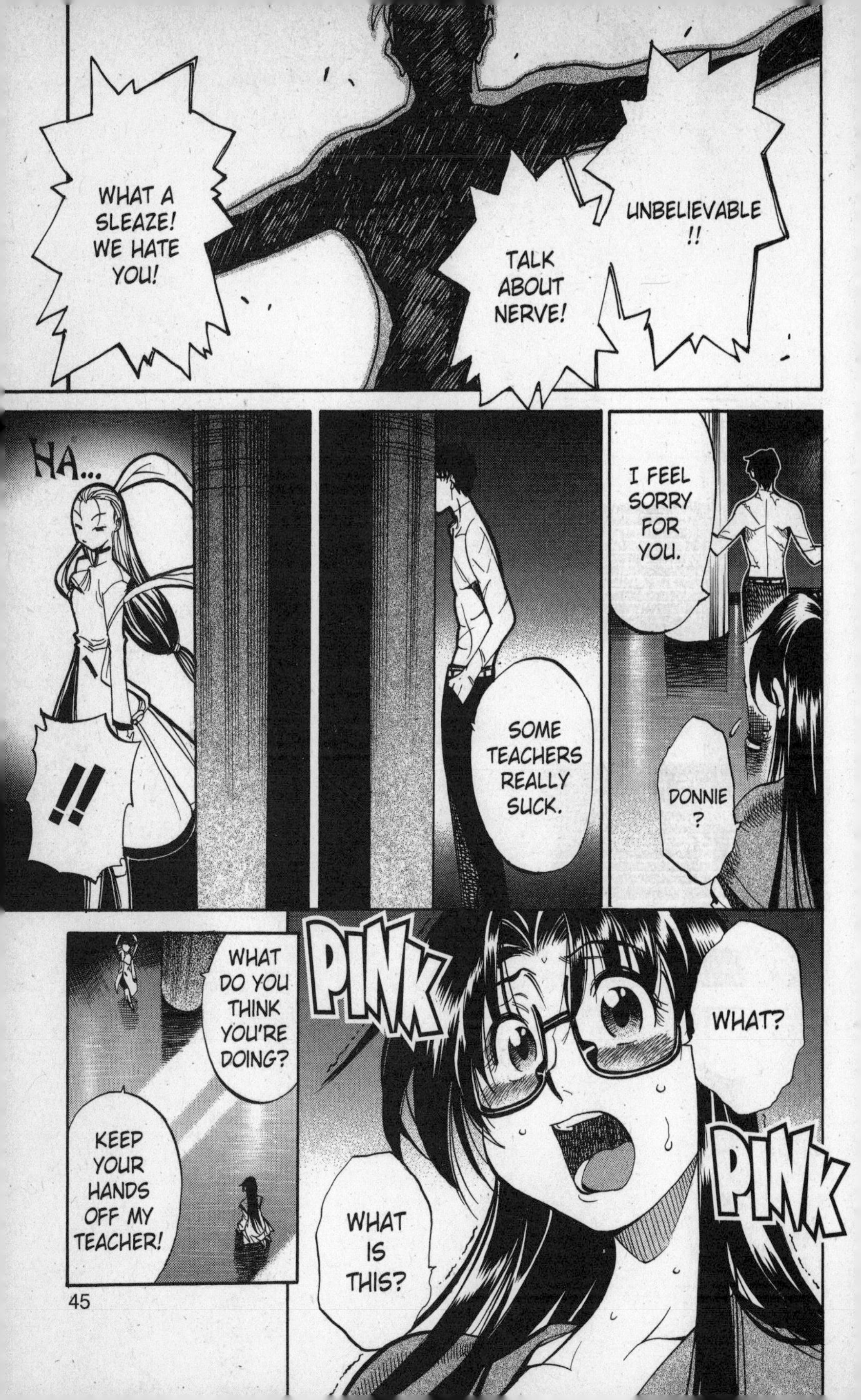

UNBELIEVABLE !!
TALK ABOUT NERVE!
WHAT A SLEAZE! WE HATE YOU!
I FEEL SORRY FOR YOU.
DONNIE ?
SOME TEACHERS REALLY SUCK.
HA...
!!
WHAT?
PINK
PINK
WHAT IS THIS?
WHAT DO YOU THINK YOU'RE DOING?
KEEP YOUR HANDS OFF MY TEACHER!

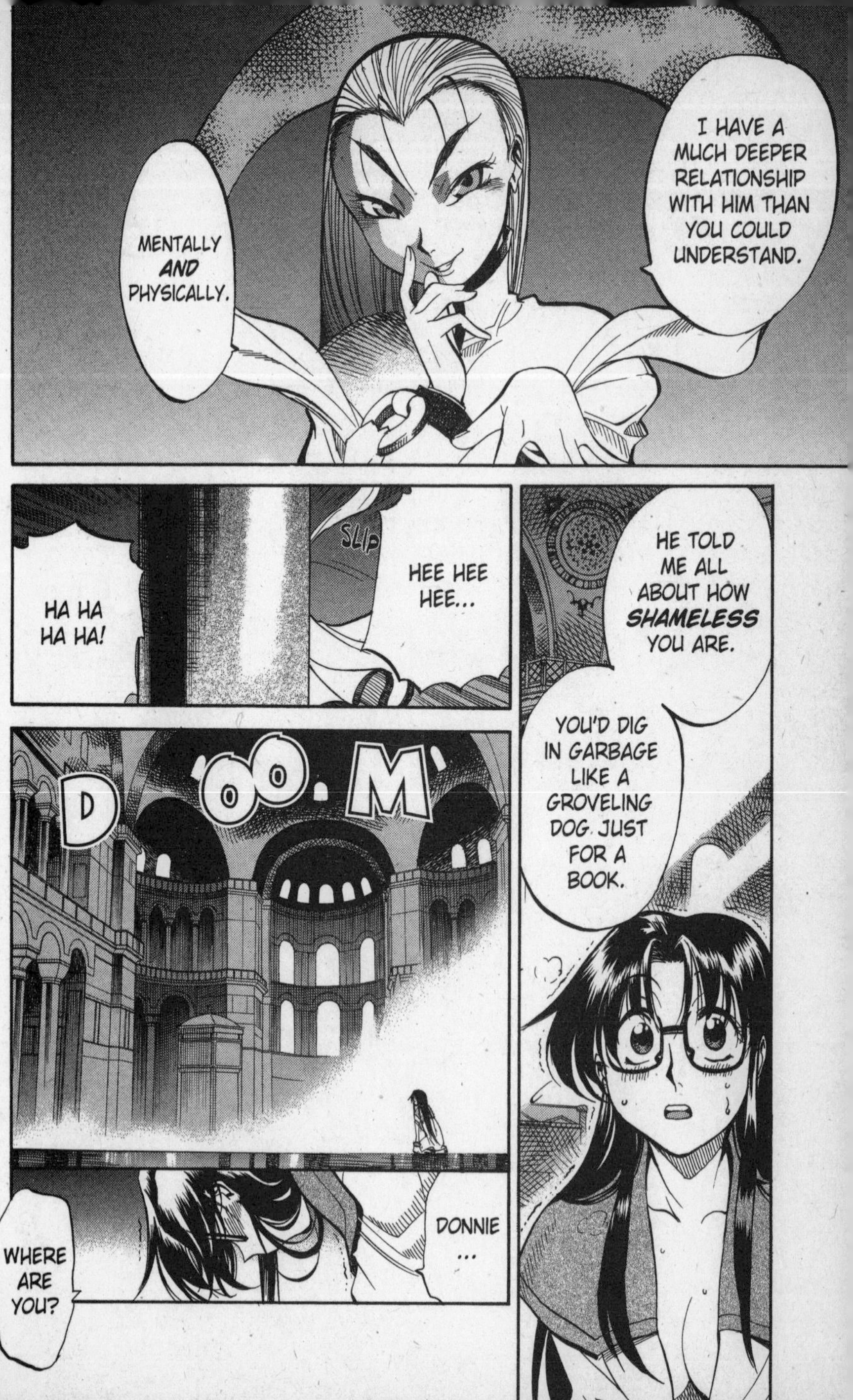
I HAVE A MUCH DEEPER RELATIONSHIP WITH HIM THAN YOU COULD UNDERSTAND.
MENTALLY **AND** PHYSICALLY.
HE TOLD ME ALL ABOUT HOW **SHAMELESS** YOU ARE.
YOU'D DIG IN GARBAGE LIKE A GROVELING DOG JUST FOR A BOOK.
SLIP
HEE HEE HEE...
HA HA HA HA!
DOOM
DONNIE ...
WHERE ARE YOU?

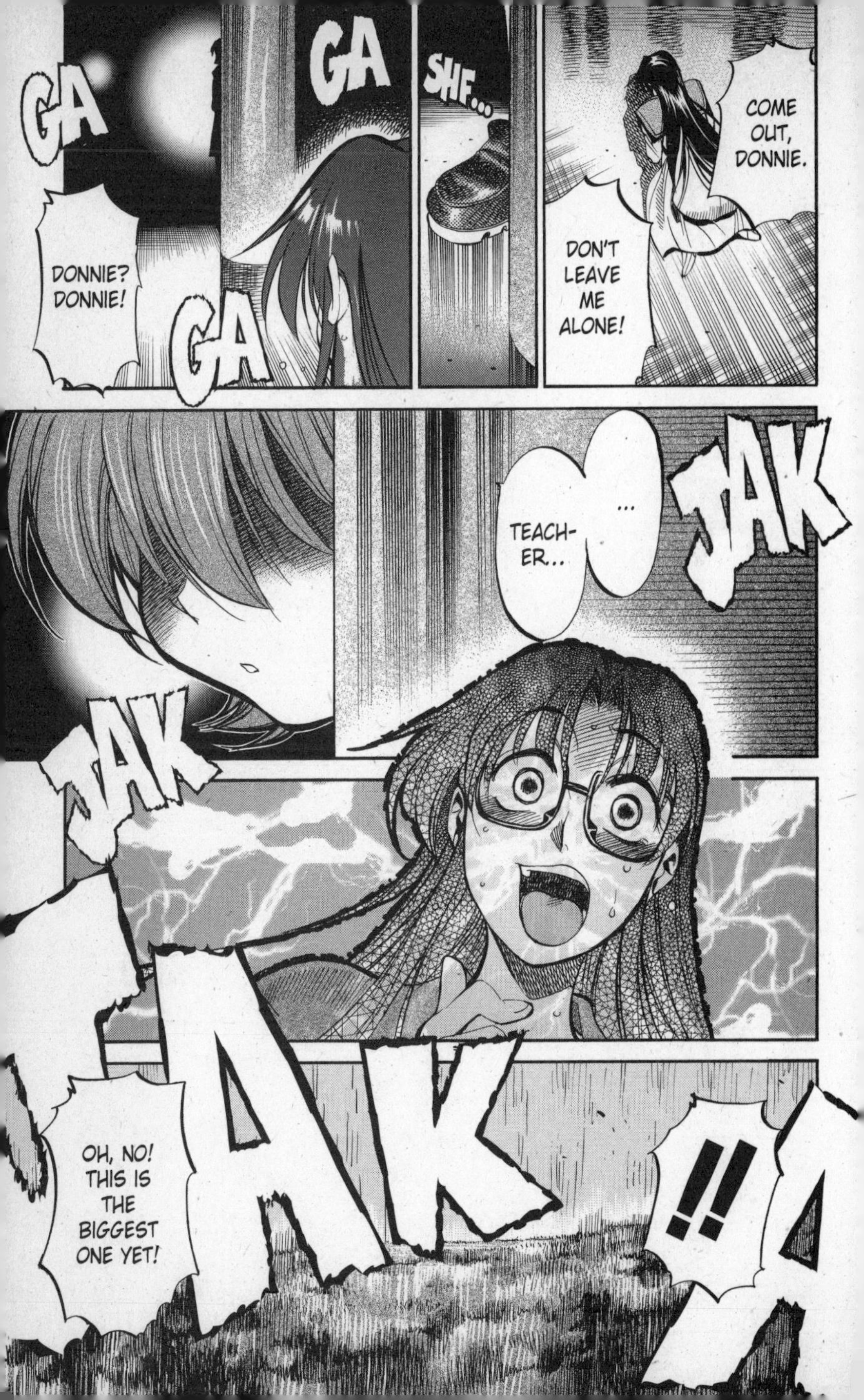
COME OUT, DONNIE.
DON'T LEAVE ME ALONE!
SHF...
GA
GA
GA
DONNIE? DONNIE!
...
TEACH-ER...
JAK
JAK
AK!!
OH, NO! THIS IS THE BIGGEST ONE YET!

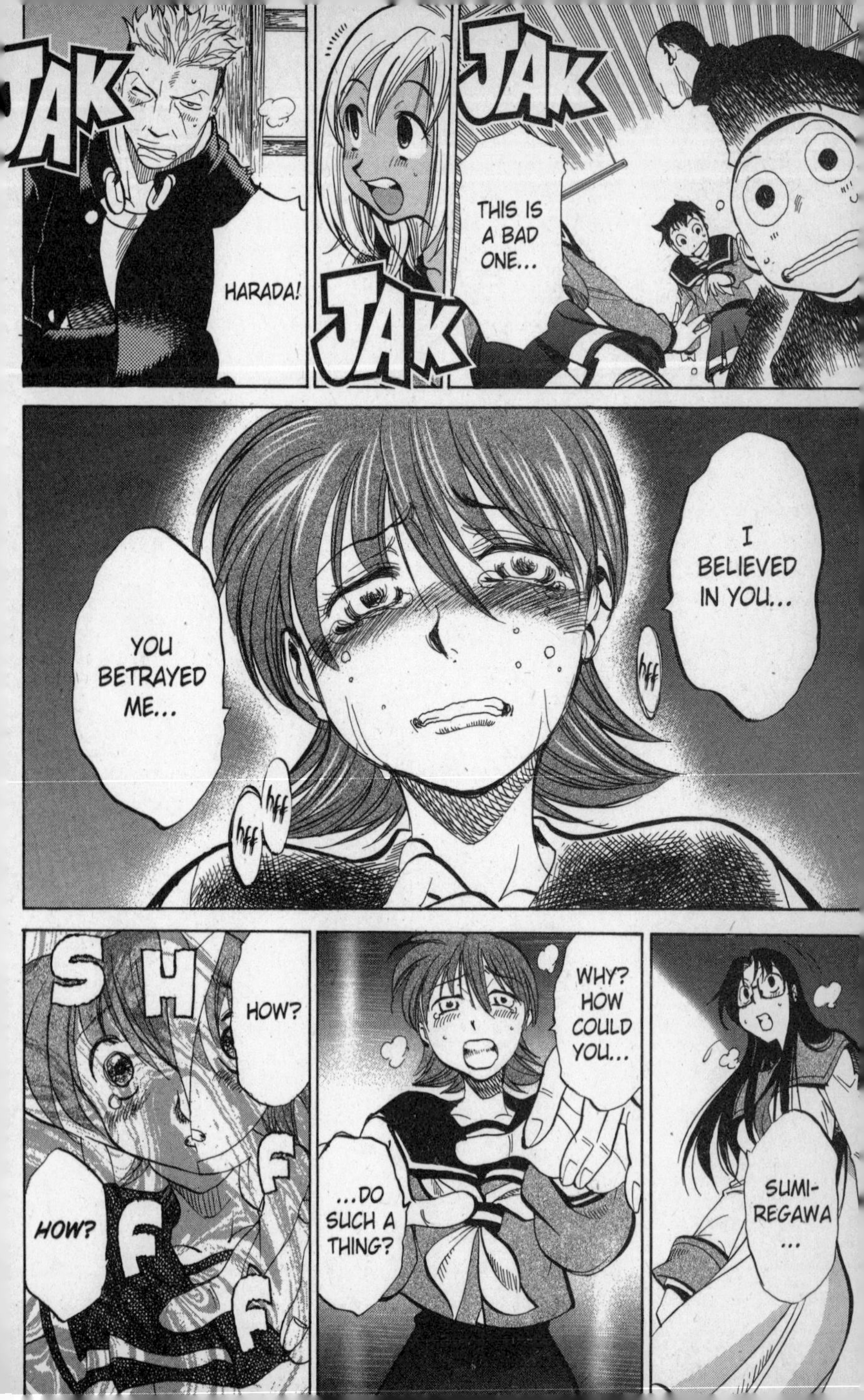
JAK
THIS IS A BAD ONE...
JAK
JAK
HARADA!
I BELIEVED IN YOU...
hff
YOU BETRAYED ME...
hff
hff
SUMI-REGAWA ...
WHY? HOW COULD YOU...
...DO SUCH A THING?
SH
HOW?
HOW?
F
F
F

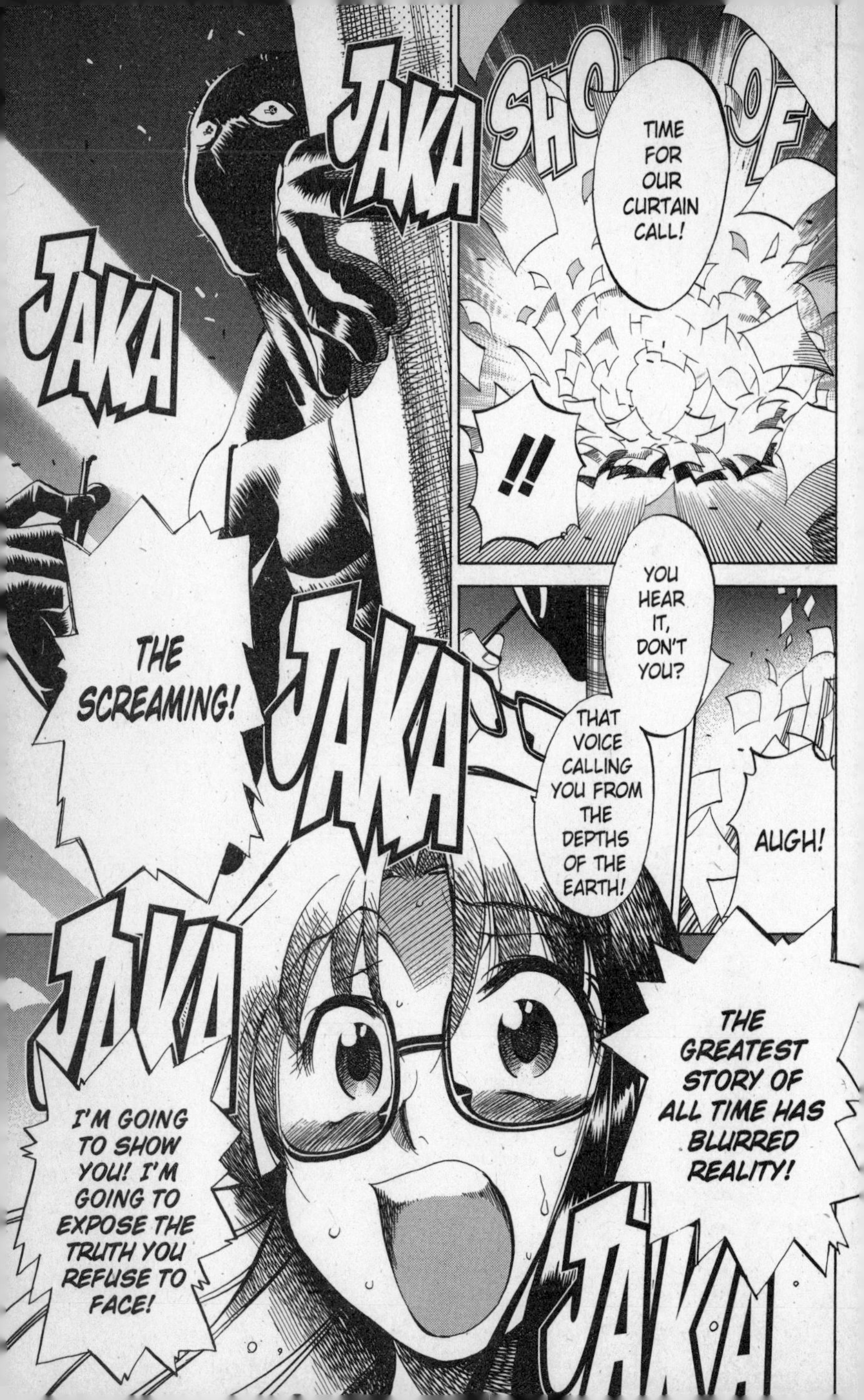
TIME FOR OUR CURTAIN CALL!
!!
YOU HEAR IT, DON'T YOU?
THAT VOICE CALLING YOU FROM THE DEPTHS OF THE EARTH!
AUGH!
JAKA
JAKA
THE SCREAMING!
JAKA
THE GREATEST STORY OF ALL TIME HAS BLURRED REALITY!
JAKA
I'M GOING TO SHOW YOU! I'M GOING TO EXPOSE THE TRUTH YOU REFUSE TO FACE!
JAKA

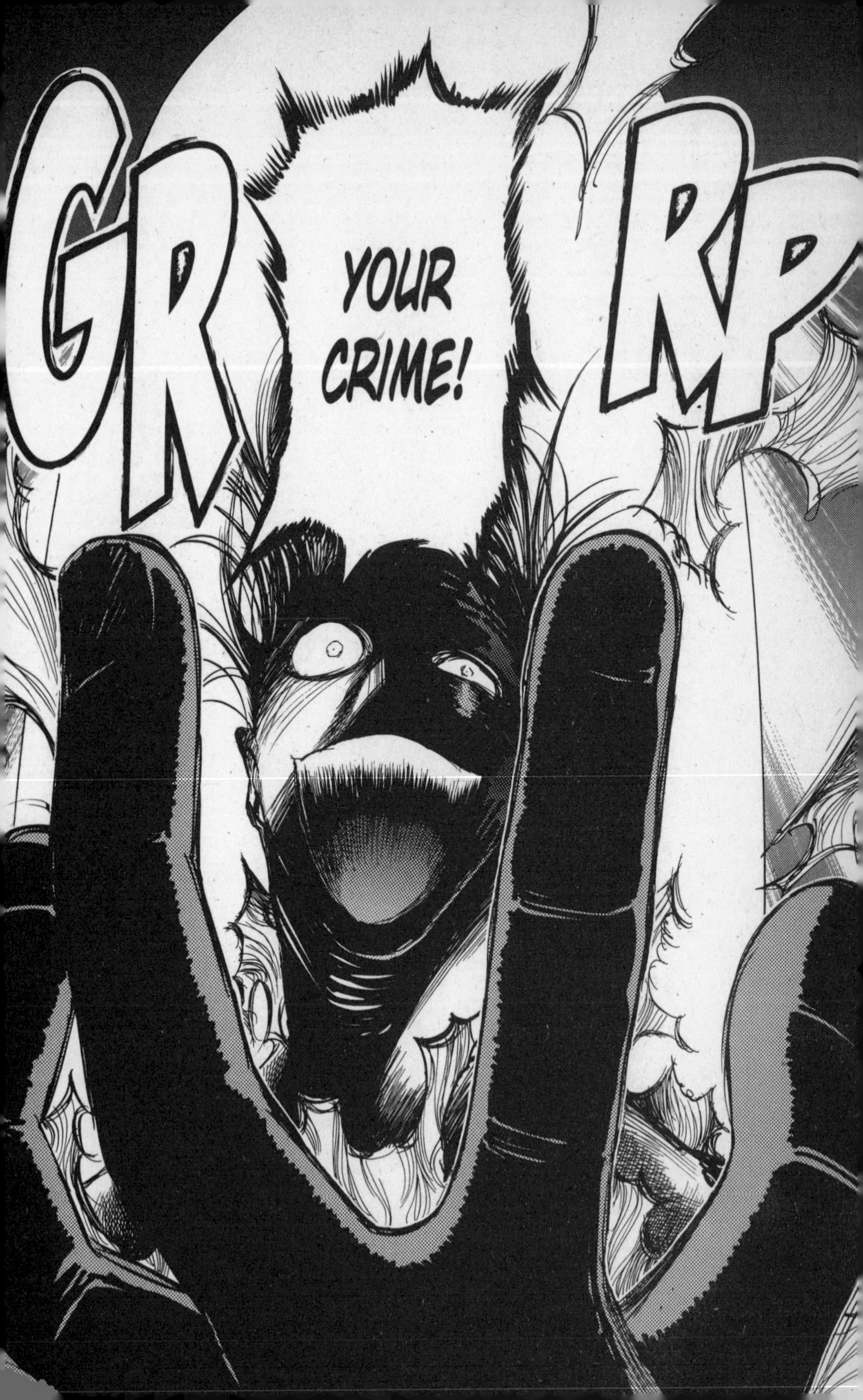
GRURP
YOUR CRIME!

EPISODE THREE

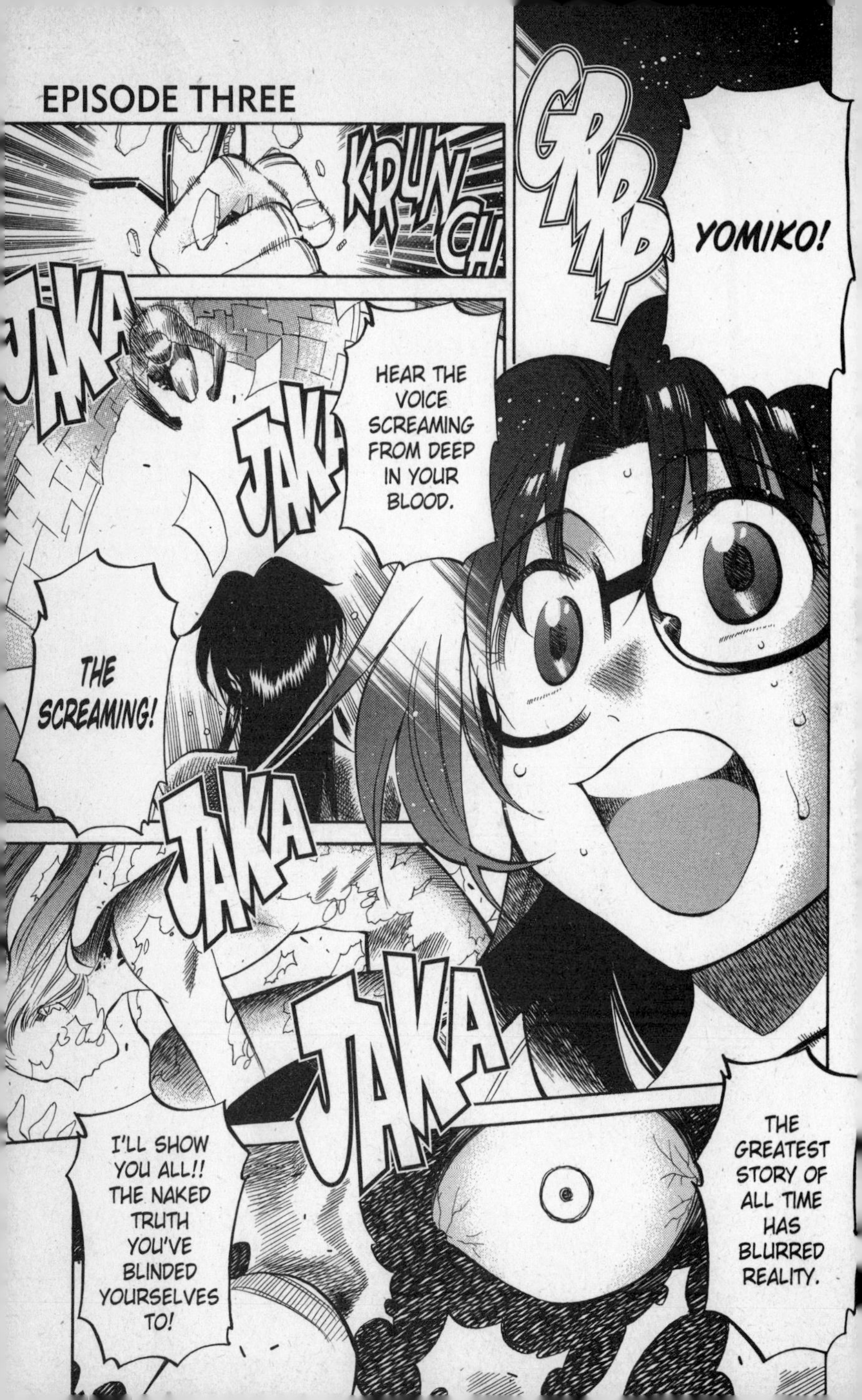

GRRR
YOMIKO!
KRUNCH
HEAR THE VOICE SCREAMING FROM DEEP IN YOUR BLOOD.
JAKA
JAKA
THE SCREAMING!
JAKA
THE GREATEST STORY OF ALL TIME HAS BLURRED REALITY.
JAKA
I'LL SHOW YOU ALL!! THE NAKED TRUTH YOU'VE BLINDED YOURSELVES TO!

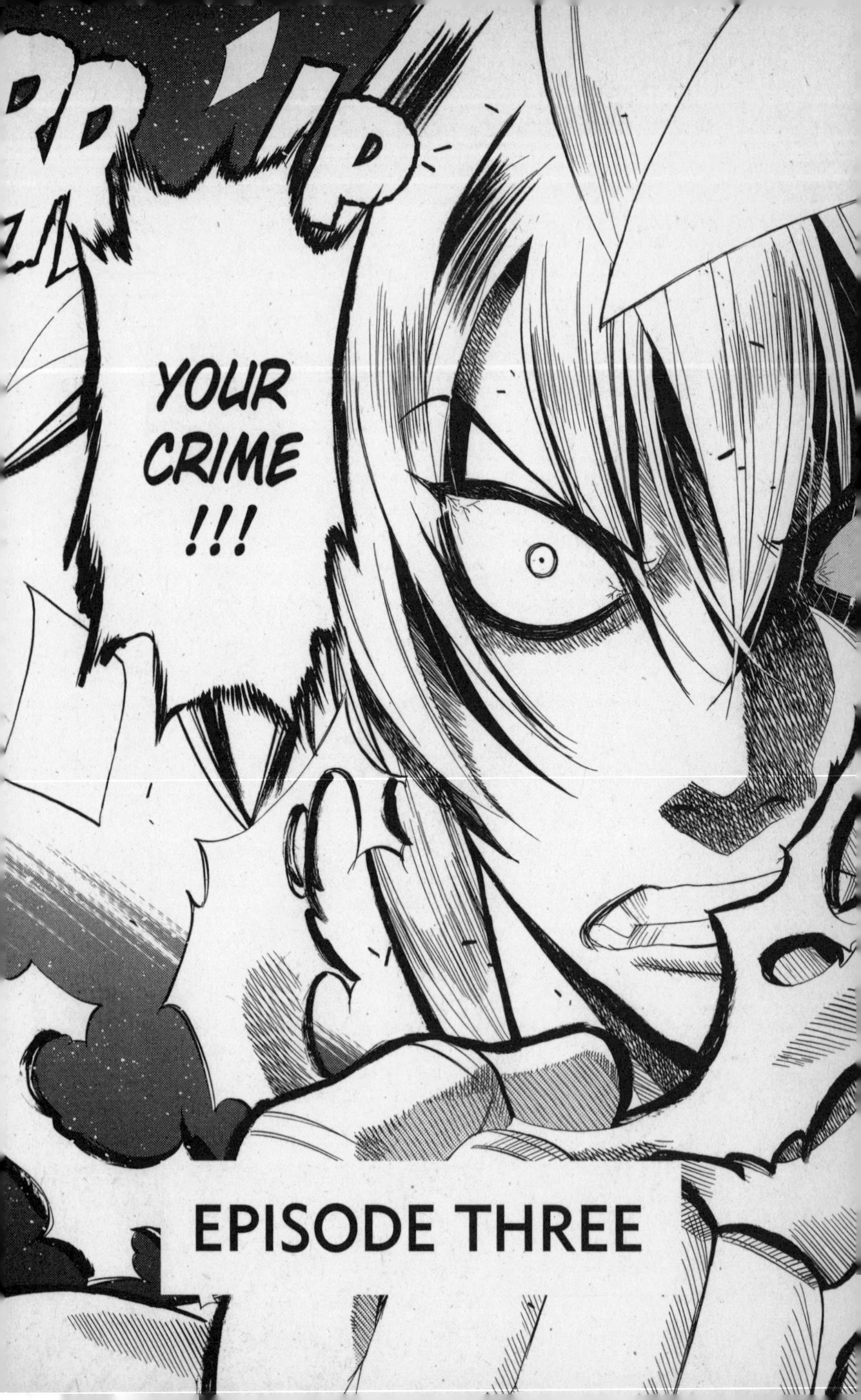
YOUR CRIME !!!

EPISODE THREE

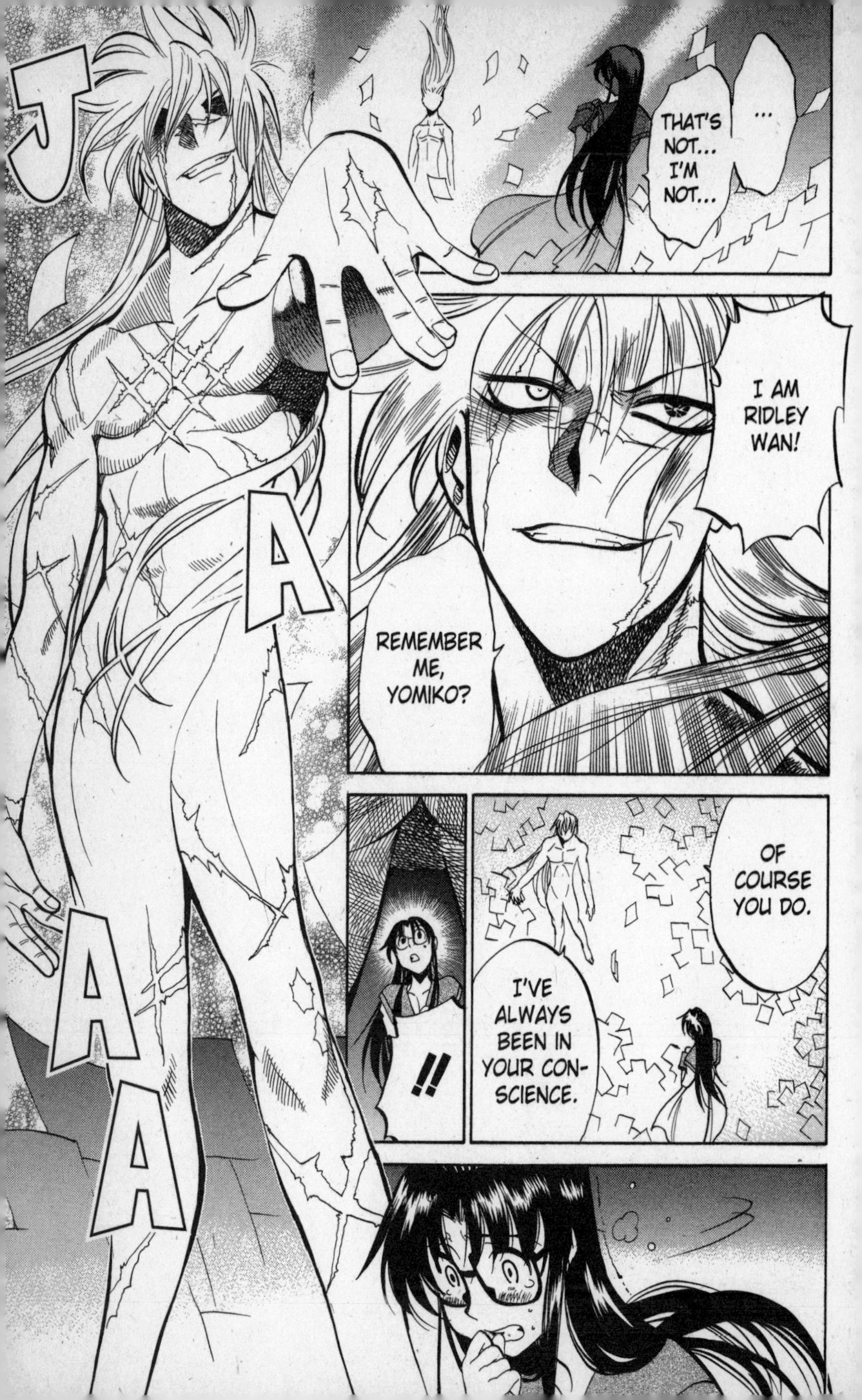
...
THAT'S NOT... I'M NOT...
I AM RIDLEY WAN!
REMEMBER ME, YOMIKO?
OF COURSE YOU DO.
I'VE ALWAYS BEEN IN YOUR CON- SCIENCE.
!!
JAAAA

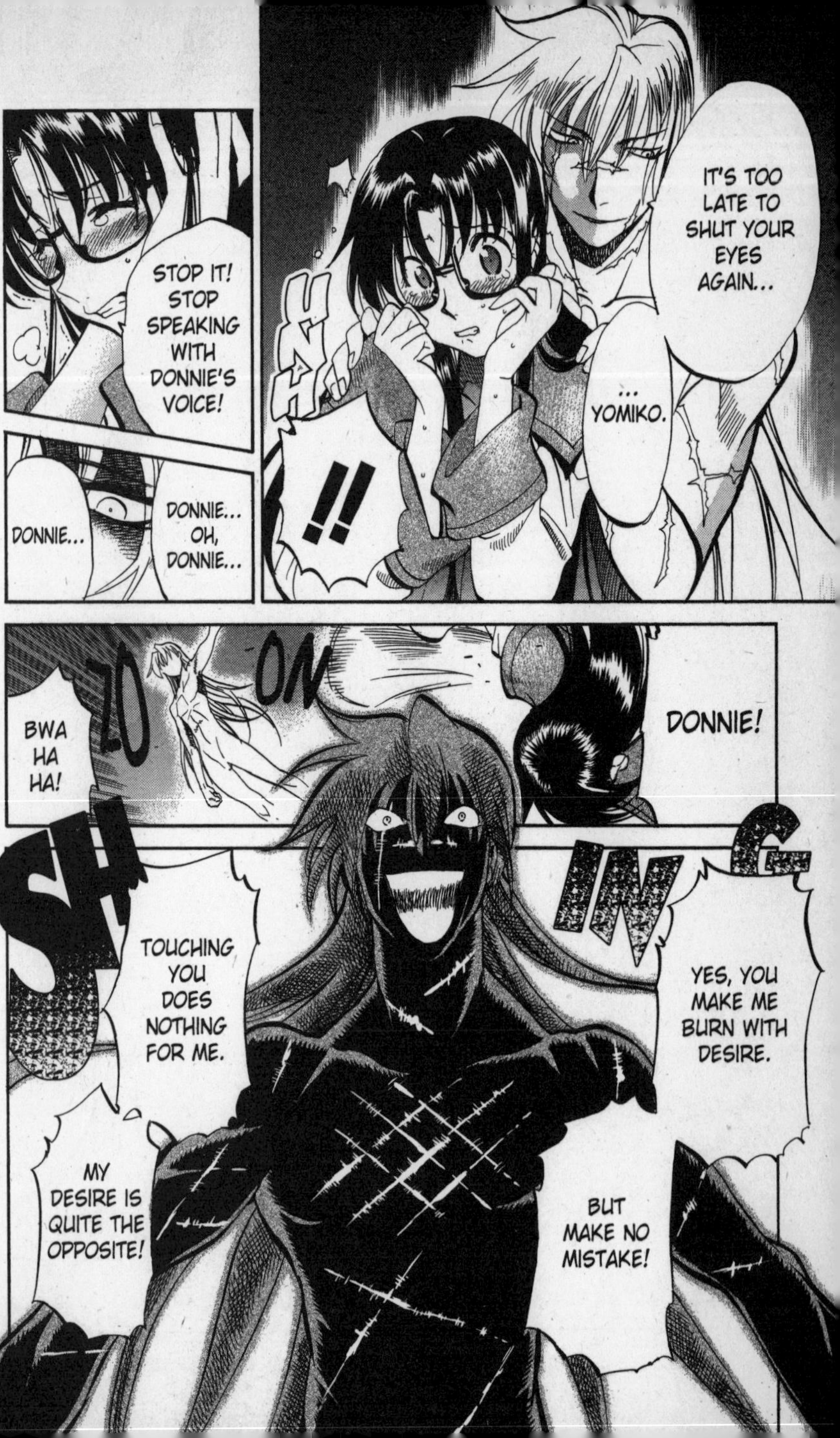
IT'S TOO LATE TO SHUT YOUR EYES AGAIN...
...YOMIKO.
SHA
!!
STOP IT! STOP SPEAKING WITH DONNIE'S VOICE!
DONNIE... OH, DONNIE...
DONNIE...
DONNIE!
ZO ON
BWA HA HA!
SHING
YES, YOU MAKE ME BURN WITH DESIRE.
TOUCHING YOU DOES NOTHING FOR ME.
BUT MAKE NO MISTAKE!
MY DESIRE IS QUITE THE OPPOSITE!

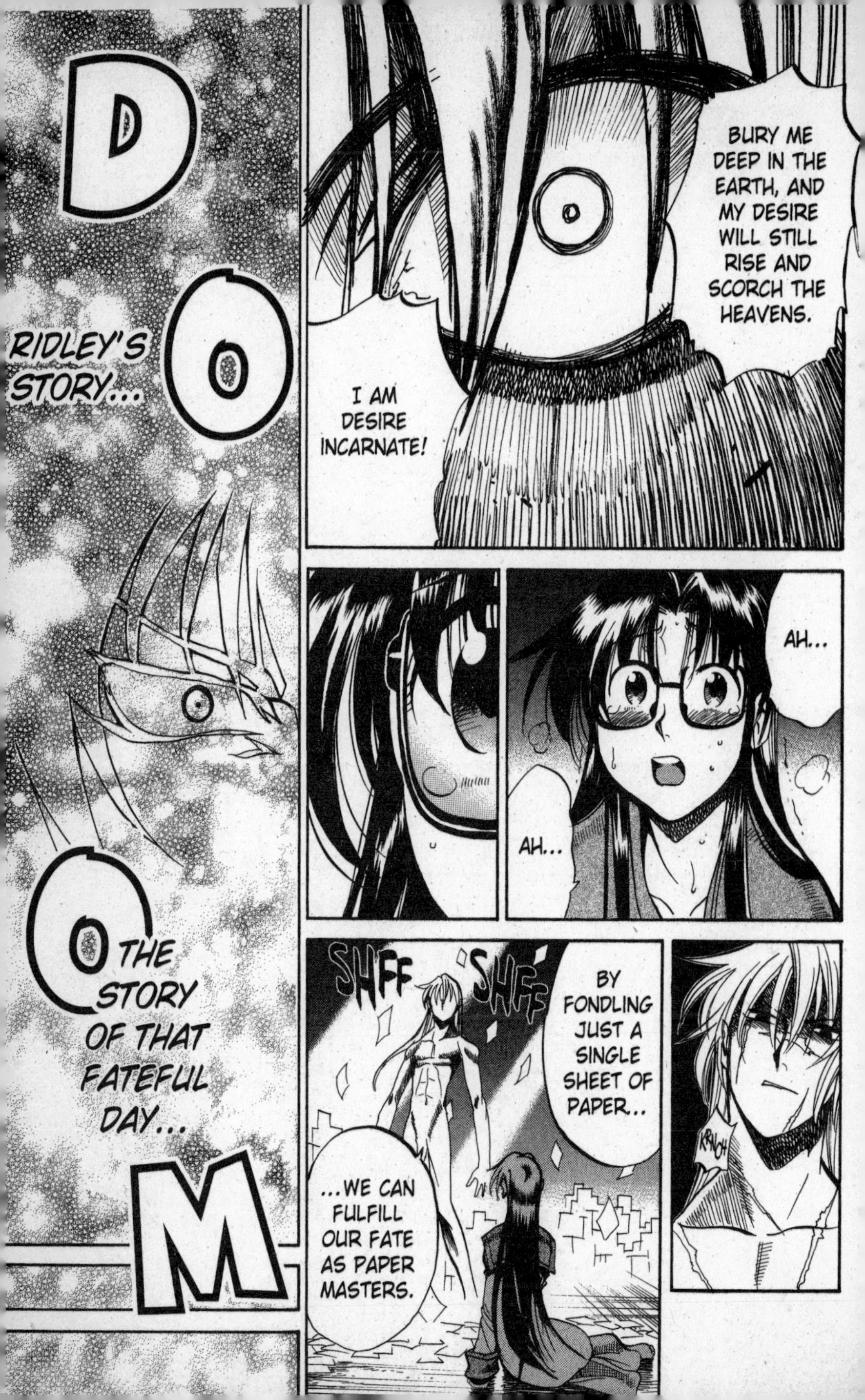
BURY ME DEEP IN THE EARTH, AND MY DESIRE WILL STILL RISE AND SCORCH THE HEAVENS.
I AM DESIRE INCARNATE!
AH...
AH...
KRNCH
SHFF
SHFF
BY FONDLING JUST A SINGLE SHEET OF PAPER...
...WE CAN FULFILL OUR FATE AS PAPER MASTERS.
DOOM
RIDLEY'S STORY...
THE STORY OF THAT FATEFUL DAY...

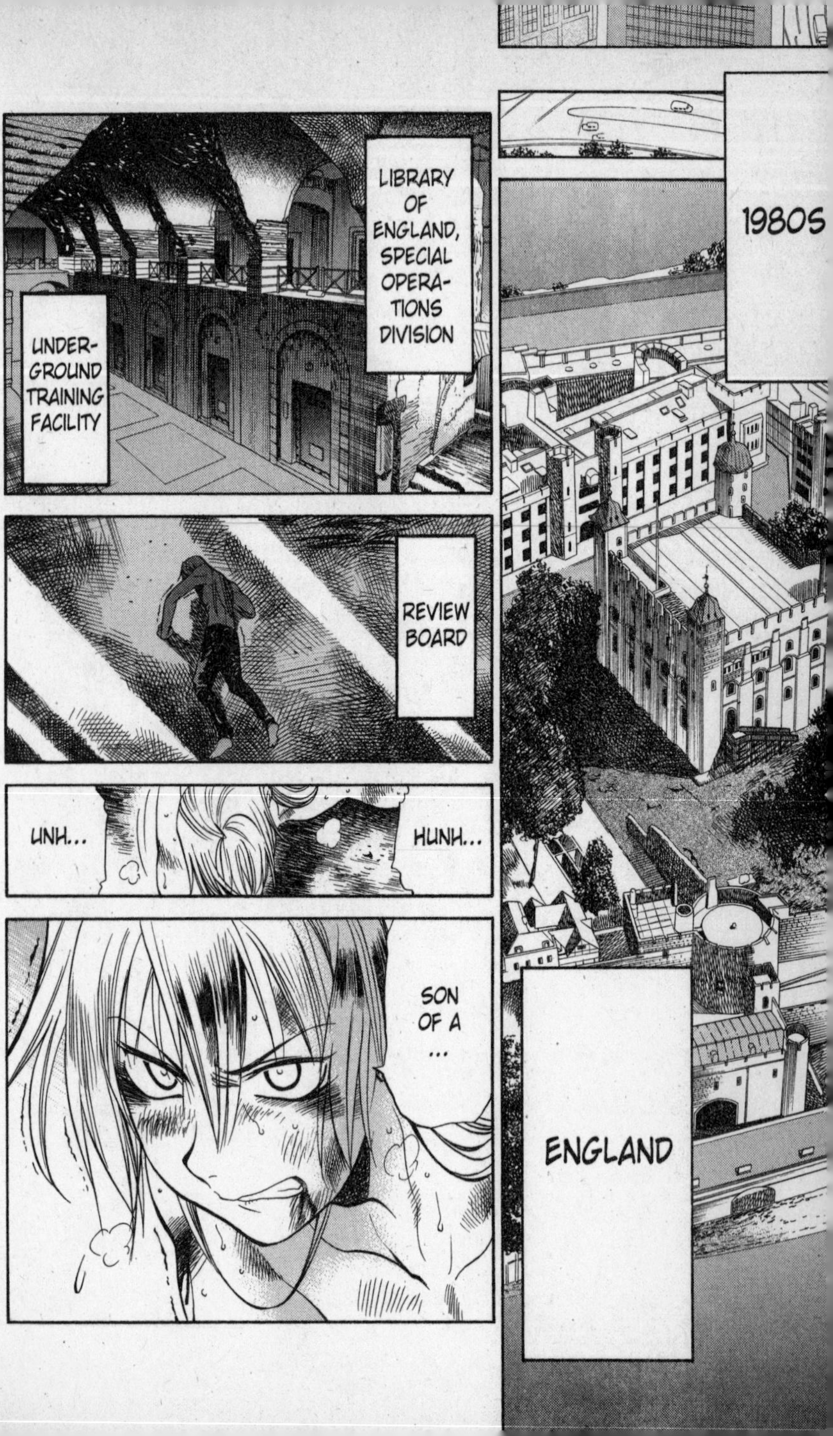
1980S
ENGLAND
LIBRARY OF ENGLAND, SPECIAL OPERA-TIONS DIVISION
UNDER-GROUND TRAINING FACILITY
REVIEW BOARD
HUNH...
UNH...
SON OF A ...

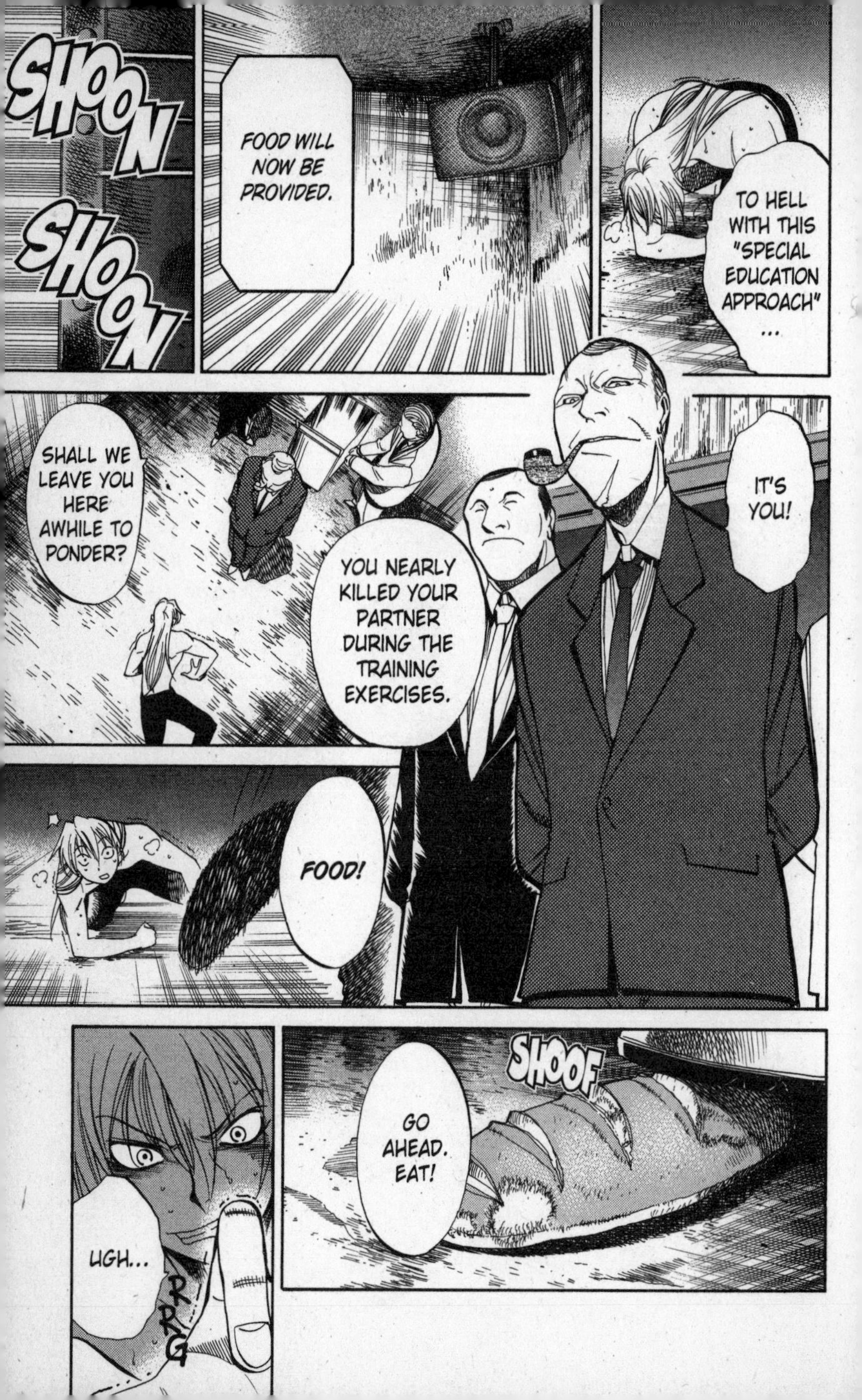
TO HELL WITH THIS "SPECIAL EDUCATION APPROACH"...
FOOD WILL NOW BE PROVIDED.
SHOON
SHOON
IT'S YOU!
YOU NEARLY KILLED YOUR PARTNER DURING THE TRAINING EXERCISES.
SHALL WE LEAVE YOU HERE AWHILE TO PONDER?
FOOD!
SHOOF
GO AHEAD. EAT!
UGH...
GRRG

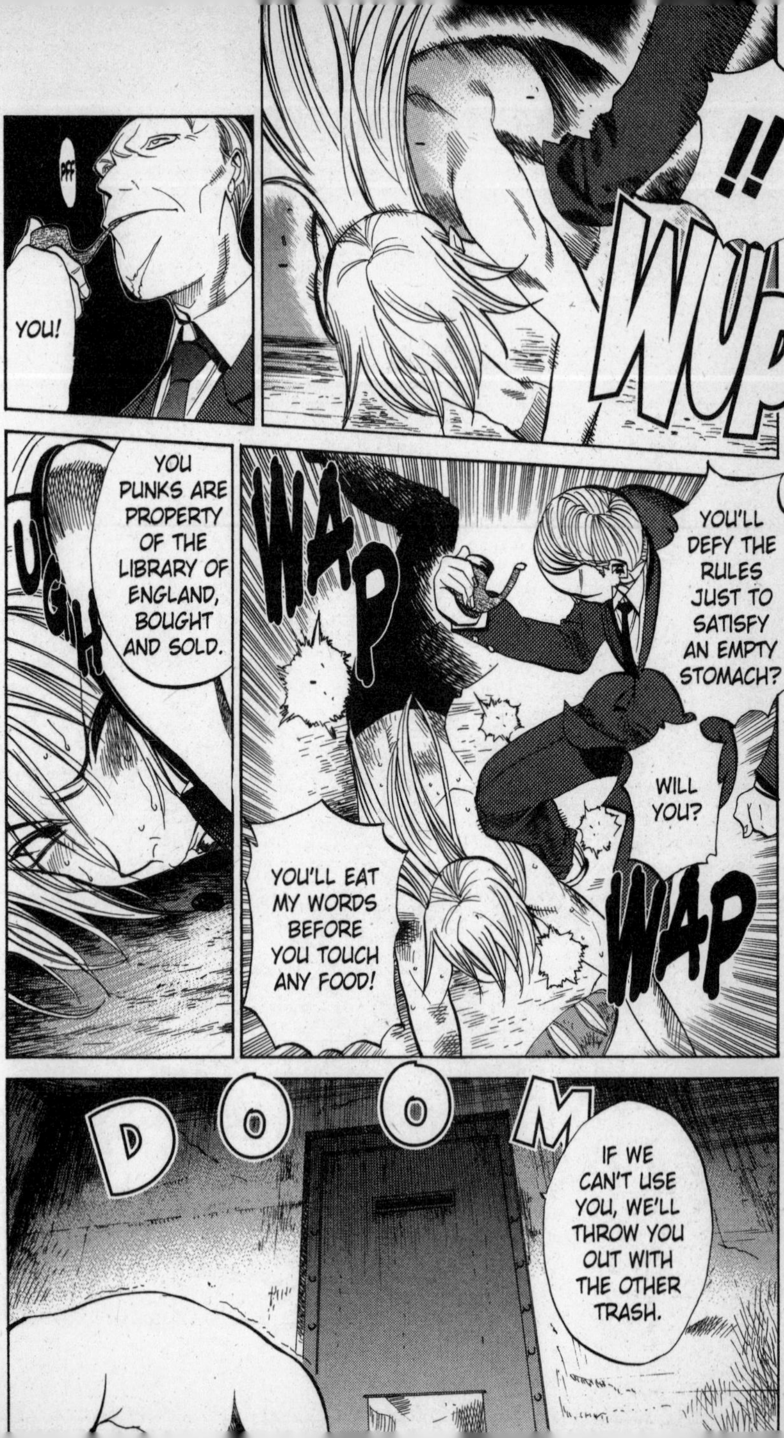
!!
WUP
PFF
YOU!
WAP
YOU'LL DEFY THE RULES JUST TO SATISFY AN EMPTY STOMACH?
WILL YOU?
WAP
YOU'LL EAT MY WORDS BEFORE YOU TOUCH ANY FOOD!
UGH
YOU PUNKS ARE PROPERTY OF THE LIBRARY OF ENGLAND, BOUGHT AND SOLD.
DOOM
IF WE CAN'T USE YOU, WE'LL THROW YOU OUT WITH THE OTHER TRASH.

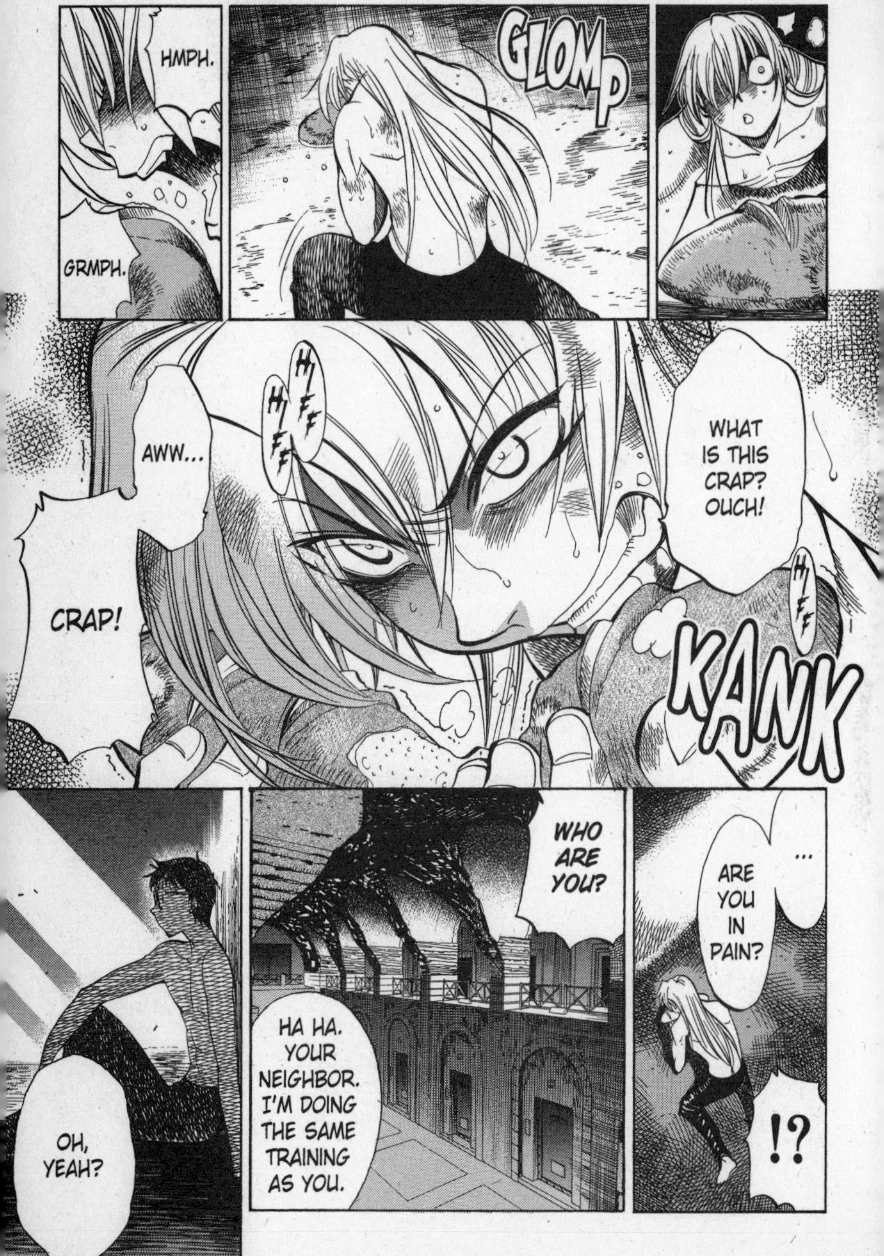
GLOMP
HMPH.
GRMPH.
WHAT IS THIS CRAP? OUCH!
HIFF HIFF
HIFF
KANK
AWW...
CRAP!
...
ARE YOU IN PAIN?
!?
WHO ARE YOU?
HA HA. YOUR NEIGHBOR. I'M DOING THE SAME TRAINING AS YOU.
OH, YEAH?

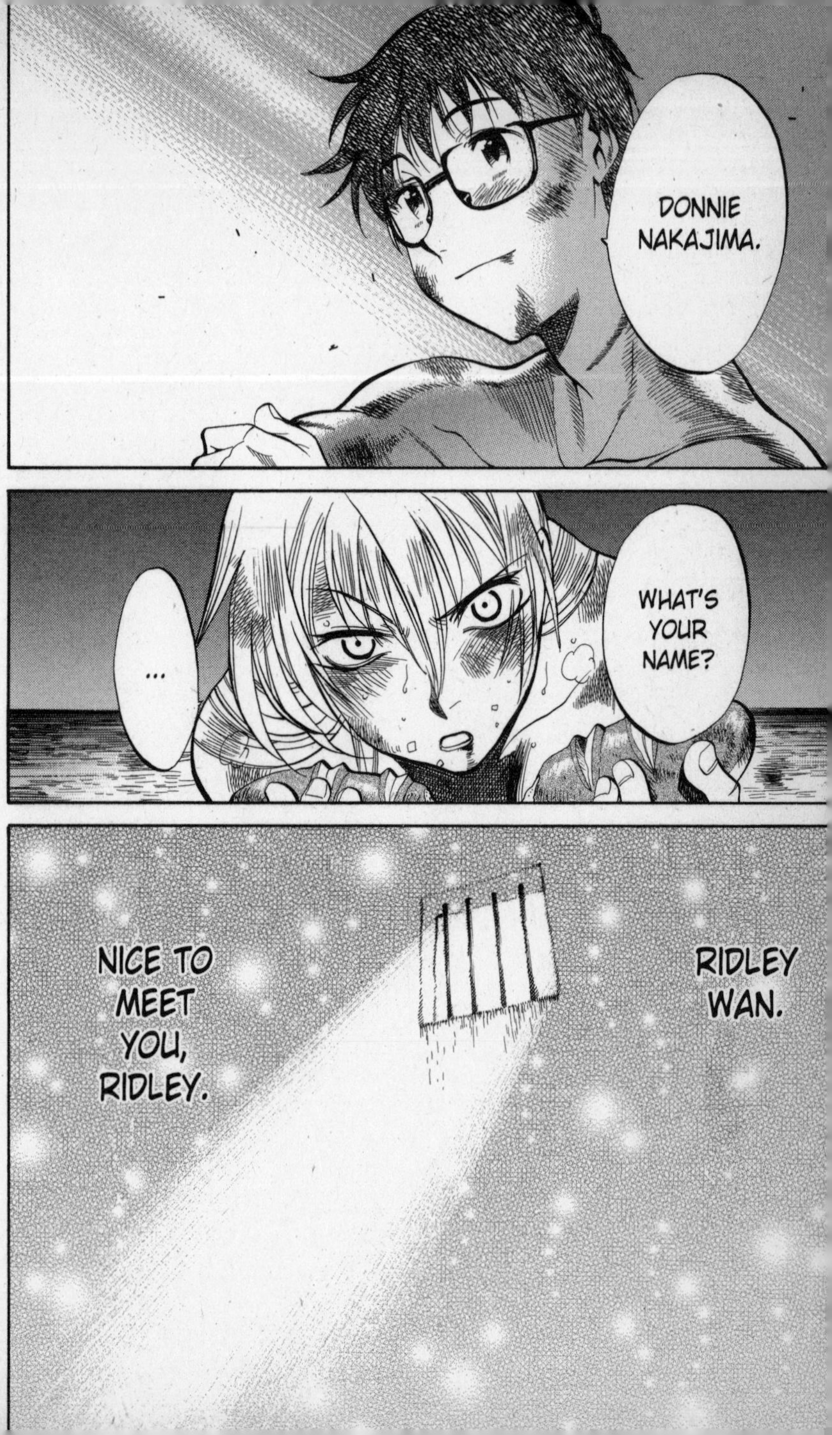
DONNIE NAKAJIMA.
WHAT'S YOUR NAME?
...
RIDLEY WAN.
NICE TO MEET YOU, RIDLEY.

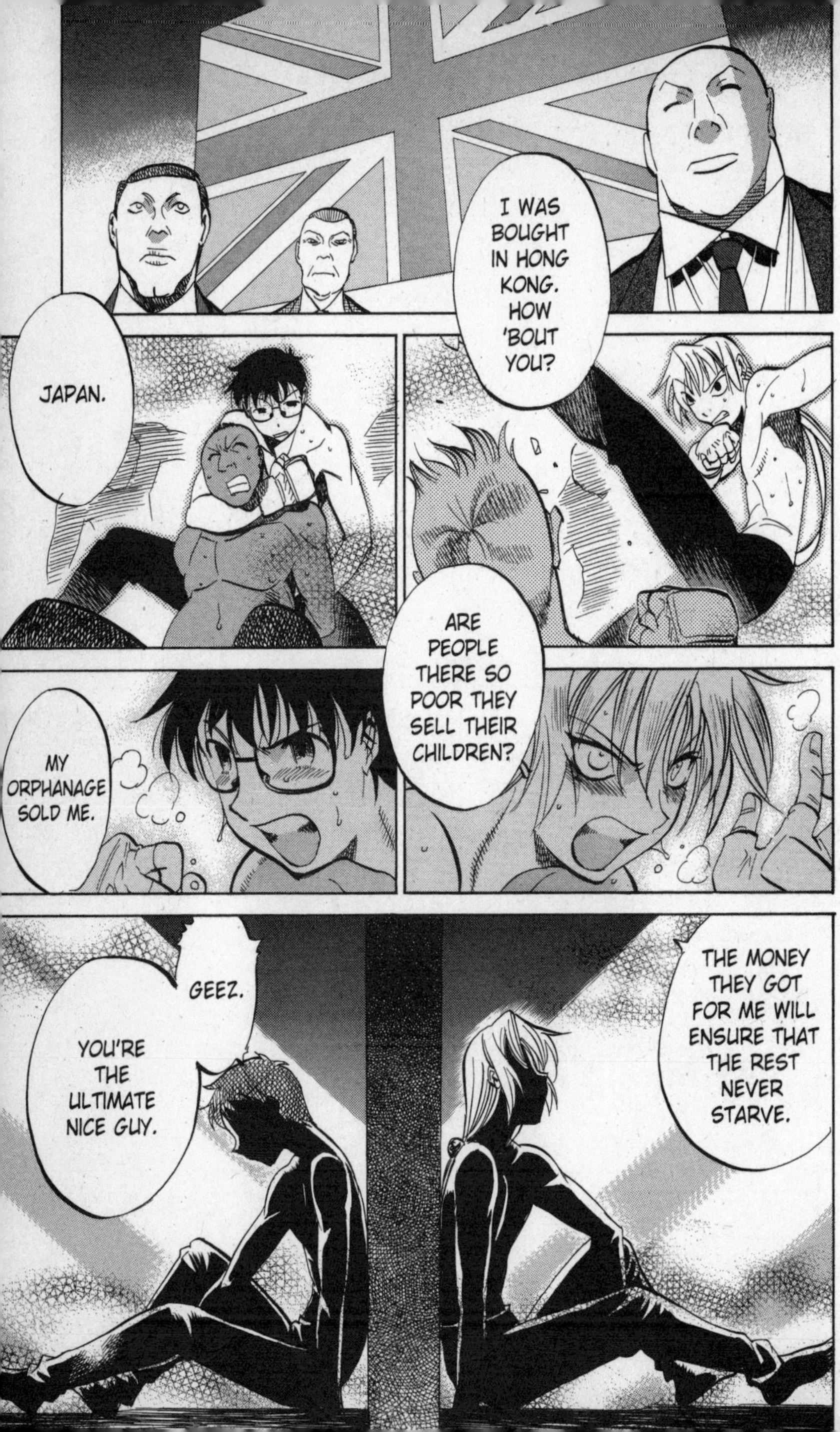
I WAS BOUGHT IN HONG KONG. HOW 'BOUT YOU?
JAPAN.
ARE PEOPLE THERE SO POOR THEY SELL THEIR CHILDREN?
MY ORPHANAGE SOLD ME.
THE MONEY THEY GOT FOR ME WILL ENSURE THAT THE REST NEVER STARVE.
GEEZ.
YOU'RE THE ULTIMATE NICE GUY.

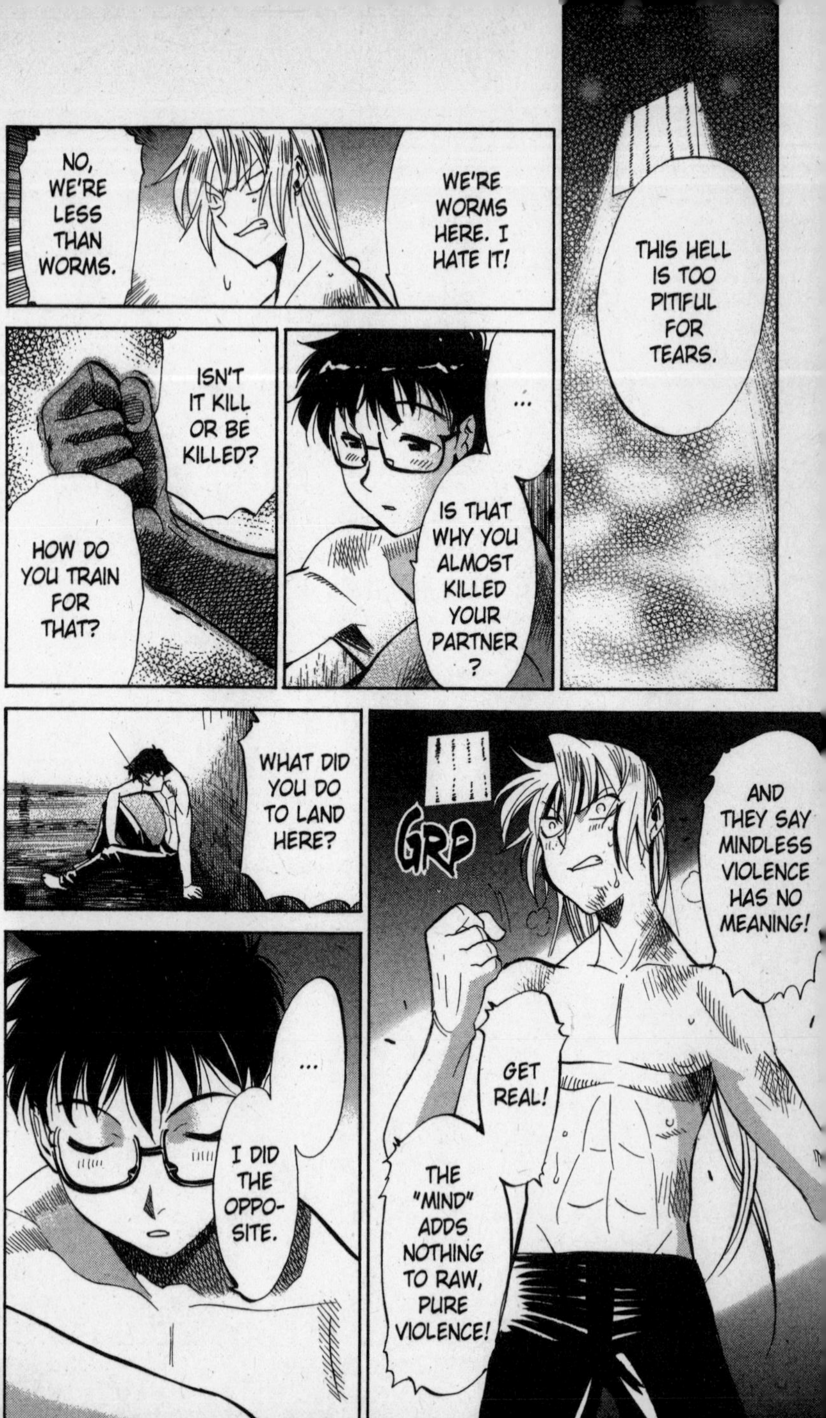
THIS HELL IS TOO PITIFUL FOR TEARS.
WE'RE WORMS HERE. I HATE IT!
NO, WE'RE LESS THAN WORMS.
...
IS THAT WHY YOU ALMOST KILLED YOUR PARTNER?
ISN'T IT KILL OR BE KILLED?
HOW DO YOU TRAIN FOR THAT?
GRP
AND THEY SAY MINDLESS VIOLENCE HAS NO MEANING!
GET REAL!
THE "MIND" ADDS NOTHING TO RAW, PURE VIOLENCE!
WHAT DID YOU DO TO LAND HERE?
...
I DID THE OPPOSITE.

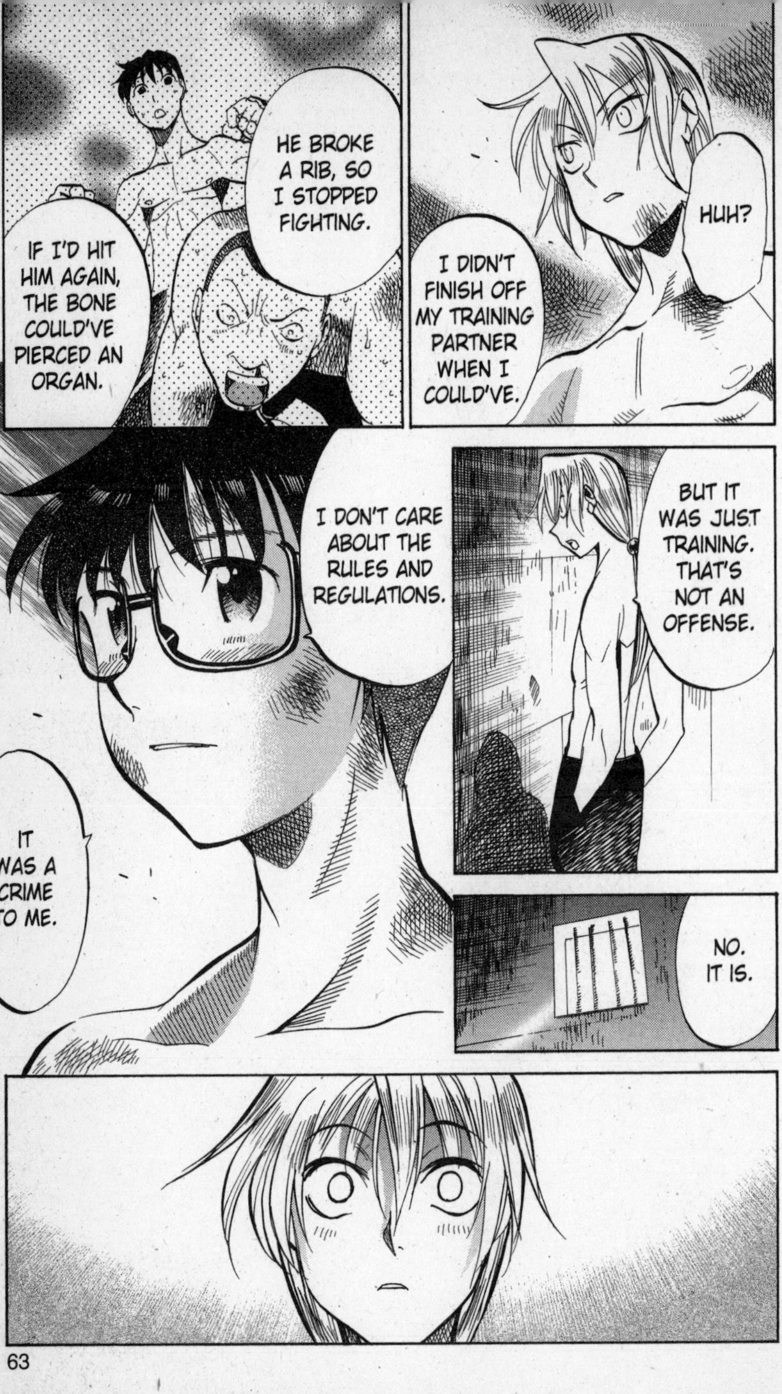
HUH?
I DIDN'T FINISH OFF MY TRAINING PARTNER WHEN I COULD'VE.
HE BROKE A RIB, SO I STOPPED FIGHTING.
IF I'D HIT HIM AGAIN, THE BONE COULD'VE PIERCED AN ORGAN.
BUT IT WAS JUST TRAINING. THAT'S NOT AN OFFENSE.
NO. IT IS.
I DON'T CARE ABOUT THE RULES AND REGULATIONS.
IT WAS A CRIME TO ME.

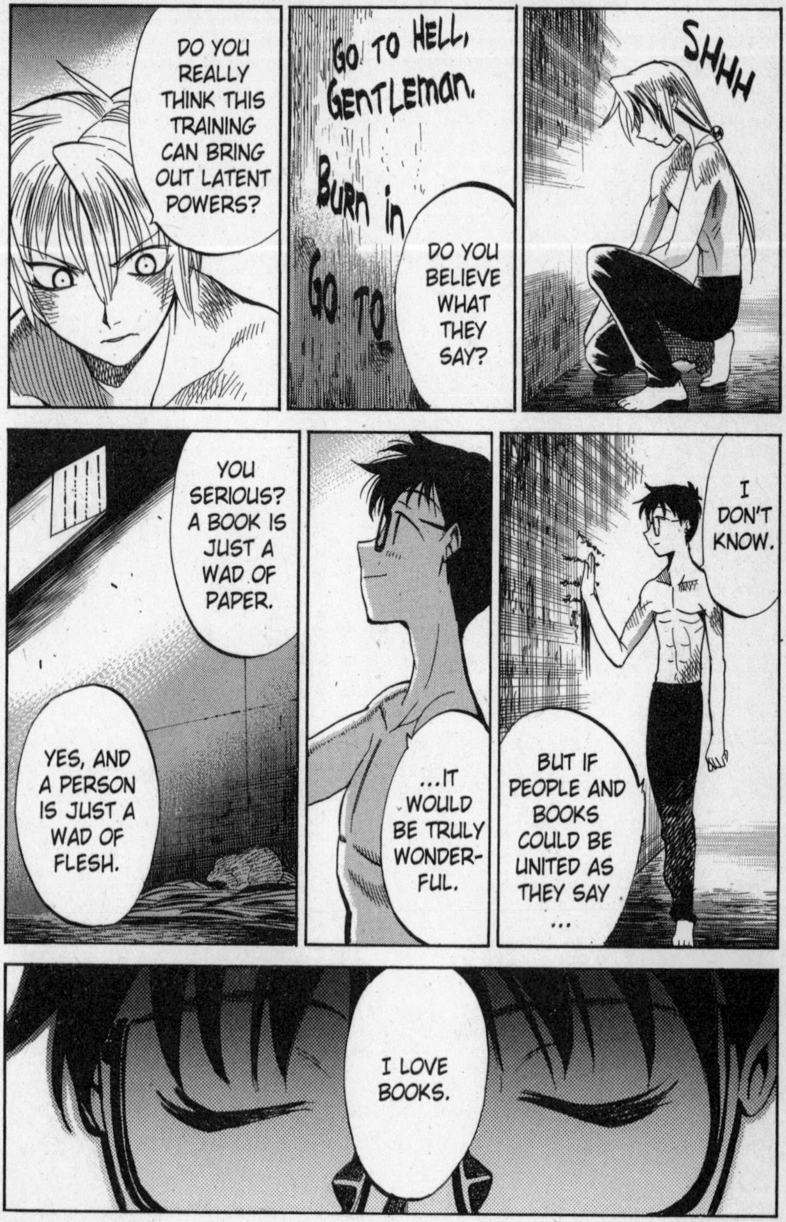
SHHH
GO TO HELL, GENTLEMAN.
BURN IN
GO TO
DO YOU BELIEVE WHAT THEY SAY?
DO YOU REALLY THINK THIS TRAINING CAN BRING OUT LATENT POWERS?
I DON'T KNOW.
BUT IF PEOPLE AND BOOKS COULD BE UNITED AS THEY SAY ...
...IT WOULD BE TRULY WONDER-FUL.
YOU SERIOUS? A BOOK IS JUST A WAD OF PAPER.
YES, AND A PERSON IS JUST A WAD OF FLESH.
I LOVE BOOKS.

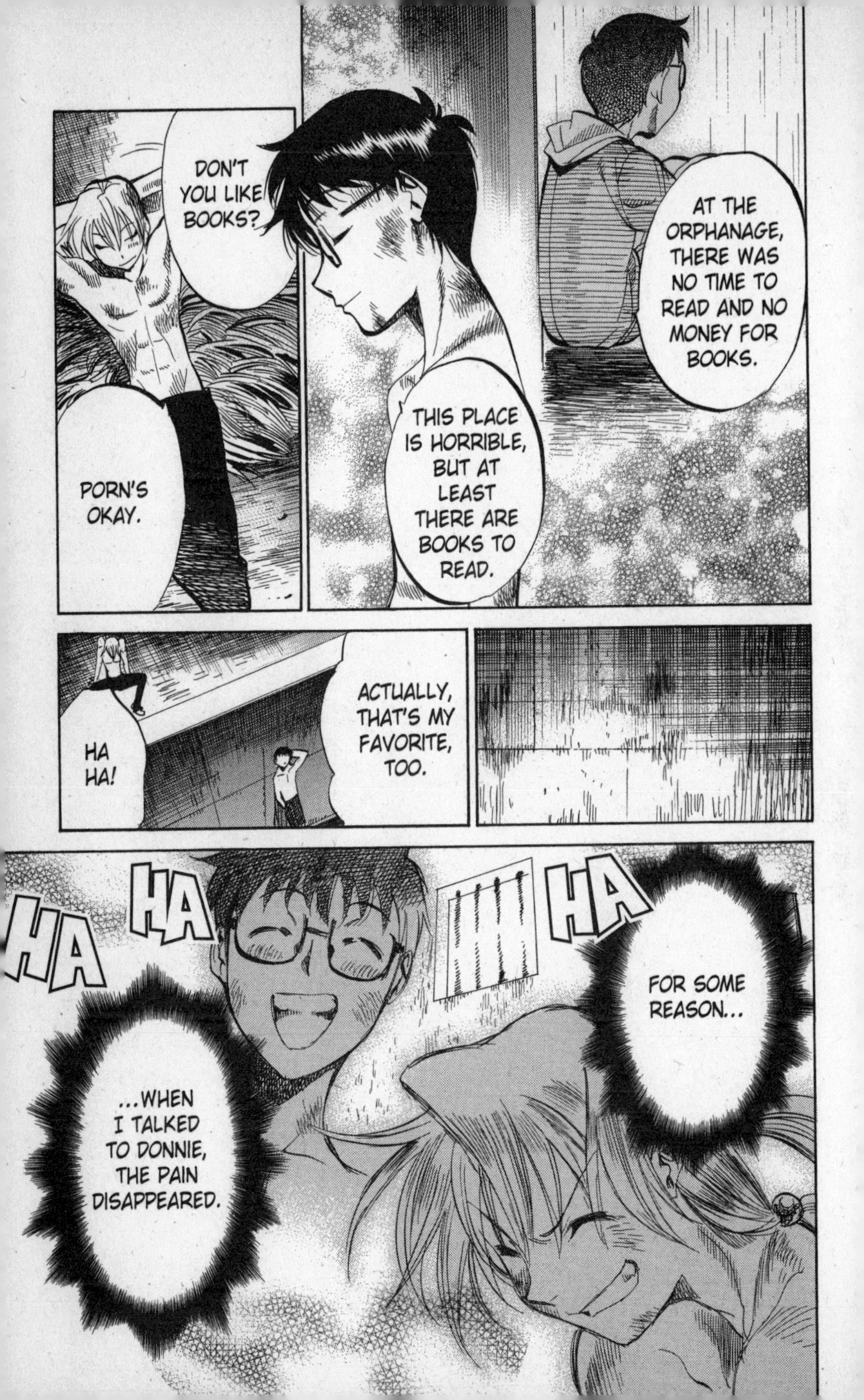
AT THE ORPHANAGE, THERE WAS NO TIME TO READ AND NO MONEY FOR BOOKS.
THIS PLACE IS HORRIBLE, BUT AT LEAST THERE ARE BOOKS TO READ.
DON'T YOU LIKE BOOKS?
PORN'S OKAY.
ACTUALLY, THAT'S MY FAVORITE, TOO.
HA HA!
HA
HA
HA
FOR SOME REASON...
...WHEN I TALKED TO DONNIE, THE PAIN DISAPPEARED.

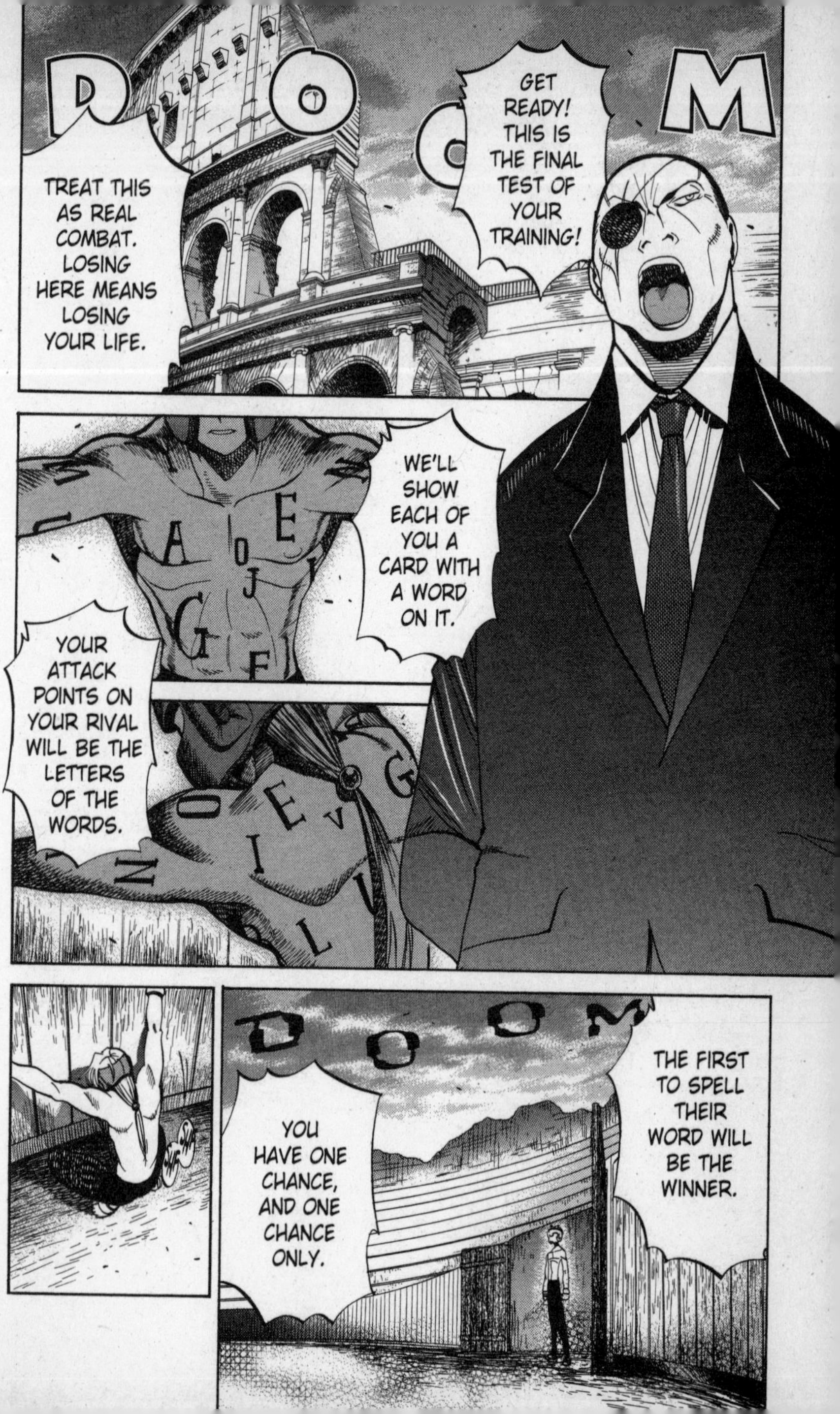
DOOM
GET READY! THIS IS THE FINAL TEST OF YOUR TRAINING!
TREAT THIS AS REAL COMBAT. LOSING HERE MEANS LOSING YOUR LIFE.
WE'LL SHOW EACH OF YOU A CARD WITH A WORD ON IT.
YOUR ATTACK POINTS ON YOUR RIVAL WILL BE THE LETTERS OF THE WORDS.
DOOM
THE FIRST TO SPELL THEIR WORD WILL BE THE WINNER.
YOU HAVE ONE CHANCE, AND ONE CHANCE ONLY.

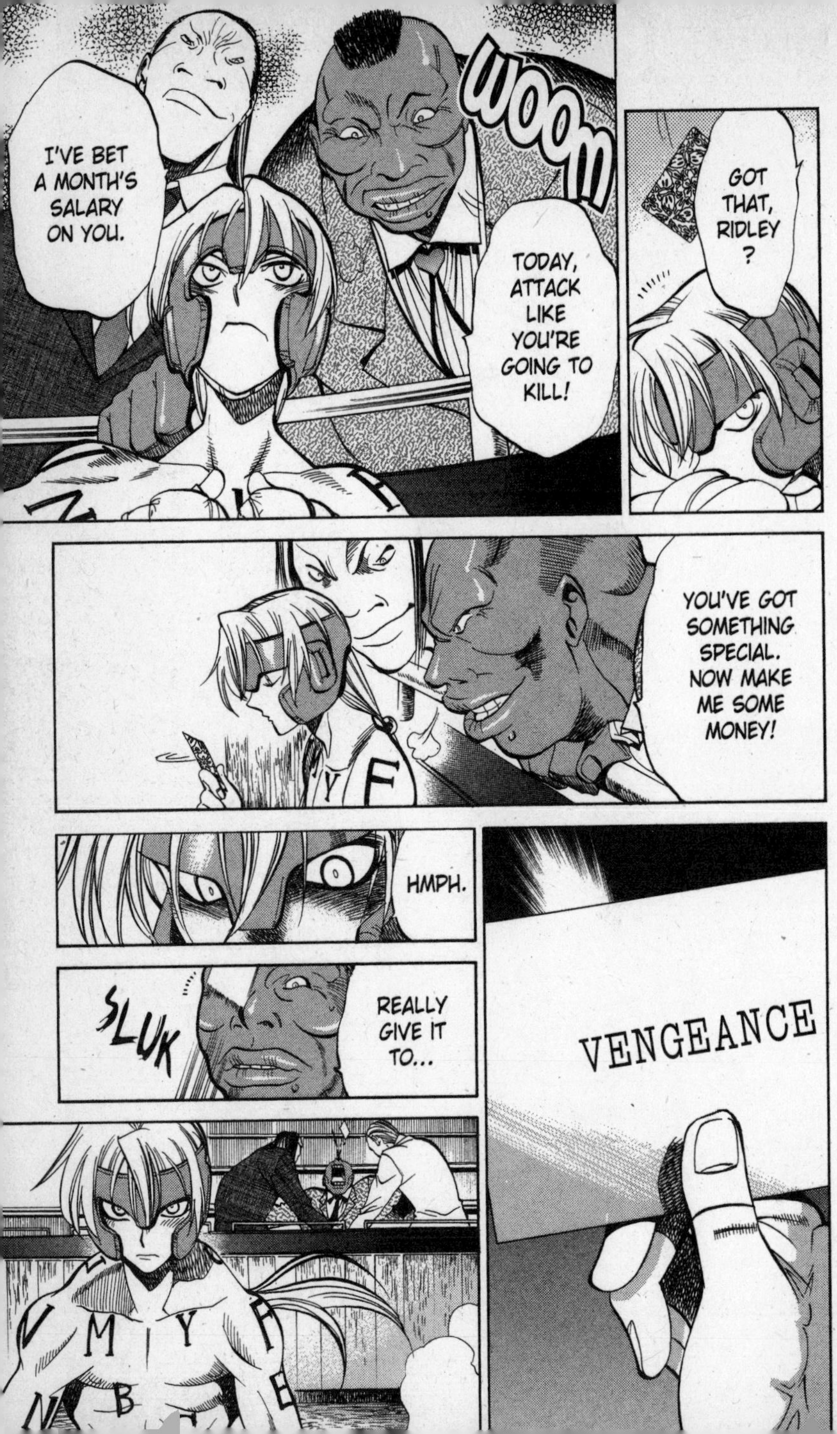
GOT THAT, RIDLEY?
WOOM
TODAY, ATTACK LIKE YOU'RE GOING TO KILL!
I'VE BET A MONTH'S SALARY ON YOU.
YOU'VE GOT SOMETHING SPECIAL. NOW MAKE ME SOME MONEY!
VENGEANCE
HMPH.
REALLY GIVE IT TO...
SLUK

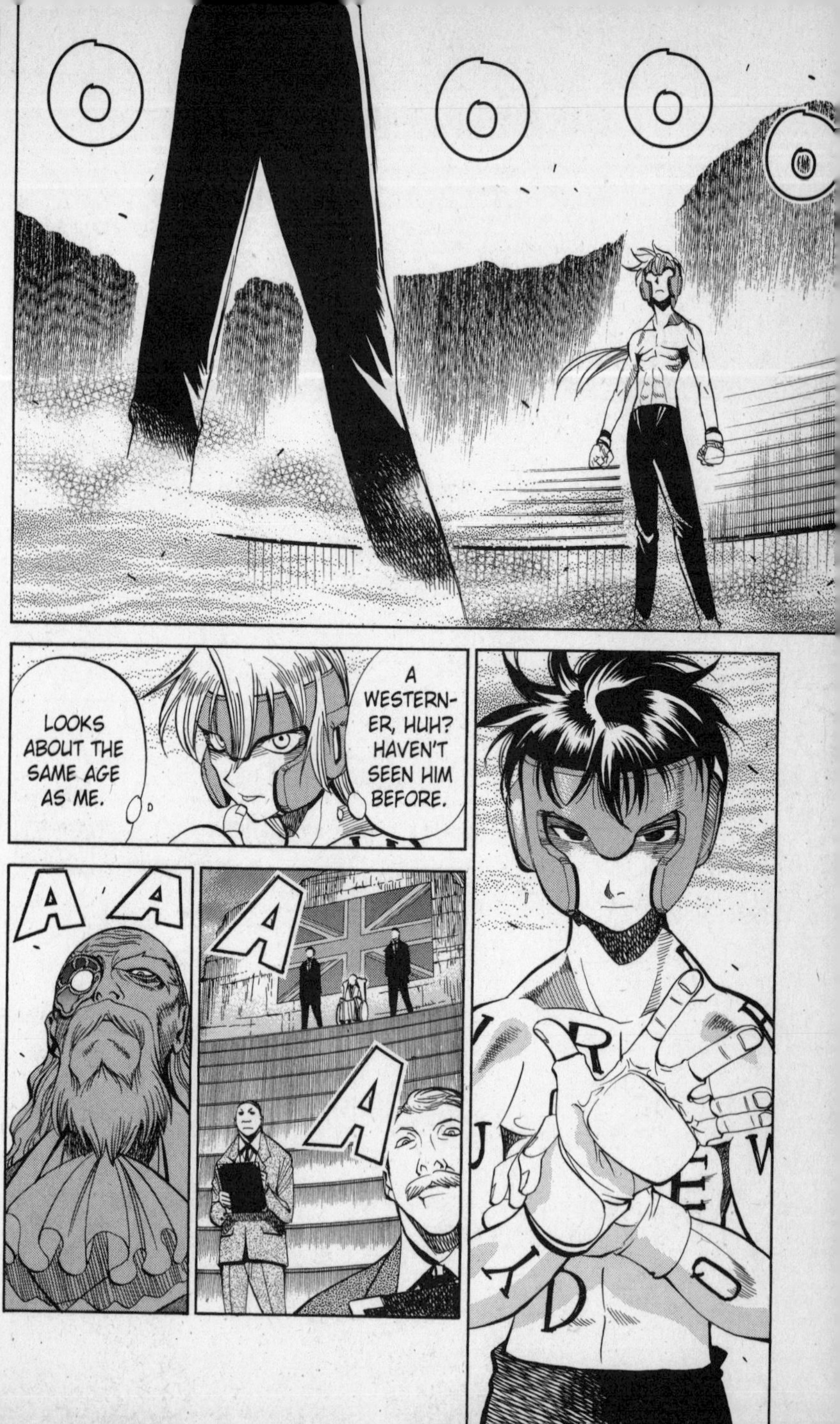
O O O O
A WESTERNER, HUH? HAVEN'T SEEN HIM BEFORE.
LOOKS ABOUT THE SAME AGE AS ME.
A
A
A A

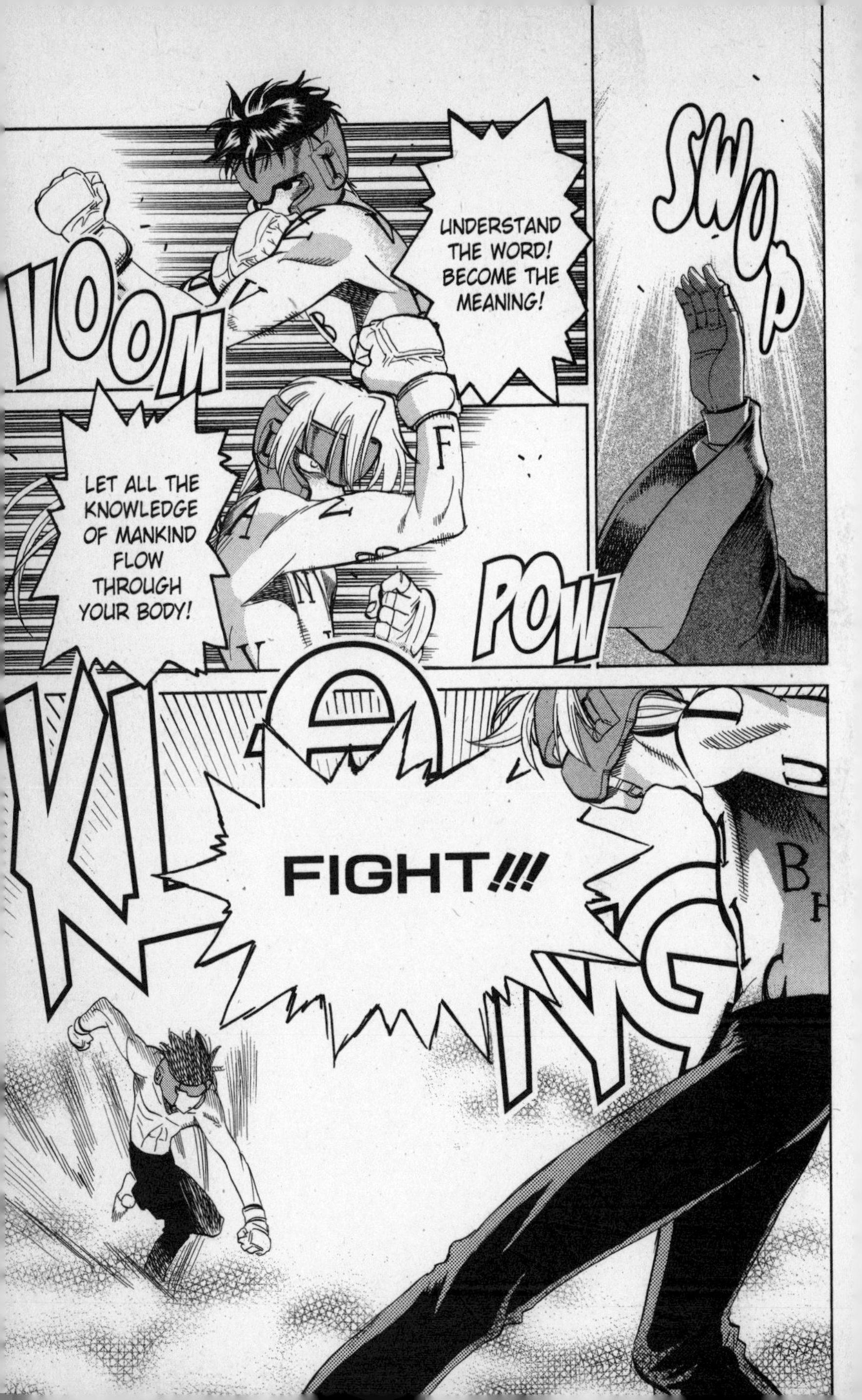
SWOOP
UNDERSTAND THE WORD! BECOME THE MEANING!
VOOM
LET ALL THE KNOWLEDGE OF MANKIND FLOW THROUGH YOUR BODY!
POW
FIGHT!!!

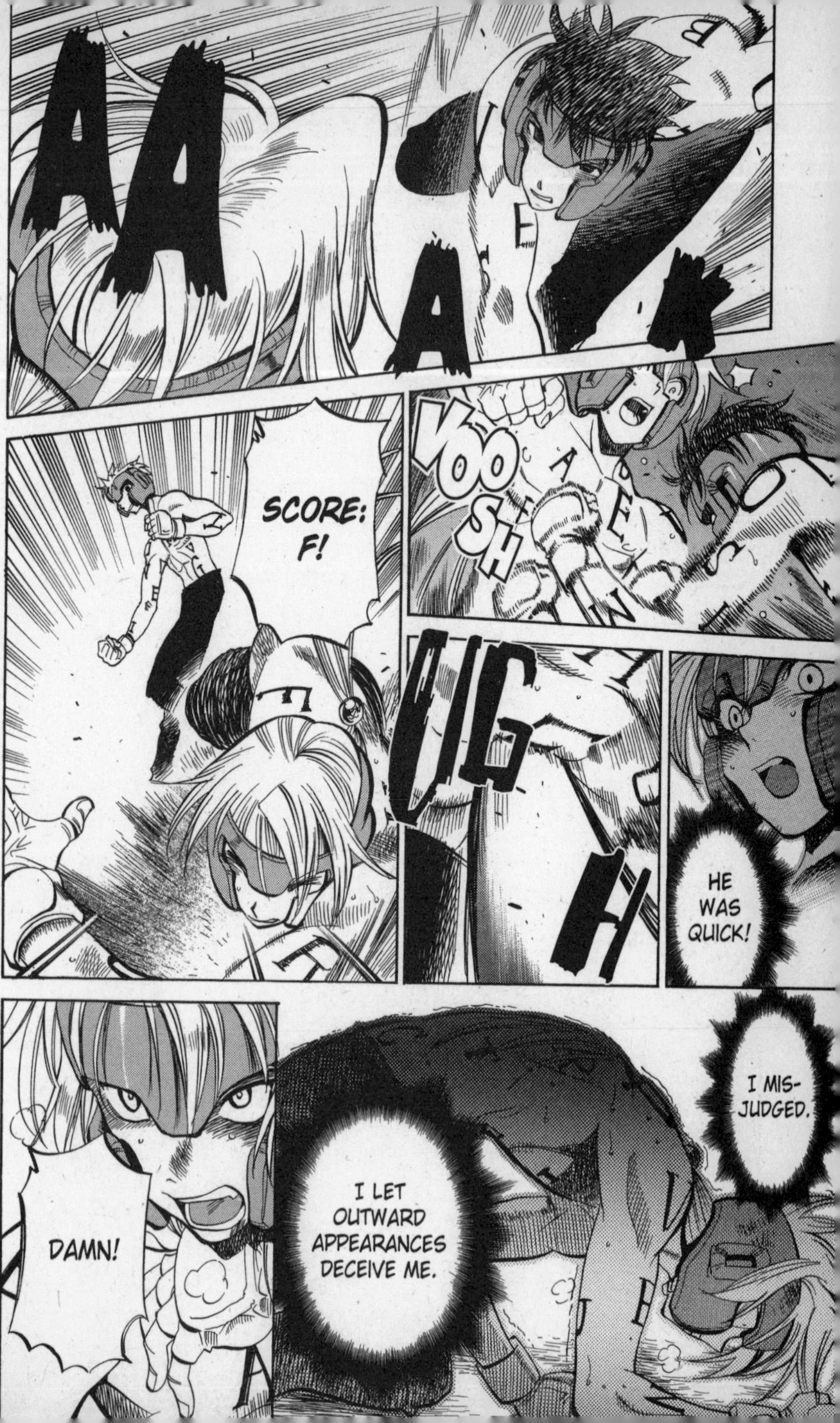
AAAA
VOOSH
HE WAS QUICK!
UGH
SCORE: F!
I MIS-JUDGED.
I LET OUTWARD APPEARANCES DECEIVE ME.
DAMN!

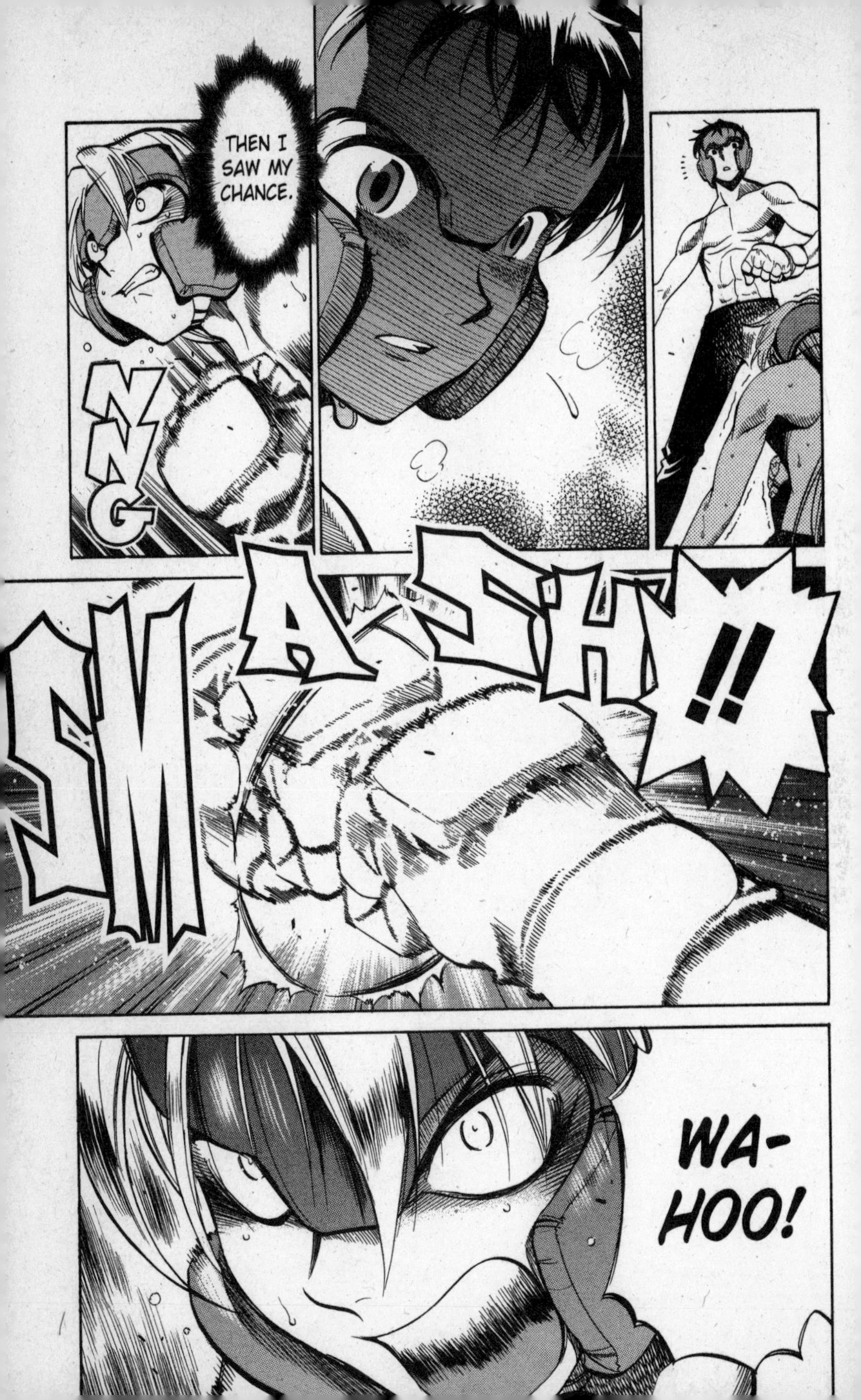
THEN I SAW MY CHANCE.
NNG
SMASH!!
WA-HOO!

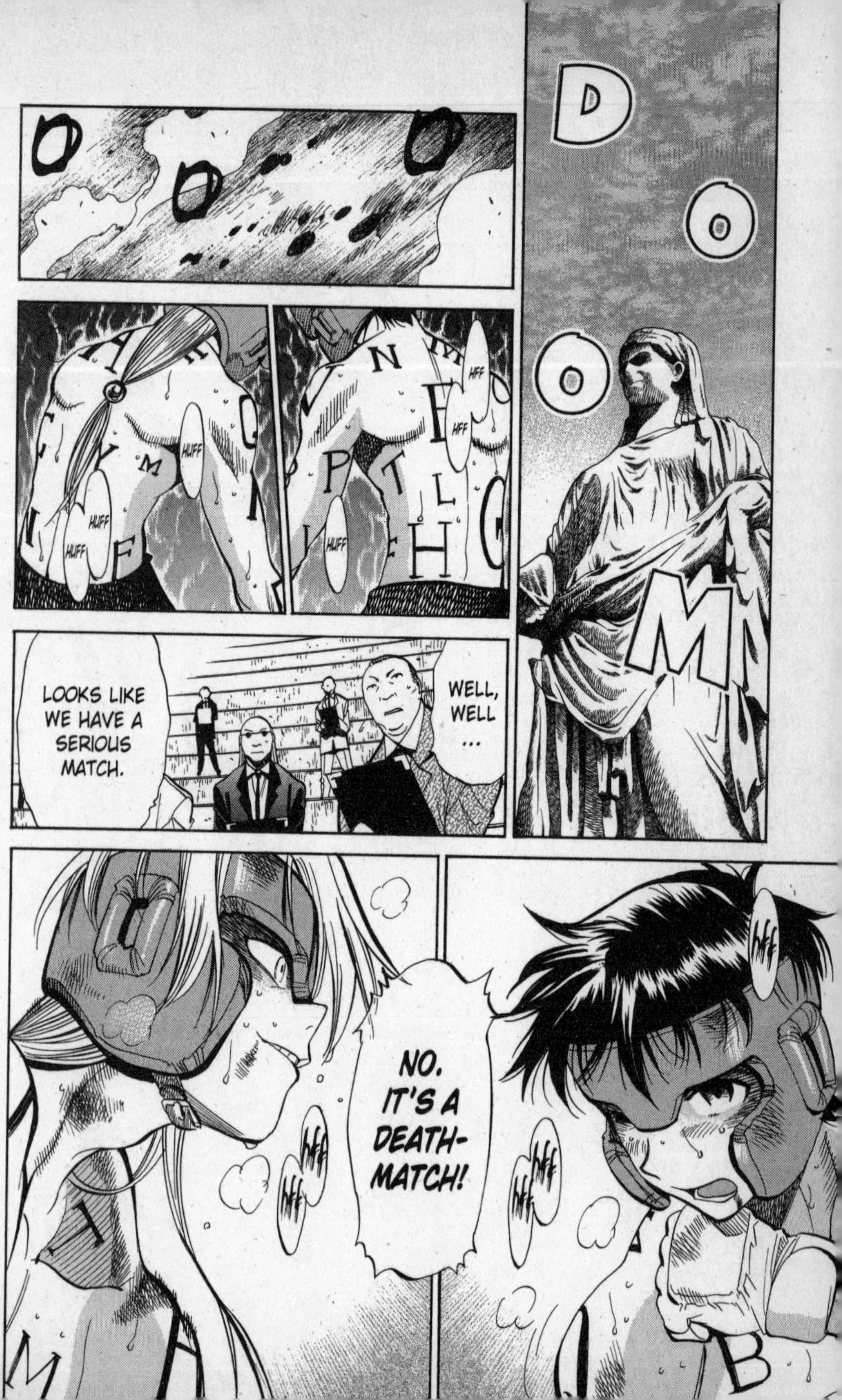
DOOOM
OOOO
HFF
HFF
HUFF
HUFF
HUFF
HUFF
WELL, WELL ...
LOOKS LIKE WE HAVE A SERIOUS MATCH.
hff
hff
NO. IT'S A DEATH-MATCH!
hff
hff

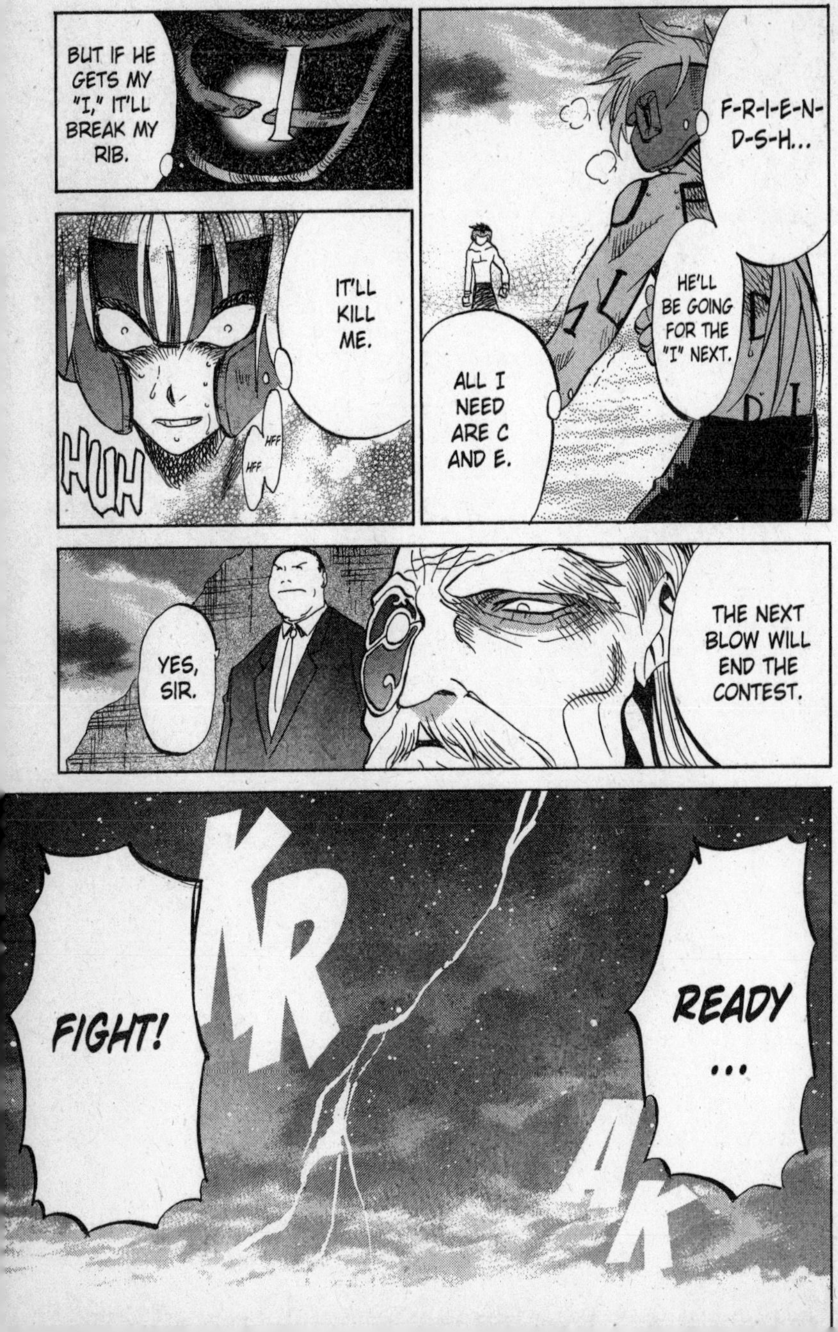
F-R-I-E-N-D-S-H...
BUT IF HE GETS MY "I," IT'LL BREAK MY RIB.
HE'LL BE GOING FOR THE "I" NEXT.
ALL I NEED ARE C AND E.
IT'LL KILL ME.
HFF
HFF
HUH
THE NEXT BLOW WILL END THE CONTEST.
YES, SIR.
READY...
KRAAK
FIGHT!

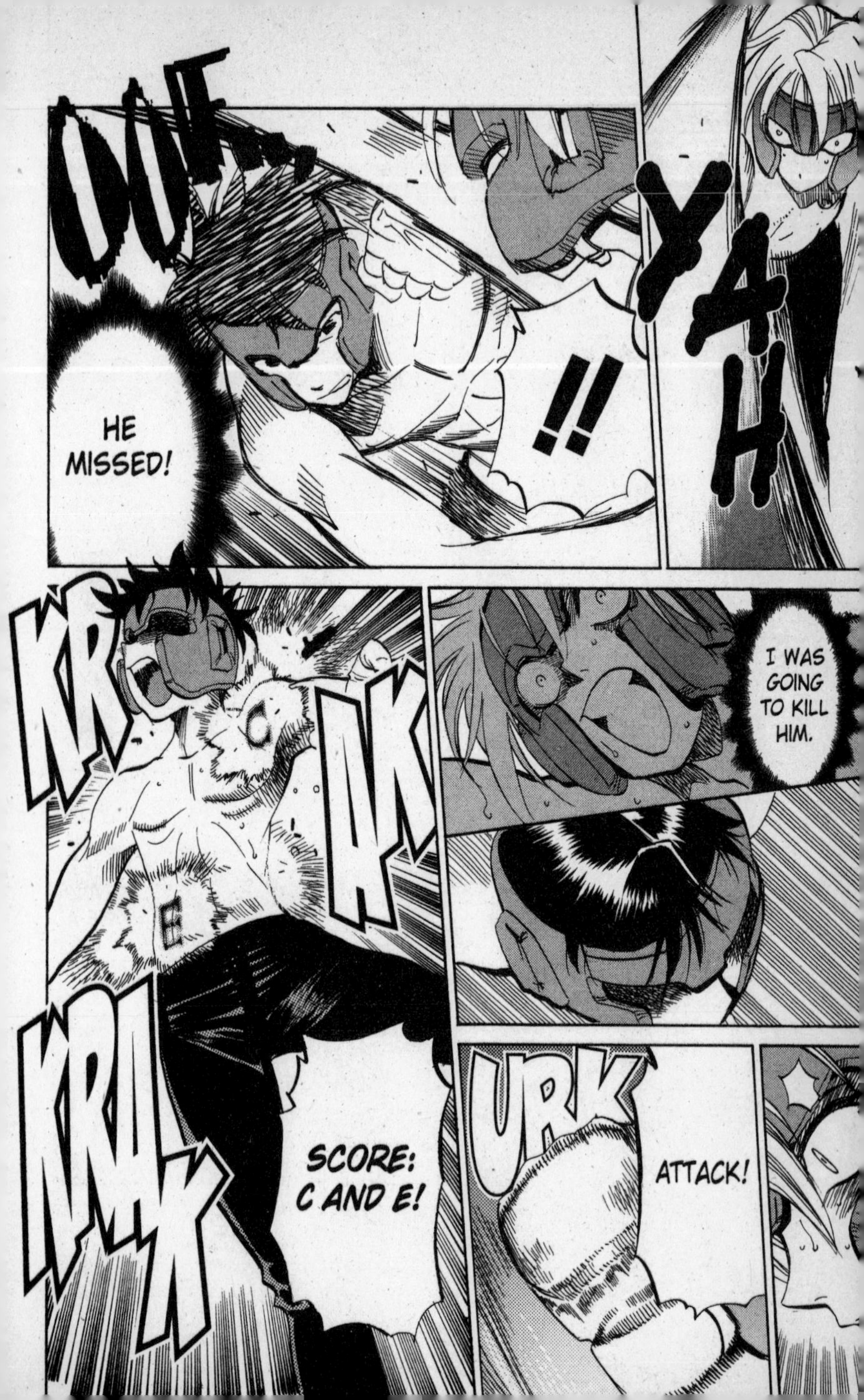
YAAH
OOF
!!
HE MISSED!
I WAS GOING TO KILL HIM.
ATTACK!
URK
SCORE: C AND E!
KRAK
KRAK

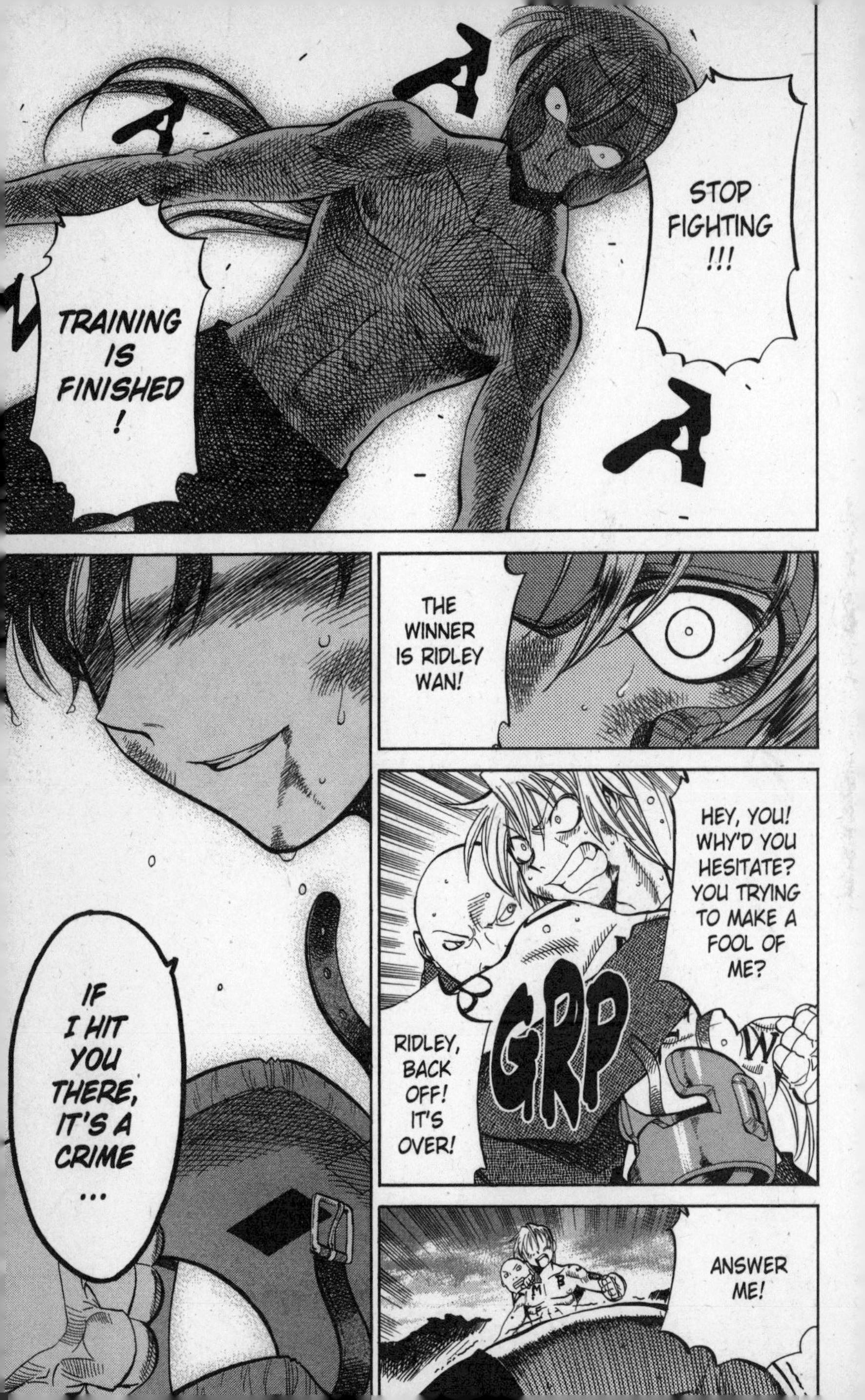
A
A
STOP FIGHTING !!!
A
TRAINING IS FINISHED !
THE WINNER IS RIDLEY WAN!
HEY, YOU! WHY'D YOU HESITATE? YOU TRYING TO MAKE A FOOL OF ME?
GRP
RIDLEY, BACK OFF! IT'S OVER!
ANSWER ME!
IF I HIT YOU THERE, IT'S A CRIME ...

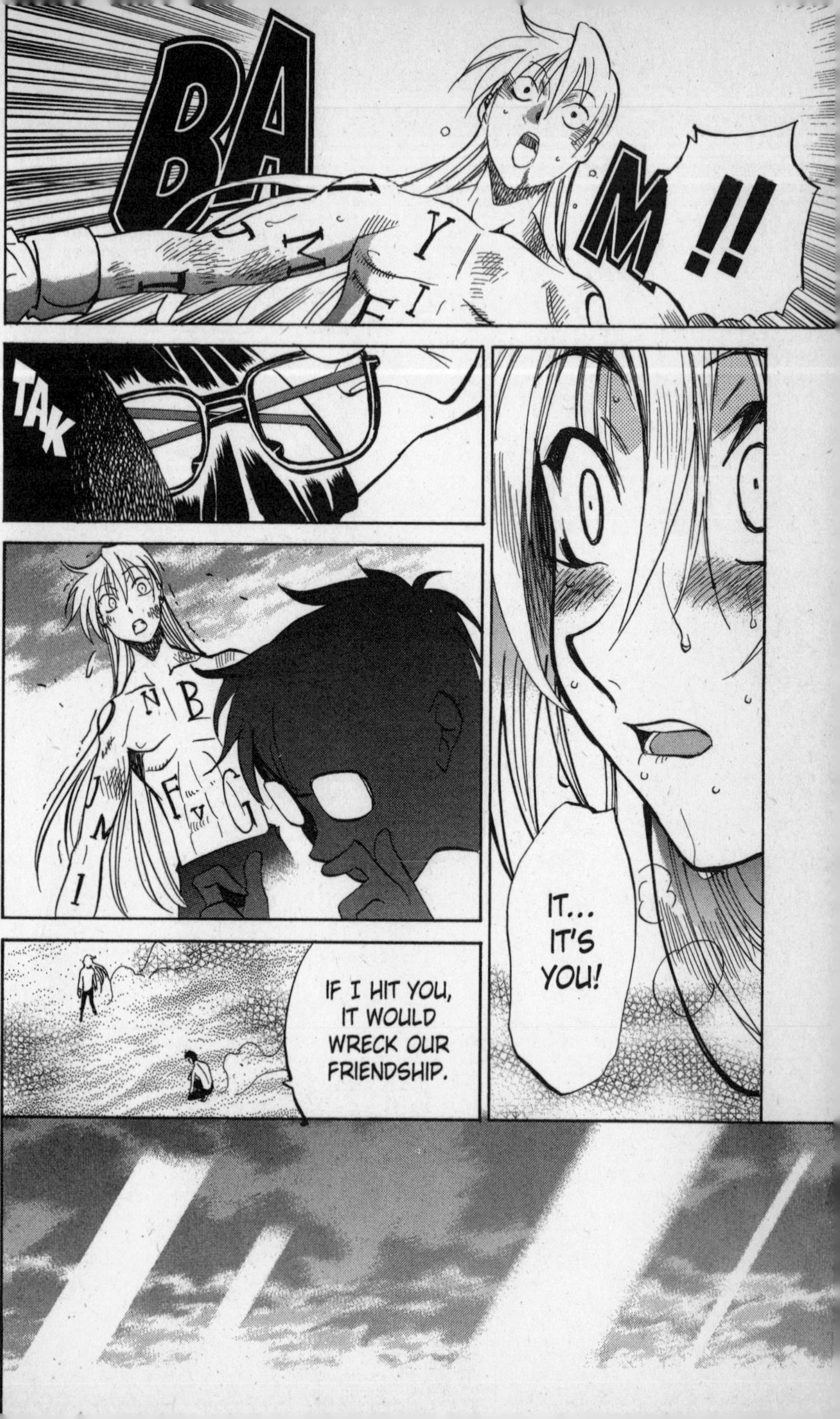
BAM!!
IT... IT'S YOU!
TAK
IF I HIT YOU, IT WOULD WRECK OUR FRIENDSHIP.

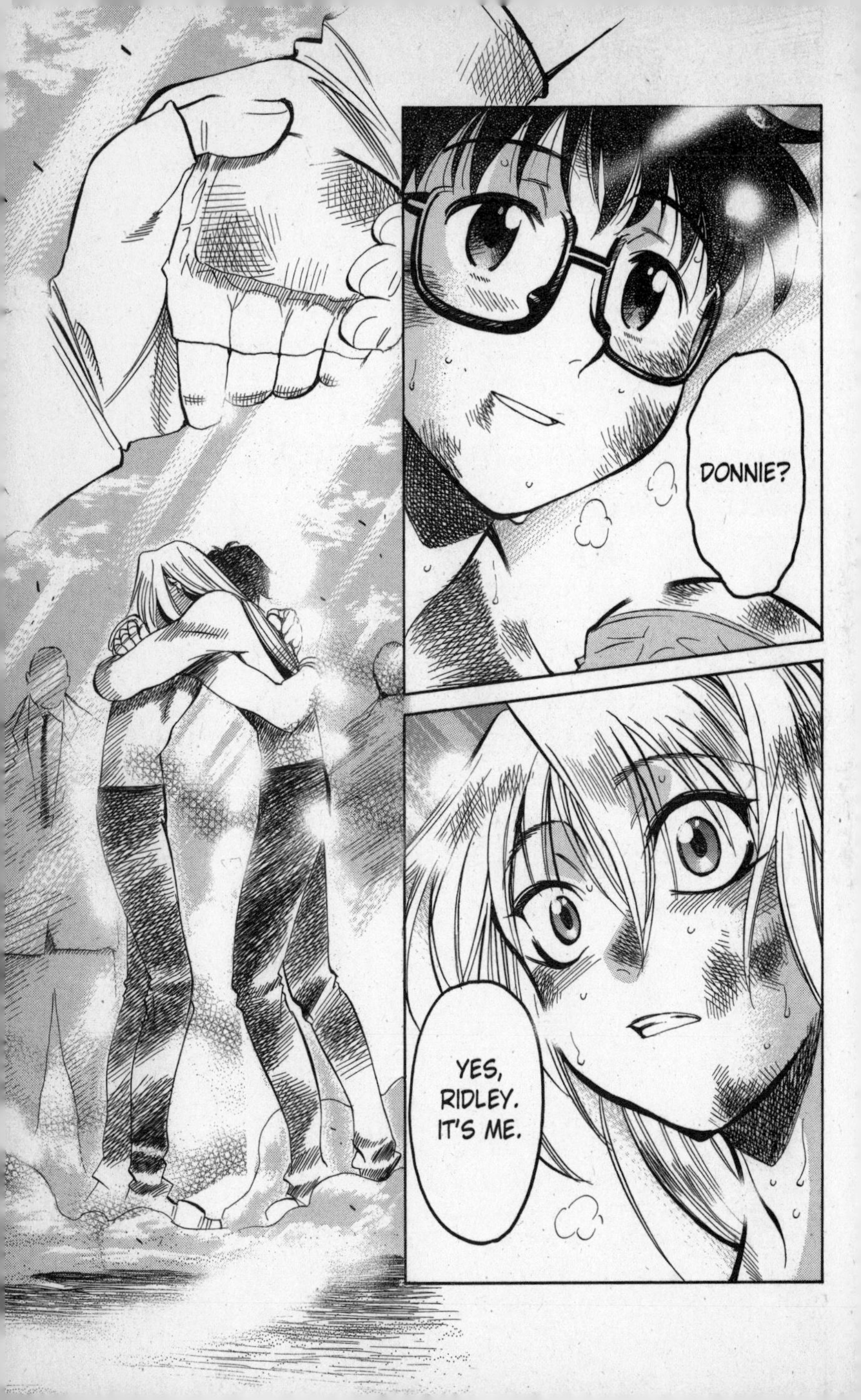
DONNIE?
YES, RIDLEY. IT'S ME.

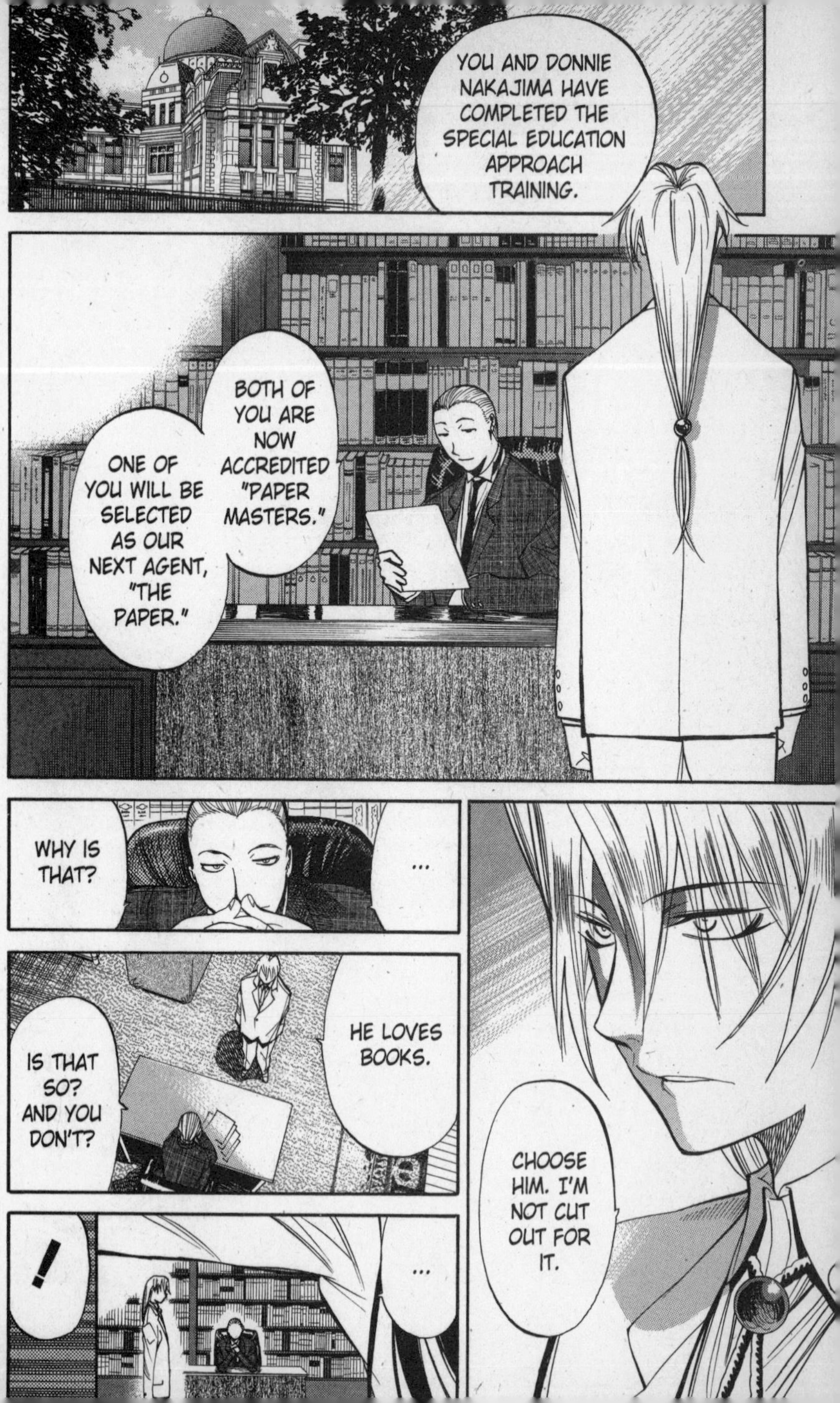
YOU AND DONNIE NAKAJIMA HAVE COMPLETED THE SPECIAL EDUCATION APPROACH TRAINING.
BOTH OF YOU ARE NOW ACCREDITED "PAPER MASTERS."
ONE OF YOU WILL BE SELECTED AS OUR NEXT AGENT, "THE PAPER."
CHOOSE HIM. I'M NOT CUT OUT FOR IT.
...
WHY IS THAT?
HE LOVES BOOKS.
IS THAT SO? AND YOU DON'T?
...
!

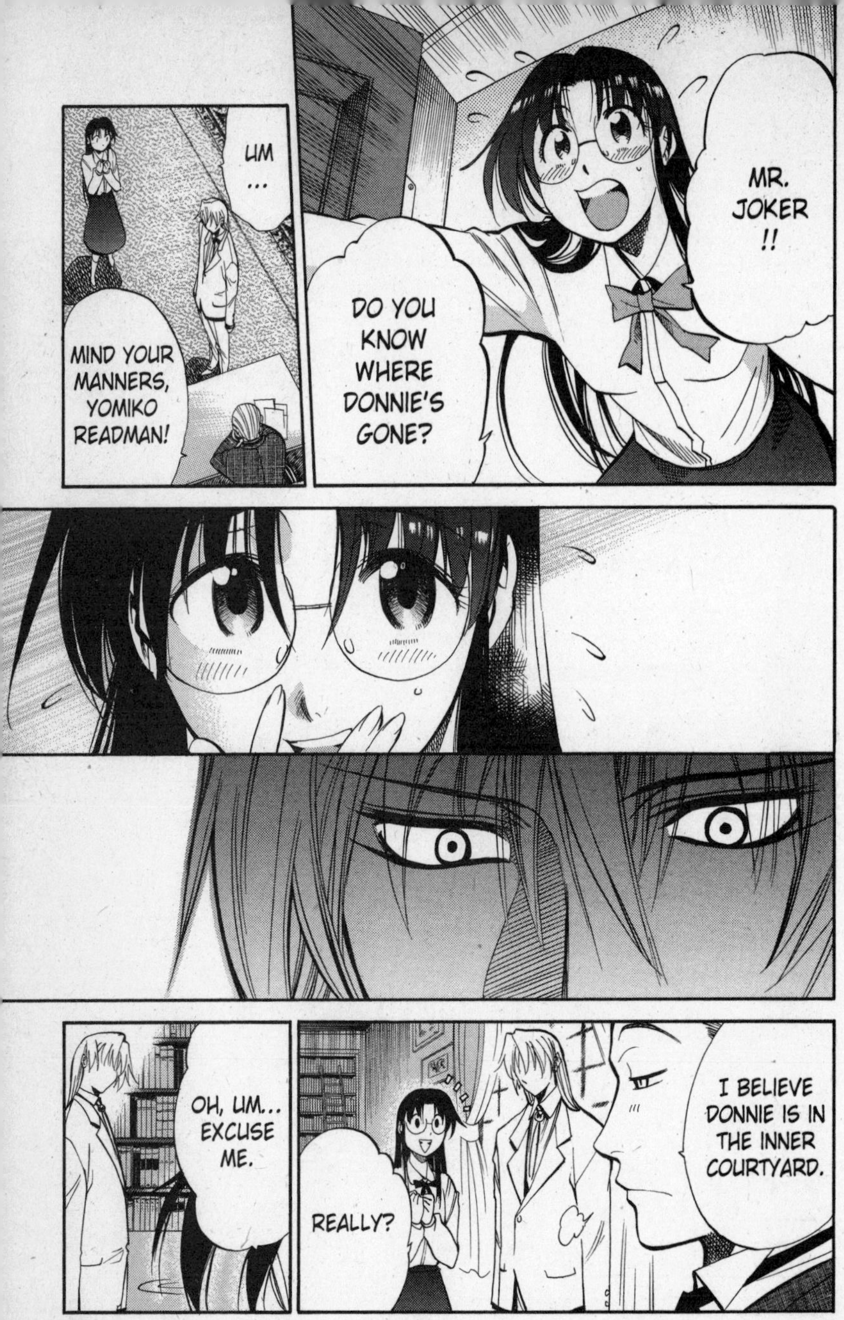
MR. JOKER !!
DO YOU KNOW WHERE DONNIE'S GONE?
UM ...
MIND YOUR MANNERS, YOMIKO READMAN!
I BELIEVE DONNIE IS IN THE INNER COURTYARD.
REALLY?
OH, UM... EXCUSE ME.

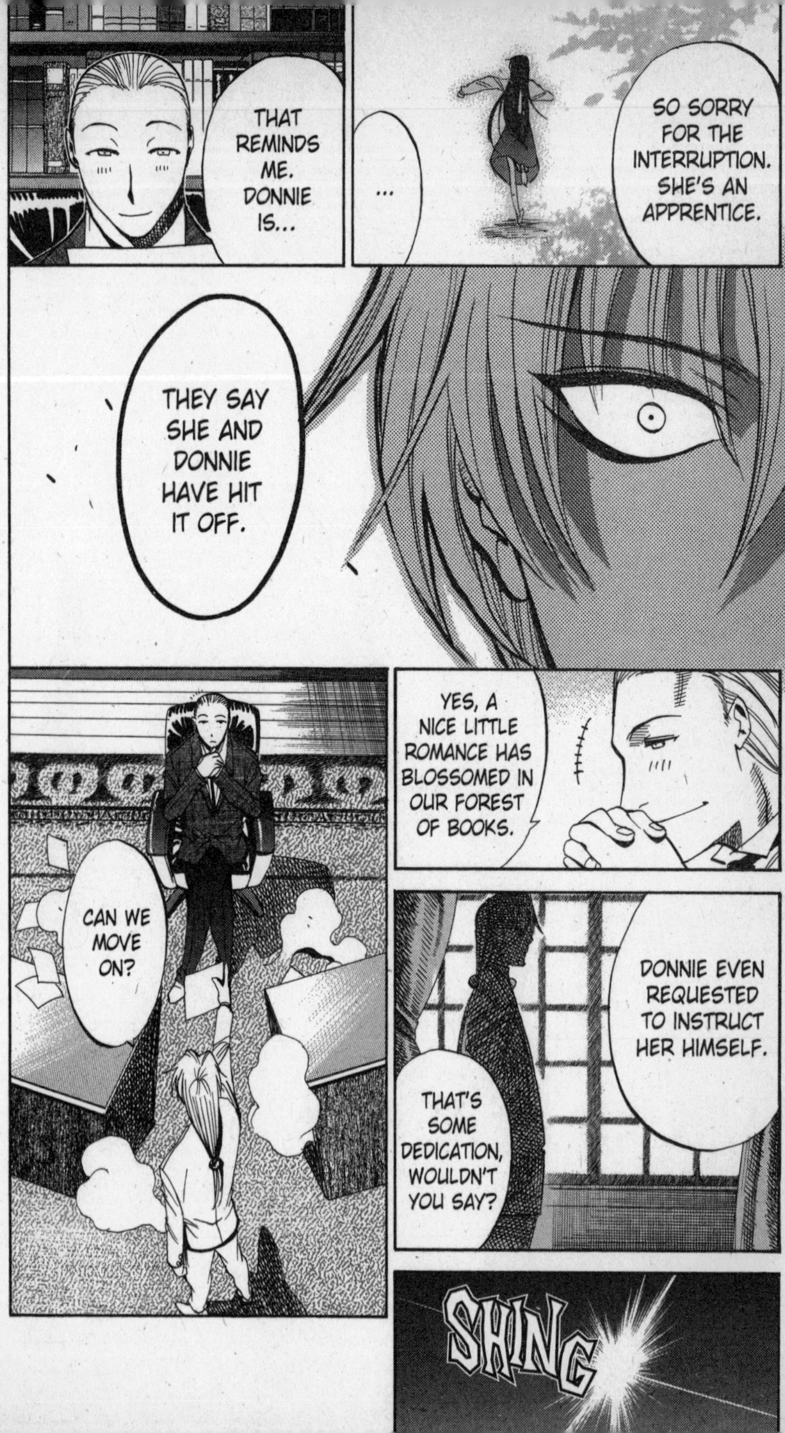
SO SORRY FOR THE INTERRUPTION. SHE'S AN APPRENTICE.
...
THAT REMINDS ME. DONNIE IS...
THEY SAY SHE AND DONNIE HAVE HIT IT OFF.
YES, A NICE LITTLE ROMANCE HAS BLOSSOMED IN OUR FOREST OF BOOKS.
DONNIE EVEN REQUESTED TO INSTRUCT HER HIMSELF.
THAT'S SOME DEDICATION, WOULDN'T YOU SAY?
SHING
CAN WE MOVE ON?

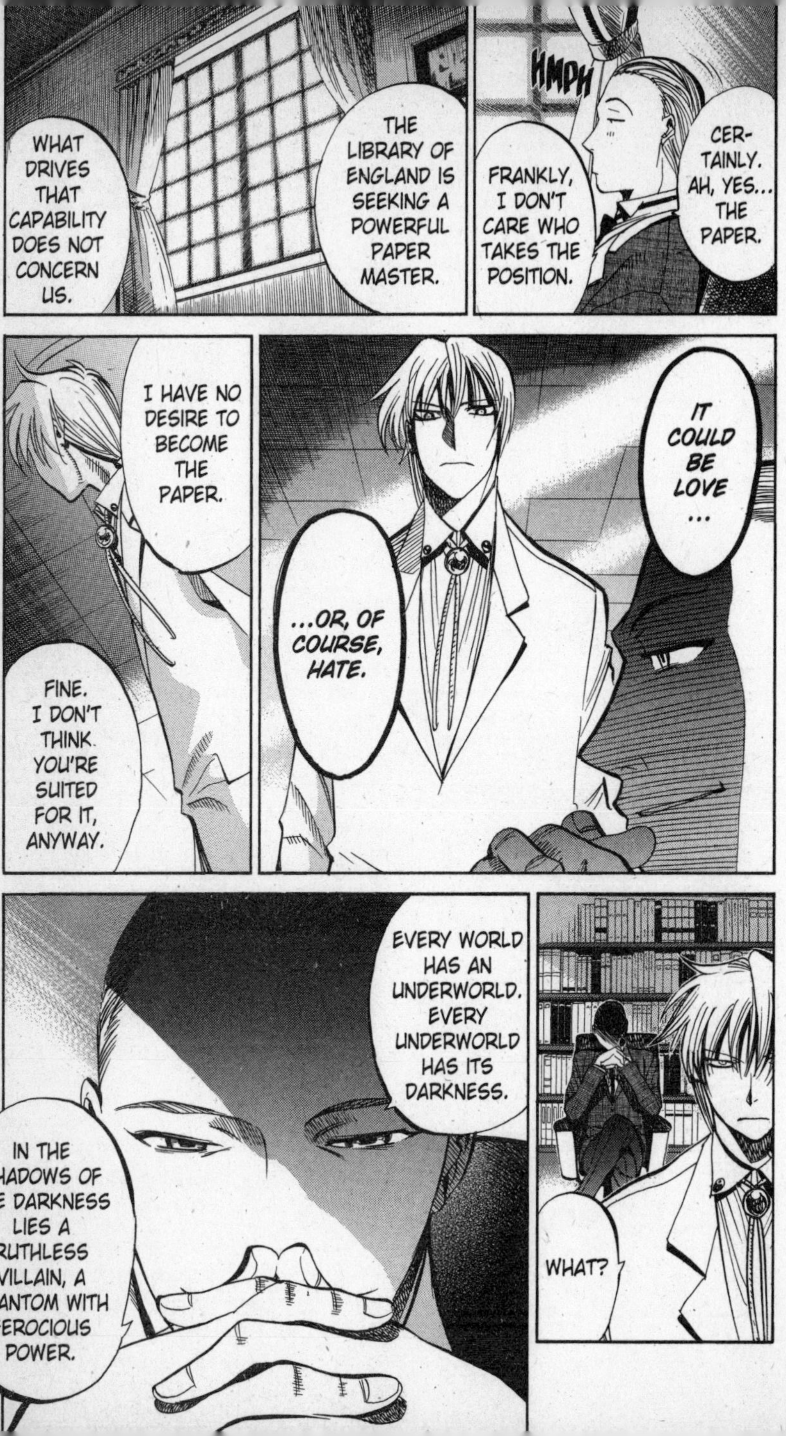
HMPH
CERTAINLY. AH, YES... THE PAPER.
FRANKLY, I DON'T CARE WHO TAKES THE POSITION.
THE LIBRARY OF ENGLAND IS SEEKING A POWERFUL PAPER MASTER.
WHAT DRIVES THAT CAPABILITY DOES NOT CONCERN US.
IT COULD BE LOVE ...
...OR, OF COURSE, HATE.
I HAVE NO DESIRE TO BECOME THE PAPER.
FINE. I DON'T THINK YOU'RE SUITED FOR IT, ANYWAY.
WHAT?
EVERY WORLD HAS AN UNDERWORLD. EVERY UNDERWORLD HAS ITS DARKNESS.
IN THE SHADOWS OF THE DARKNESS LIES A RUTHLESS VILLAIN, A PHANTOM WITH FEROCIOUS POWER.

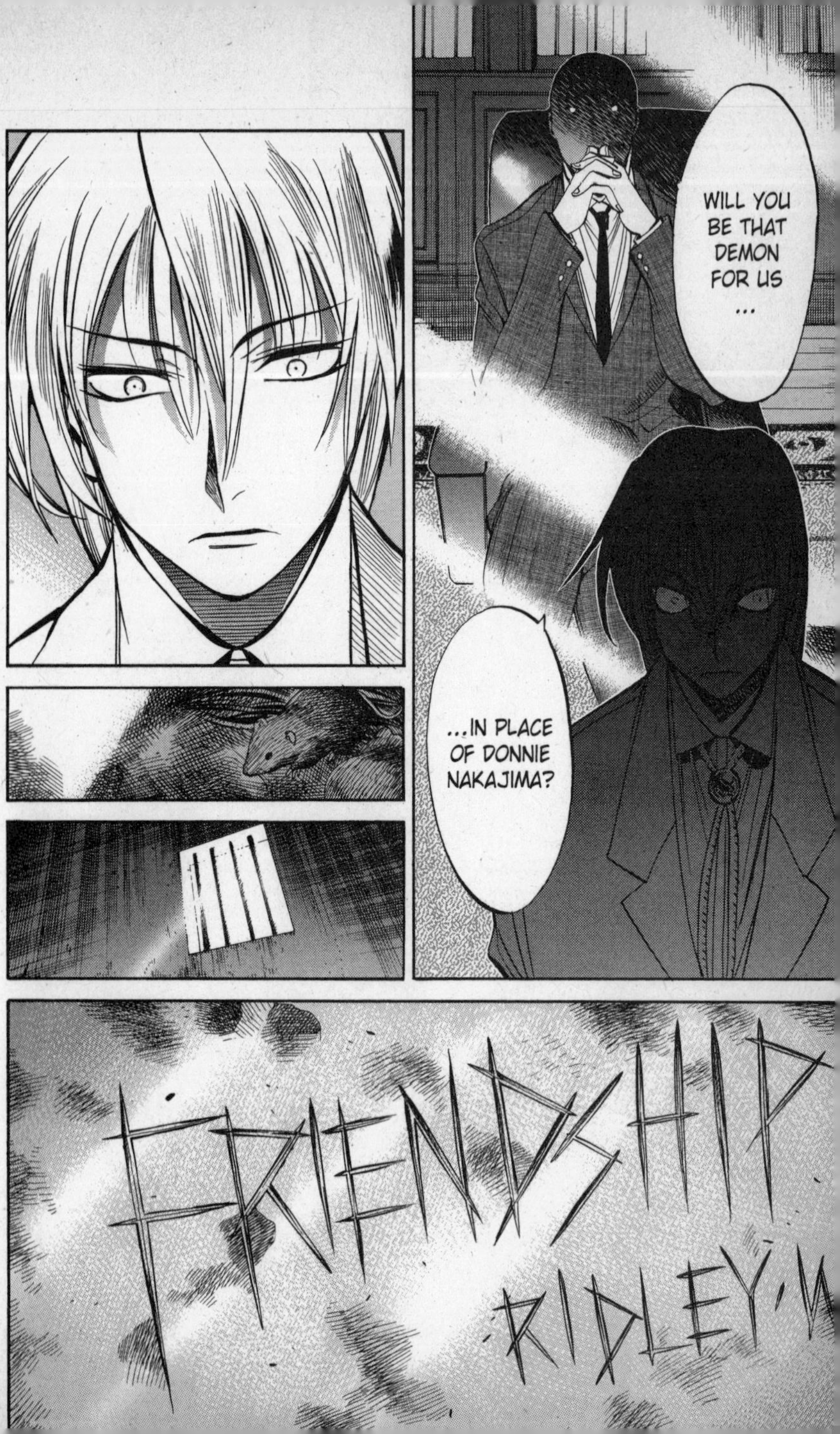
WILL YOU BE THAT DEMON FOR US ...
...IN PLACE OF DONNIE NAKAJIMA?
FRIENDSHIP
RIDLEY'

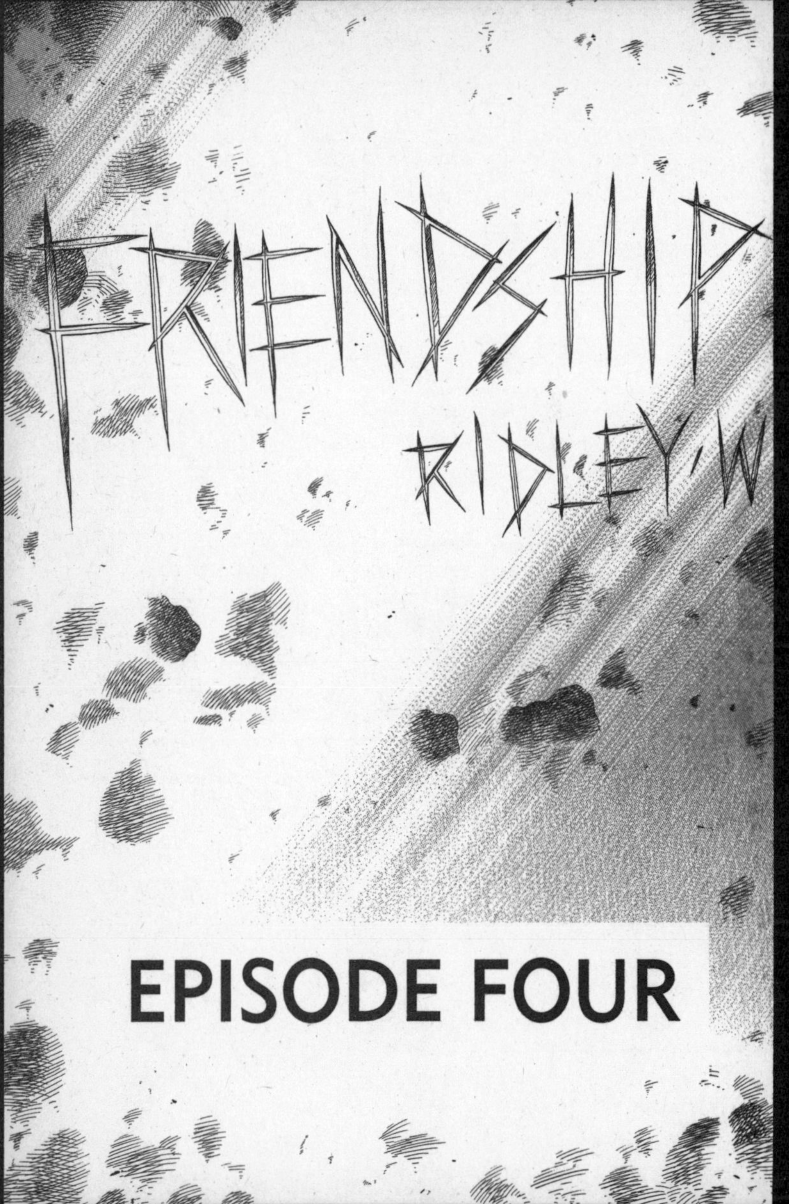
FRIENDSHIP
RIDLEY'W

EPISODE FOUR

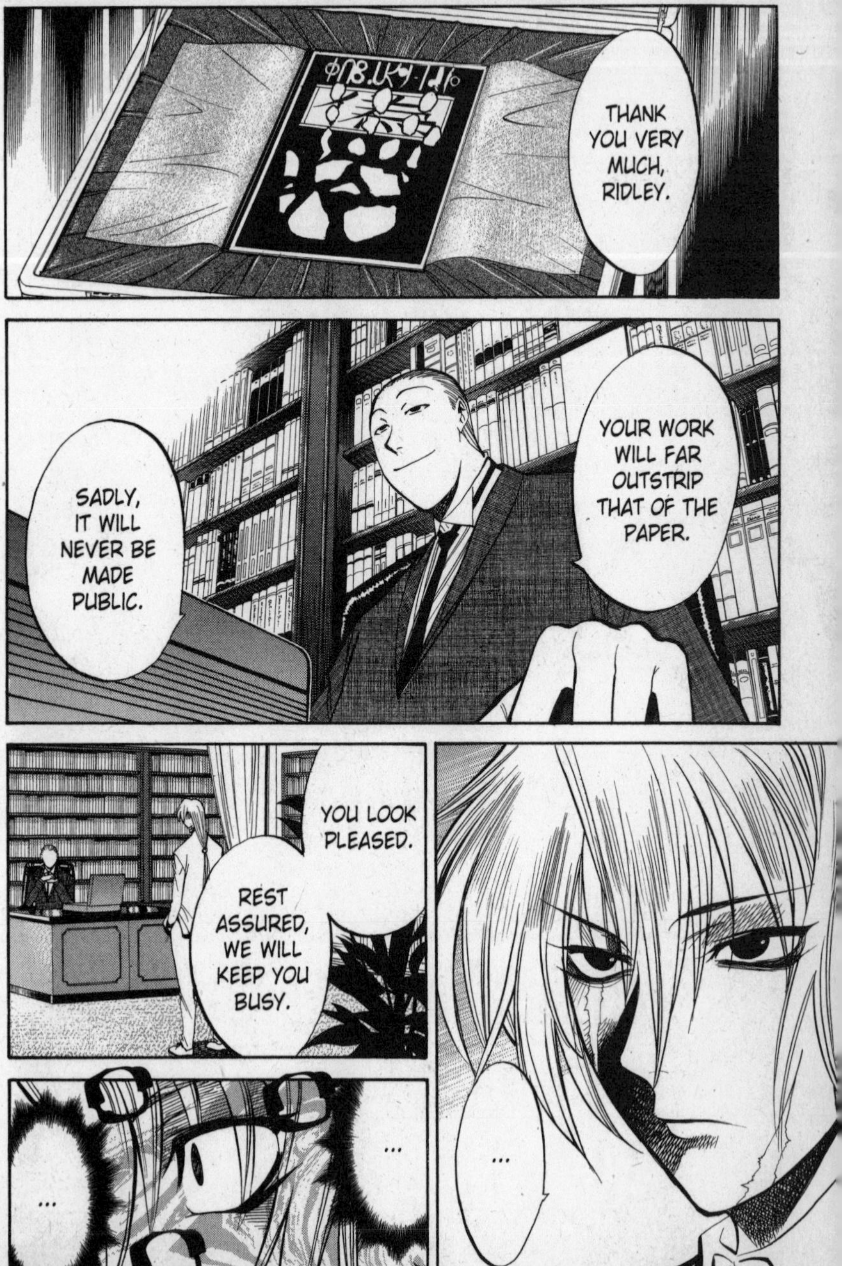
THANK YOU VERY MUCH, RIDLEY.
YOUR WORK WILL FAR OUTSTRIP THAT OF THE PAPER.
SADLY, IT WILL NEVER BE MADE PUBLIC.
...
YOU LOOK PLEASED.
REST ASSURED, WE WILL KEEP YOU BUSY.
...
...

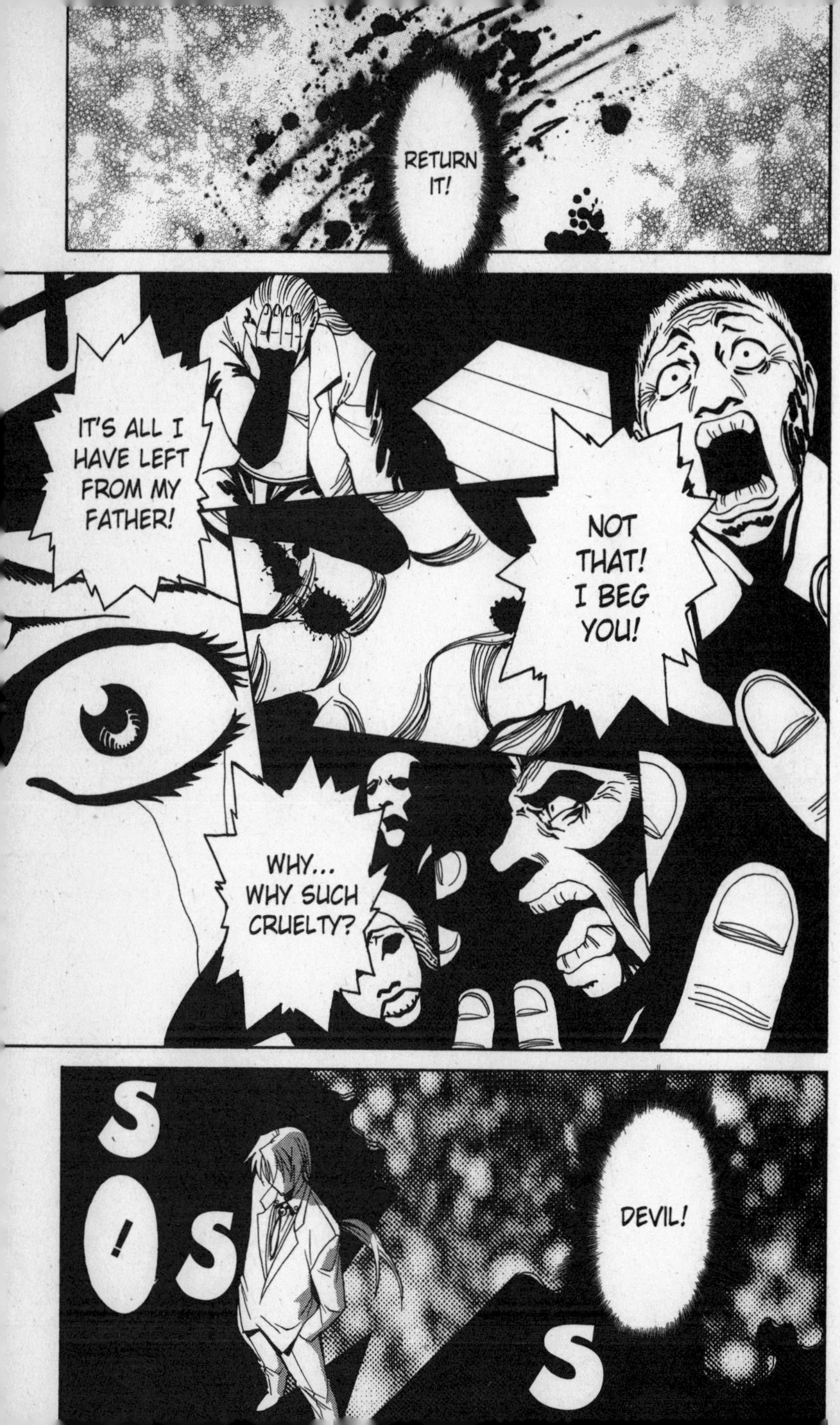
RETURN IT!
NOT THAT! I BEG YOU!
IT'S ALL I HAVE LEFT FROM MY FATHER!
WHY... WHY SUCH CRUELTY?
DEVIL!
!
S S S

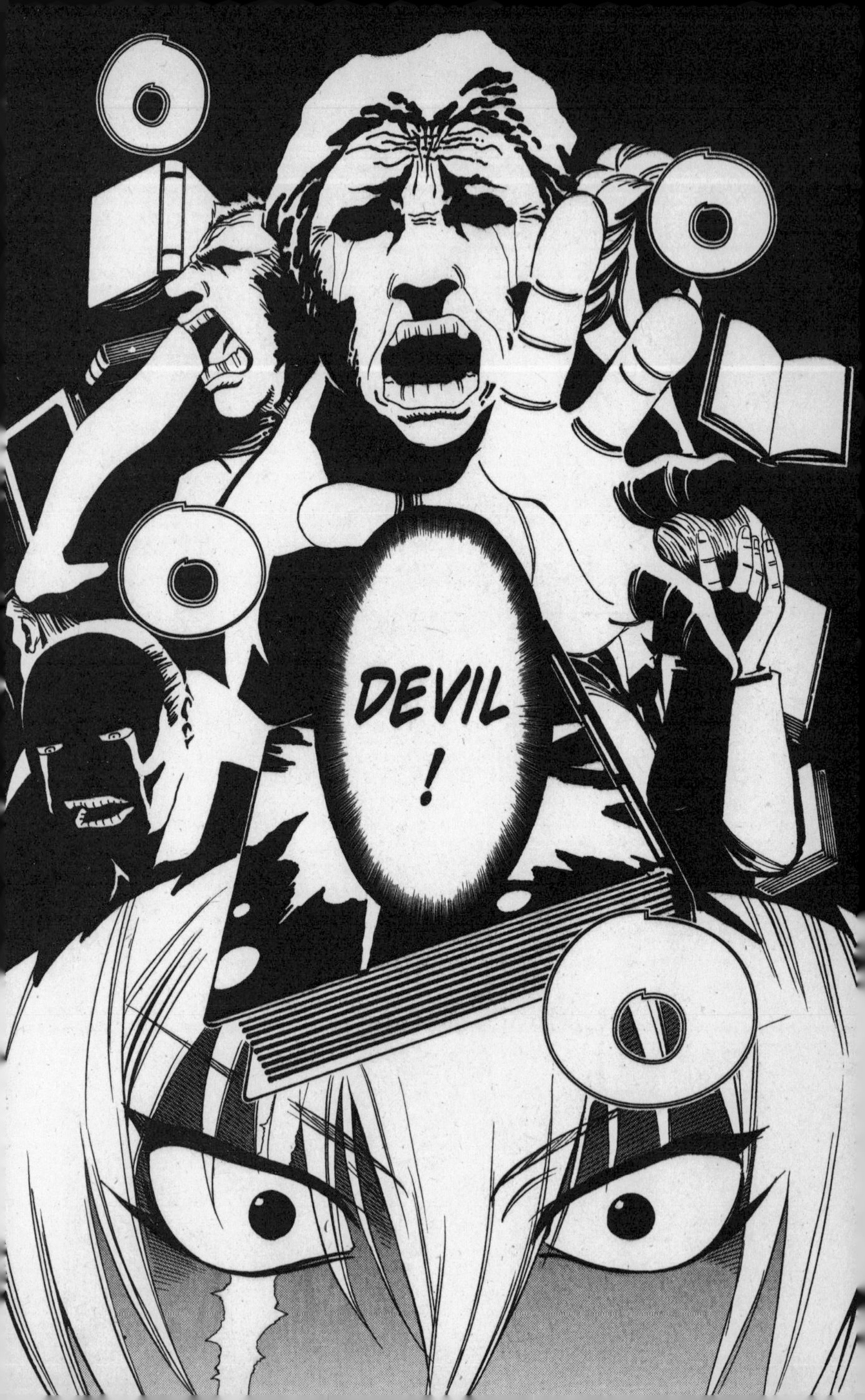
DEVIL!

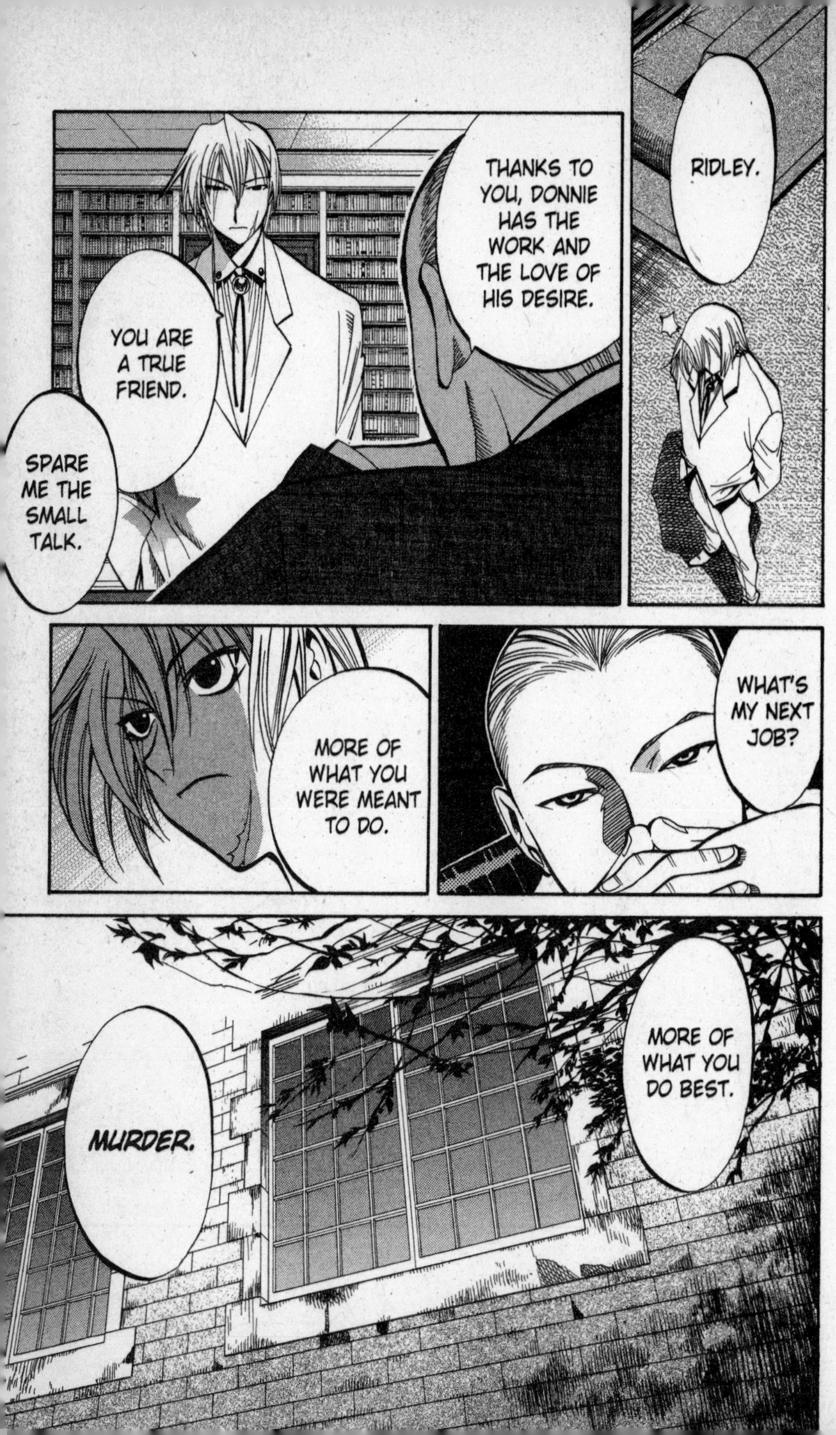
RIDLEY.
THANKS TO YOU, DONNIE HAS THE WORK AND THE LOVE OF HIS DESIRE.
YOU ARE A TRUE FRIEND.
SPARE ME THE SMALL TALK.
WHAT'S MY NEXT JOB?
MORE OF WHAT YOU WERE MEANT TO DO.
MORE OF WHAT YOU DO BEST.
MURDER.

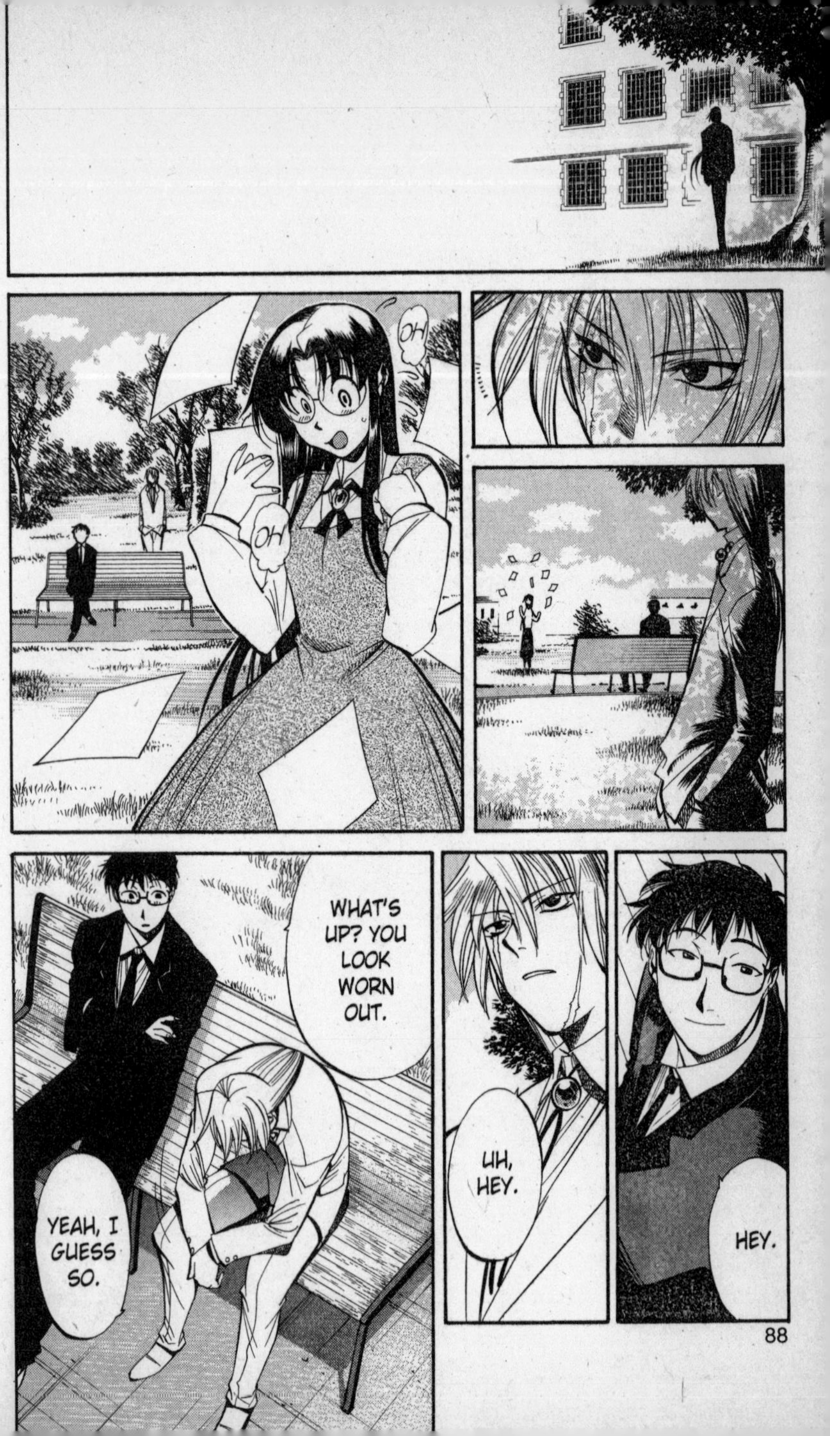
OH
OH
HEY.
UH, HEY.
WHAT'S UP? YOU LOOK WORN OUT.
YEAH, I GUESS SO.

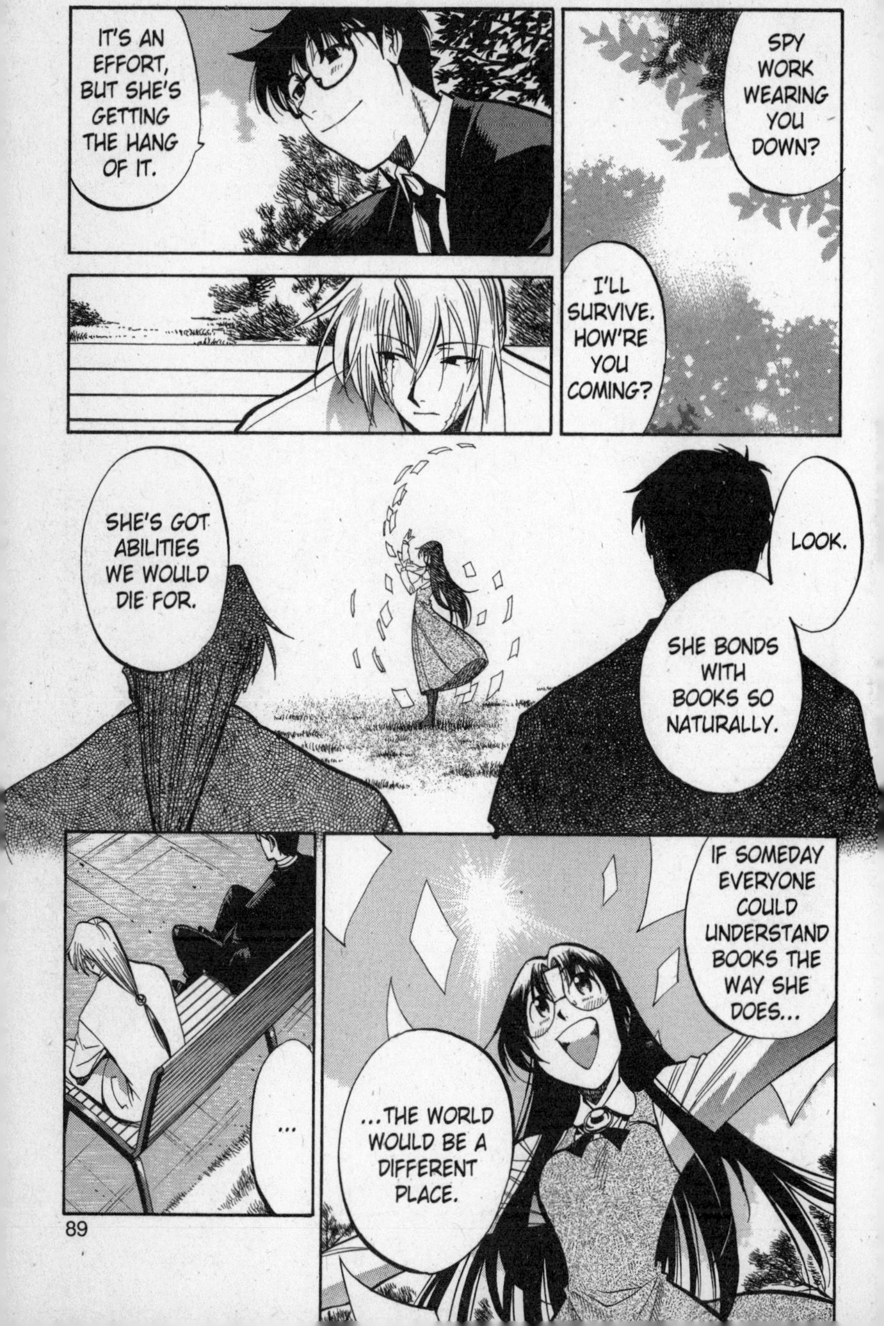

SPY WORK WEARING YOU DOWN?
I'LL SURVIVE. HOW'RE YOU COMING?
IT'S AN EFFORT, BUT SHE'S GETTING THE HANG OF IT.
LOOK.
SHE BONDS WITH BOOKS SO NATURALLY.
SHE'S GOT ABILITIES WE WOULD DIE FOR.
IF SOMEDAY EVERYONE COULD UNDERSTAND BOOKS THE WAY SHE DOES...
...THE WORLD WOULD BE A DIFFERENT PLACE.
...

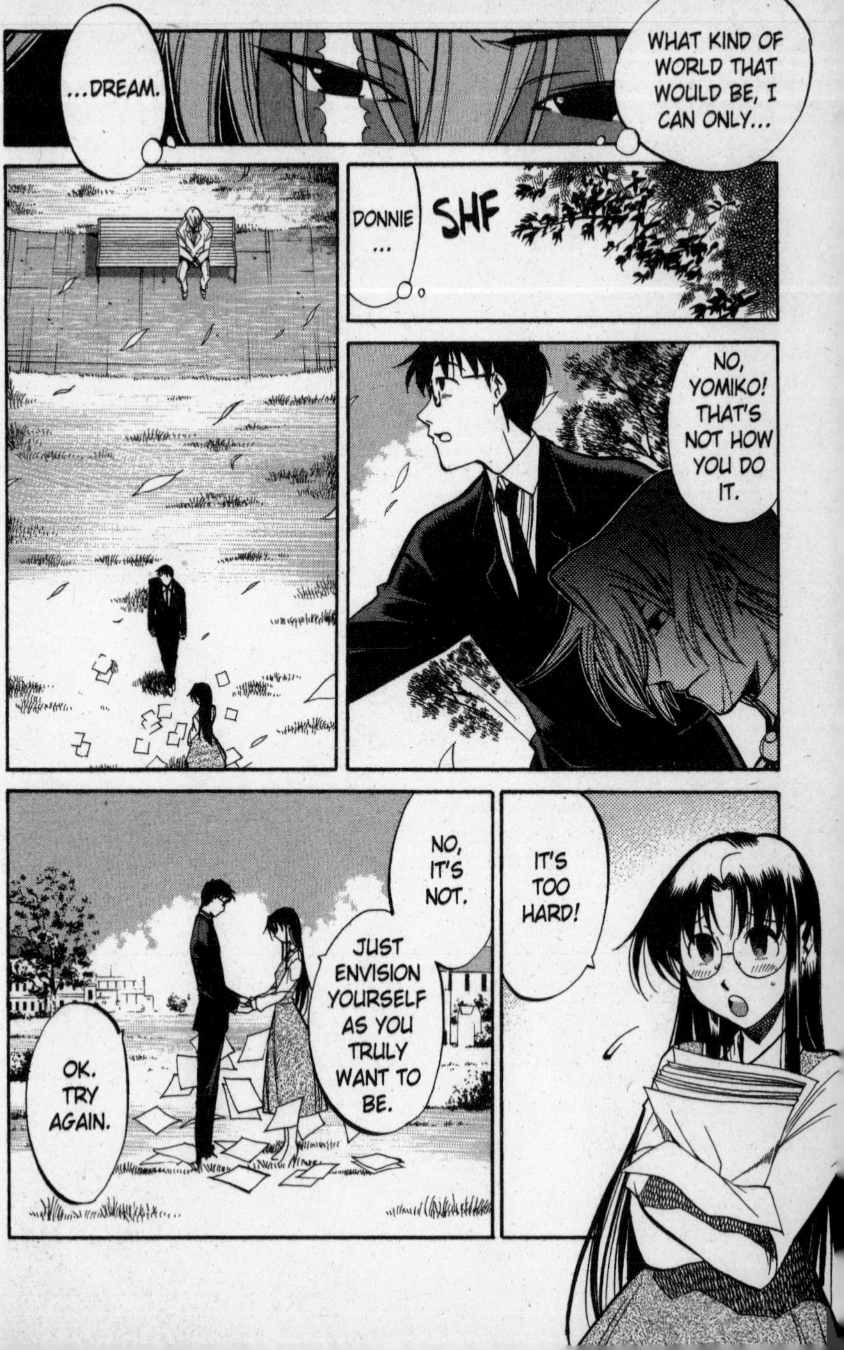
WHAT KIND OF WORLD THAT WOULD BE, I CAN ONLY...
...DREAM.
SHF
DONNIE ...
NO, YOMIKO! THAT'S NOT HOW YOU DO IT.
IT'S TOO HARD!
NO, IT'S NOT.
JUST ENVISION YOURSELF AS YOU TRULY WANT TO BE.
OK. TRY AGAIN.

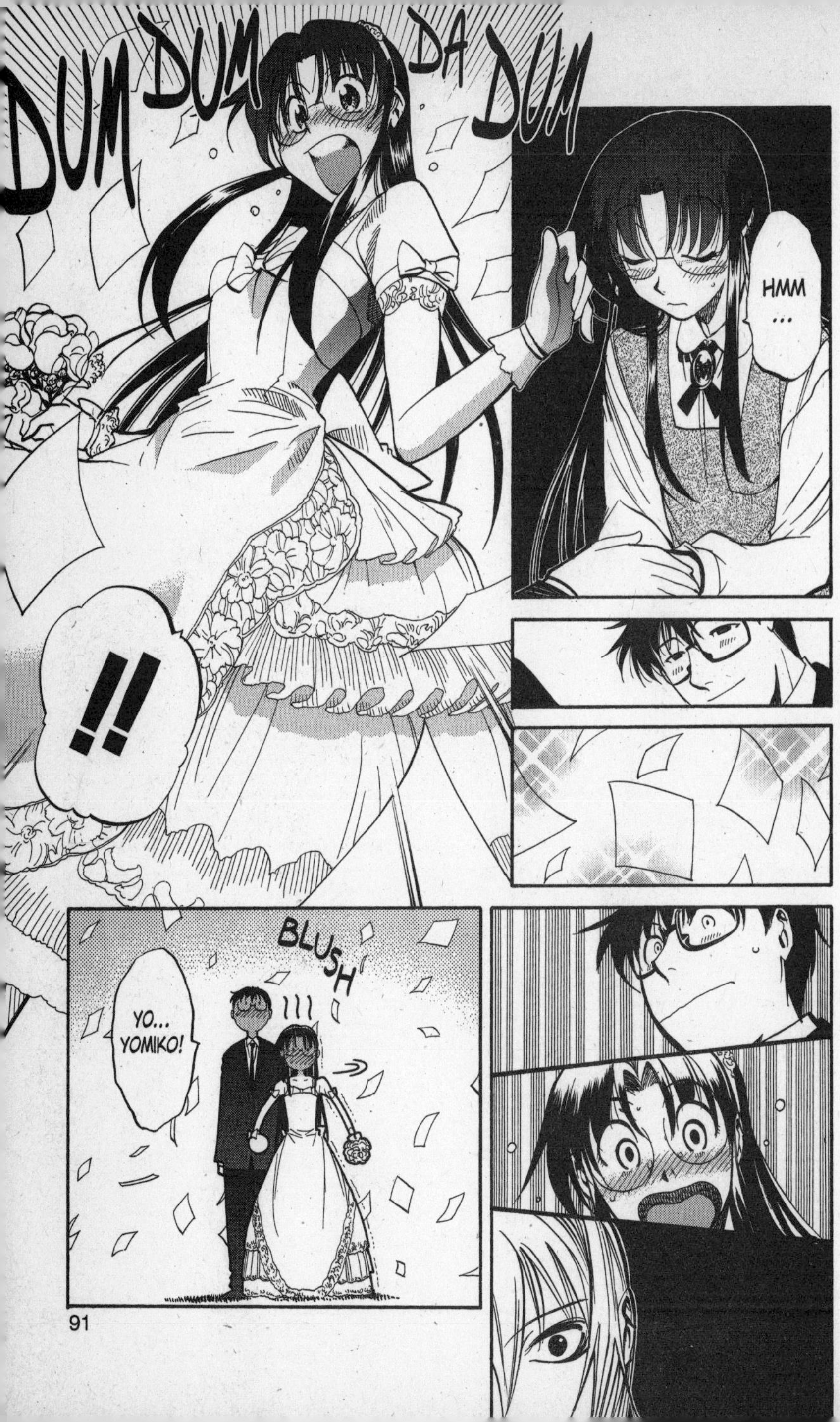
HMM ...
DUM DUM DA DUM
!!
YO... YOMIKO!
BLUSH
!!!

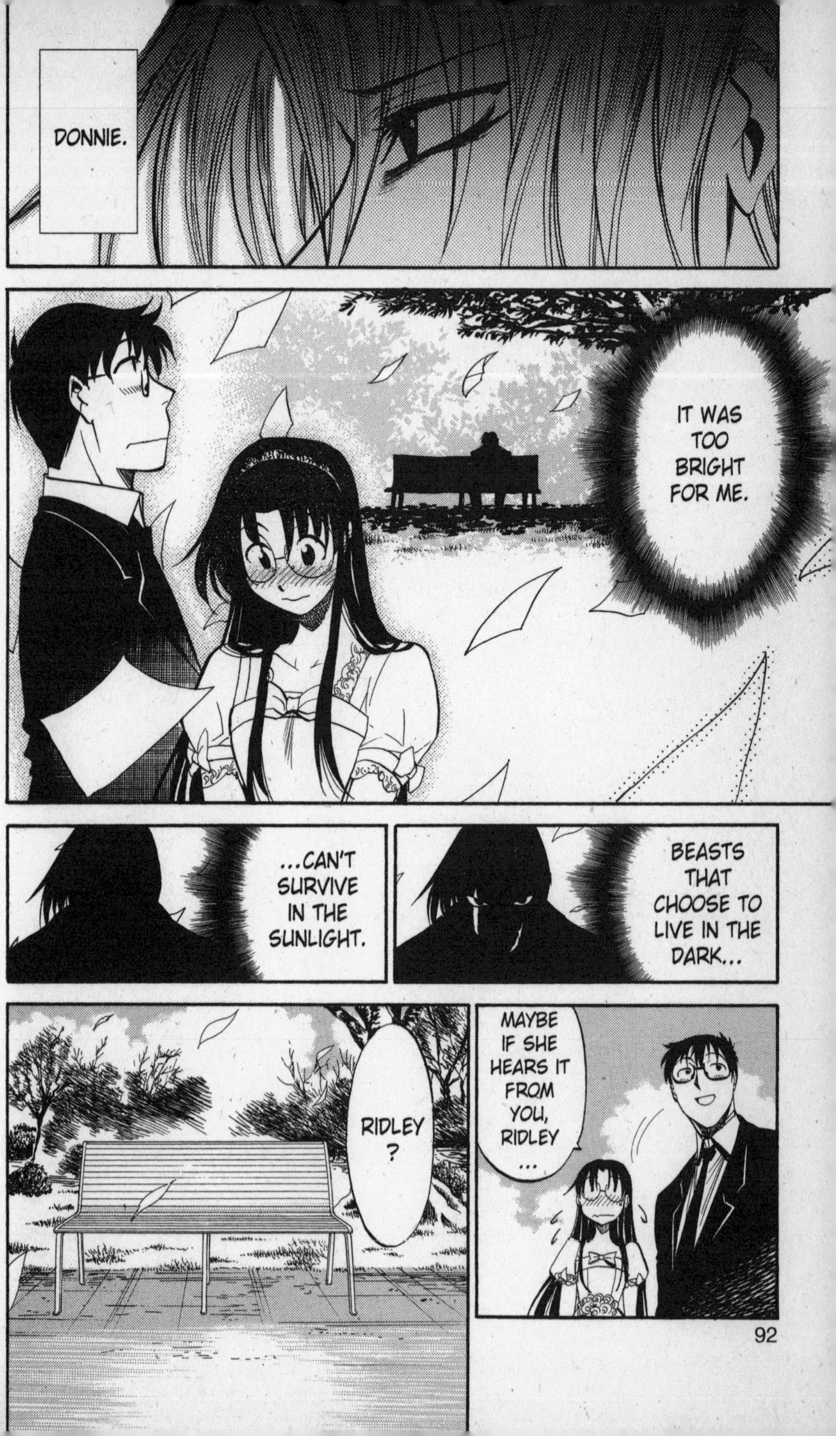
DONNIE.
IT WAS TOO BRIGHT FOR ME.
BEASTS THAT CHOOSE TO LIVE IN THE DARK...
...CAN'T SURVIVE IN THE SUNLIGHT.
MAYBE IF SHE HEARS IT FROM YOU, RIDLEY ...
RIDLEY?

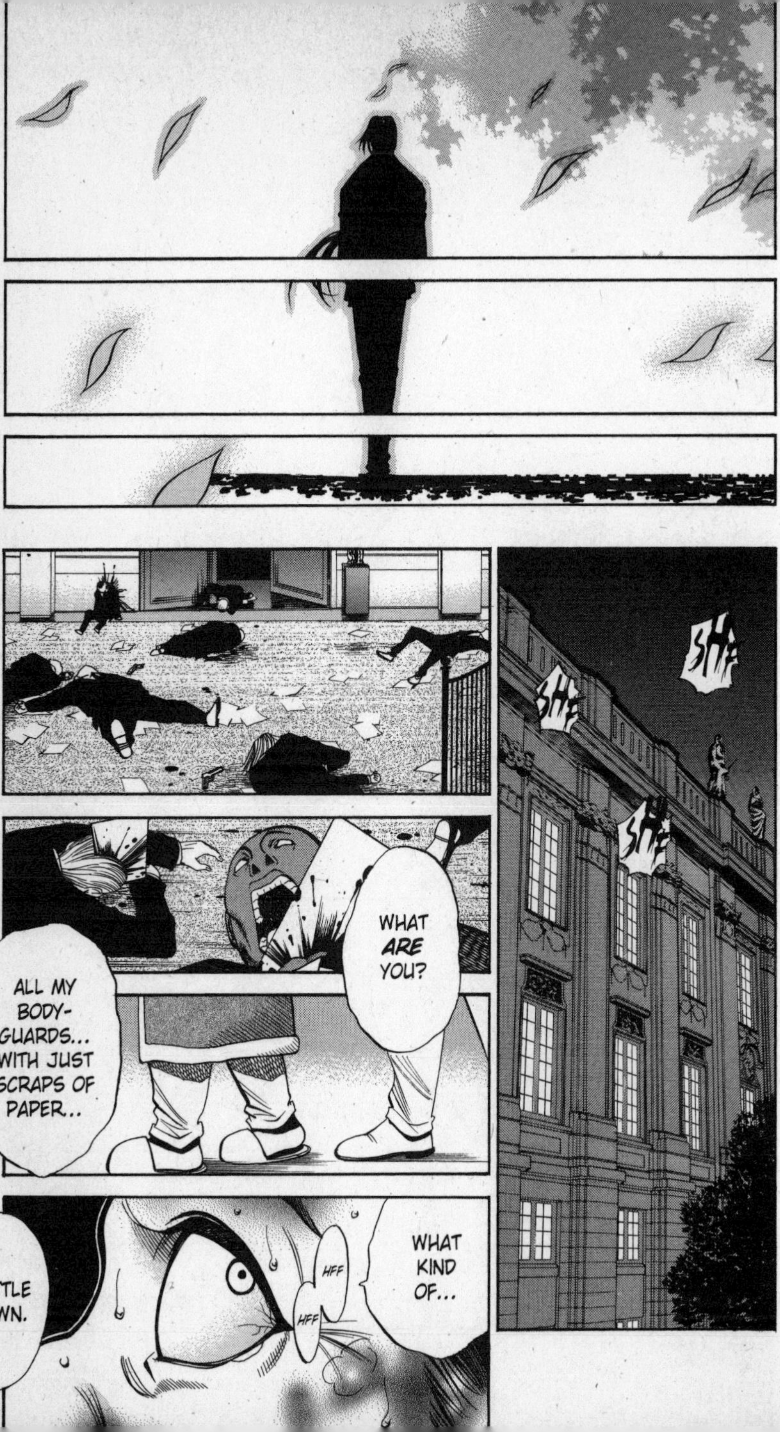
SHF
SHF
SHF
WHAT ARE YOU?
ALL MY BODY-GUARDS... WITH JUST SCRAPS OF PAPER...
WHAT KIND OF...
HFF
HFF
SETTLE DOWN.

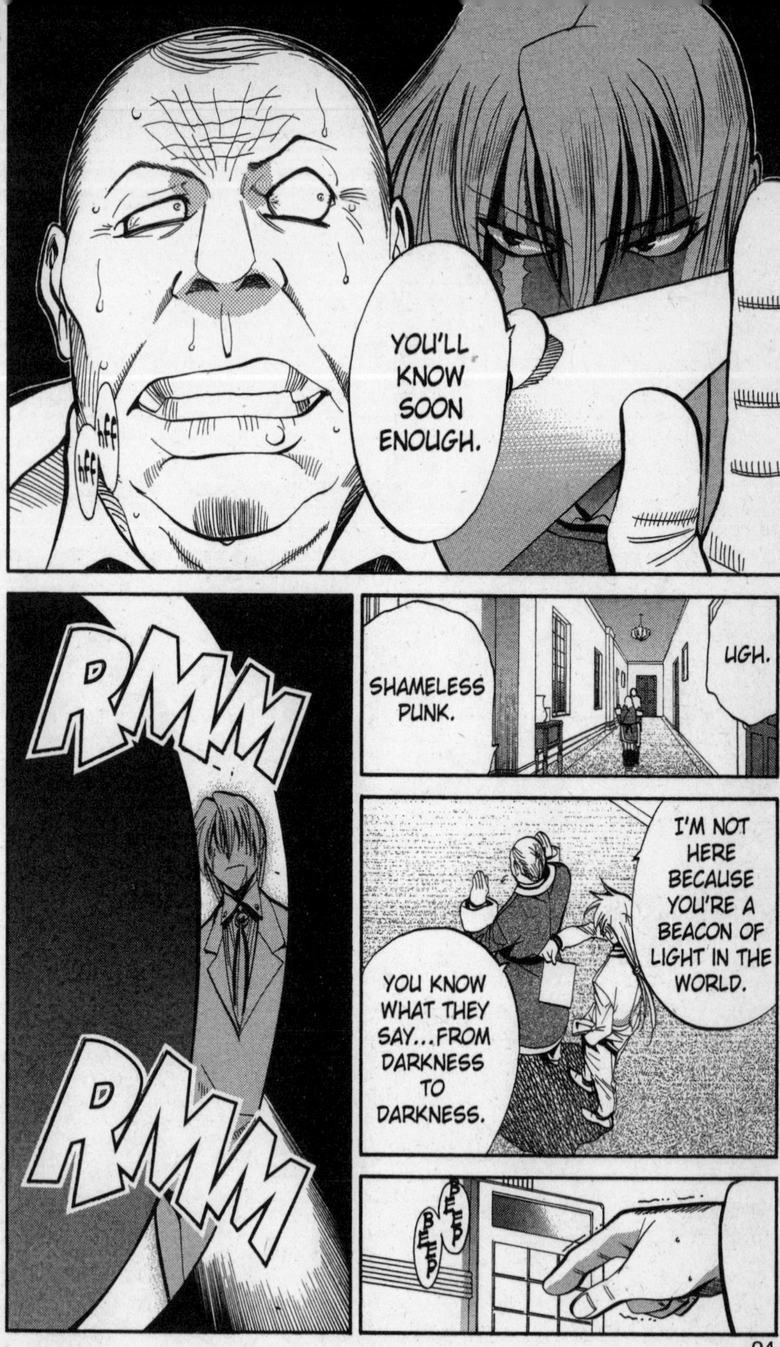
YOU'LL KNOW SOON ENOUGH.
hff hff
UGH.
SHAMELESS PUNK.
I'M NOT HERE BECAUSE YOU'RE A BEACON OF LIGHT IN THE WORLD.
YOU KNOW WHAT THEY SAY...FROM DARKNESS TO DARKNESS.
BEEP BEEP
RMM RMM

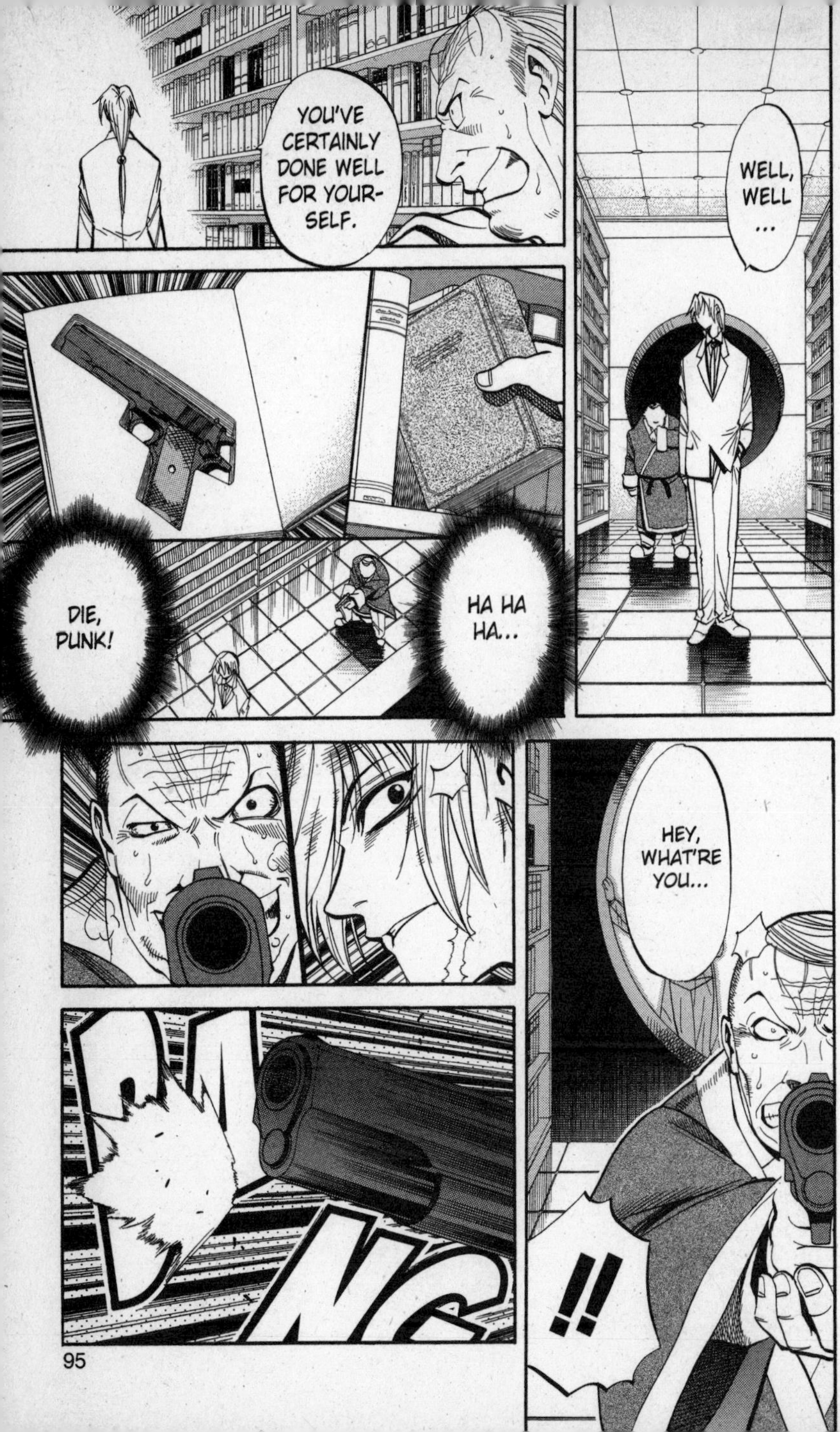

WELL, WELL ...
YOU'VE CERTAINLY DONE WELL FOR YOURSELF.
HA HA HA...
DIE, PUNK!
HEY, WHAT'RE YOU...
!!

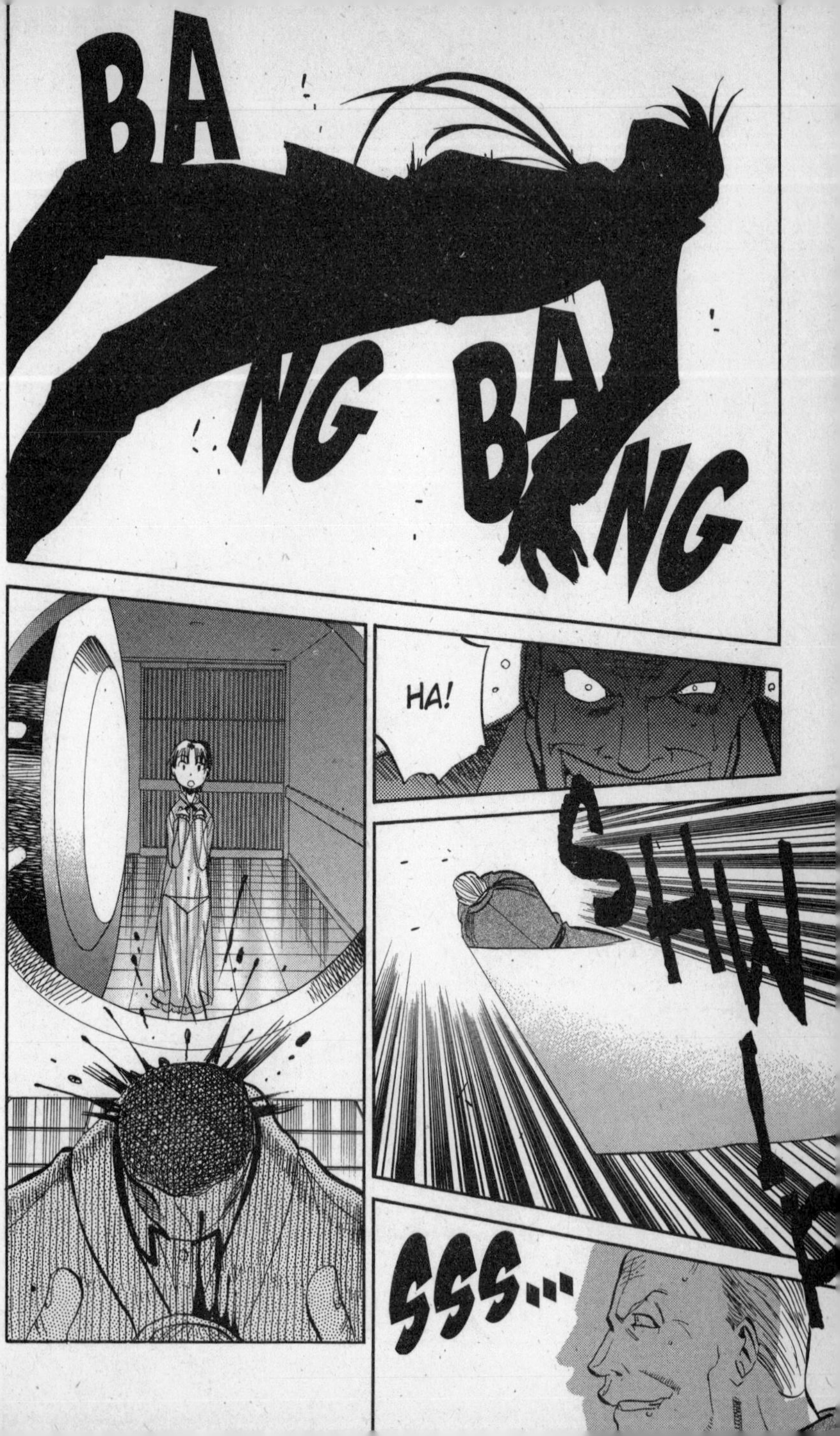
BANG
BANG
HA!
SHWI
SSS...

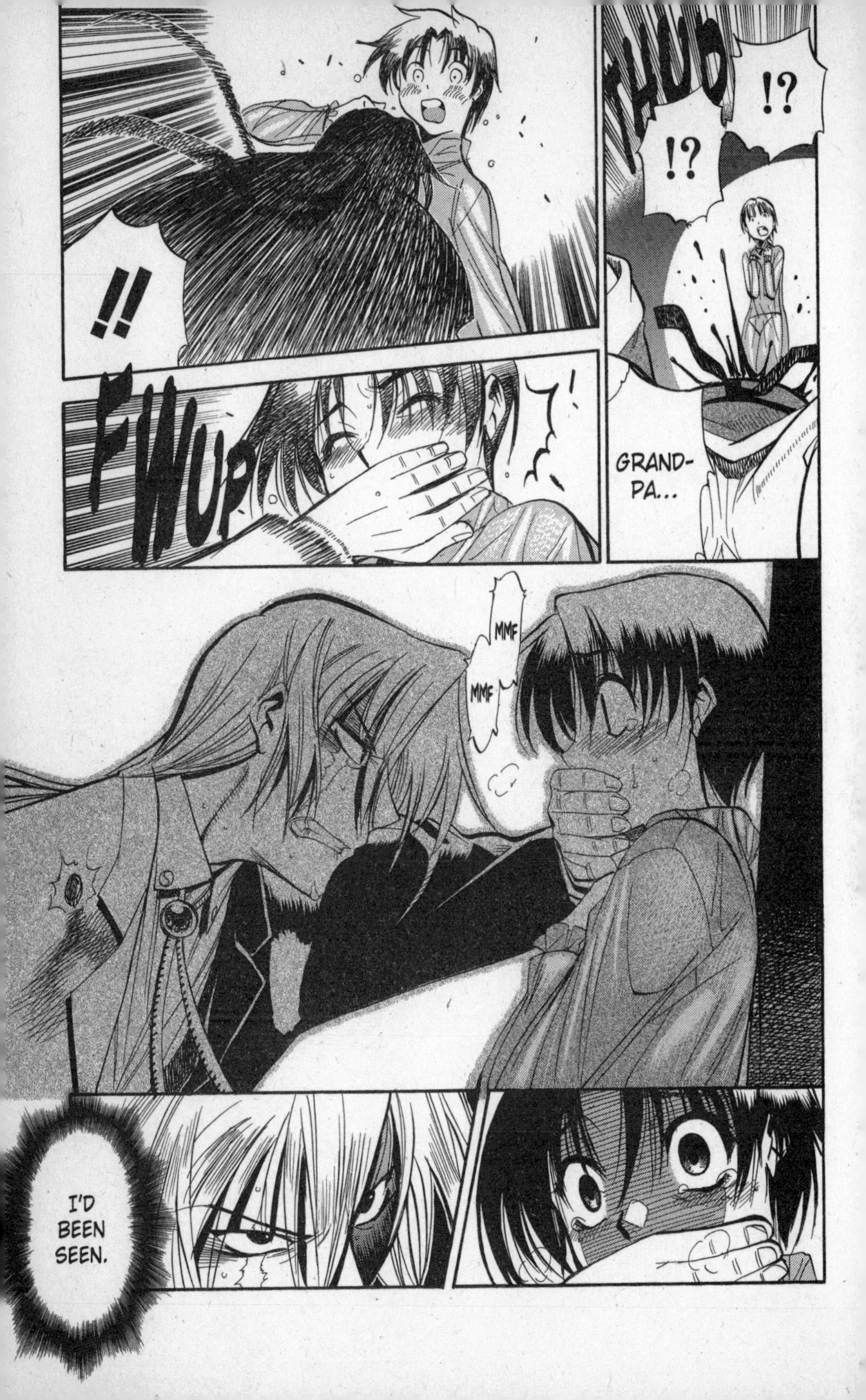
THUD
!?
!?
GRAND-PA...
!!
FWUP
MMF
MMF
I'D BEEN SEEN.

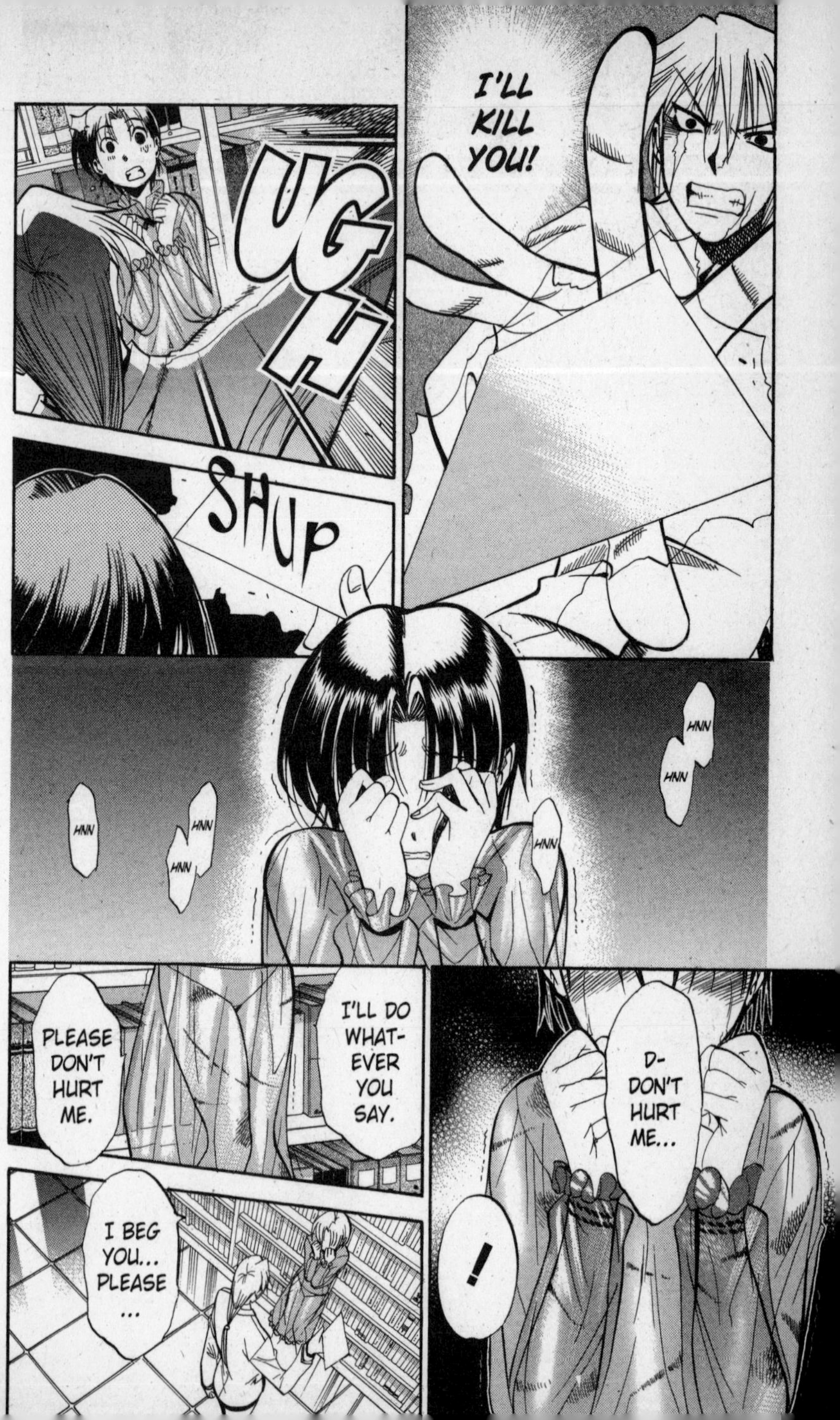
I'LL KILL YOU!
UGH
SHUP
HNN
HNN
HNN
HNN
HNN
HNN
D- DON'T HURT ME...
!
I'LL DO WHAT-EVER YOU SAY.
PLEASE DON'T HURT ME.
I BEG YOU... PLEASE ...

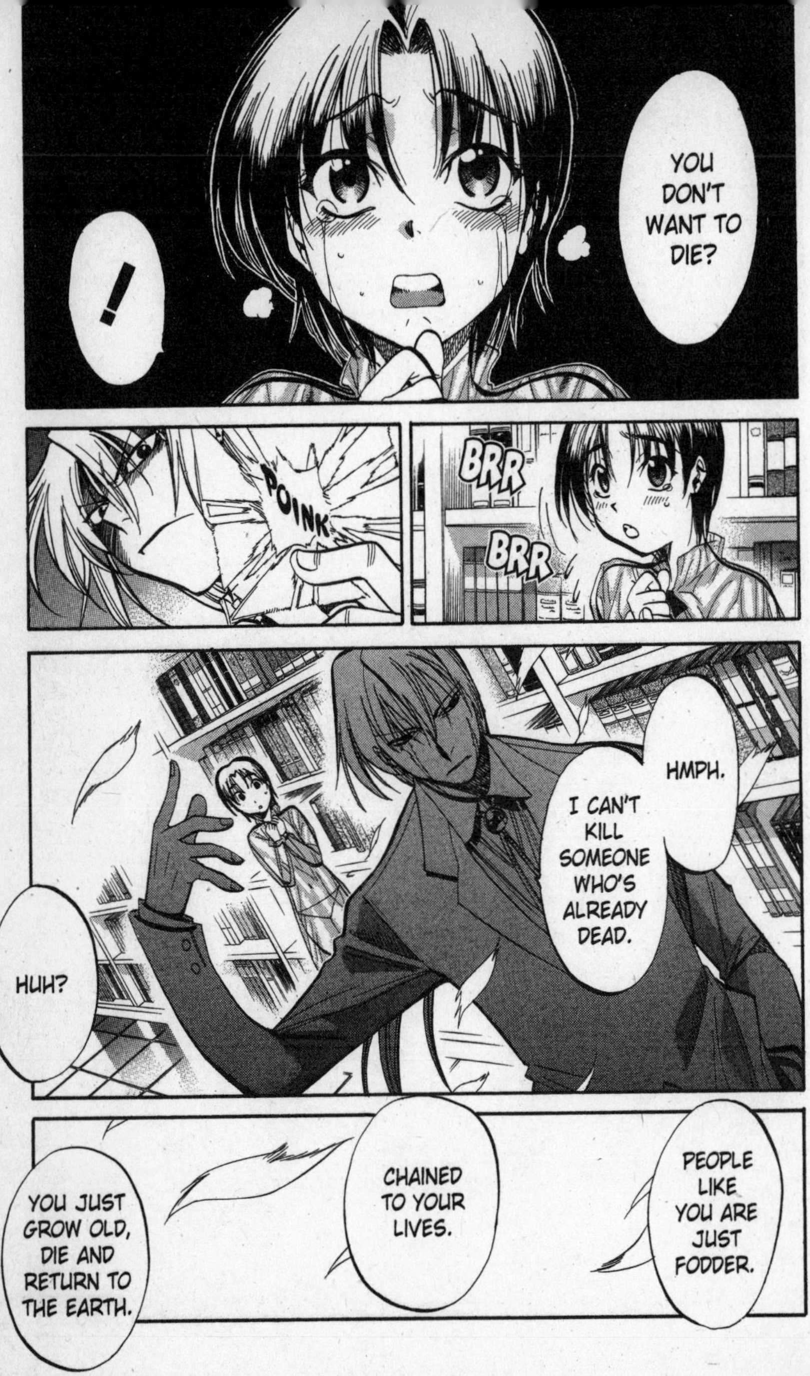
YOU DON'T WANT TO DIE?
!
BRR
BRR
POINK
HMPH.
I CAN'T KILL SOMEONE WHO'S ALREADY DEAD.
HUH?
PEOPLE LIKE YOU ARE JUST FODDER.
CHAINED TO YOUR LIVES.
YOU JUST GROW OLD, DIE AND RETURN TO THE EARTH.

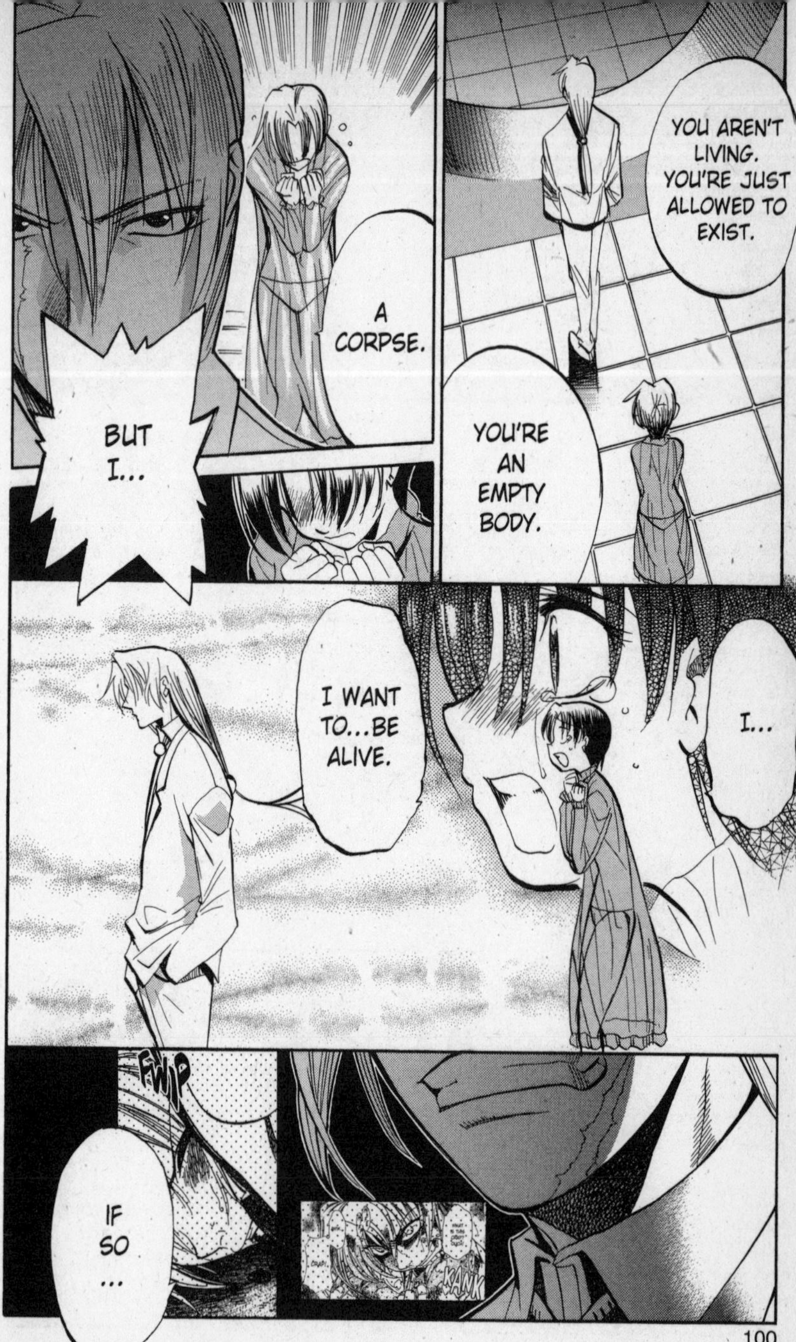
YOU AREN'T LIVING. YOU'RE JUST ALLOWED TO EXIST.
YOU'RE AN EMPTY BODY.
A CORPSE.
BUT I...
I...
I WANT TO...BE ALIVE.
KANK
FWIP
IF SO ...

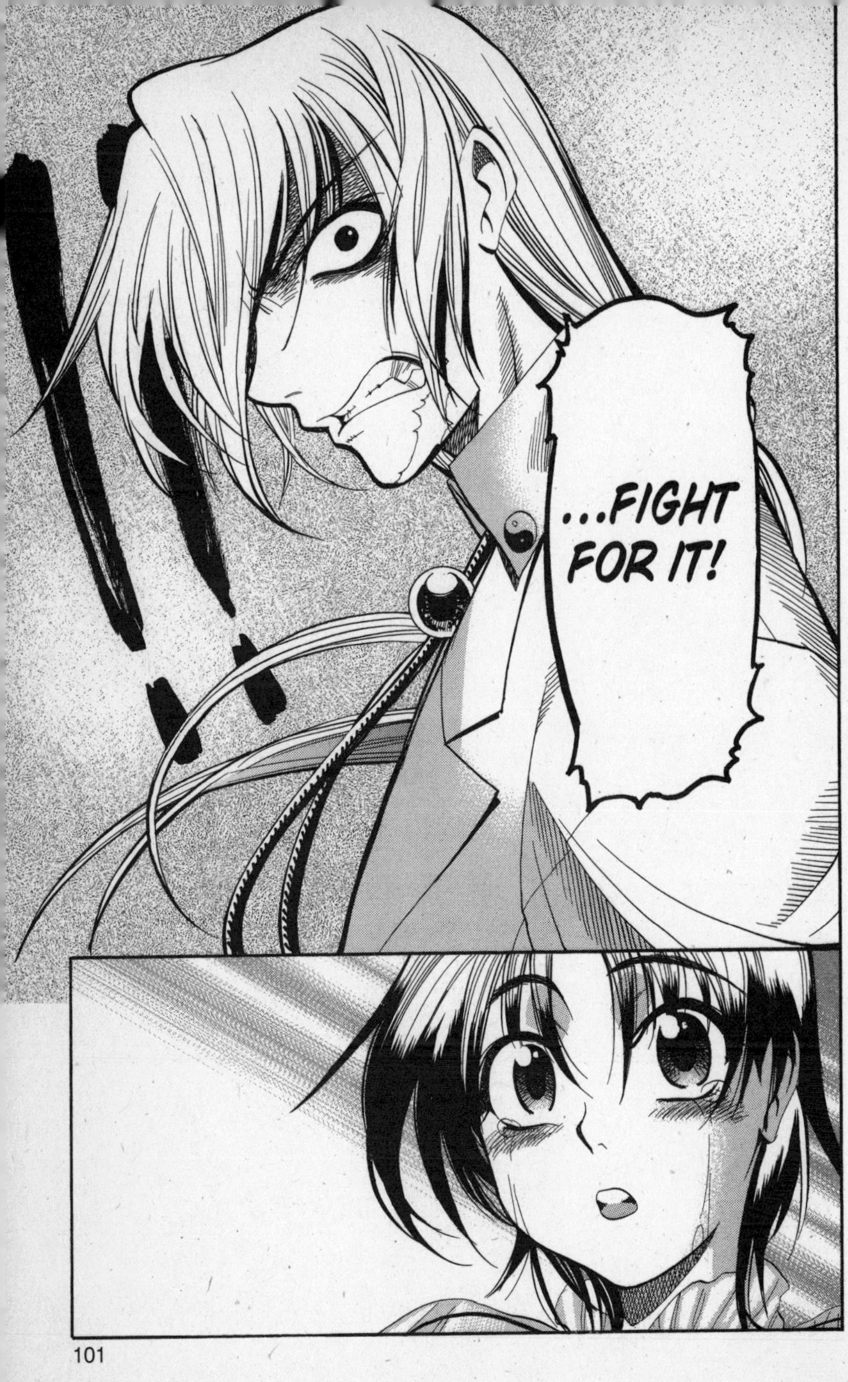
...FIGHT FOR IT!

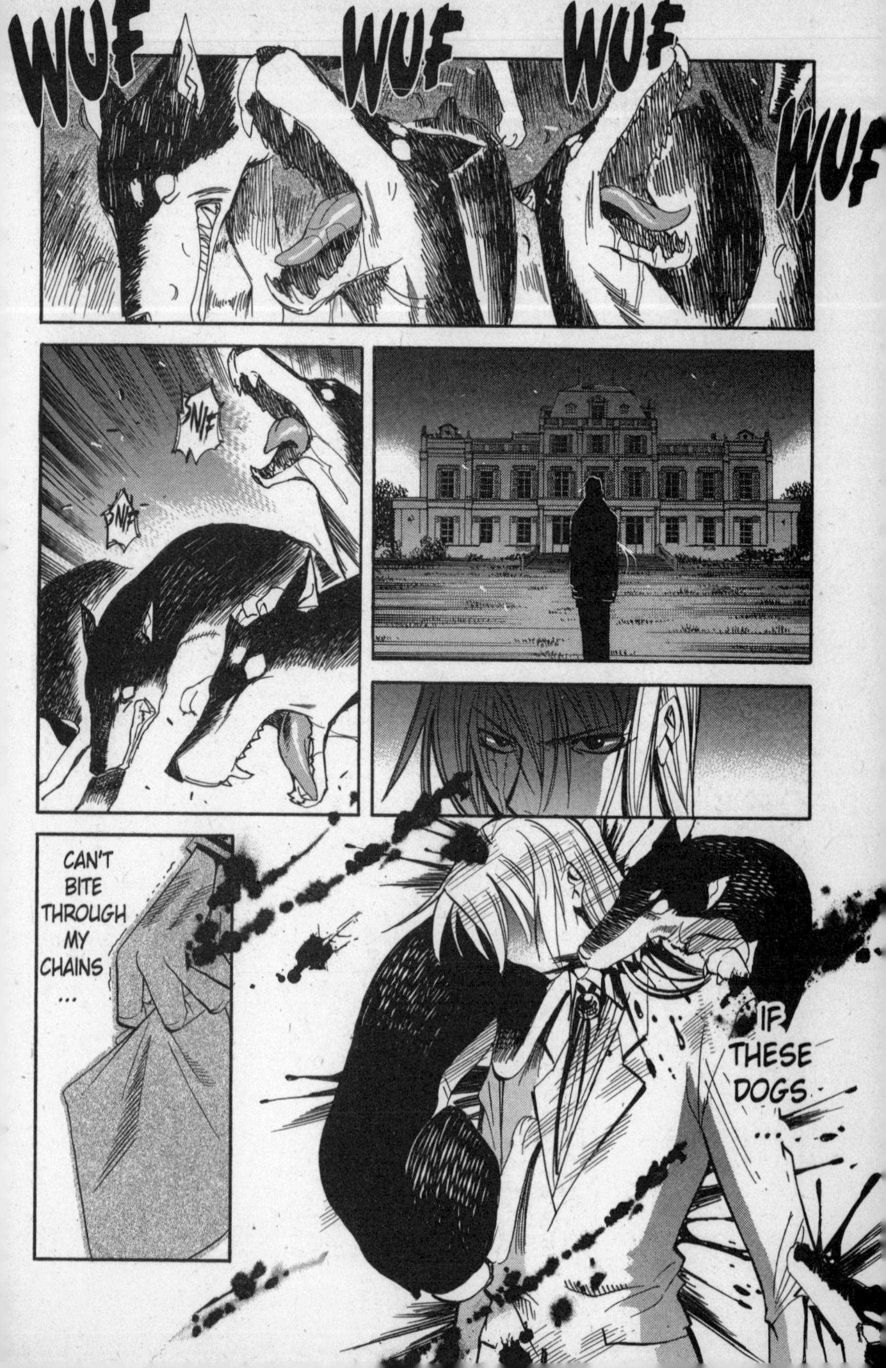
WUF
WUF
WUF
WUF
SNIF
SNIF
IF THESE DOGS ...
CAN'T BITE THROUGH MY CHAINS ...

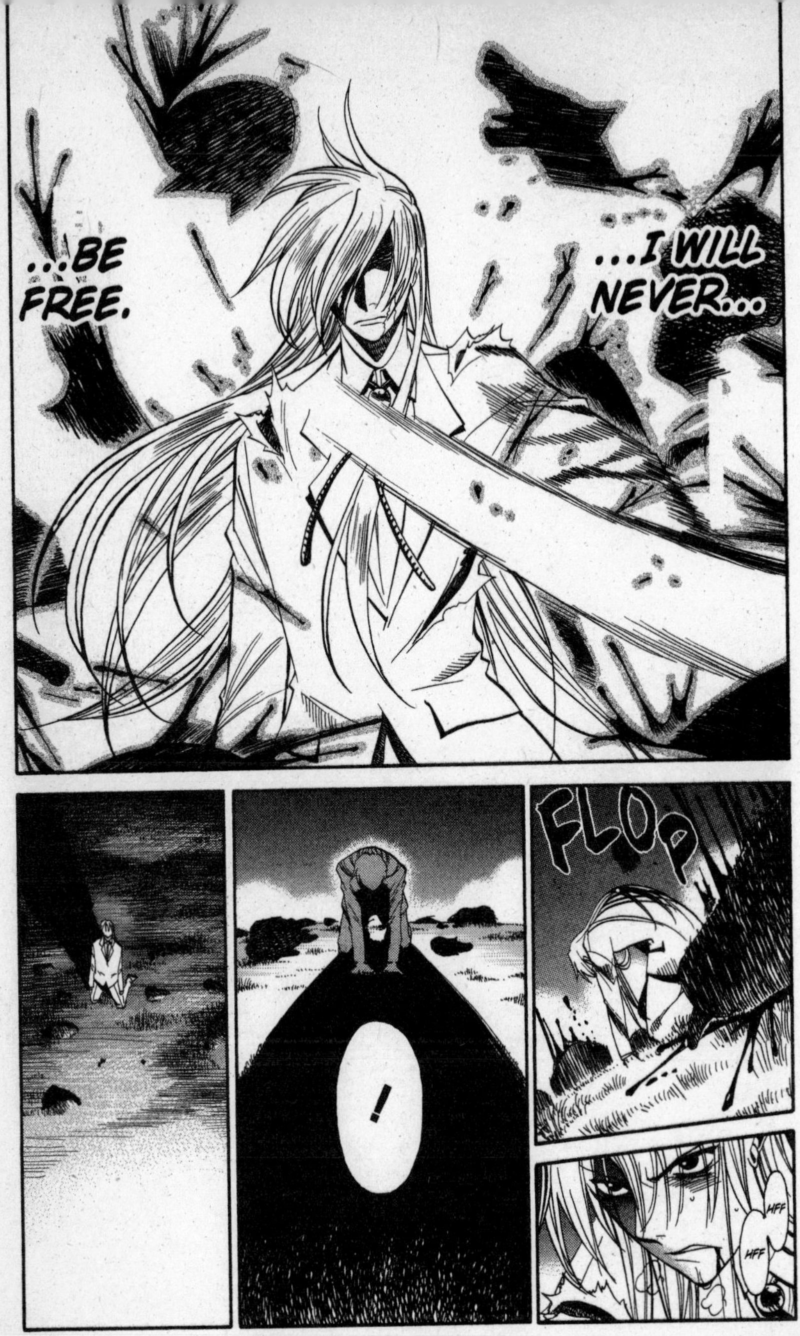
...I WILL NEVER...
...BE FREE.
FLOP
HFF
HFF
!

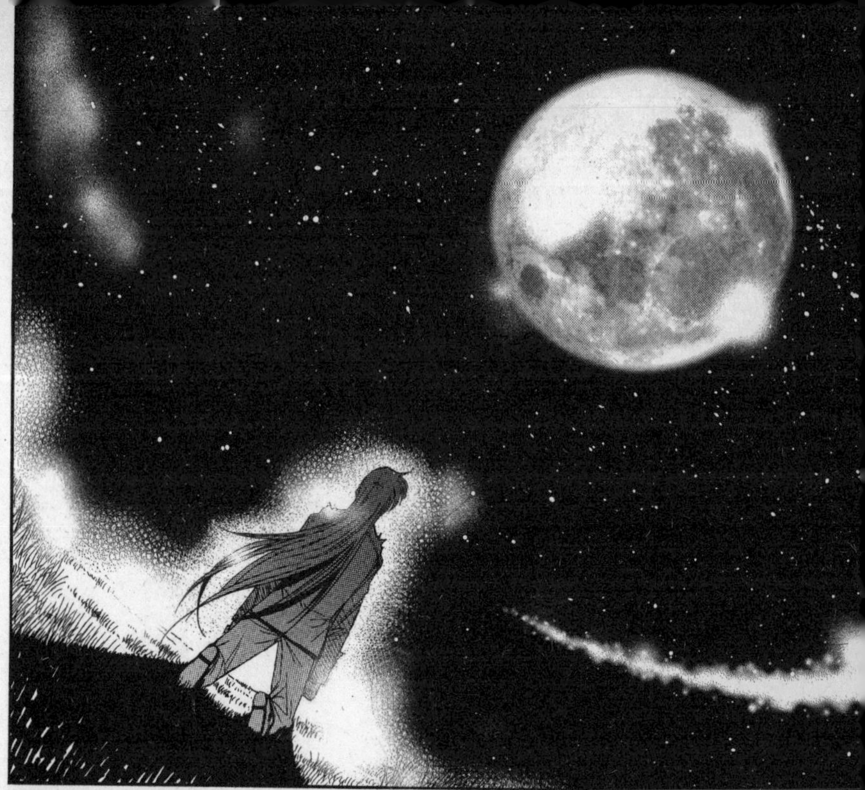

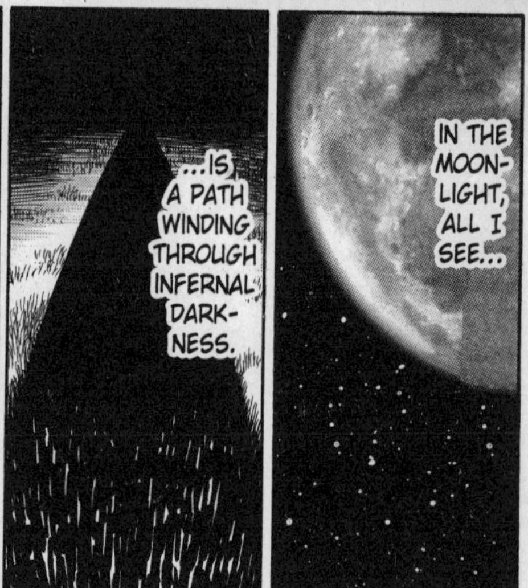
IN THE MOON-LIGHT, ALL I SEE...
...IS A PATH WINDING THROUGH INFERNAL DARK-NESS.

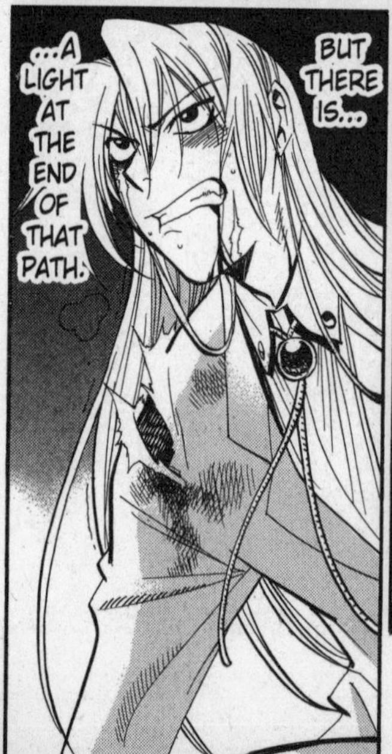
BUT THERE IS...
...A LIGHT AT THE END OF THAT PATH.

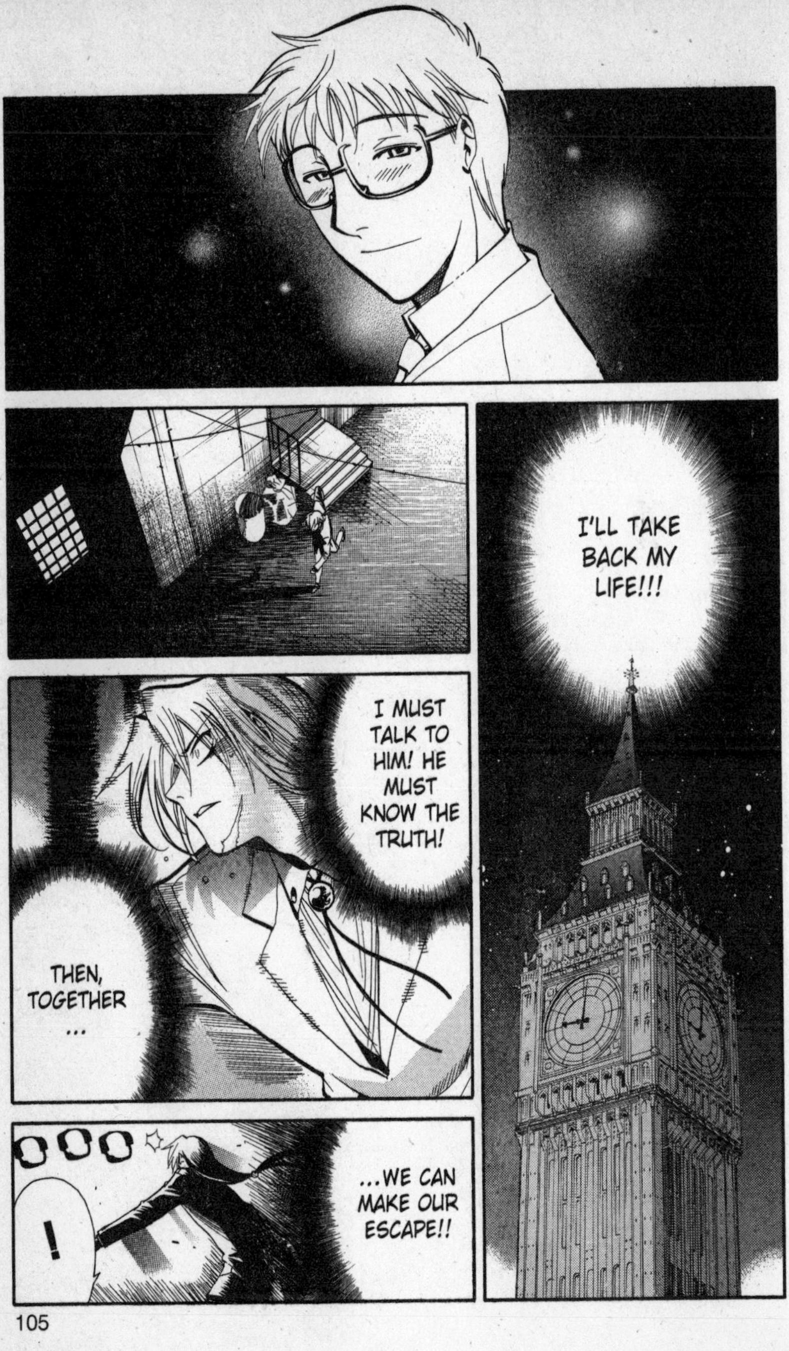
I'LL TAKE BACK MY LIFE!!!
I MUST TALK TO HIM! HE MUST KNOW THE TRUTH!
THEN, TOGETHER ...
...WE CAN MAKE OUR ESCAPE!!
!

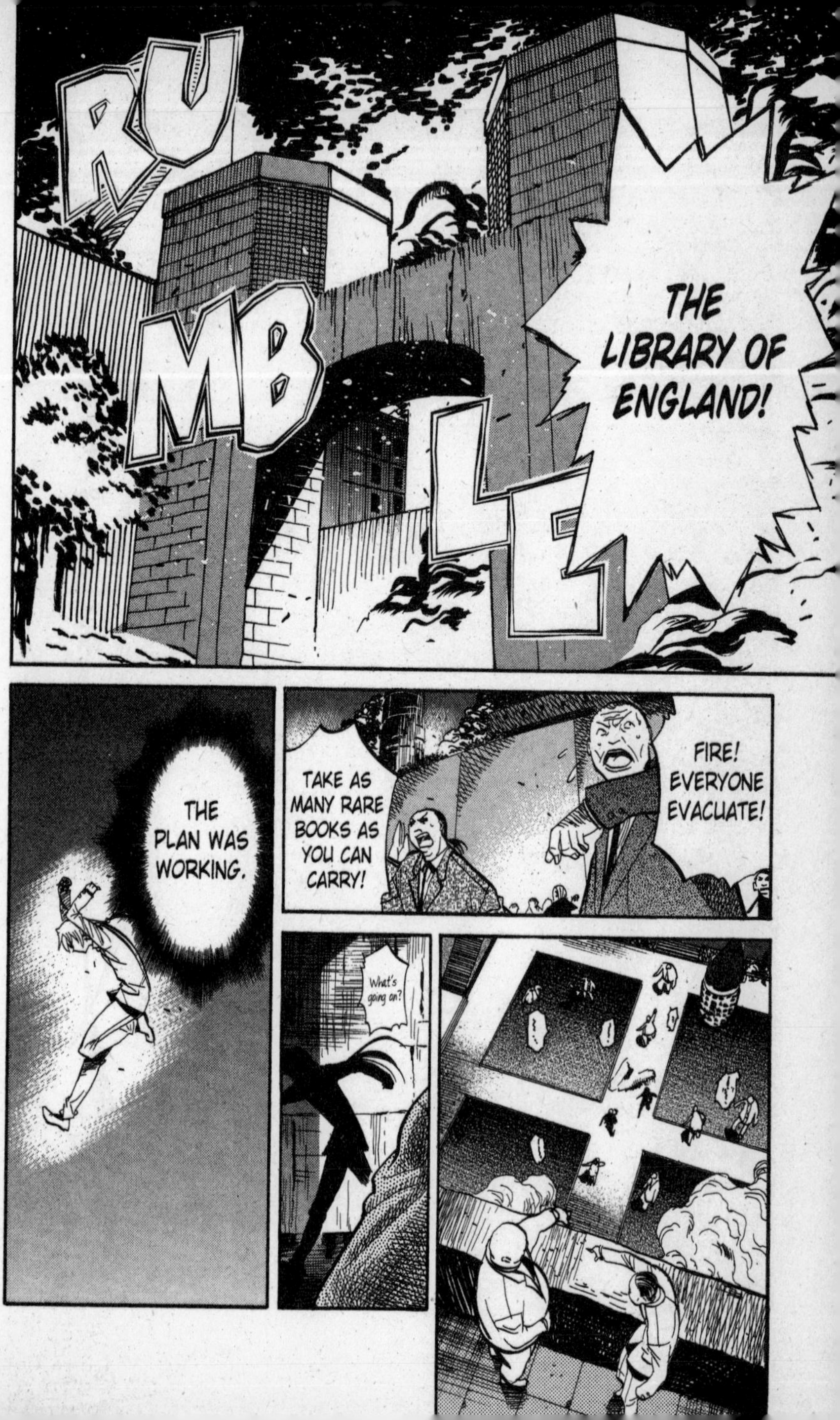
RUMBLE
THE LIBRARY OF ENGLAND!
FIRE! EVERYONE EVACUATE!
TAKE AS MANY RARE BOOKS AS YOU CAN CARRY!
What's going on?
THE PLAN WAS WORKING.

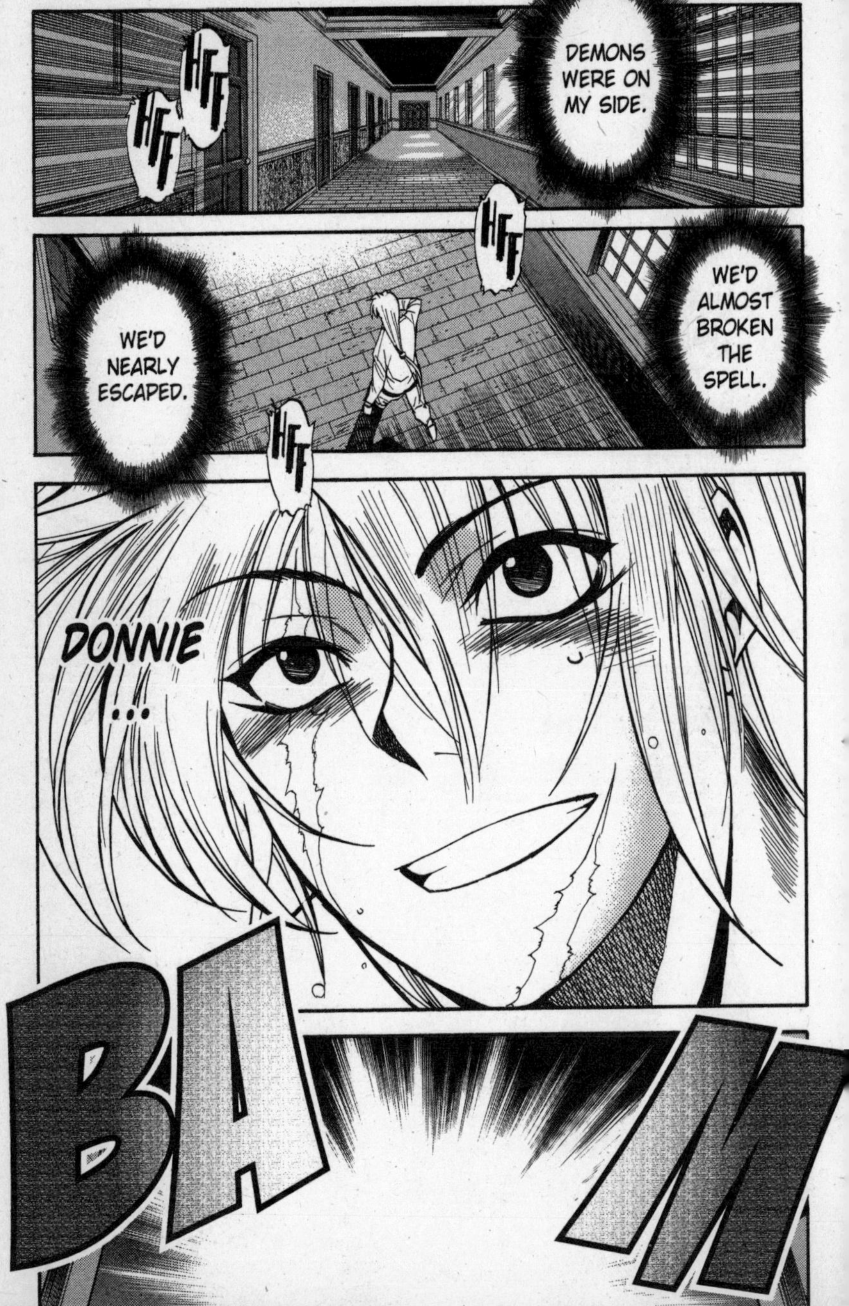
DEMONS WERE ON MY SIDE.
HFF
HFF
WE'D ALMOST BROKEN THE SPELL.
HFF
WE'D NEARLY ESCAPED.
HFF
DONNIE
!...
BAM

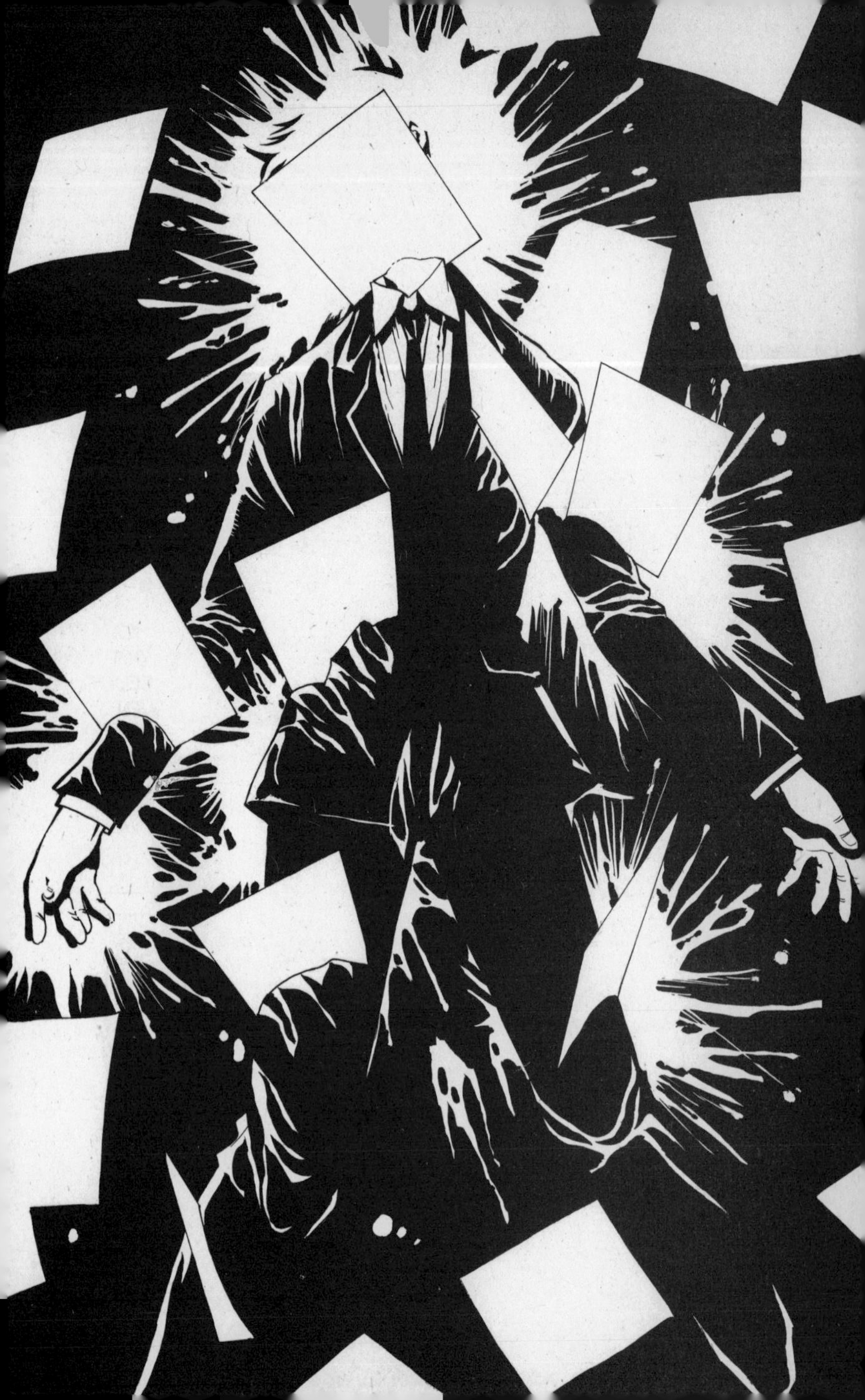

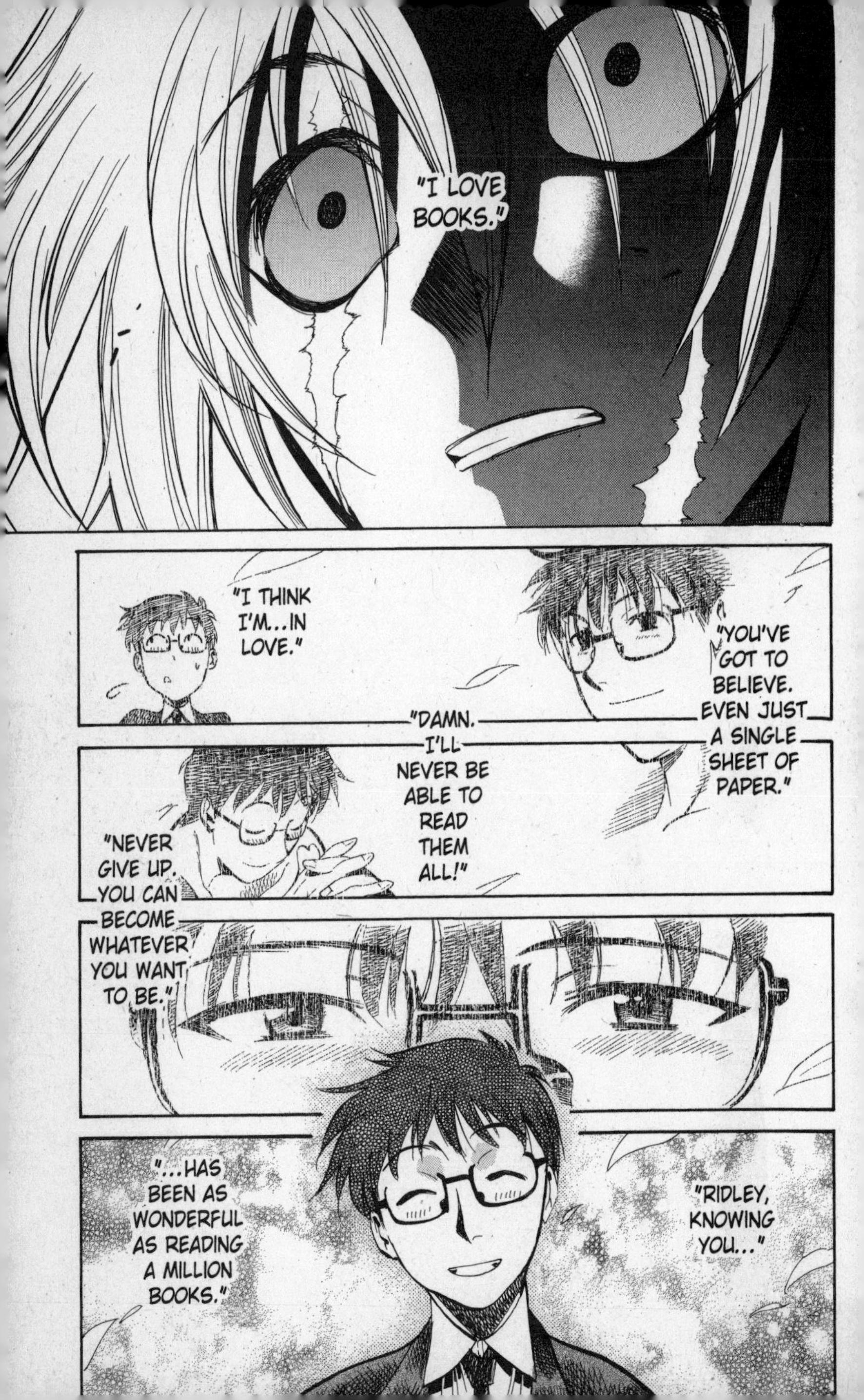
"I LOVE BOOKS."
"YOU'VE GOT TO BELIEVE. EVEN JUST A SINGLE SHEET OF PAPER."
"I THINK I'M...IN LOVE."
"DAMN. I'LL NEVER BE ABLE TO READ THEM ALL!"
"NEVER GIVE UP. YOU CAN BECOME WHATEVER YOU WANT TO BE."
"RIDLEY, KNOWING YOU..."
"...HAS BEEN AS WONDERFUL AS READING A MILLION BOOKS."

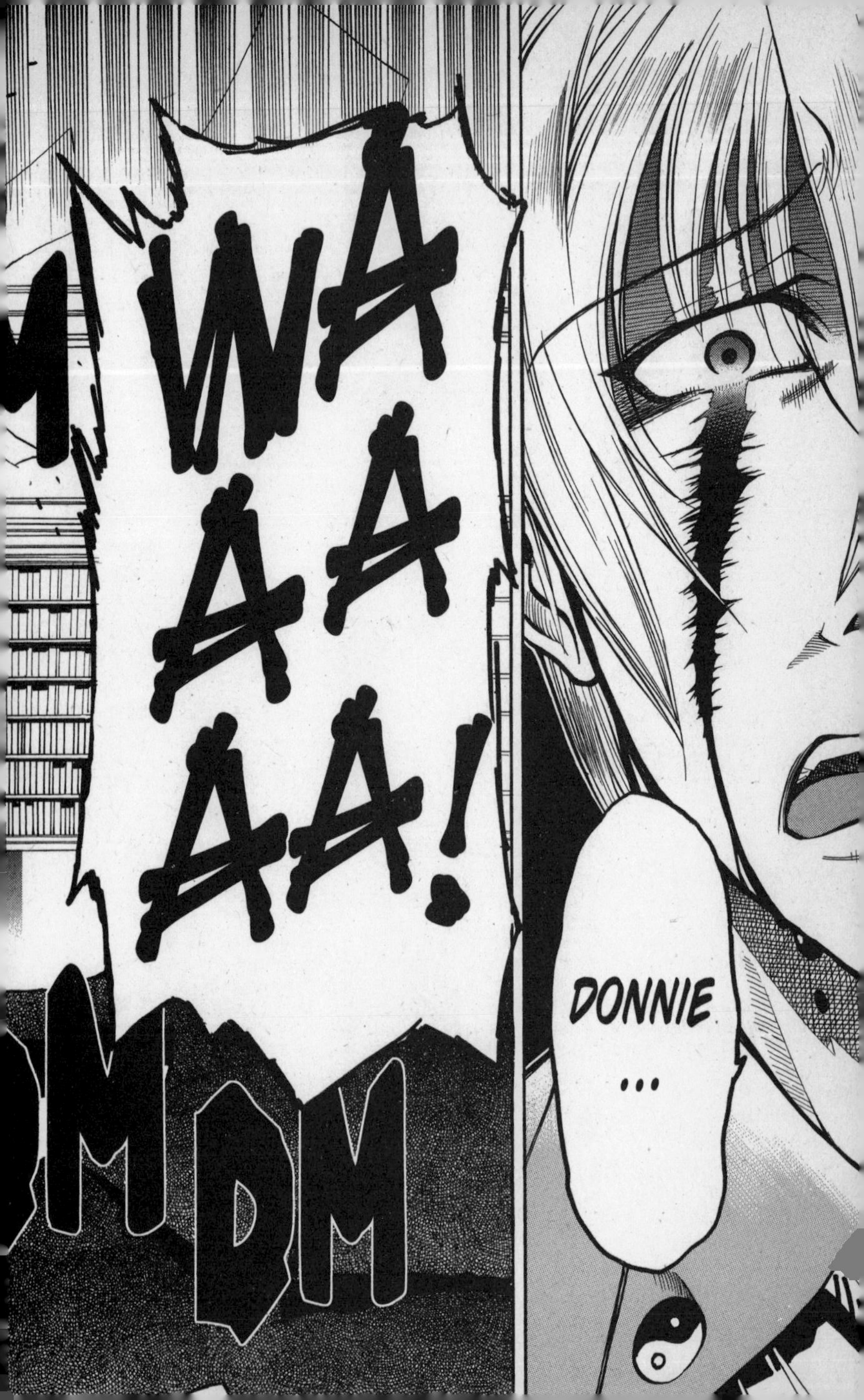
DONNIE ...
WAAAAAA!
DMDM

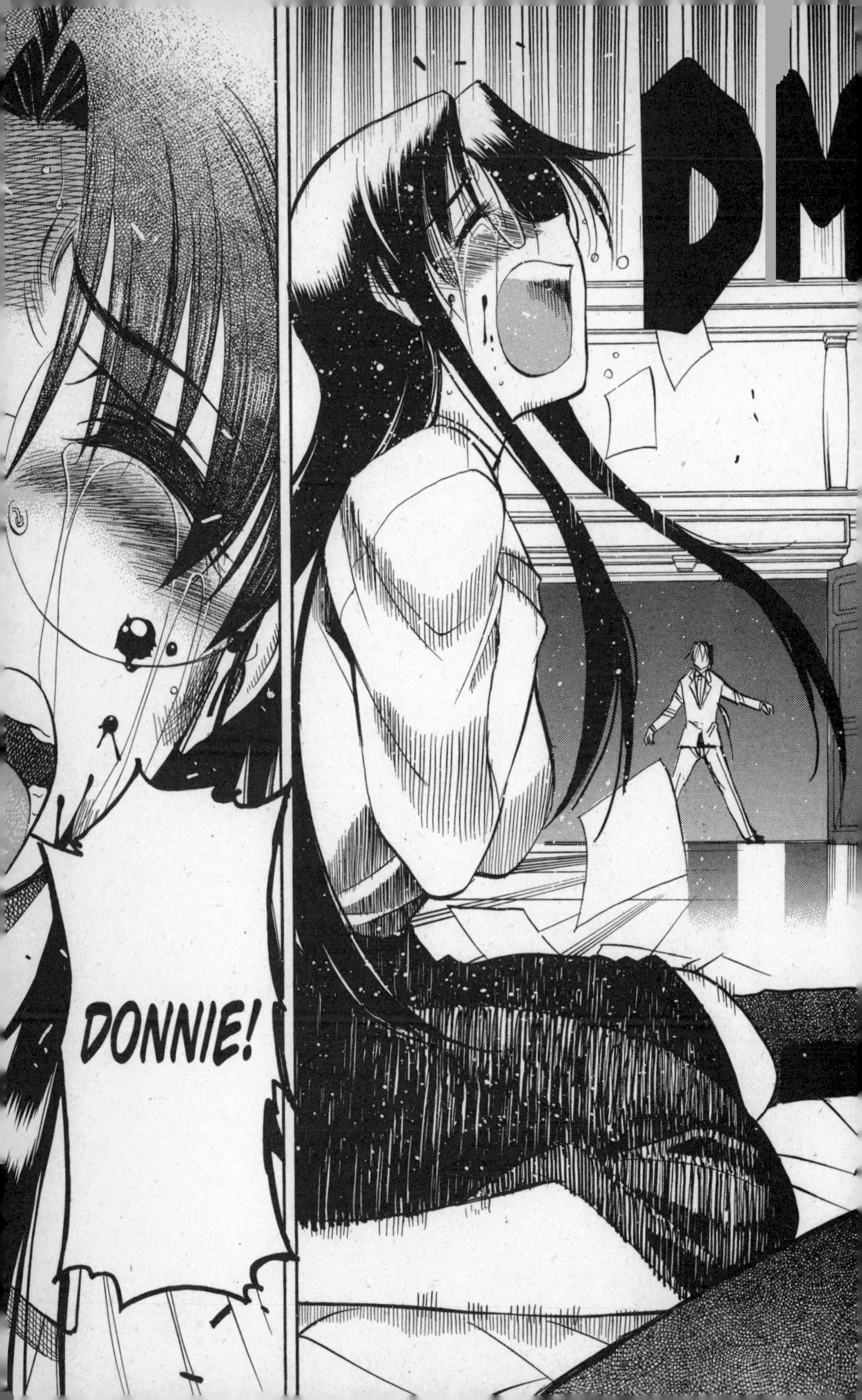
DM
DONNIE!

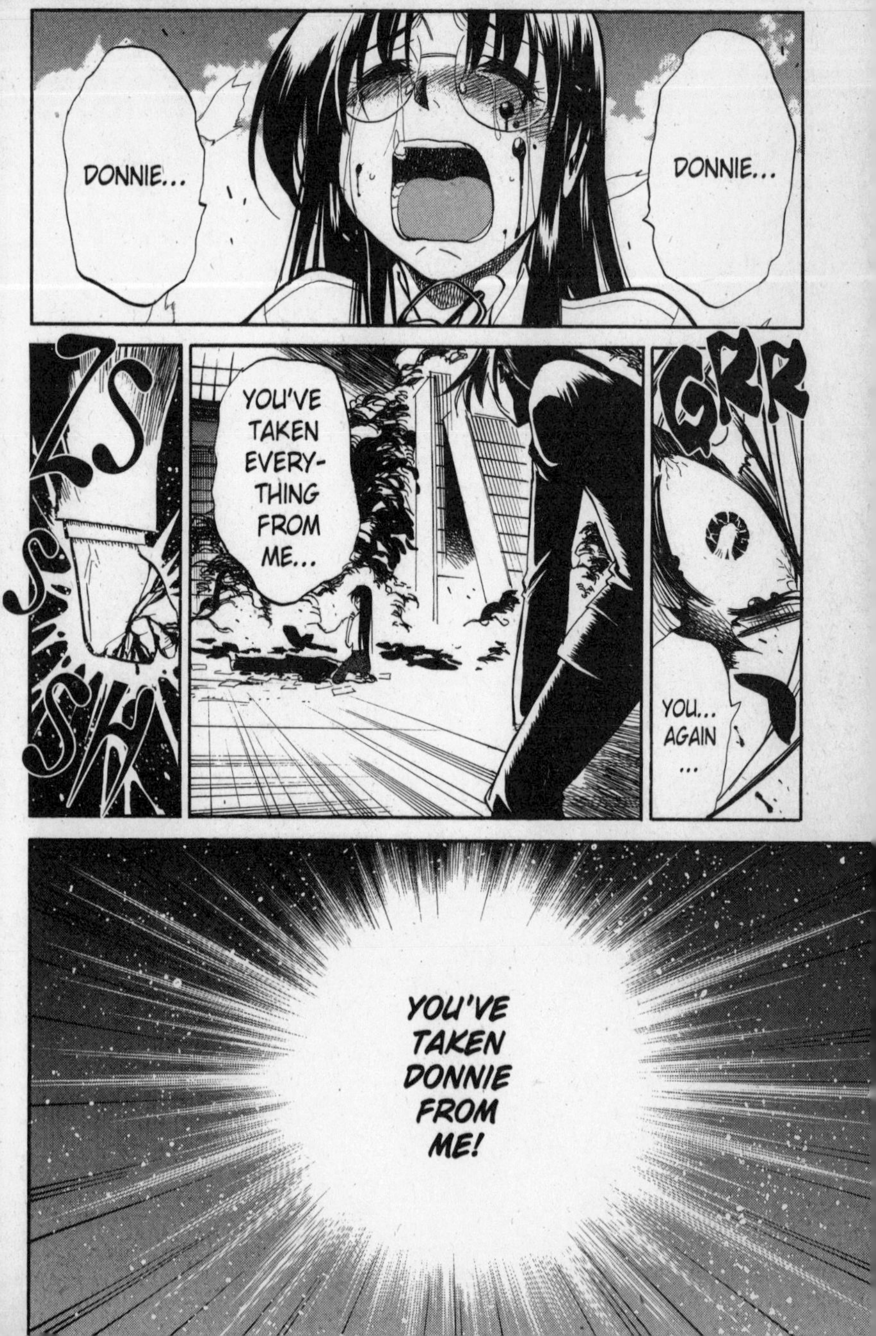
DONNIE...
DONNIE...
GRR
YOU... AGAIN ...
YOU'VE TAKEN EVERY-THING FROM ME...
YOU'VE TAKEN DONNIE FROM ME!

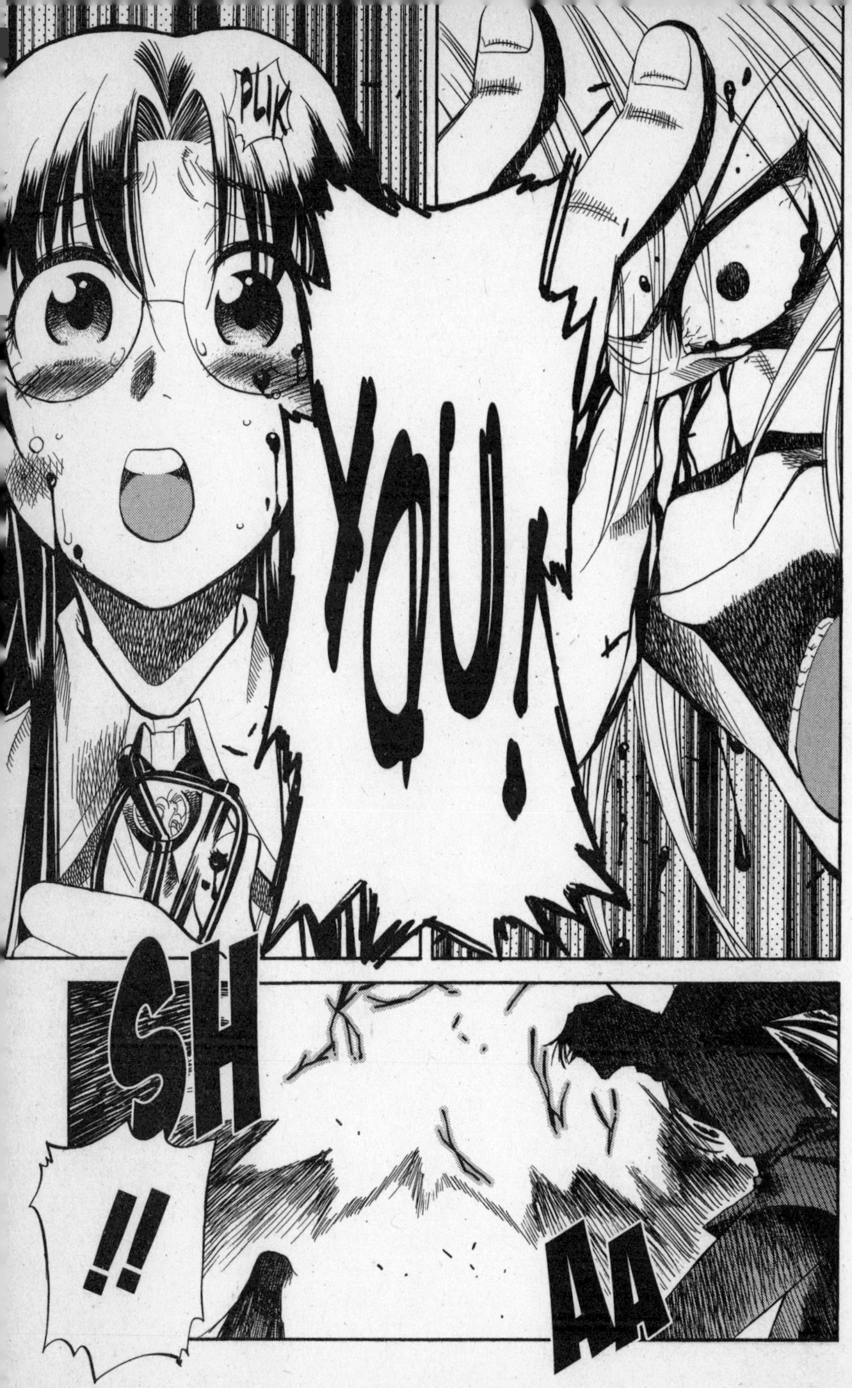
PLIK
YOU!
SH
AA
!!

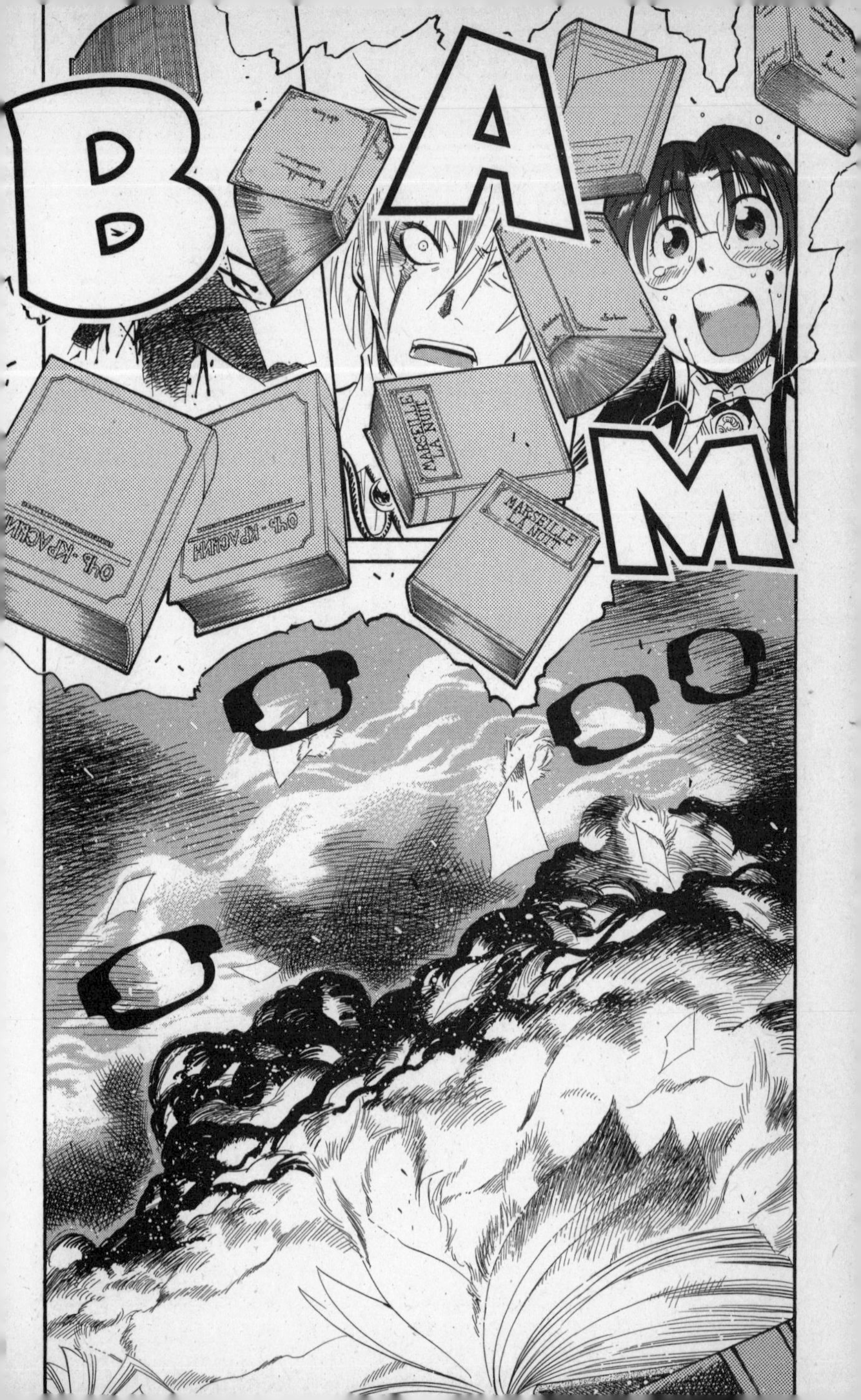
BAM
MARSEILLE LA NUIT
MARSEILLE LA NUIT

EPISODE FIVE

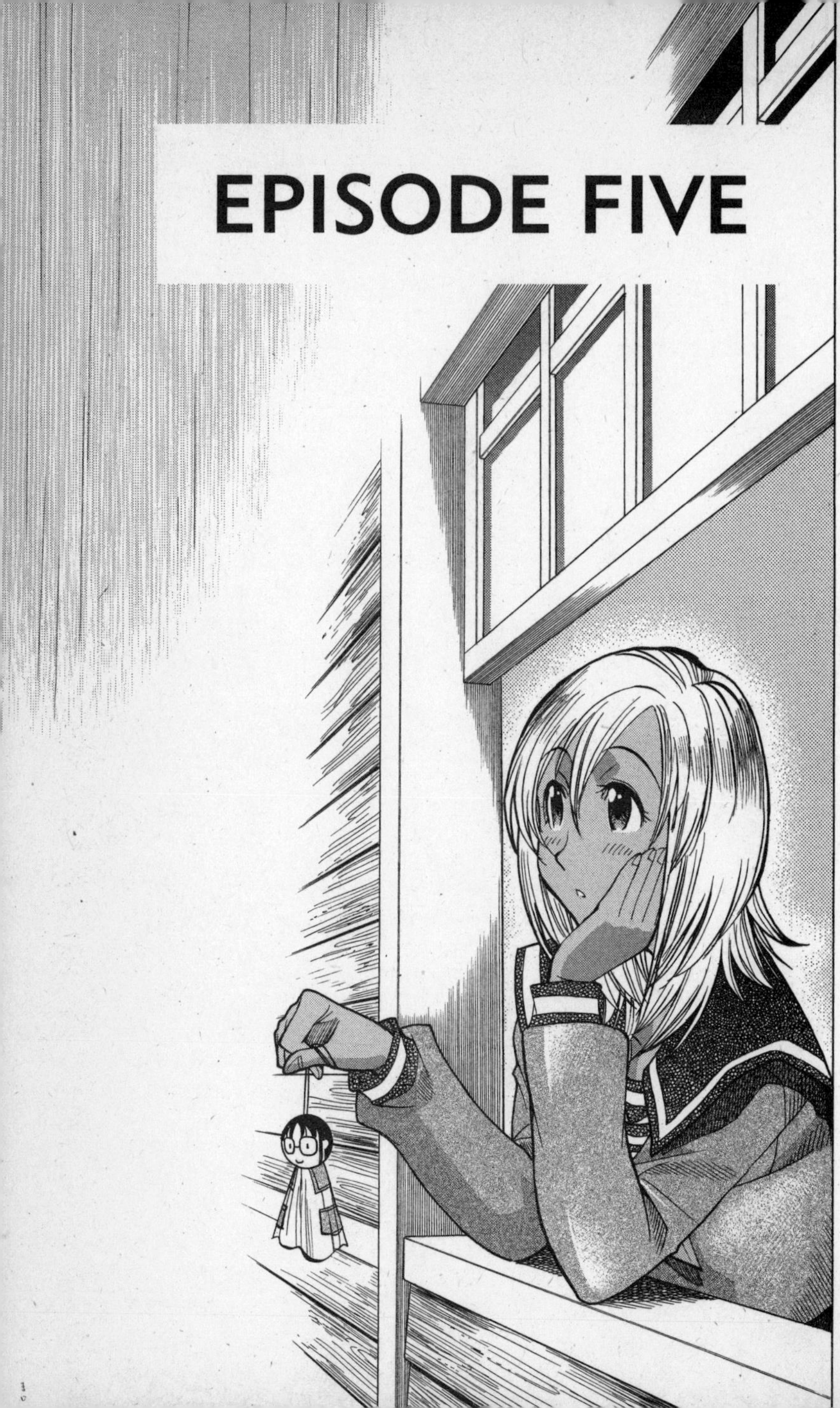

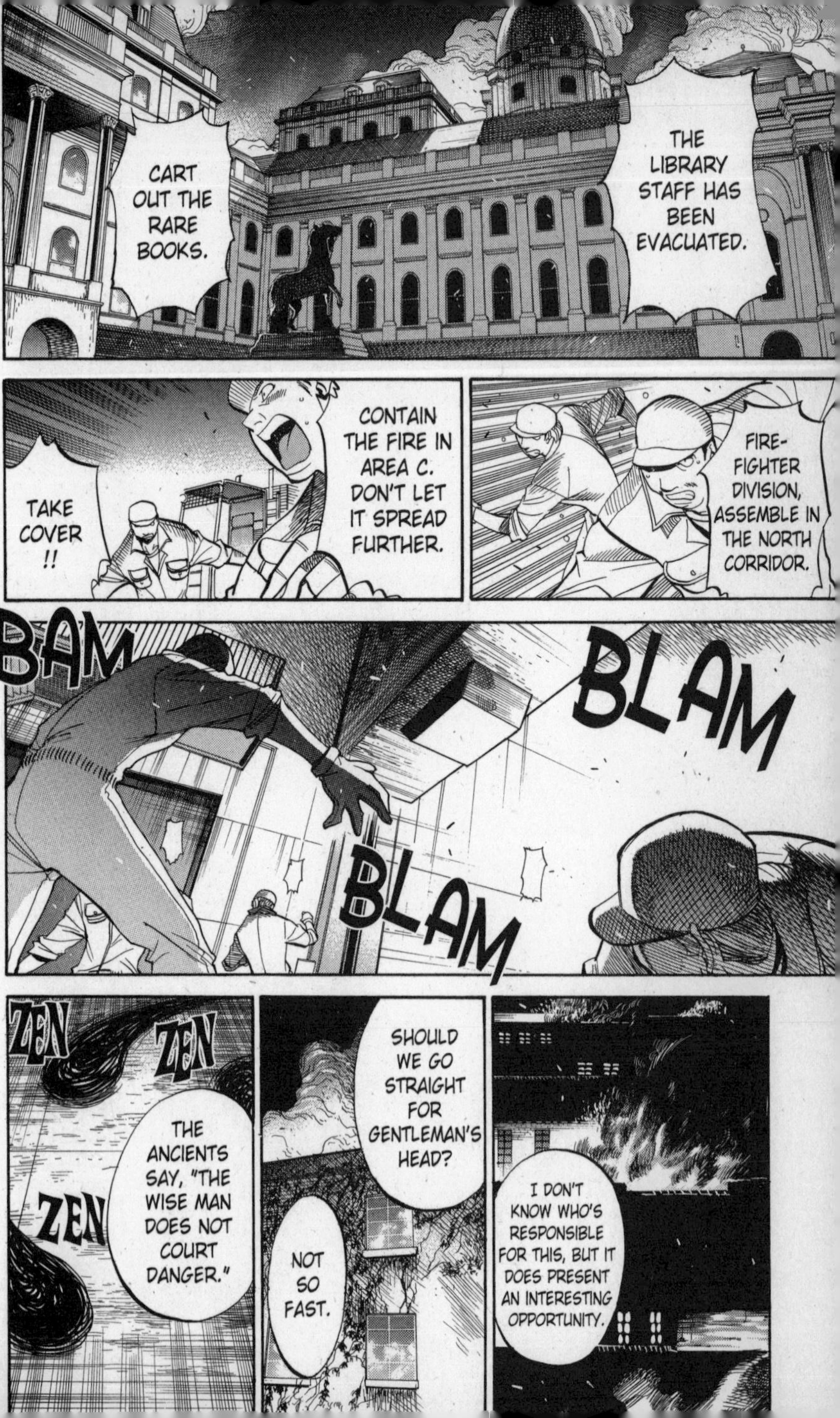
THE LIBRARY STAFF HAS BEEN EVACUATED.
CART OUT THE RARE BOOKS.
FIRE-FIGHTER DIVISION, ASSEMBLE IN THE NORTH CORRIDOR.
CONTAIN THE FIRE IN AREA C. DON'T LET IT SPREAD FURTHER.
TAKE COVER !!
BLAM
BAM
BLAM
I DON'T KNOW WHO'S RESPONSIBLE FOR THIS, BUT IT DOES PRESENT AN INTERESTING OPPORTUNITY.
SHOULD WE GO STRAIGHT FOR GENTLEMAN'S HEAD?
NOT SO FAST.
ZEN
ZEN
ZEN
THE ANCIENTS SAY, "THE WISE MAN DOES NOT COURT DANGER."

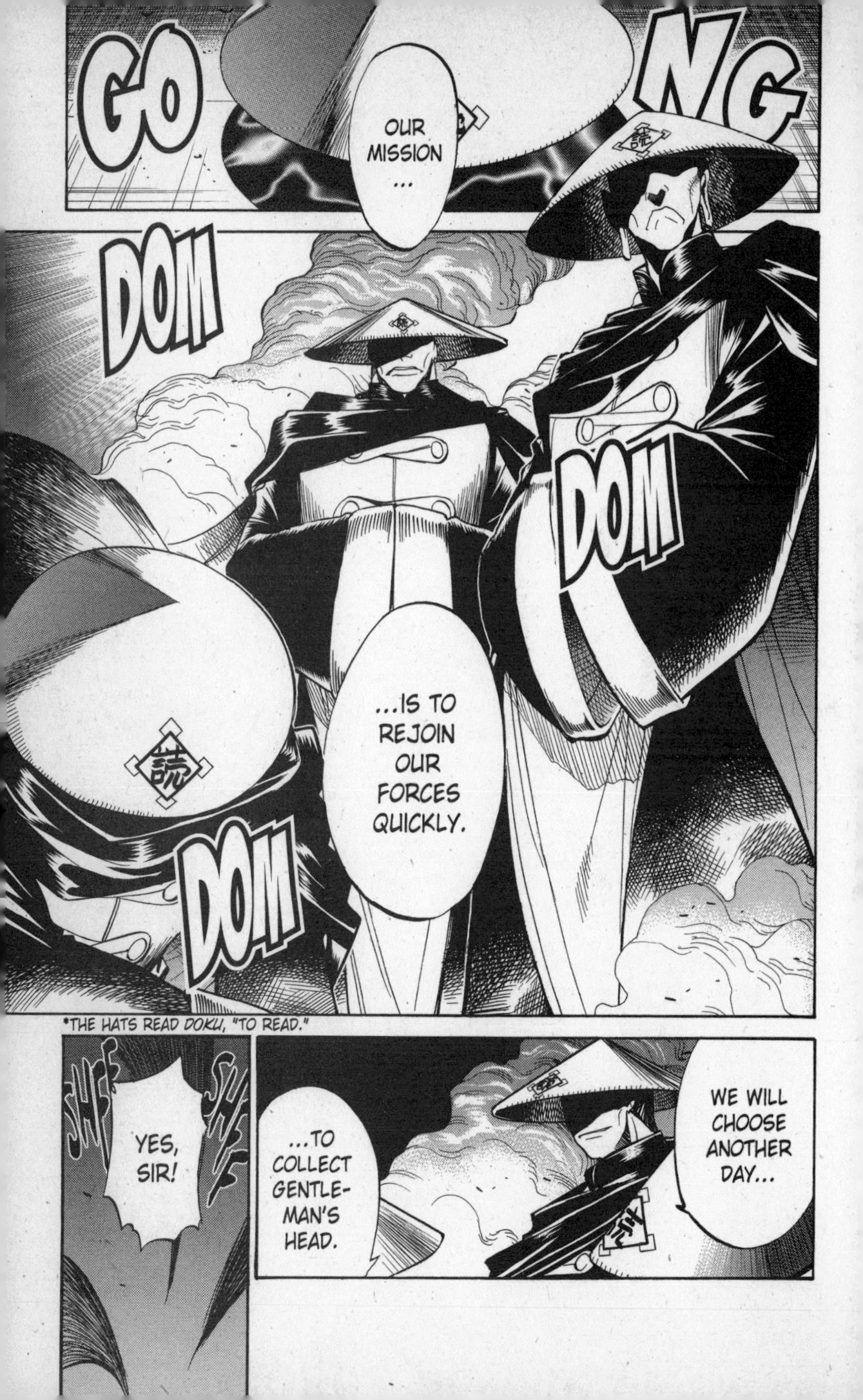
GO
NG
OUR MISSION ...
DOM
DOM
...IS TO REJOIN OUR FORCES QUICKLY.
DOM
WE WILL CHOOSE ANOTHER DAY...
...TO COLLECT GENTLE-MAN'S HEAD.
YES, SIR!

*THE HATS READ *DOKU*, "TO READ."

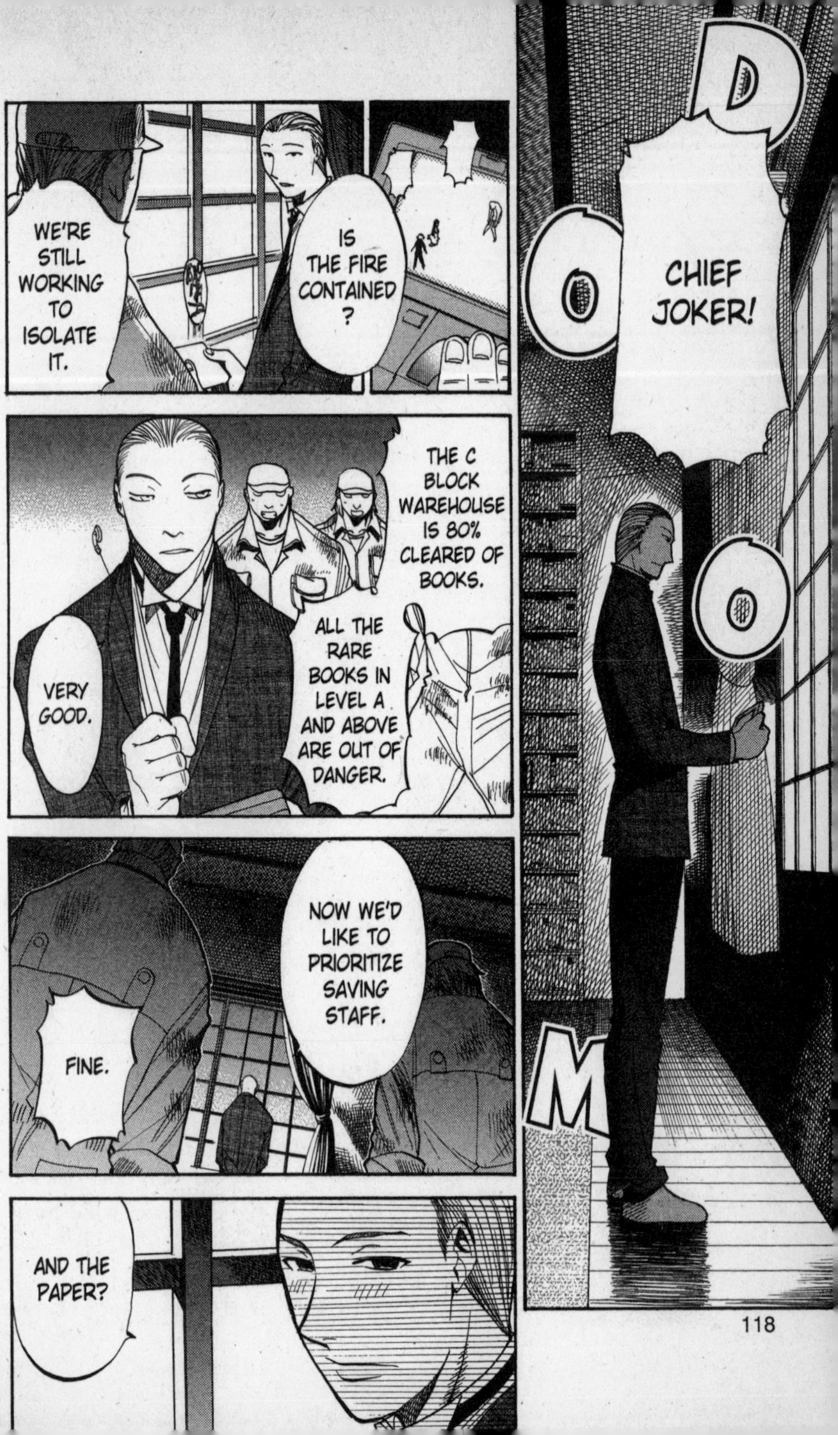
DOOM
CHIEF JOKER!
IS THE FIRE CONTAINED?
WE'RE STILL WORKING TO ISOLATE IT.
THE C BLOCK WAREHOUSE IS 80% CLEARED OF BOOKS.
ALL THE RARE BOOKS IN LEVEL A AND ABOVE ARE OUT OF DANGER.
VERY GOOD.
NOW WE'D LIKE TO PRIORITIZE SAVING STAFF.
FINE.
AND THE PAPER?

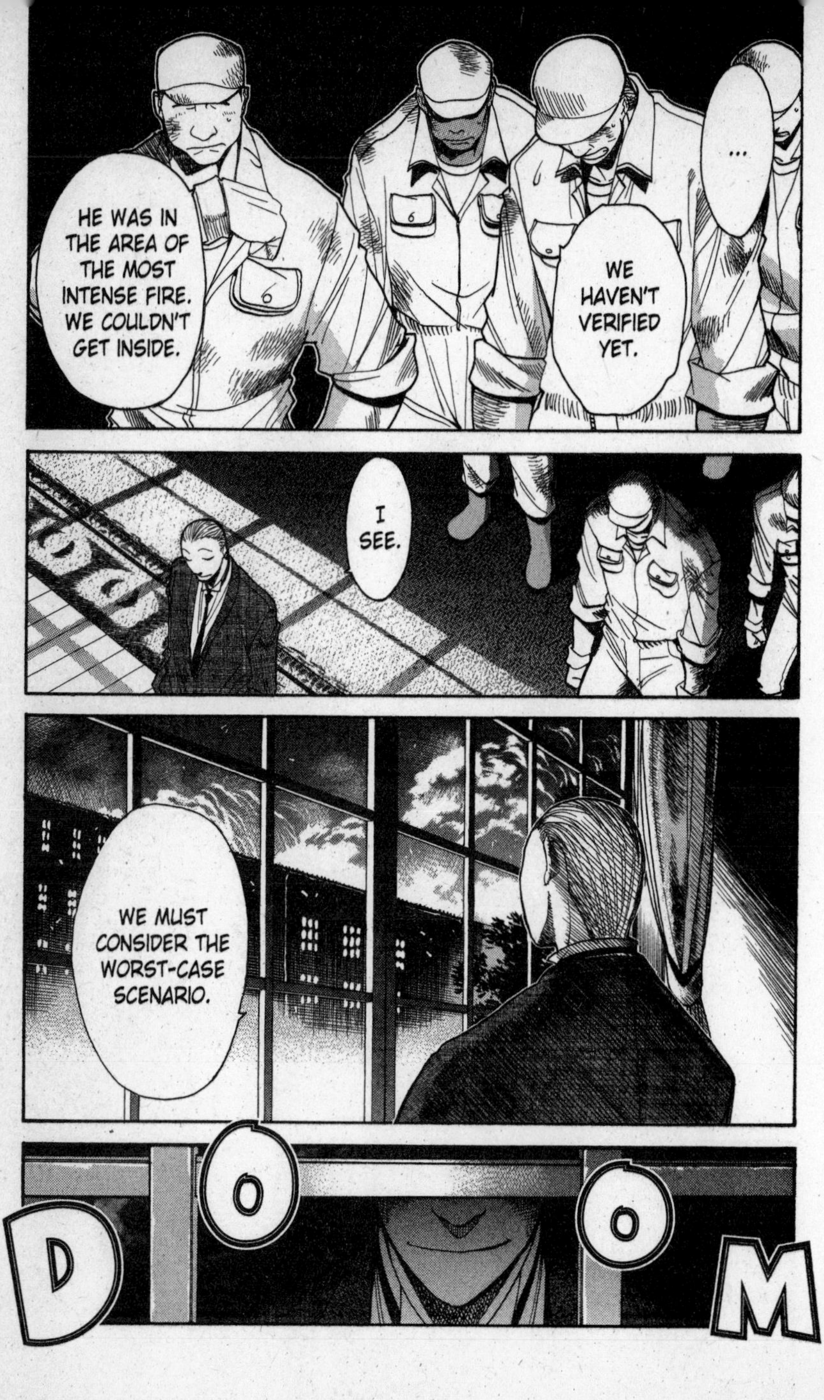
...
WE HAVEN'T VERIFIED YET.
HE WAS IN THE AREA OF THE MOST INTENSE FIRE. WE COULDN'T GET INSIDE.
I SEE.
WE MUST CONSIDER THE WORST-CASE SCENARIO.
DOOM

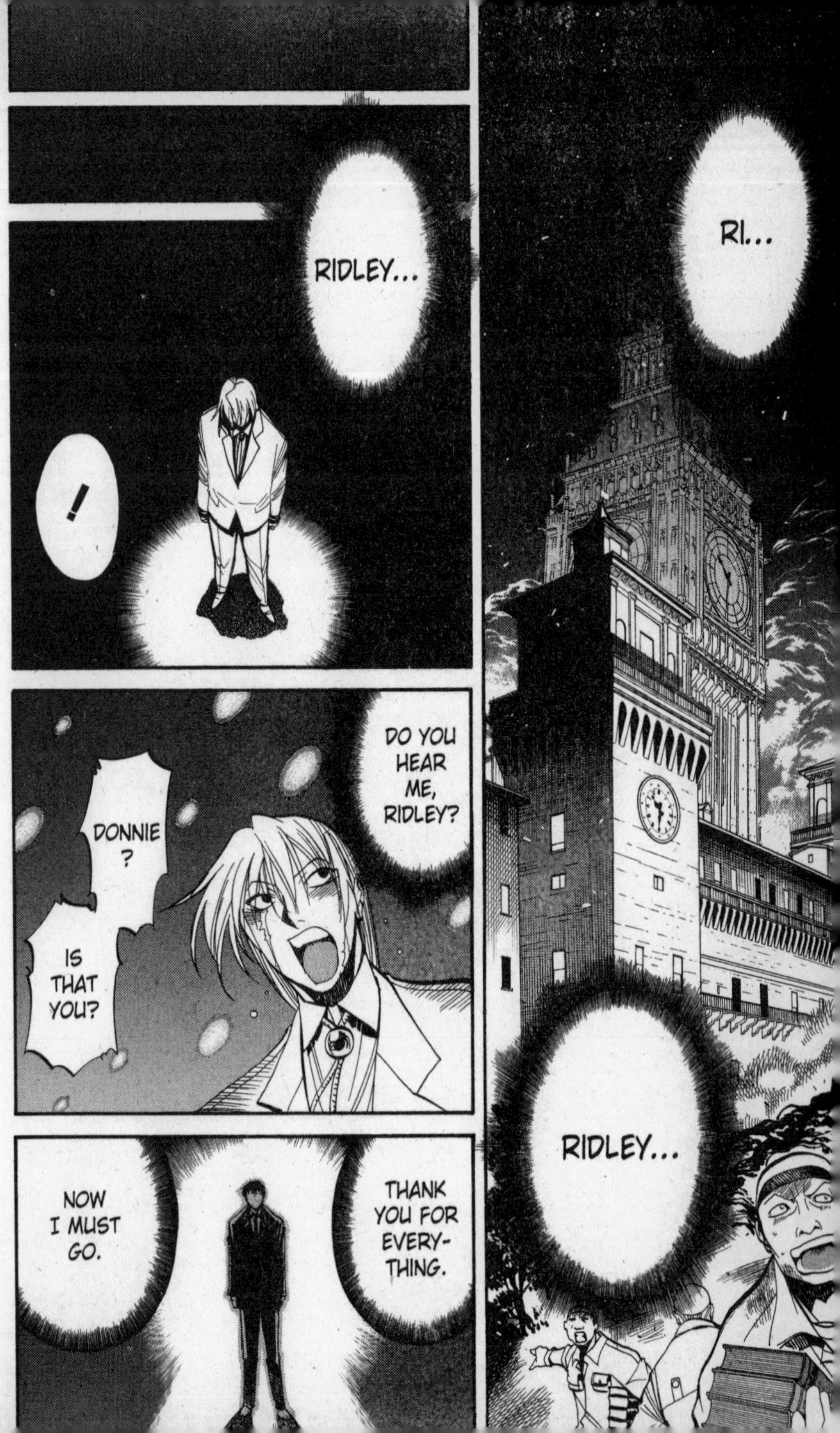
RI...
RIDLEY...
RIDLEY...
!
DO YOU HEAR ME, RIDLEY?
DONNIE?
IS THAT YOU?
THANK YOU FOR EVERYTHING.
NOW I MUST GO.

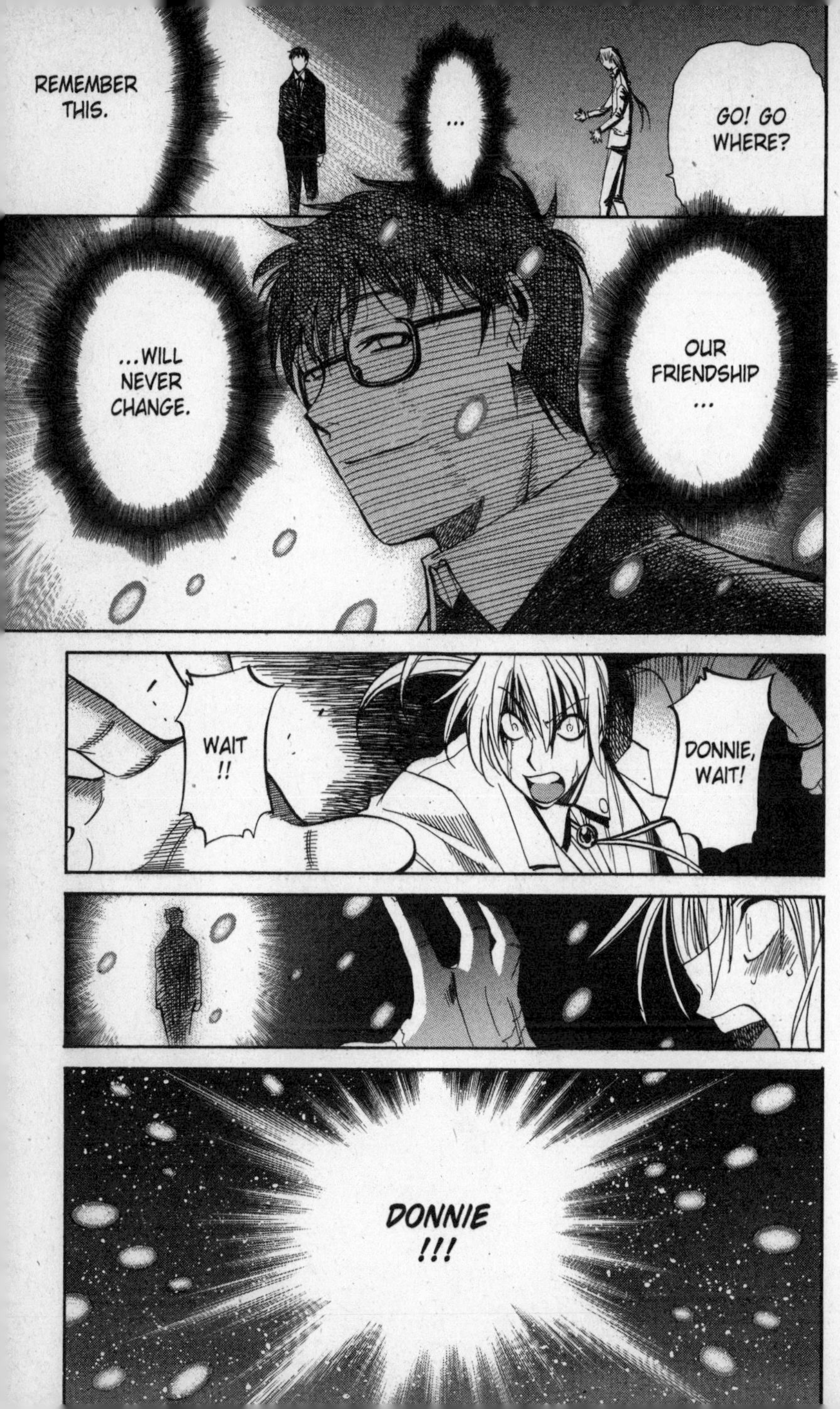
GO! GO WHERE?
...
REMEMBER THIS.
OUR FRIENDSHIP ...
...WILL NEVER CHANGE.
DONNIE, WAIT!
WAIT !!
DONNIE !!!

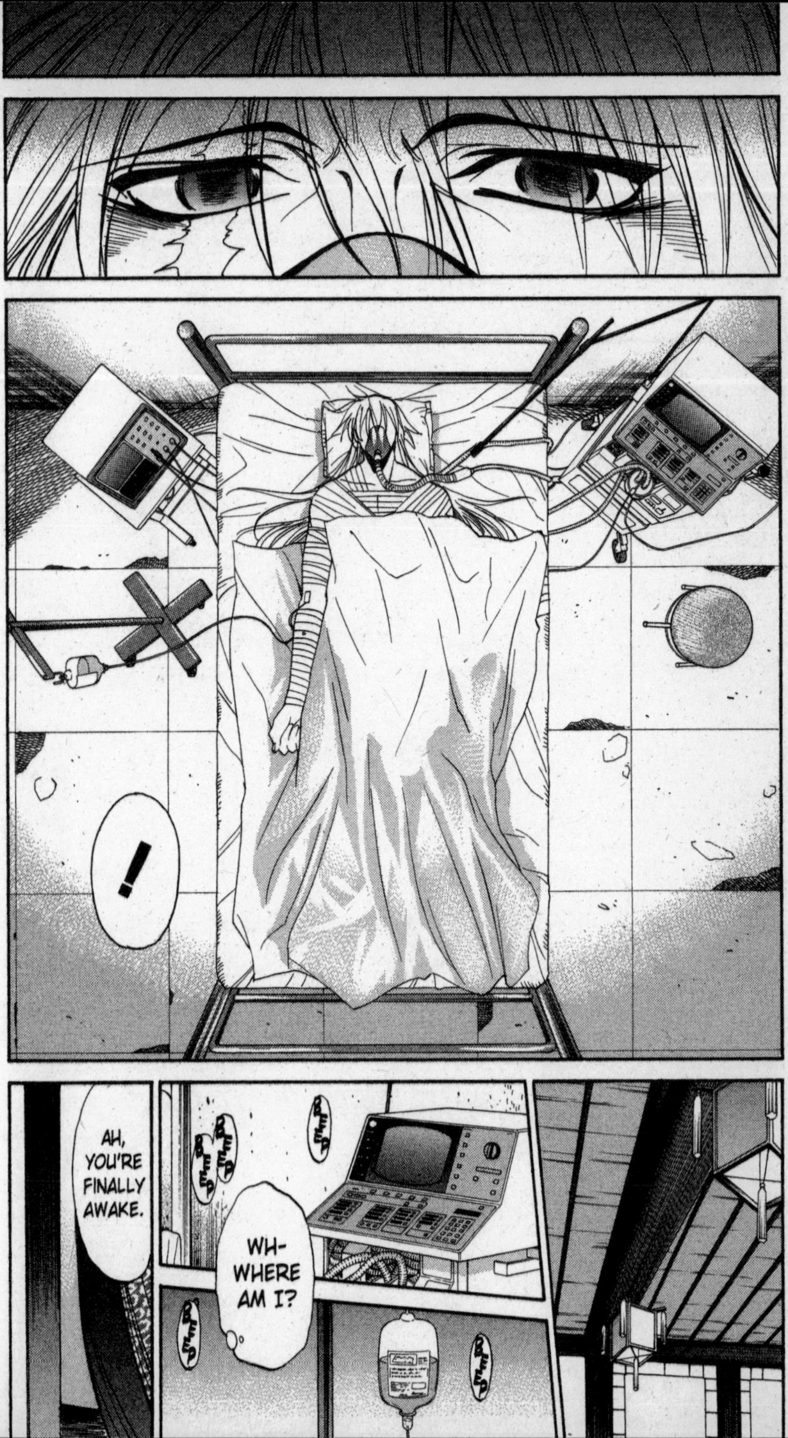
!
WH- WHERE AM I?
AH, YOU'RE FINALLY AWAKE.

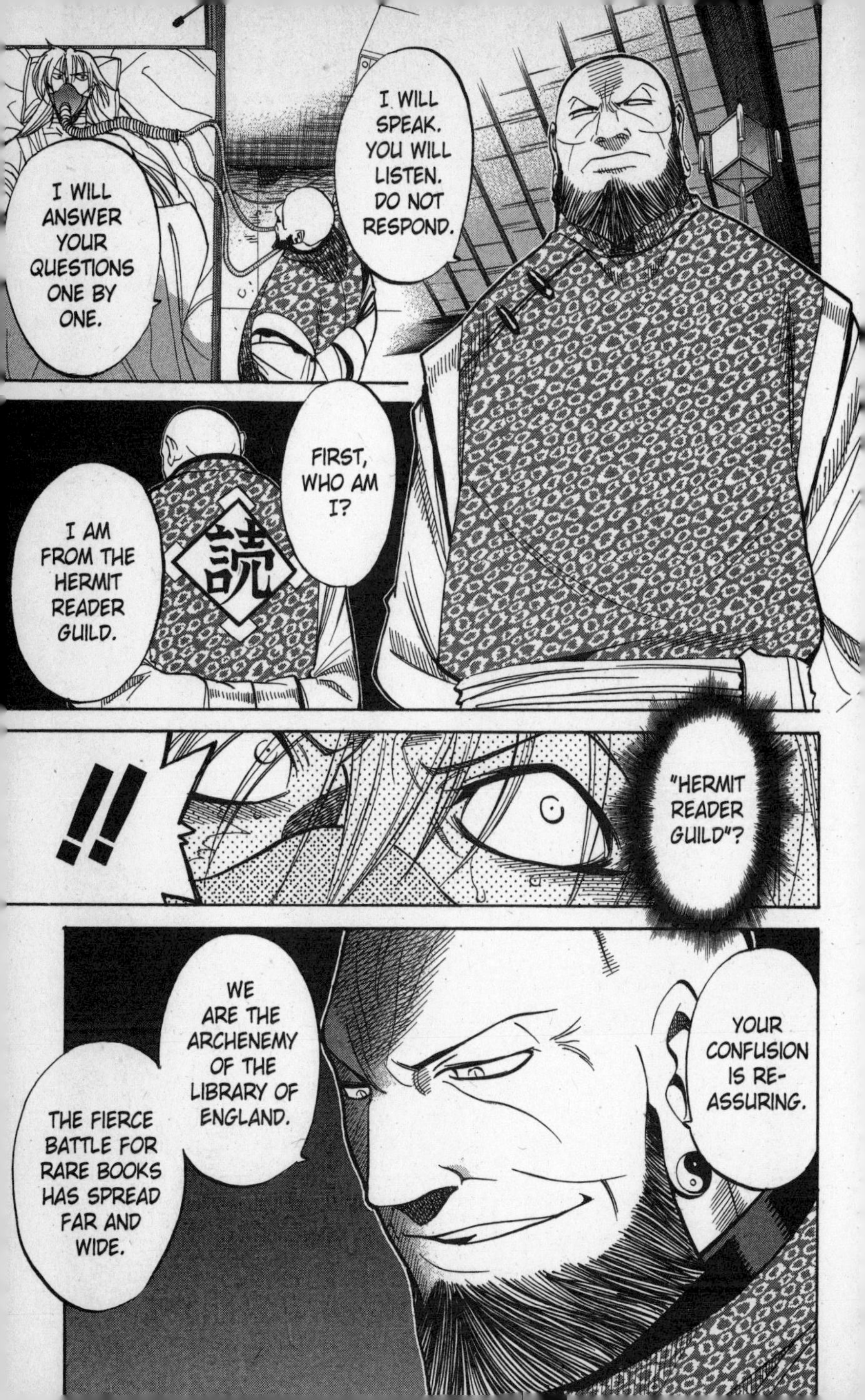
I WILL SPEAK. YOU WILL LISTEN. DO NOT RESPOND.
I WILL ANSWER YOUR QUESTIONS ONE BY ONE.
FIRST, WHO AM I?
I AM FROM THE HERMIT READER GUILD.
読
"HERMIT READER GUILD"?
!!
YOUR CONFUSION IS RE-ASSURING.
WE ARE THE ARCHENEMY OF THE LIBRARY OF ENGLAND.
THE FIERCE BATTLE FOR RARE BOOKS HAS SPREAD FAR AND WIDE.

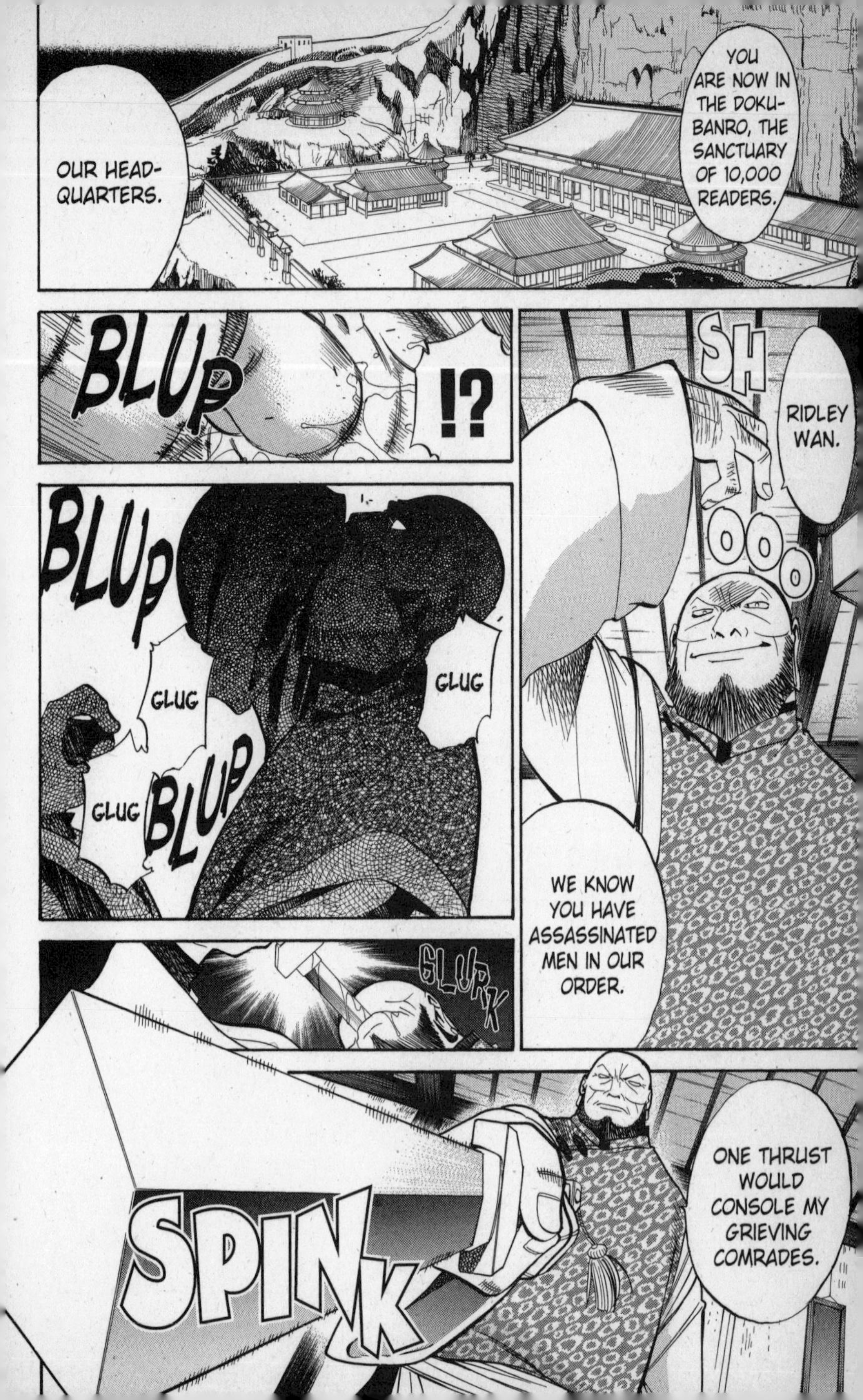
YOU ARE NOW IN THE DOKU-BANRO, THE SANCTUARY OF 10,000 READERS.
OUR HEAD-QUARTERS.
SHOOO
RIDLEY WAN.
WE KNOW YOU HAVE ASSASSINATED MEN IN OUR ORDER.
!?
BLUP
GLUG
BLUP
GLUG
BLUP
GLUG
GLURK
ONE THRUST WOULD CONSOLE MY GRIEVING COMRADES.
SPINK

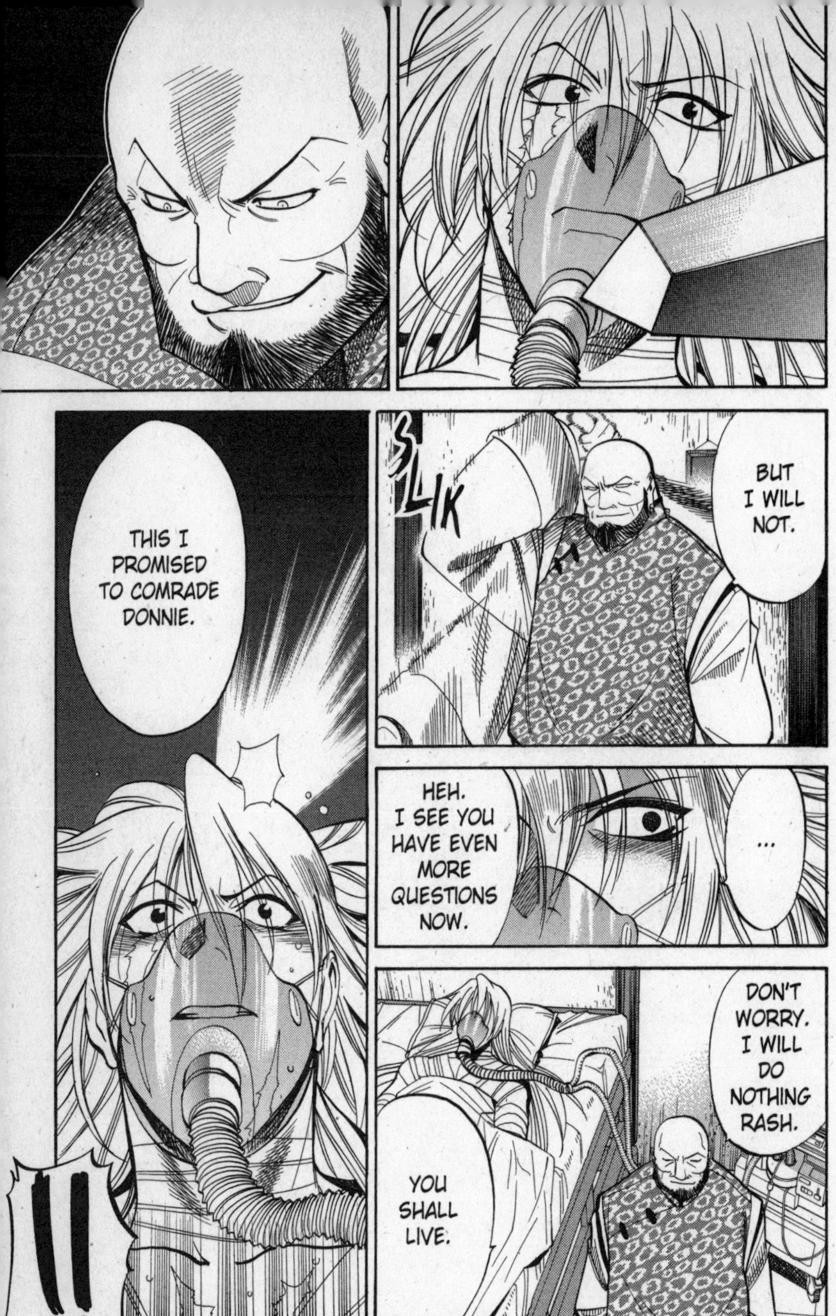
BUT I WILL NOT.
SLIK
...
HEH. I SEE YOU HAVE EVEN MORE QUESTIONS NOW.
DON'T WORRY. I WILL DO NOTHING RASH.
YOU SHALL LIVE.
THIS I PROMISED TO COMRADE DONNIE.
!!

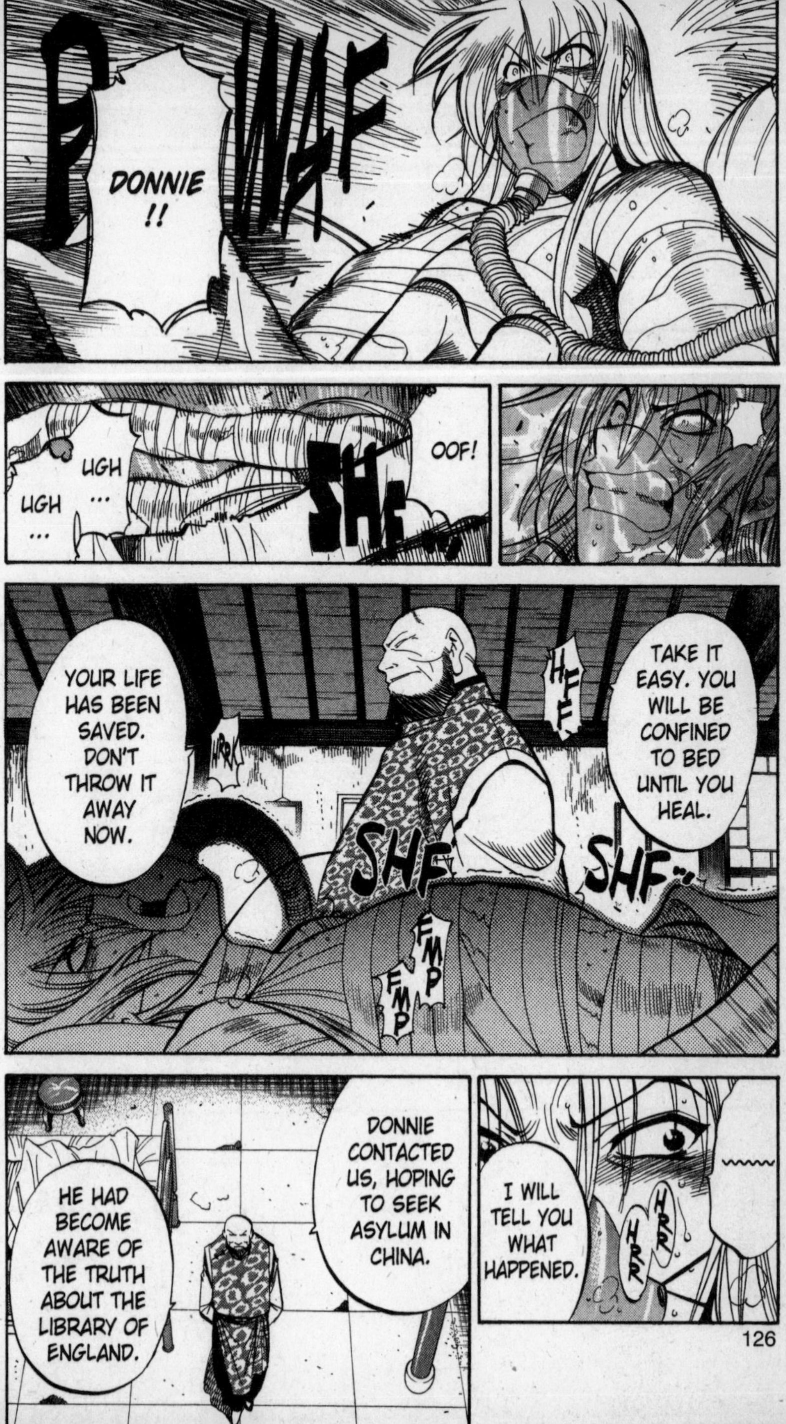
PWAF
DONNIE !!
OOF!
SHF
UGH ...
UGH ...
TAKE IT EASY. YOU WILL BE CONFINED TO BED UNTIL YOU HEAL.
HFF
YOUR LIFE HAS BEEN SAVED. DON'T THROW IT AWAY NOW.
HRRK
SHF
SHF...
FMP
FMP
HRR
HRR
I WILL TELL YOU WHAT HAPPENED.
DONNIE CONTACTED US, HOPING TO SEEK ASYLUM IN CHINA.
HE HAD BECOME AWARE OF THE TRUTH ABOUT THE LIBRARY OF ENGLAND.

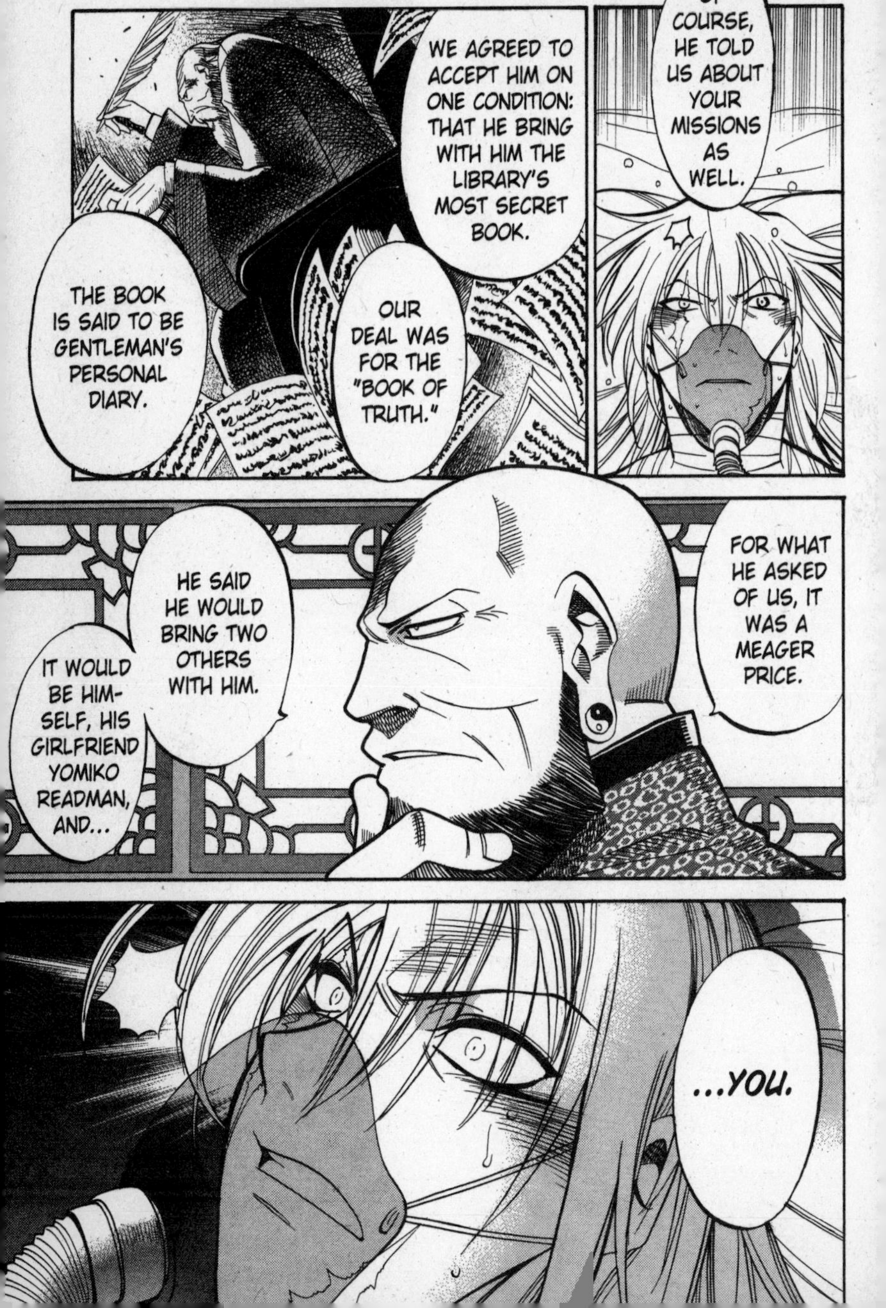
OF COURSE, HE TOLD US ABOUT YOUR MISSIONS AS WELL.
WE AGREED TO ACCEPT HIM ON ONE CONDITION: THAT HE BRING WITH HIM THE LIBRARY'S MOST SECRET BOOK.
OUR DEAL WAS FOR THE "BOOK OF TRUTH."
THE BOOK IS SAID TO BE GENTLEMAN'S PERSONAL DIARY.
FOR WHAT HE ASKED OF US, IT WAS A MEAGER PRICE.
HE SAID HE WOULD BRING TWO OTHERS WITH HIM.
IT WOULD BE HIM-SELF, HIS GIRLFRIEND YOMIKO READMAN, AND...
...YOU.

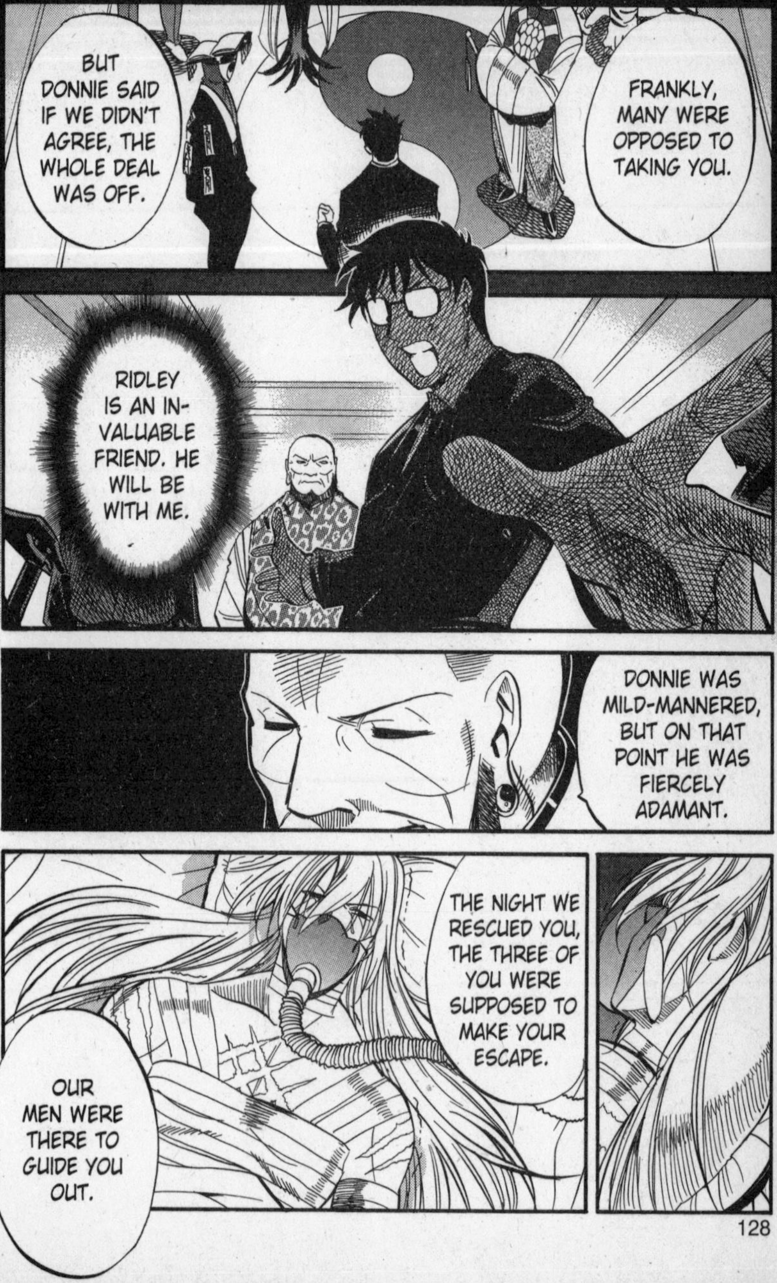
FRANKLY, MANY WERE OPPOSED TO TAKING YOU.
BUT DONNIE SAID IF WE DIDN'T AGREE, THE WHOLE DEAL WAS OFF.
RIDLEY IS AN IN-VALUABLE FRIEND. HE WILL BE WITH ME.
DONNIE WAS MILD-MANNERED, BUT ON THAT POINT HE WAS FIERCELY ADAMANT.
THE NIGHT WE RESCUED YOU, THE THREE OF YOU WERE SUPPOSED TO MAKE YOUR ESCAPE.
OUR MEN WERE THERE TO GUIDE YOU OUT.

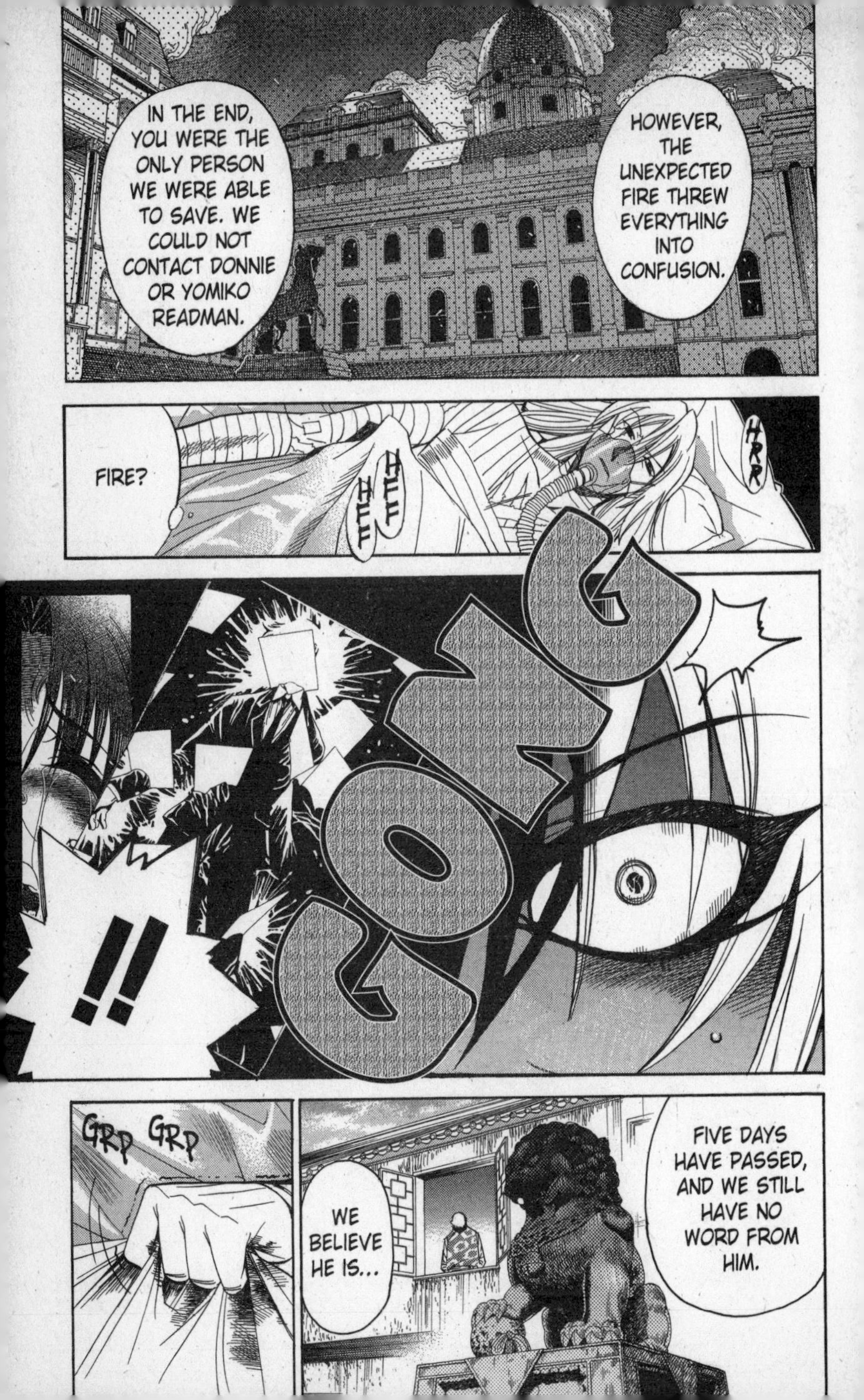
HOWEVER, THE UNEXPECTED FIRE THREW EVERYTHING INTO CONFUSION.
IN THE END, YOU WERE THE ONLY PERSON WE WERE ABLE TO SAVE. WE COULD NOT CONTACT DONNIE OR YOMIKO READMAN.
HRR
HEFF HEFF
HEFF
FIRE?
GONG
!!
FIVE DAYS HAVE PASSED, AND WE STILL HAVE NO WORD FROM HIM.
WE BELIEVE HE IS...
GRP GRP

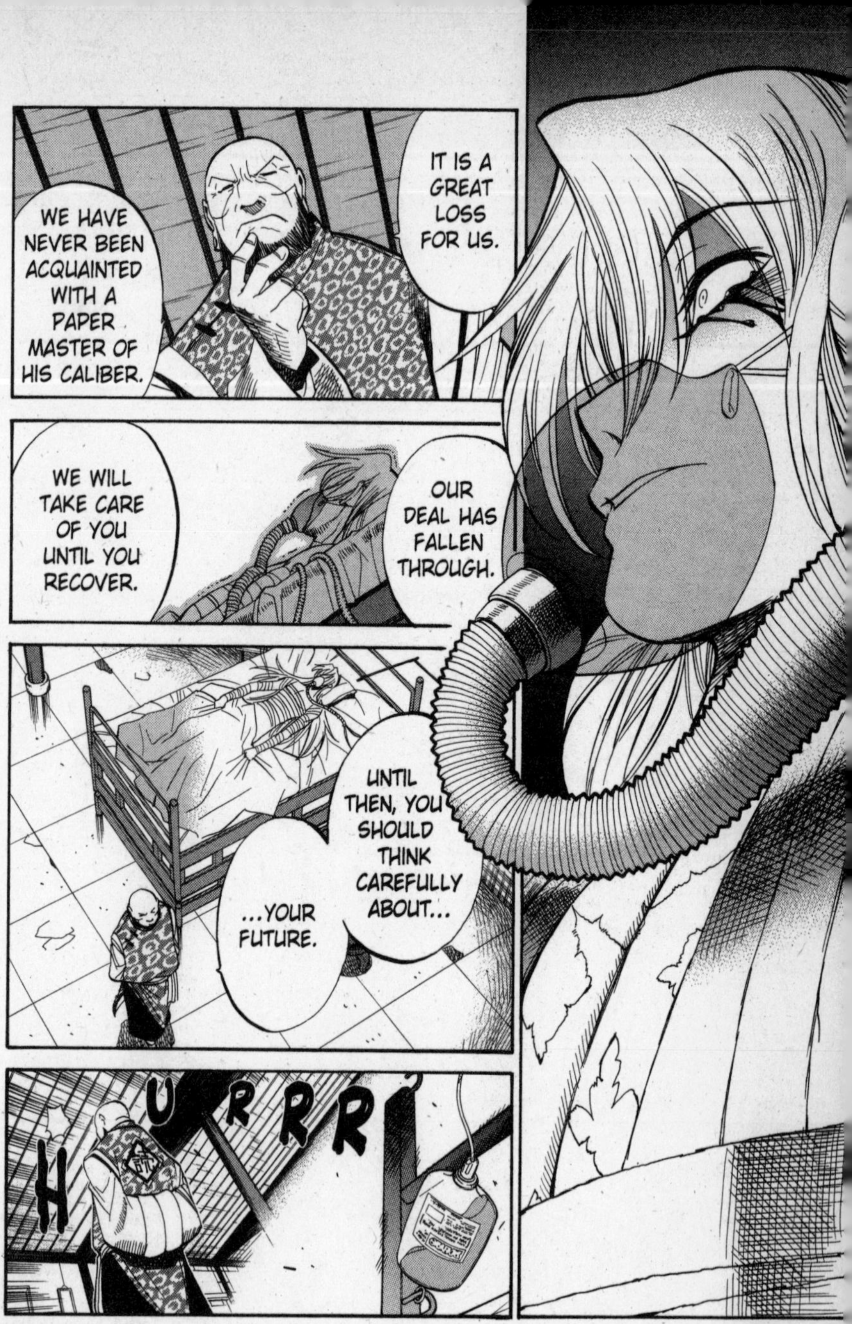
IT IS A GREAT LOSS FOR US.
WE HAVE NEVER BEEN ACQUAINTED WITH A PAPER MASTER OF HIS CALIBER.
OUR DEAL HAS FALLEN THROUGH.
WE WILL TAKE CARE OF YOU UNTIL YOU RECOVER.
UNTIL THEN, YOU SHOULD THINK CAREFULLY ABOUT...
...YOUR FUTURE.
HURRR

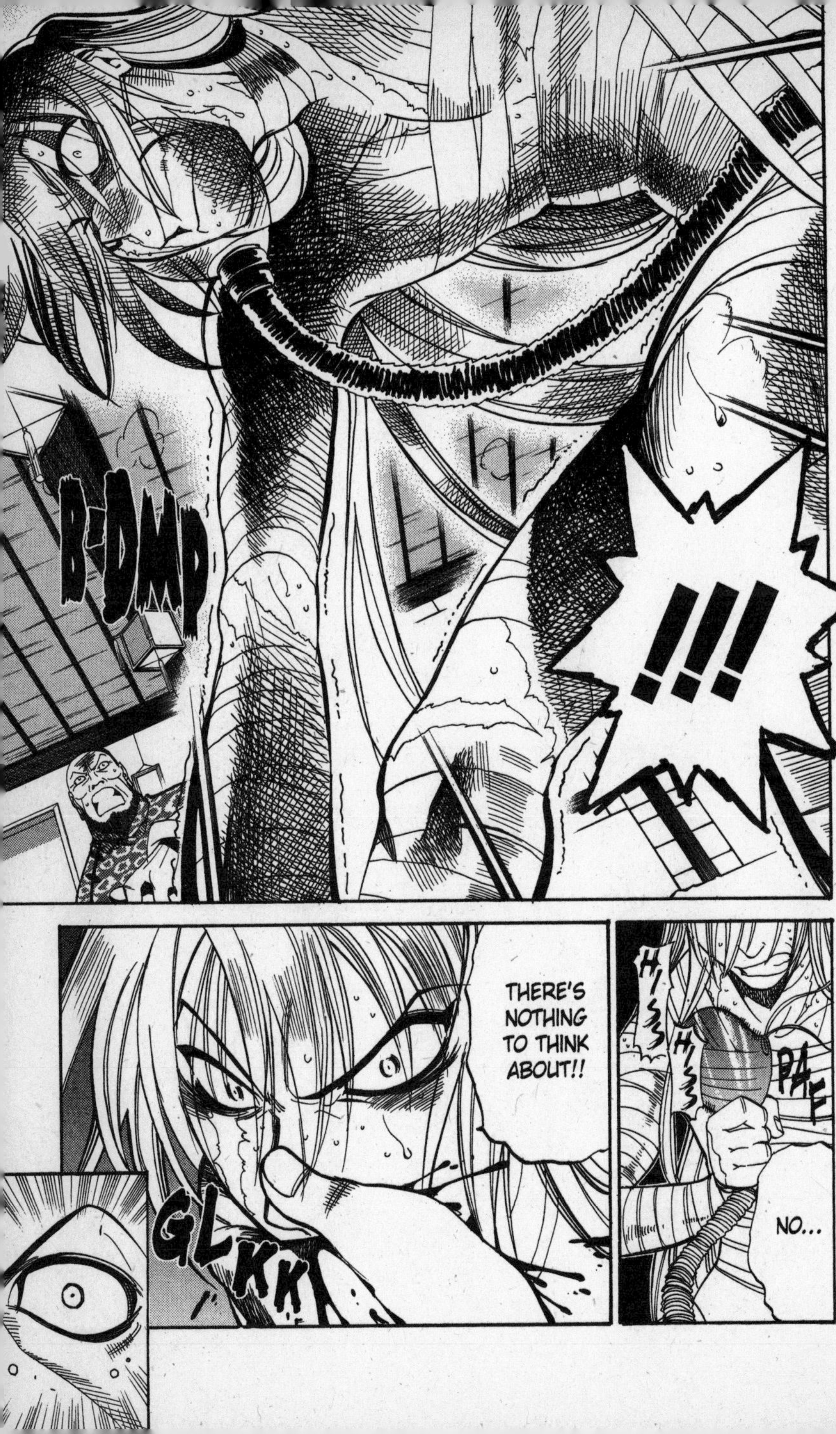
!!!
B-DMP
HISS
HISS
PAF
NO...
THERE'S NOTHING TO THINK ABOUT!!
GLKK

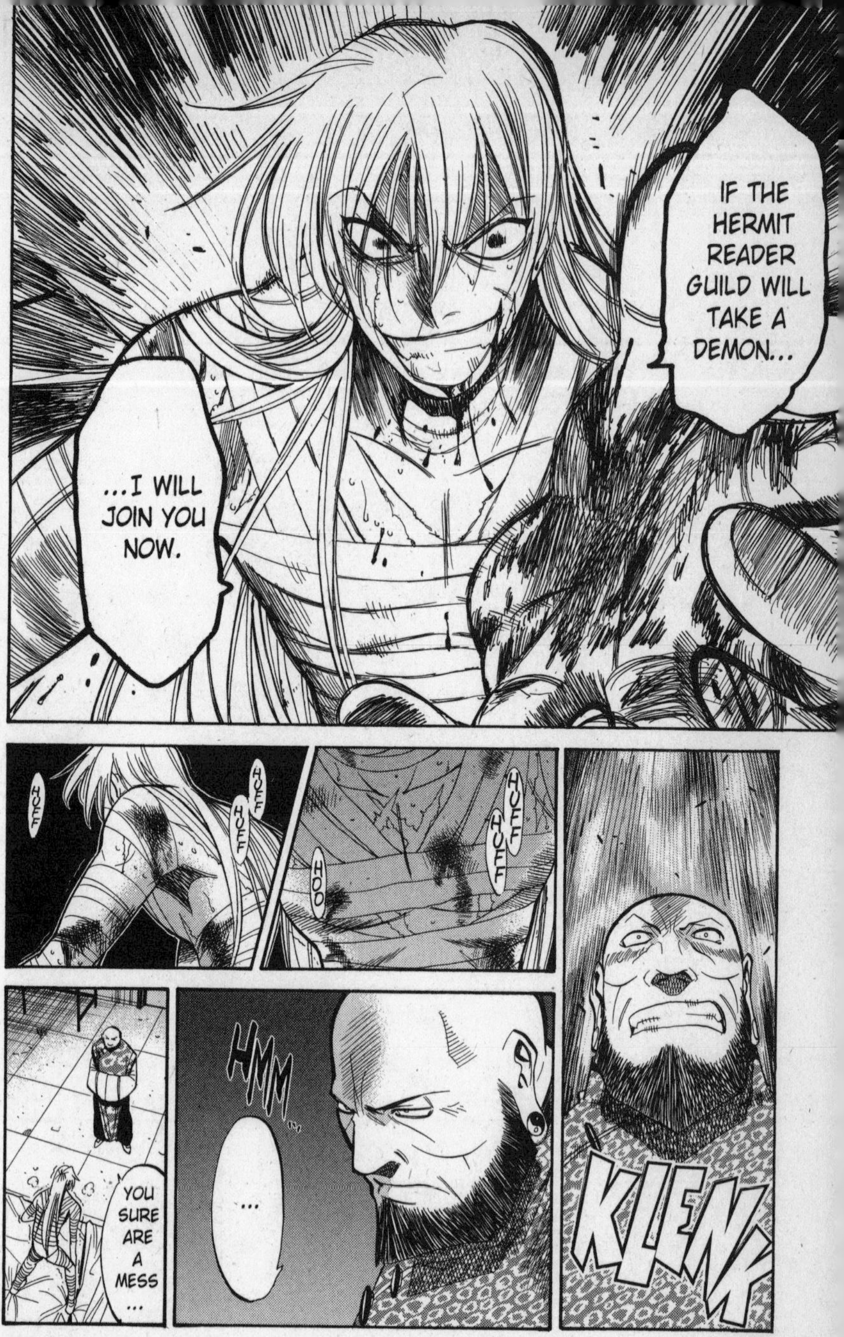
IF THE HERMIT READER GUILD WILL TAKE A DEMON...
...I WILL JOIN YOU NOW.
KLENK
HUFF HUFF
HOO
HUFF
HUFF HUFF
HMM...
...
YOU SURE ARE A MESS...

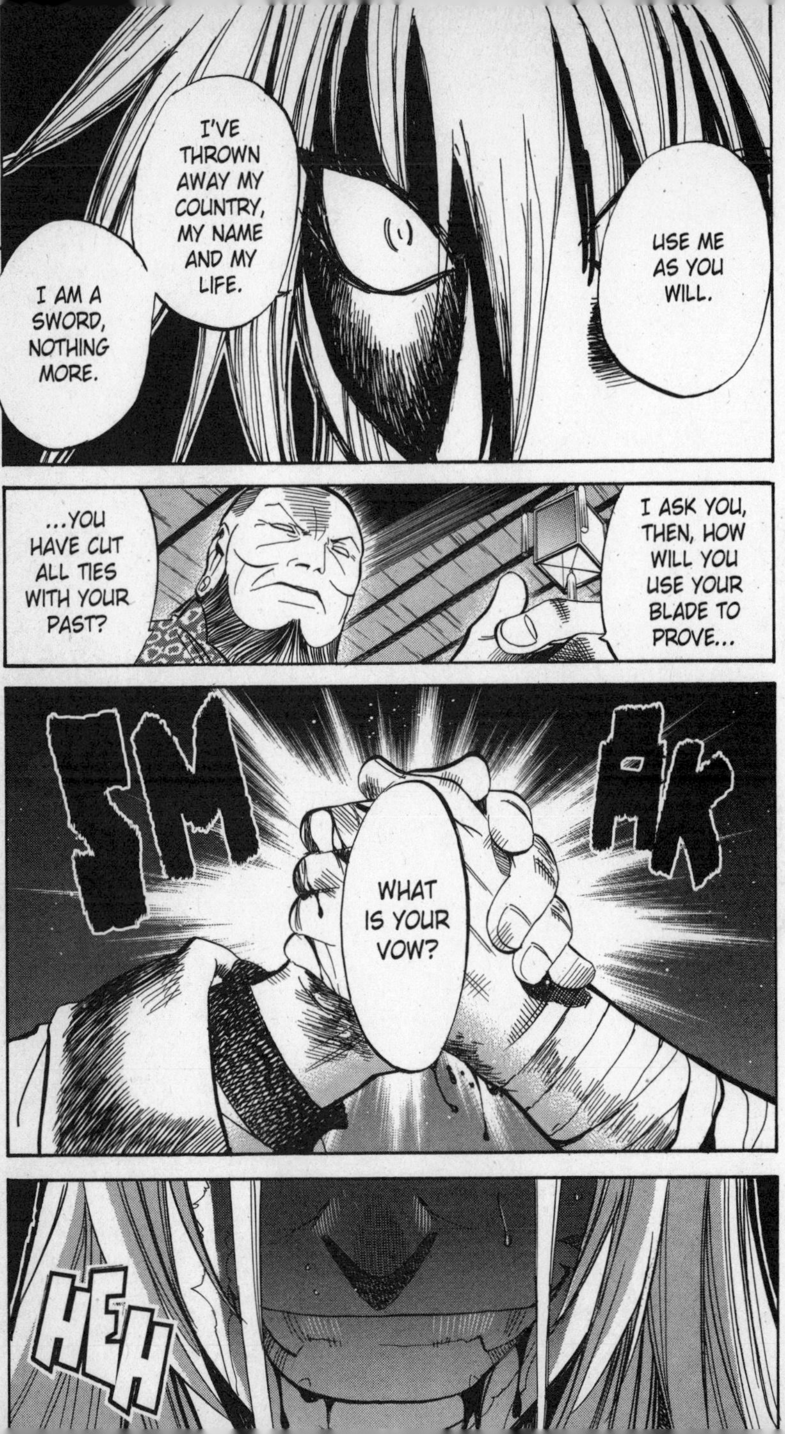
USE ME AS YOU WILL.
I'VE THROWN AWAY MY COUNTRY, MY NAME AND MY LIFE.
I AM A SWORD, NOTHING MORE.
I ASK YOU, THEN, HOW WILL YOU USE YOUR BLADE TO PROVE...
...YOU HAVE CUT ALL TIES WITH YOUR PAST?
SHAK
WHAT IS YOUR VOW?
HEH

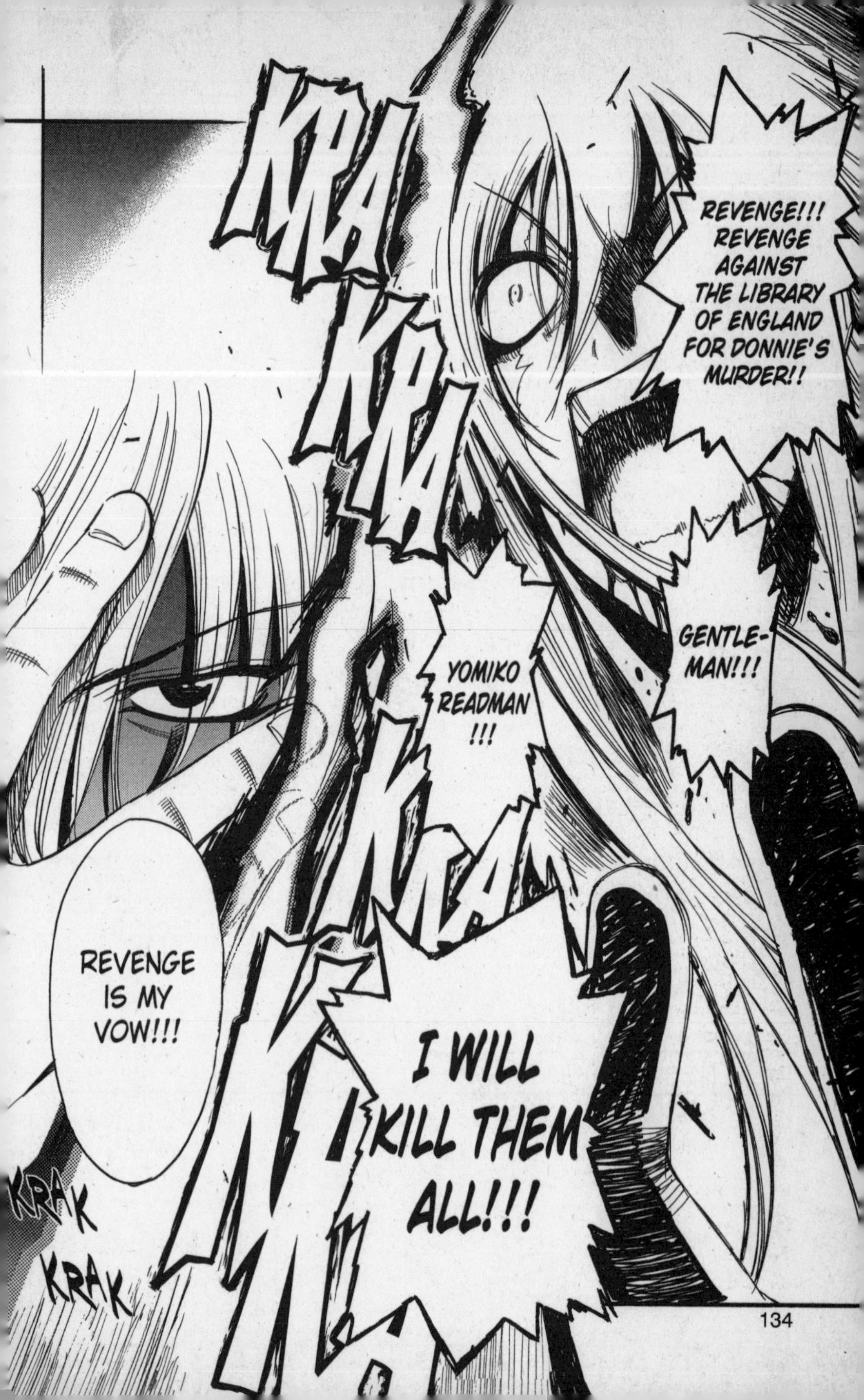
REVENGE!!! REVENGE AGAINST THE LIBRARY OF ENGLAND FOR DONNIE'S MURDER!!
GENTLE-MAN!!!
YOMIKO READMAN !!!
I WILL KILL THEM ALL!!!
REVENGE IS MY VOW!!!
KRAK
KRAK

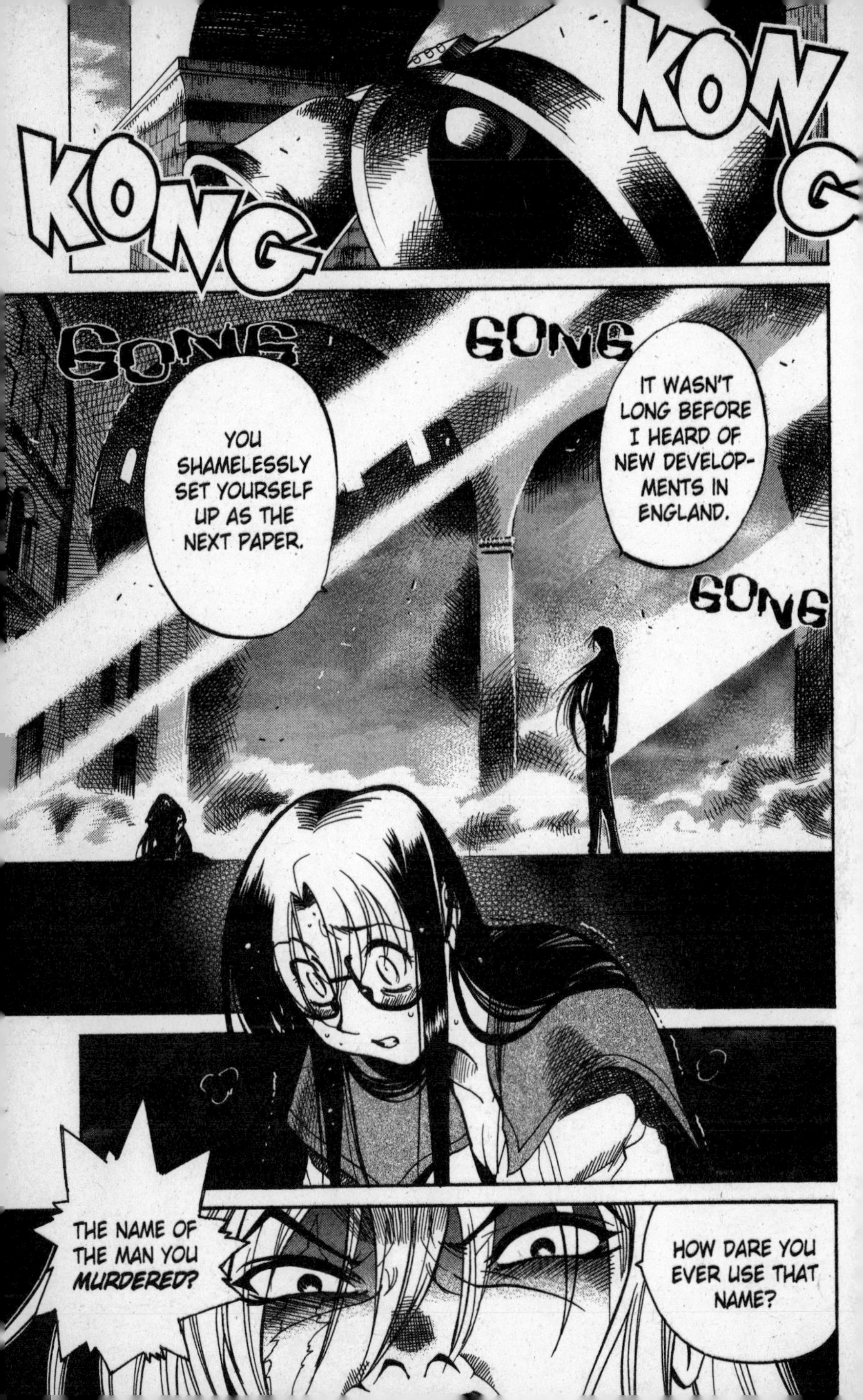
KONG
KONG
GONG
IT WASN'T LONG BEFORE I HEARD OF NEW DEVELOP-MENTS IN ENGLAND.
YOU SHAMELESSLY SET YOURSELF UP AS THE NEXT PAPER.
GONG
GONG
HOW DARE YOU EVER USE THAT NAME?
THE NAME OF THE MAN YOU *MURDERED?*

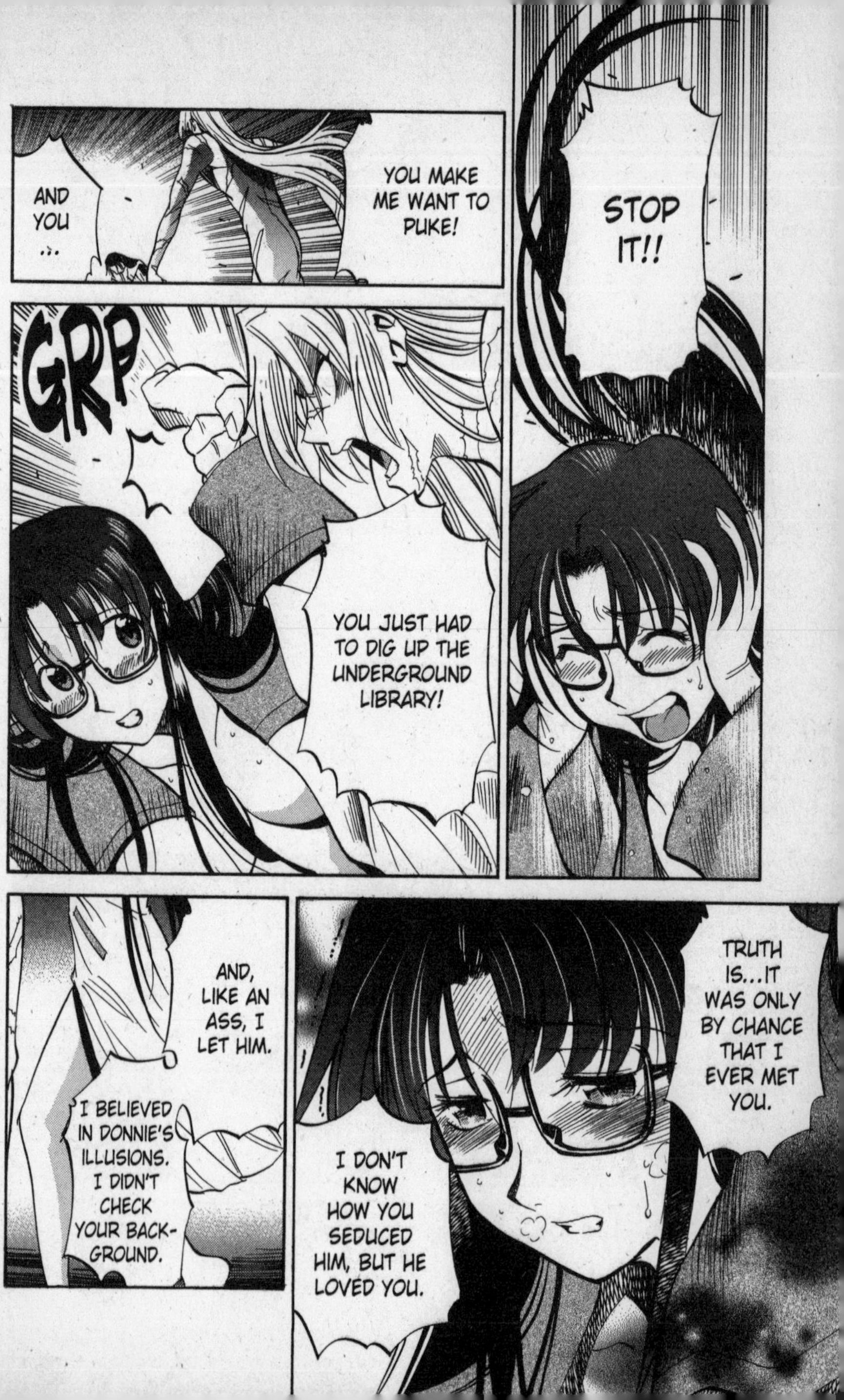
STOP IT!!
YOU MAKE ME WANT TO PUKE!
AND YOU ...
GRP
YOU JUST HAD TO DIG UP THE UNDERGROUND LIBRARY!
TRUTH IS...IT WAS ONLY BY CHANCE THAT I EVER MET YOU.
I DON'T KNOW HOW YOU SEDUCED HIM, BUT HE LOVED YOU.
AND, LIKE AN ASS, I LET HIM.
I BELIEVED IN DONNIE'S ILLUSIONS. I DIDN'T CHECK YOUR BACK-GROUND.

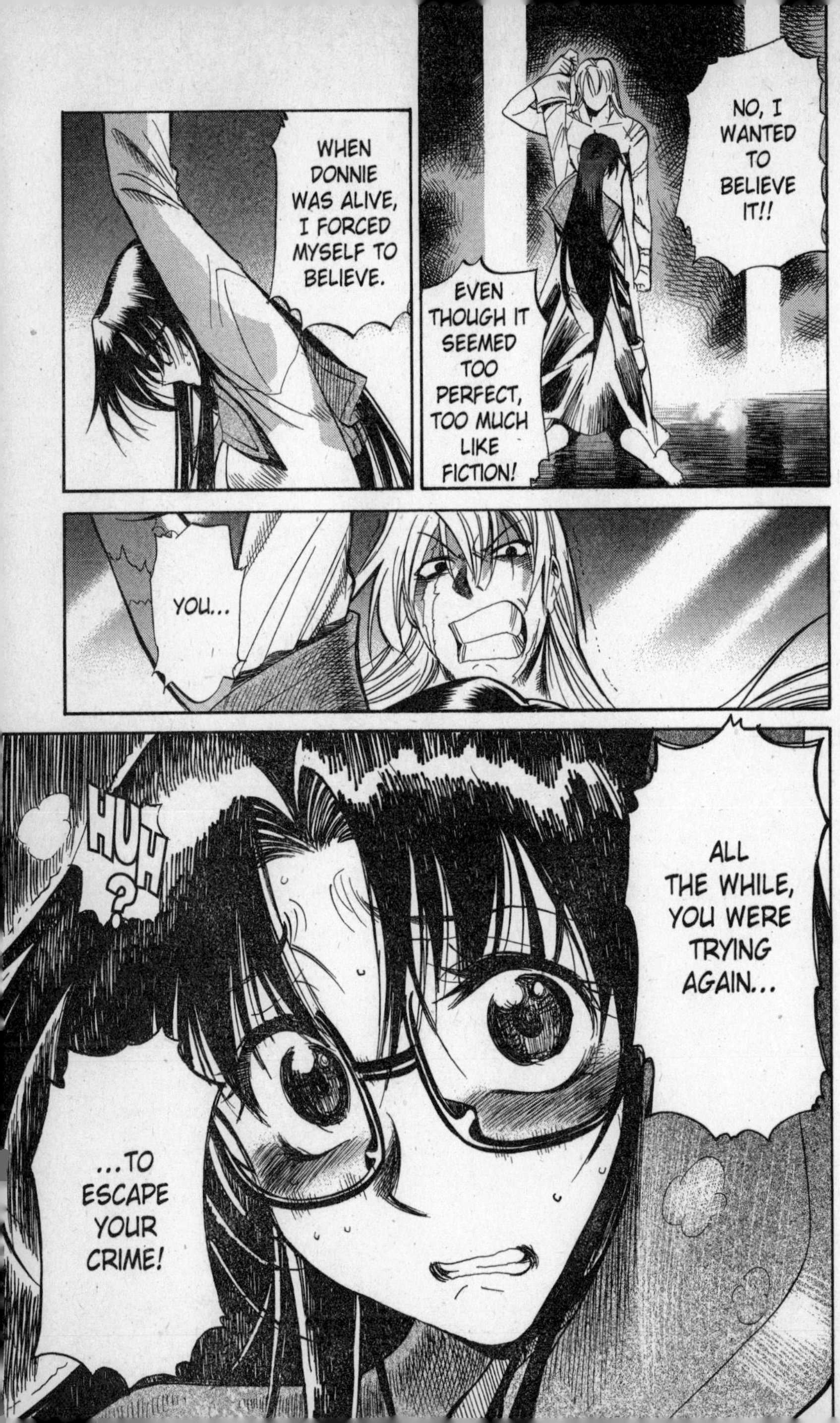
NO, I WANTED TO BELIEVE IT!!
EVEN THOUGH IT SEEMED TOO PERFECT, TOO MUCH LIKE FICTION!
WHEN DONNIE WAS ALIVE, I FORCED MYSELF TO BELIEVE.
YOU...
ALL THE WHILE, YOU WERE TRYING AGAIN...
...TO ESCAPE YOUR CRIME!
HUH?

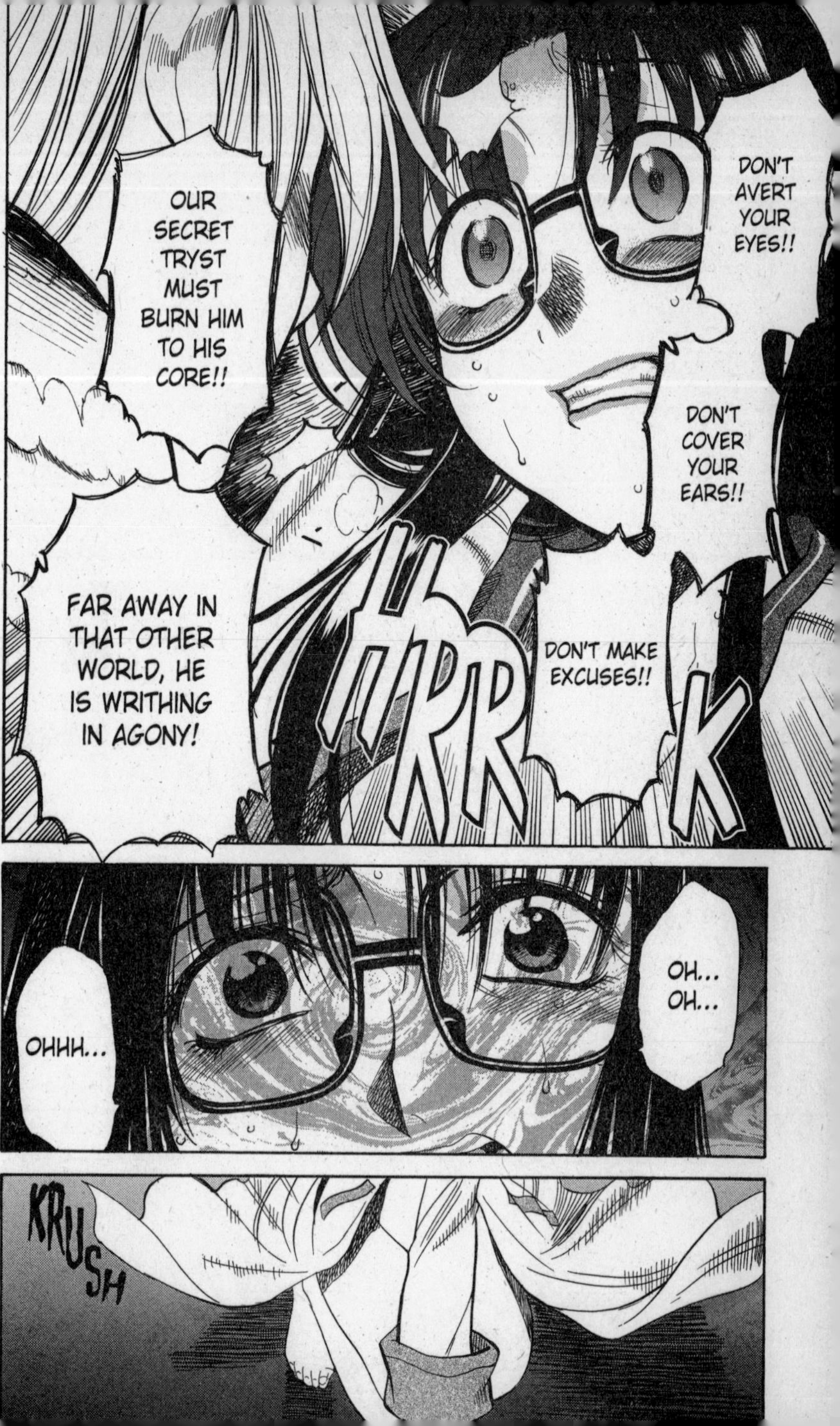
DON'T AVERT YOUR EYES!!
DON'T COVER YOUR EARS!!
DON'T MAKE EXCUSES!!
HRRK
OUR SECRET TRYST MUST BURN HIM TO HIS CORE!!
FAR AWAY IN THAT OTHER WORLD, HE IS WRITHING IN AGONY!
OH... OH...
OHHH...
KRUSH

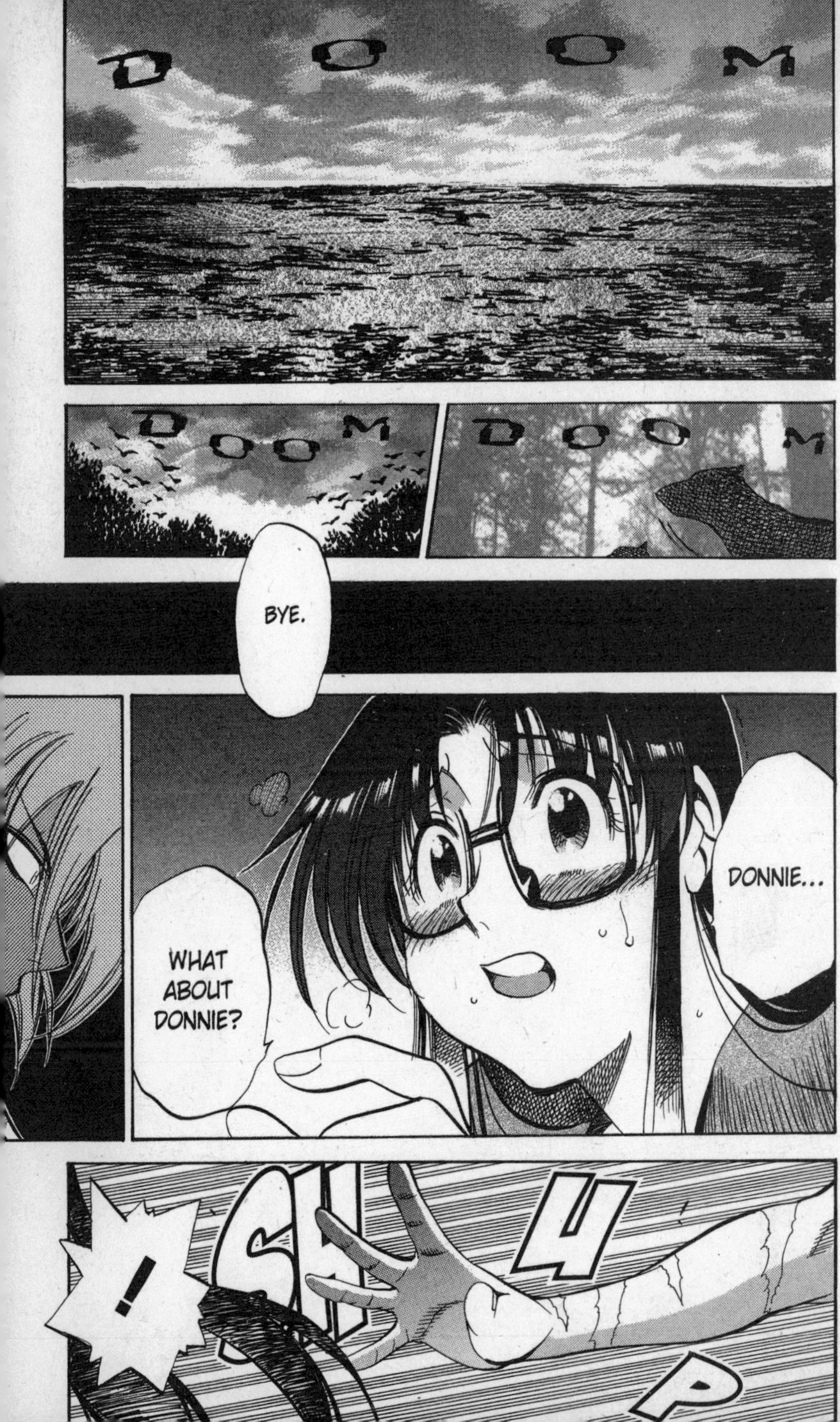
DOOM
DOOOM
DOOM
BYE.
DONNIE...
WHAT ABOUT DONNIE?
SHUP
!

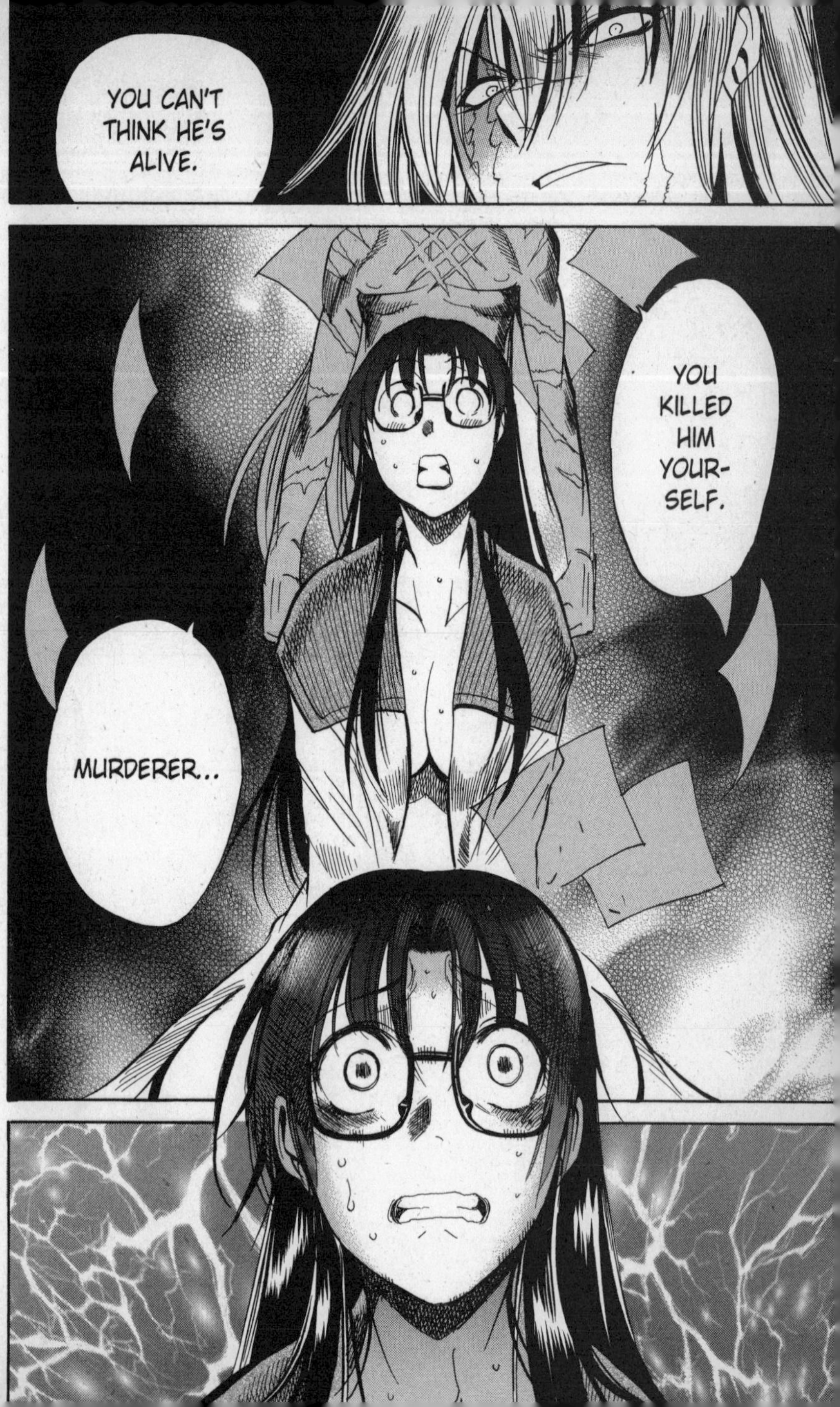
YOU CAN'T THINK HE'S ALIVE.
YOU KILLED HIM YOUR-SELF.
MURDERER...

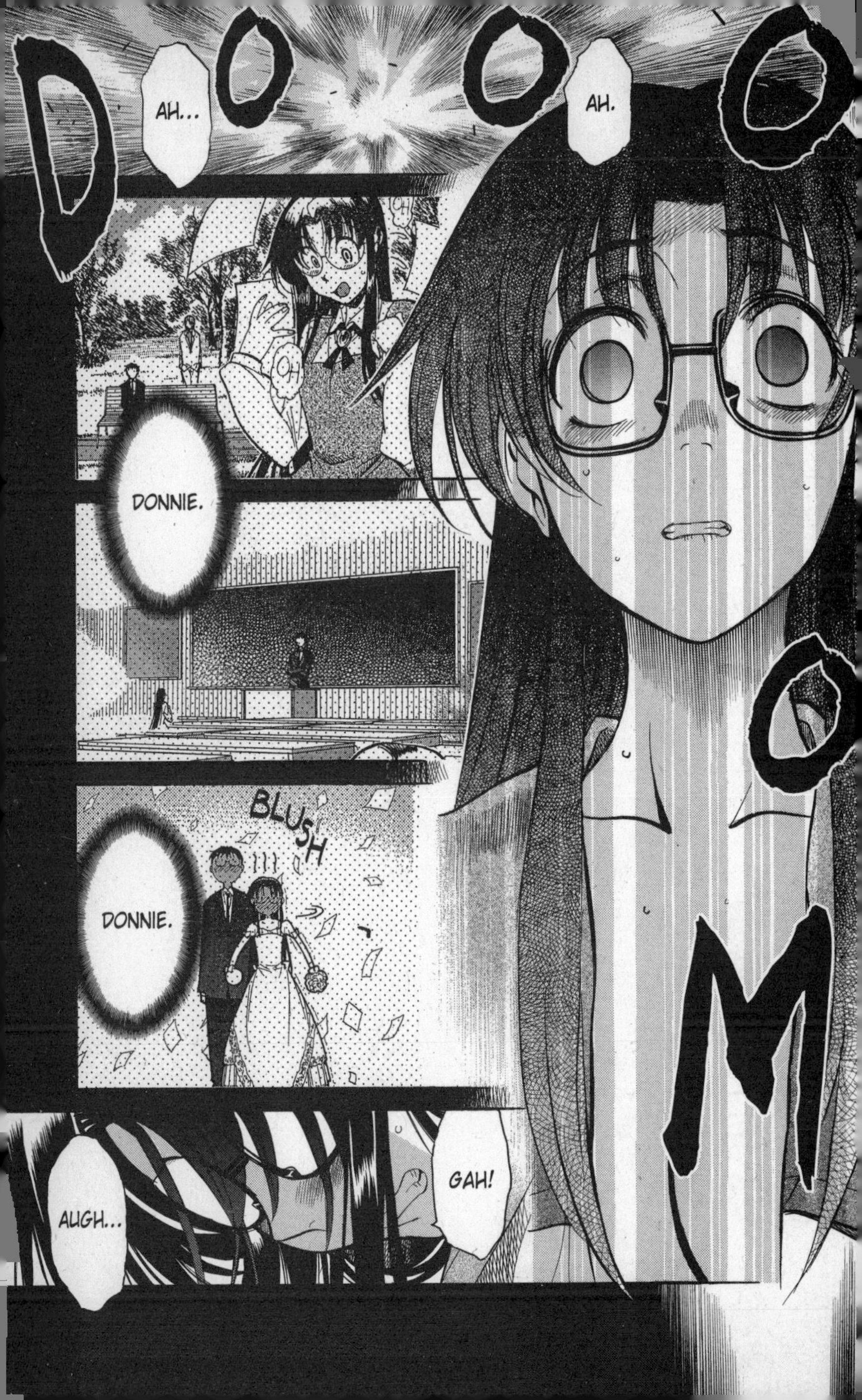
DOOOOM
AH.
AH...
DONNIE.
BLUSH
DONNIE.
GAH!
AUGH...

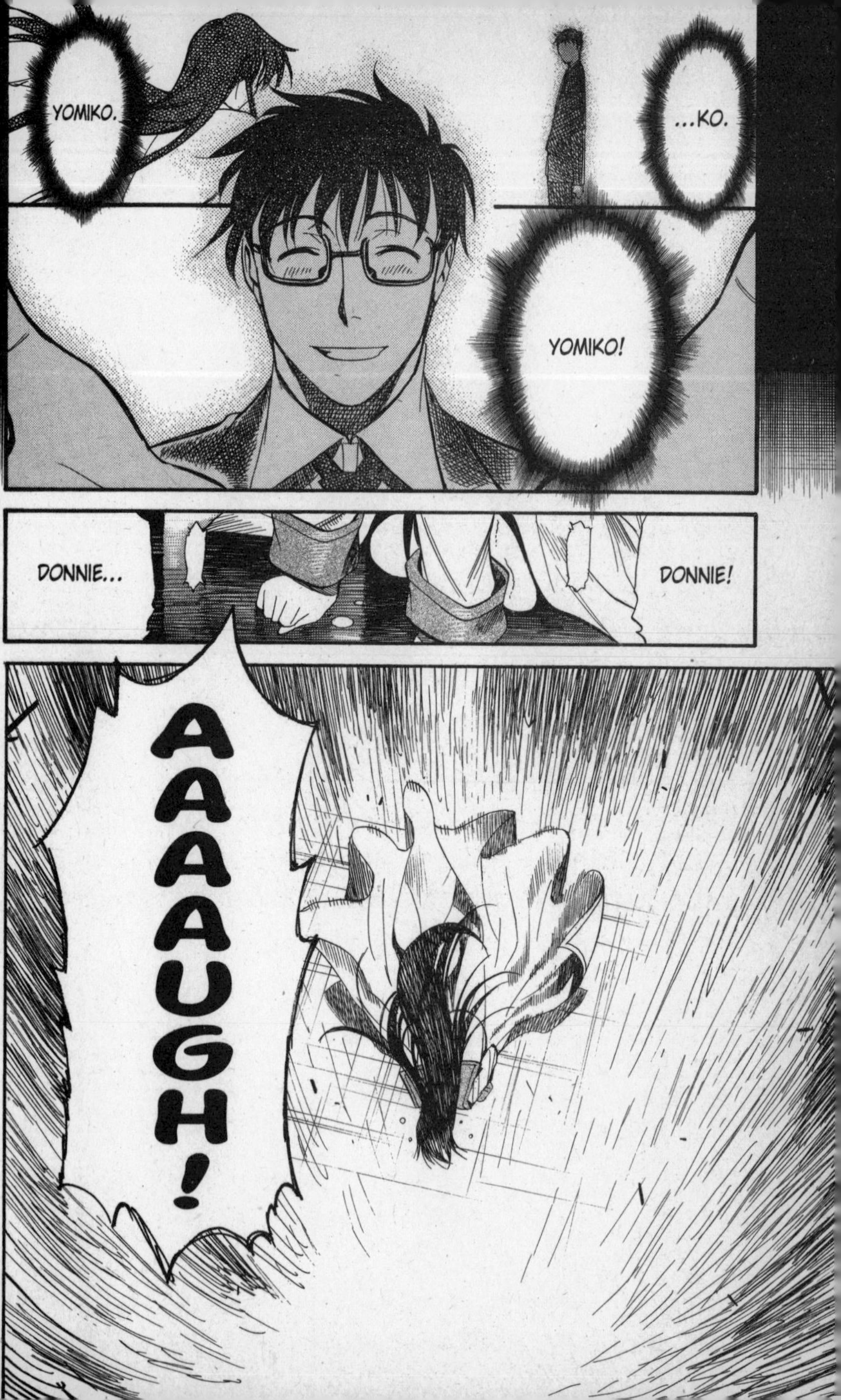
...KO.
YOMIKO.
YOMIKO!
DONNIE!
DONNIE...
AAAAUGH!

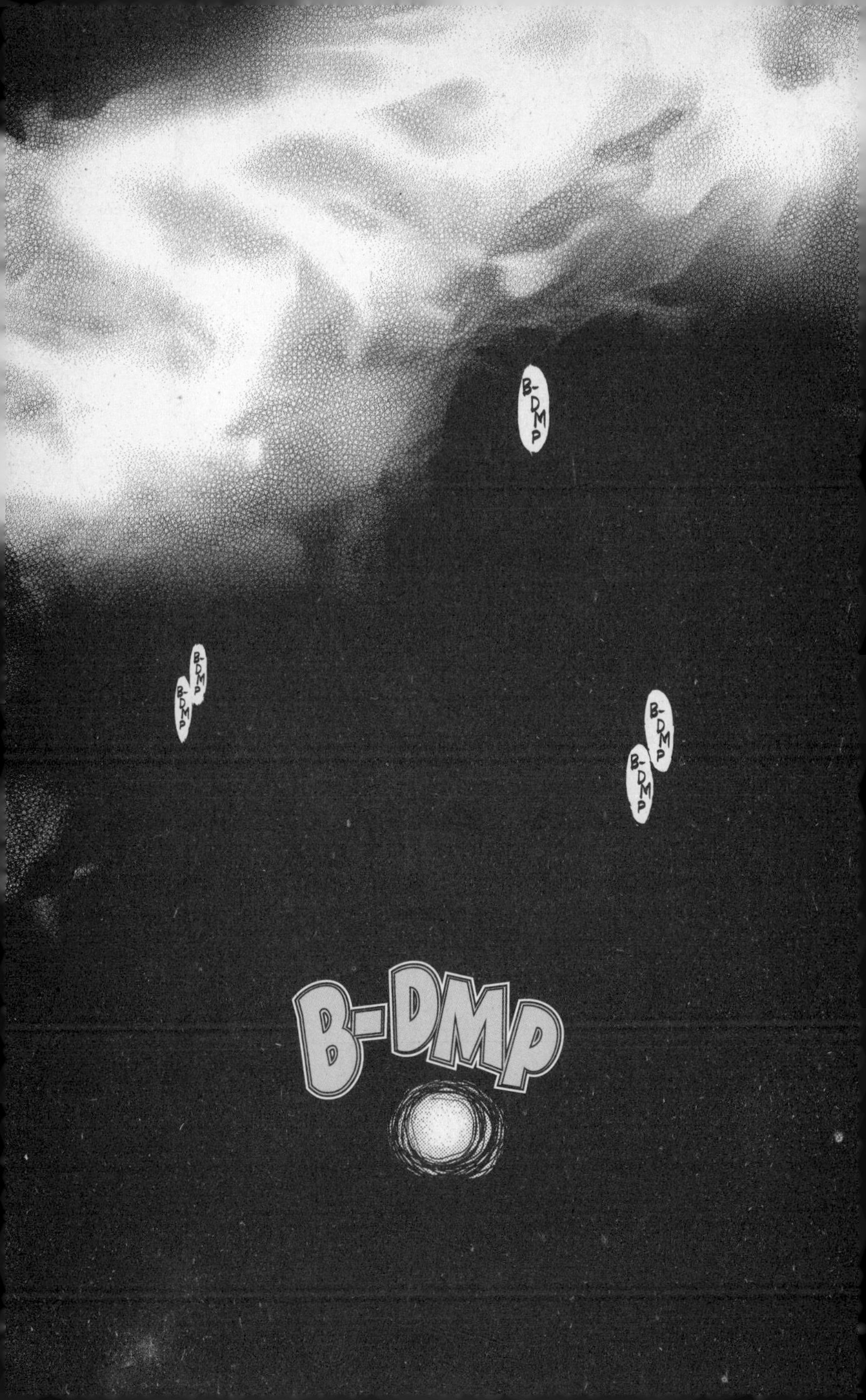
B-DMP
B-DMP
B-DMP
B-DMP
B-DMP
B-DMP

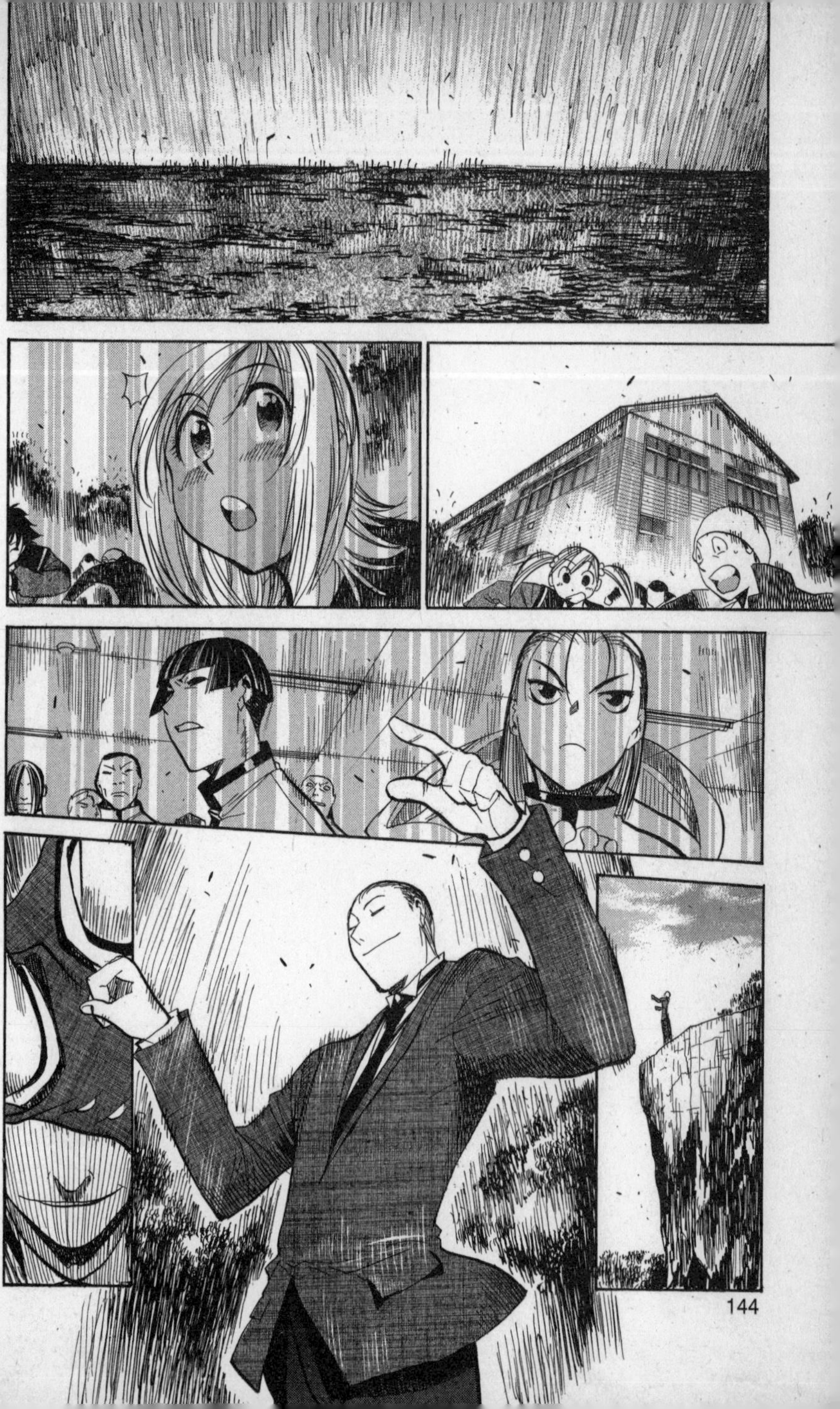

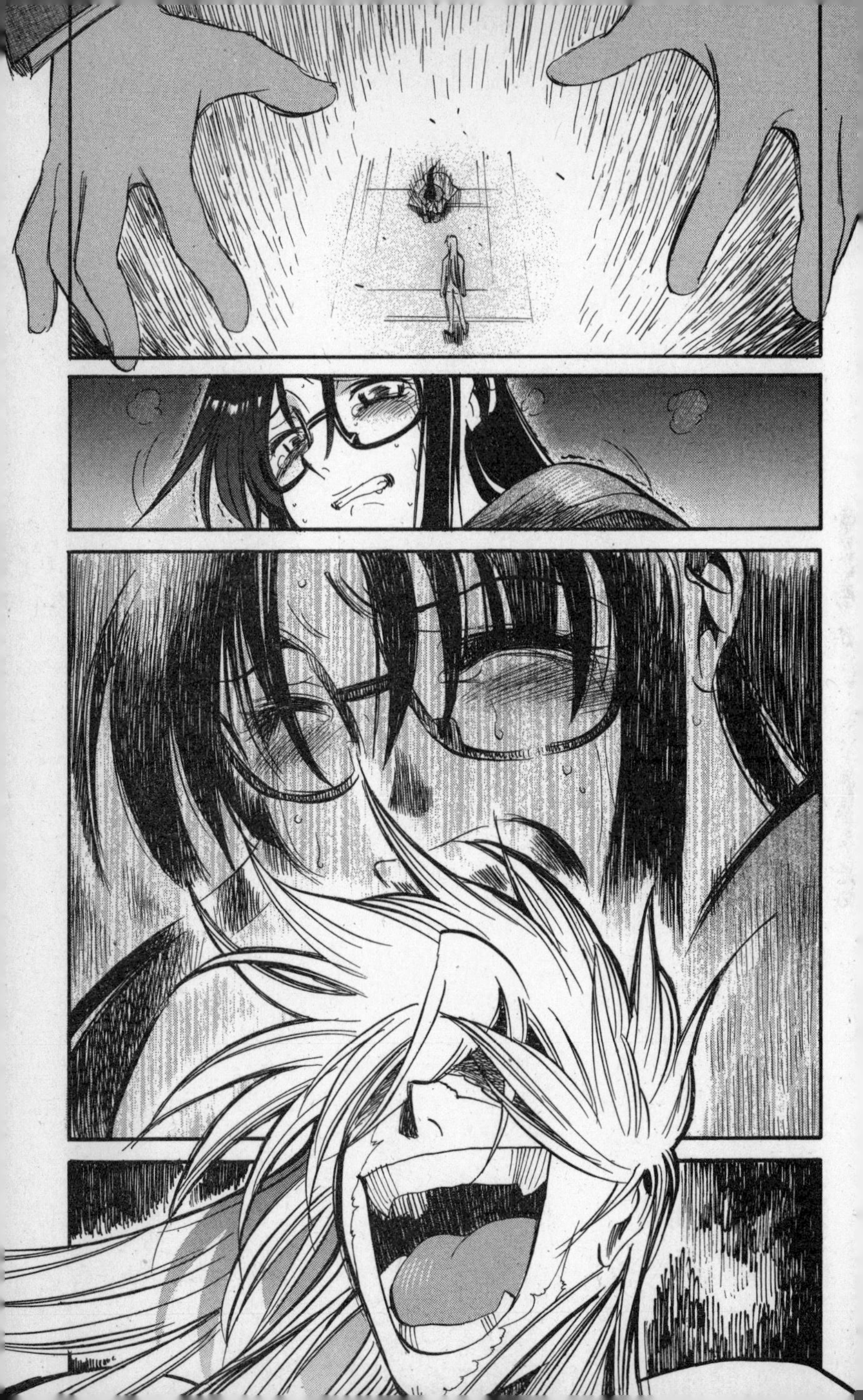

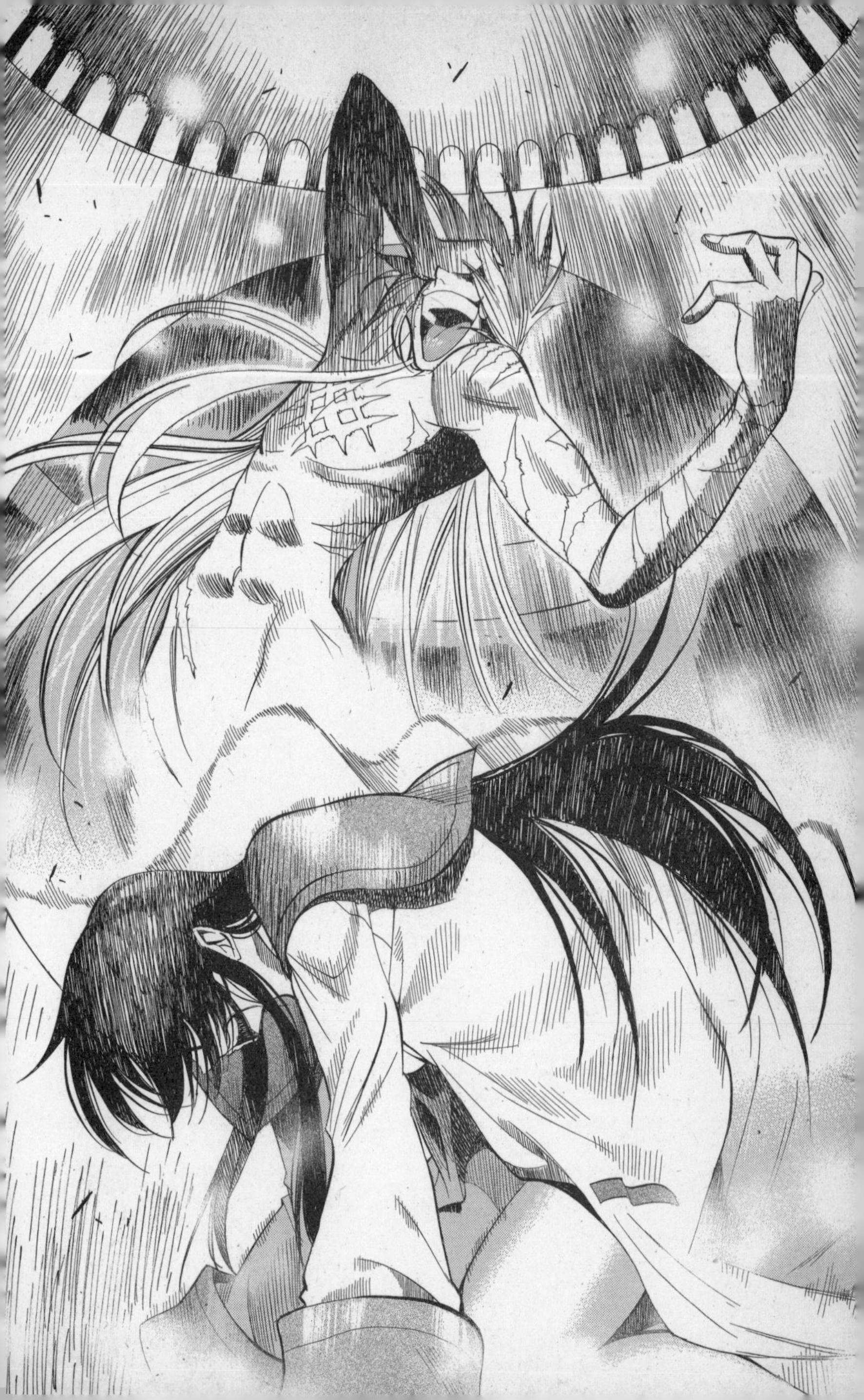

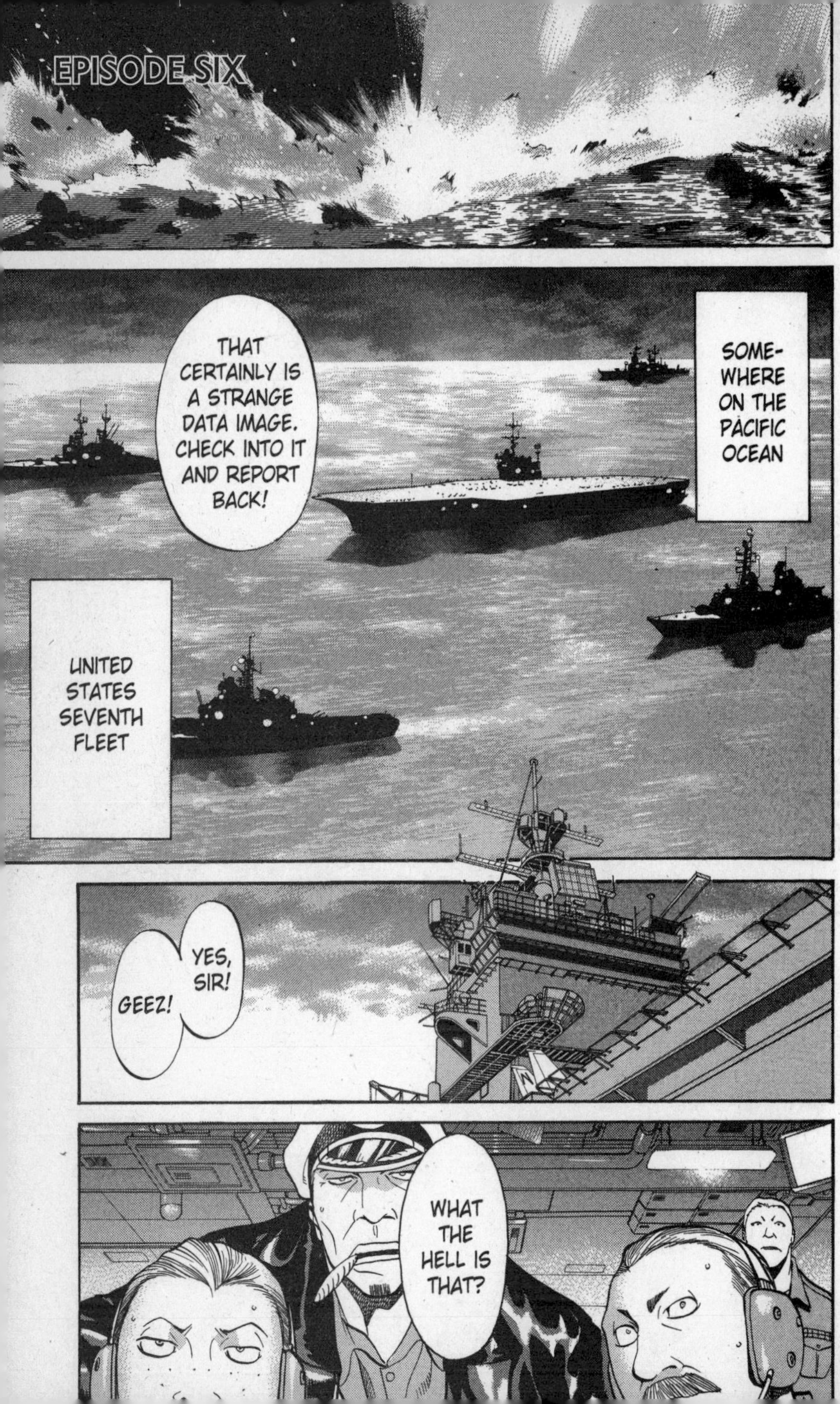
EPISODE SIX
SOME-WHERE ON THE PACIFIC OCEAN
THAT CERTAINLY IS A STRANGE DATA IMAGE. CHECK INTO IT AND REPORT BACK!
UNITED STATES SEVENTH FLEET
YES, SIR!
GEEZ!
WHAT THE HELL IS THAT?

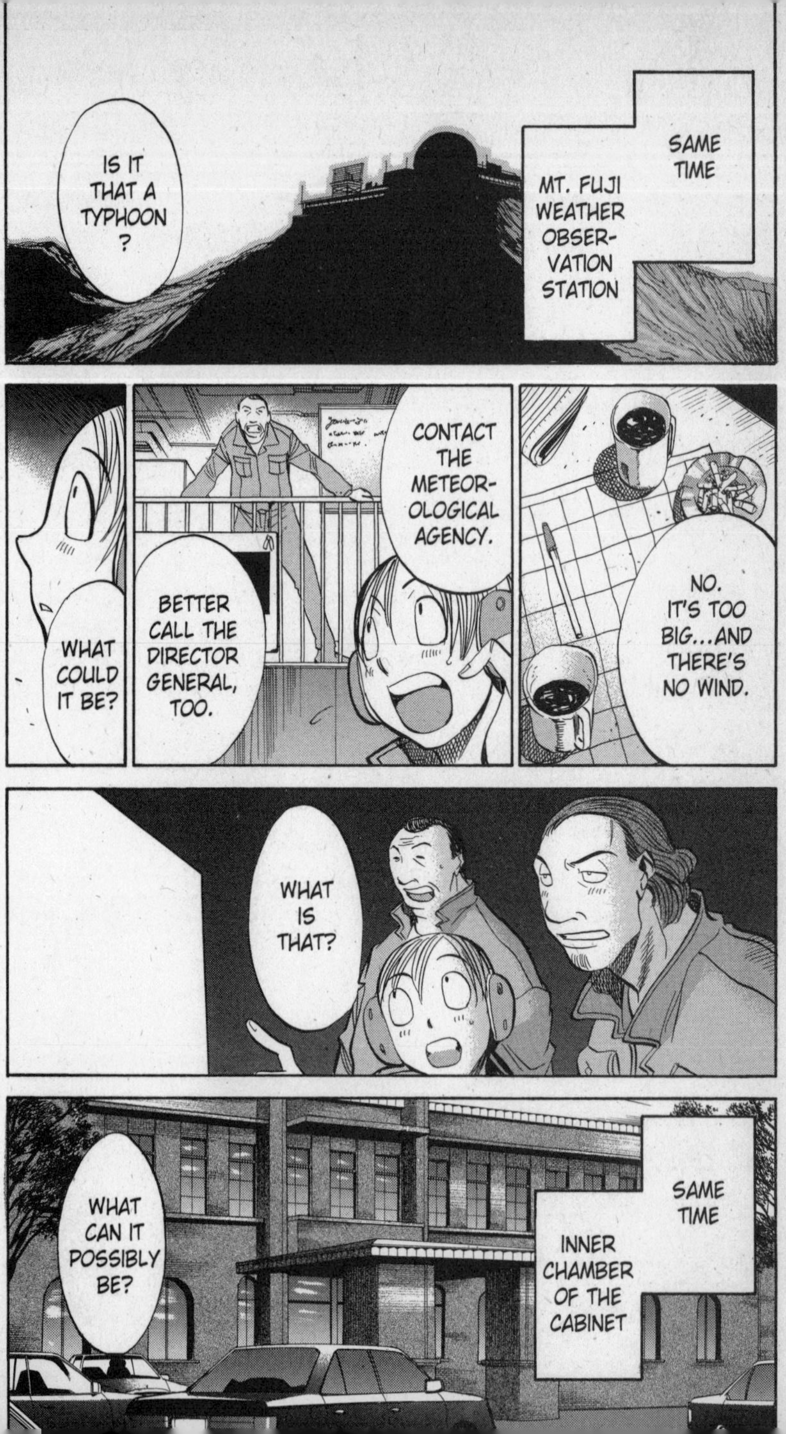
SAME TIME
MT. FUJI WEATHER OBSERVATION STATION
IS IT THAT A TYPHOON ?
NO. IT'S TOO BIG...AND THERE'S NO WIND.
CONTACT THE METEOROLOGICAL AGENCY.
BETTER CALL THE DIRECTOR GENERAL, TOO.
WHAT COULD IT BE?
WHAT IS THAT?
SAME TIME
INNER CHAMBER OF THE CABINET
WHAT CAN IT POSSIBLY BE?

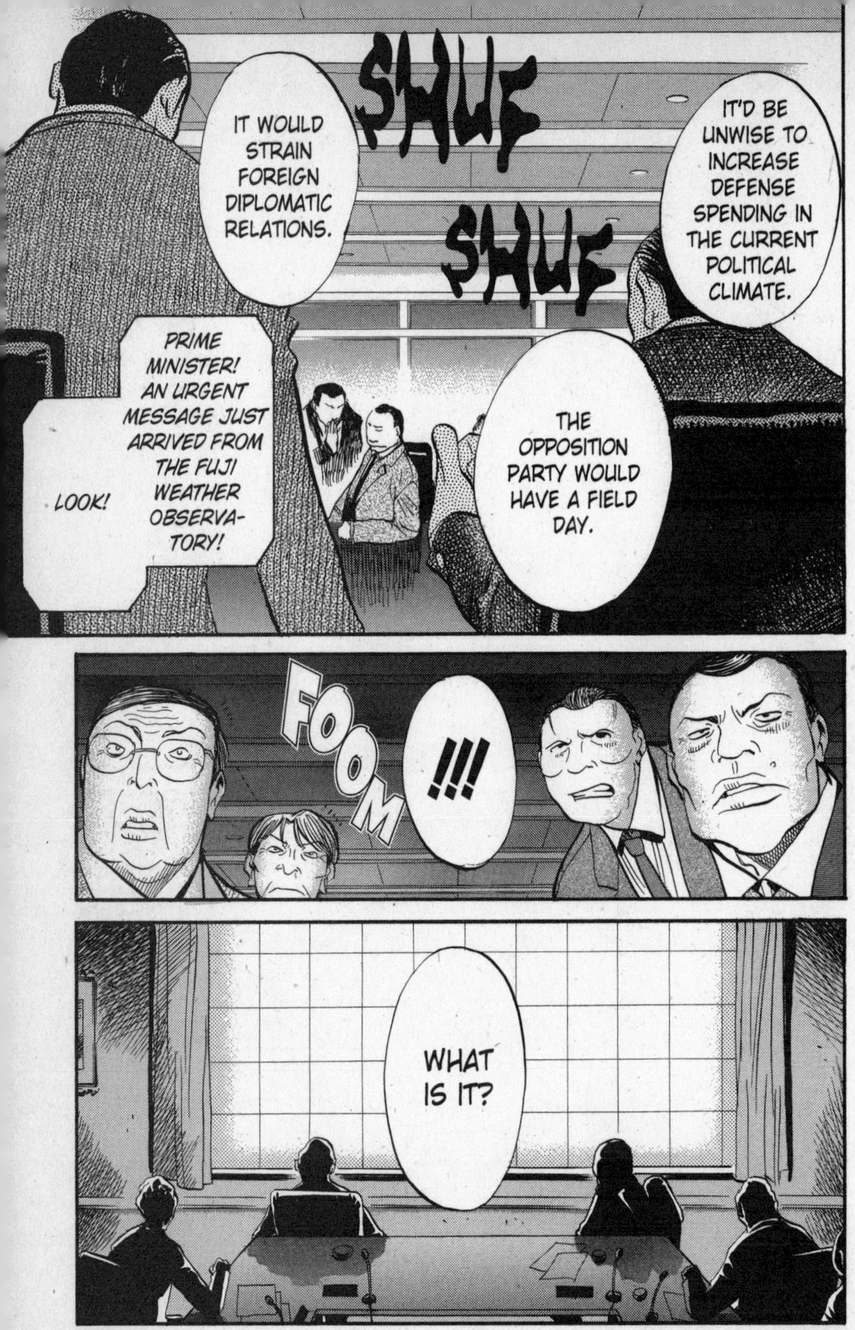
IT'D BE UNWISE TO INCREASE DEFENSE SPENDING IN THE CURRENT POLITICAL CLIMATE.
SHUF
SHUF
IT WOULD STRAIN FOREIGN DIPLOMATIC RELATIONS.
THE OPPOSITION PARTY WOULD HAVE A FIELD DAY.
PRIME MINISTER! AN URGENT MESSAGE JUST ARRIVED FROM THE FUJI WEATHER OBSERVATORY!
LOOK!
!!!
FOOM
WHAT IS IT?

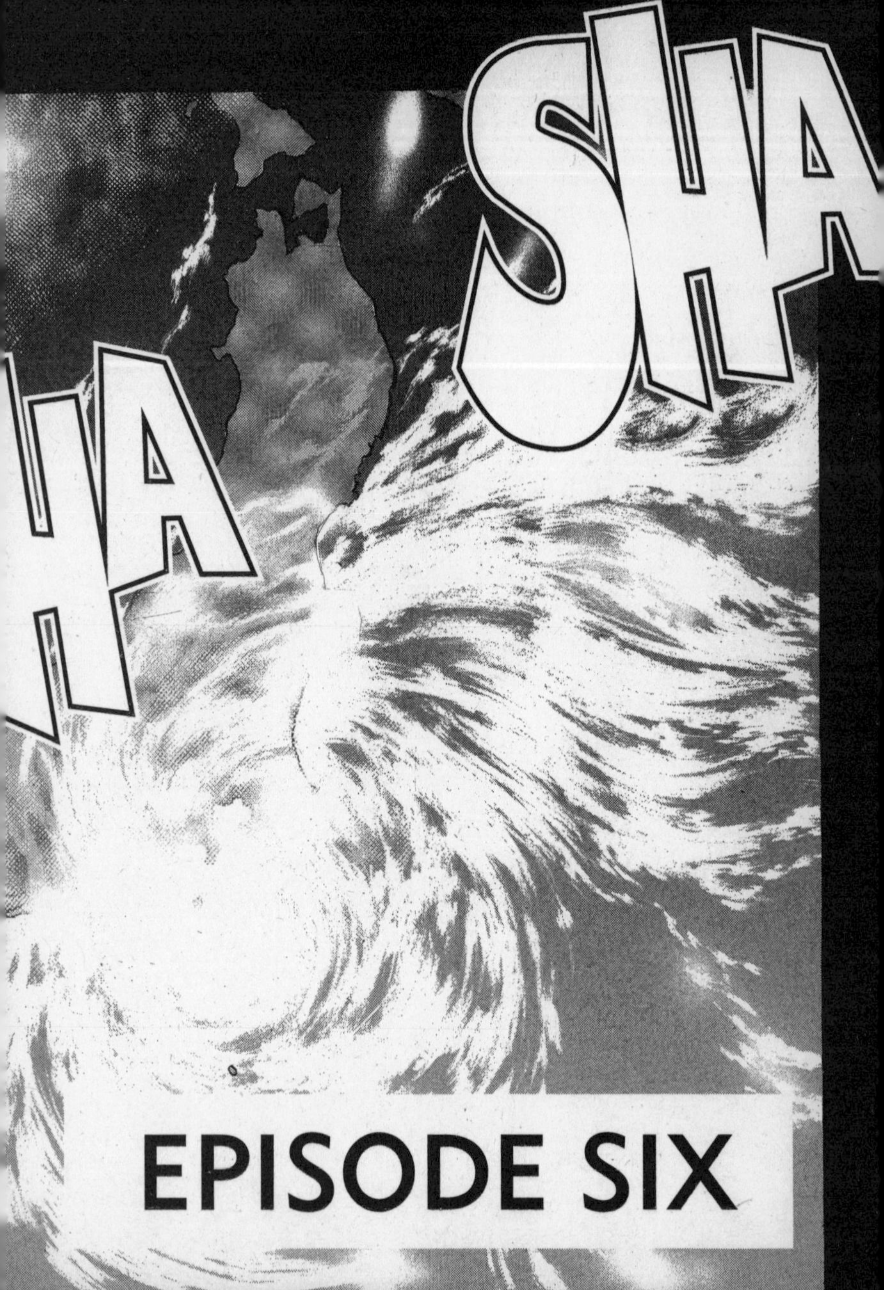
SHA
HA

EPISODE SIX

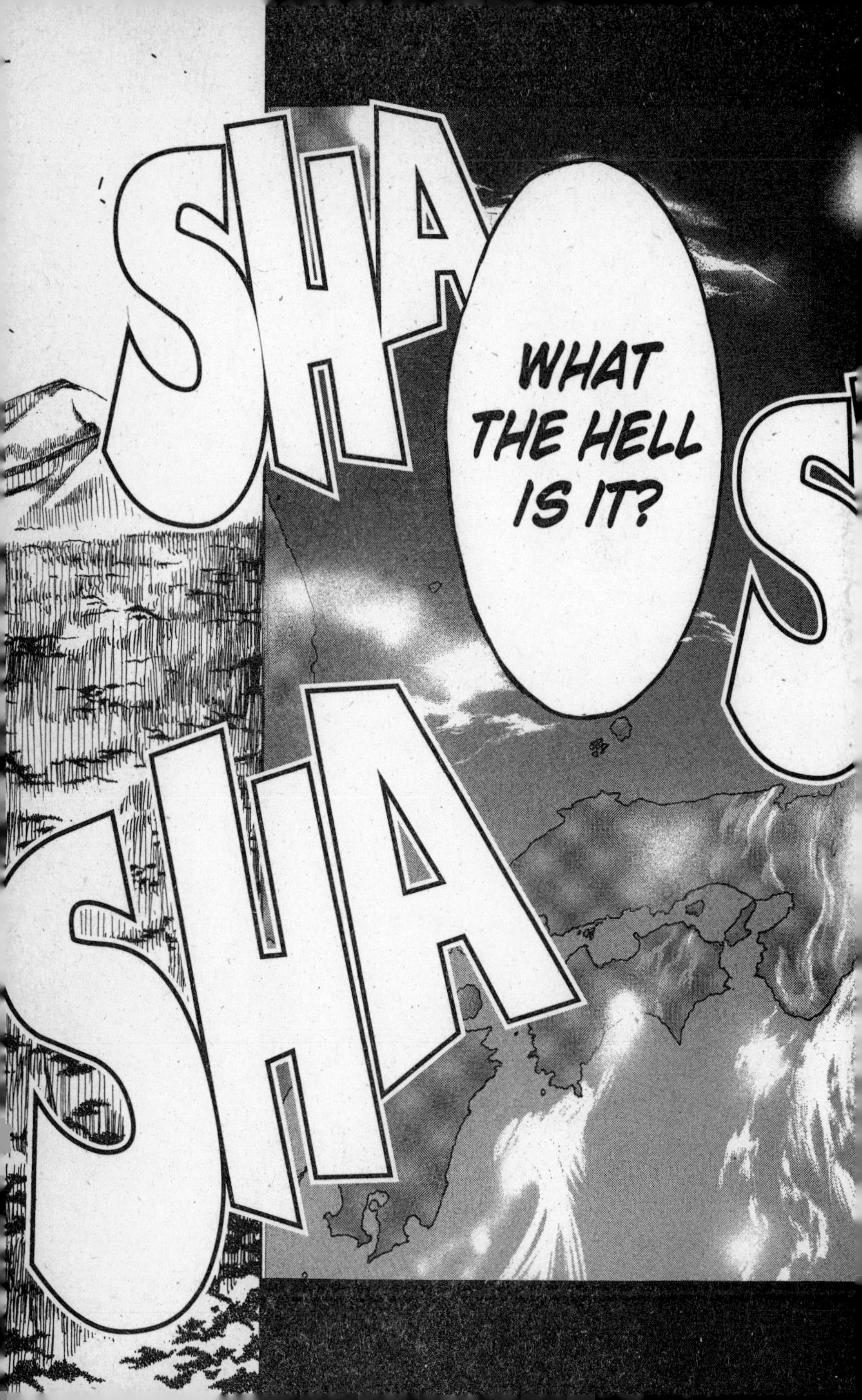
SHA
WHAT THE HELL IS IT?
S
SHA

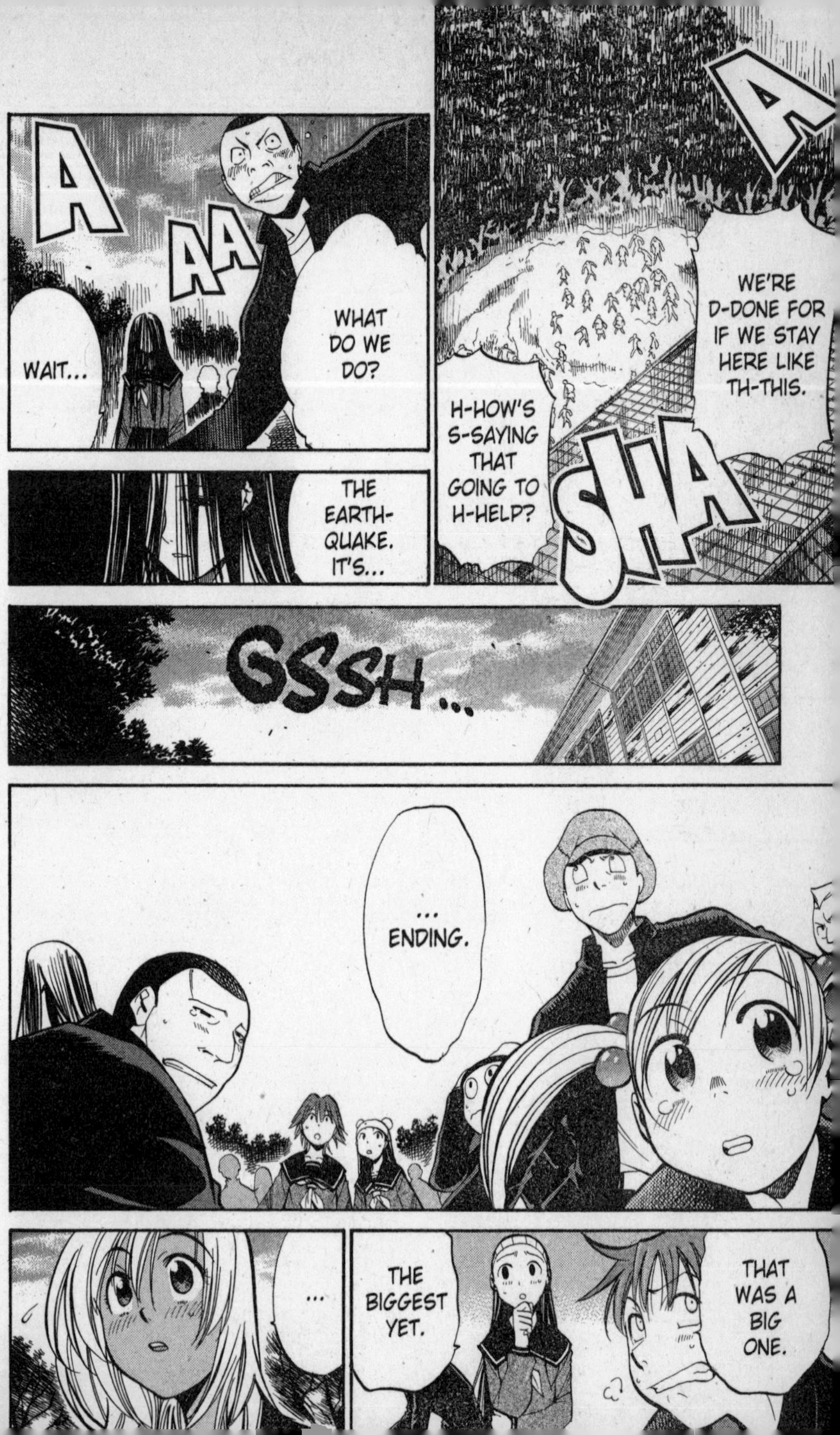
A
WE'RE D-DONE FOR IF WE STAY HERE LIKE TH-THIS.
H-HOW'S S-SAYING THAT GOING TO H-HELP?
SHA
A
AA
WHAT DO WE DO?
WAIT...
THE EARTH-QUAKE. IT'S...
GSSH...
... ENDING.
THAT WAS A BIG ONE.
THE BIGGEST YET.
...

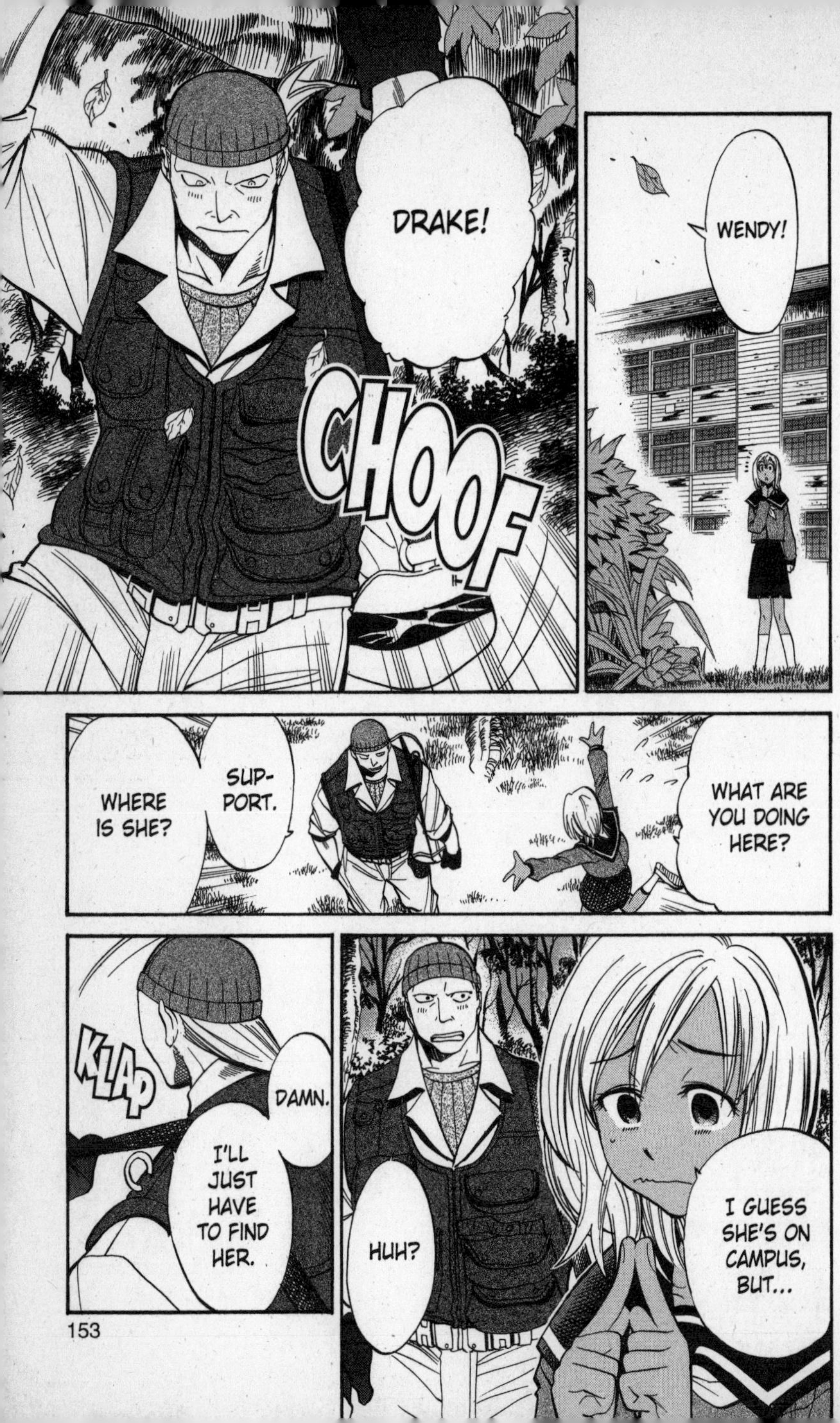
WENDY!
DRAKE!
CHOOF
WHAT ARE YOU DOING HERE?
SUP-PORT.
WHERE IS SHE?
I GUESS SHE'S ON CAMPUS, BUT...
HUH?
DAMN.
KLAP
I'LL JUST HAVE TO FIND HER.

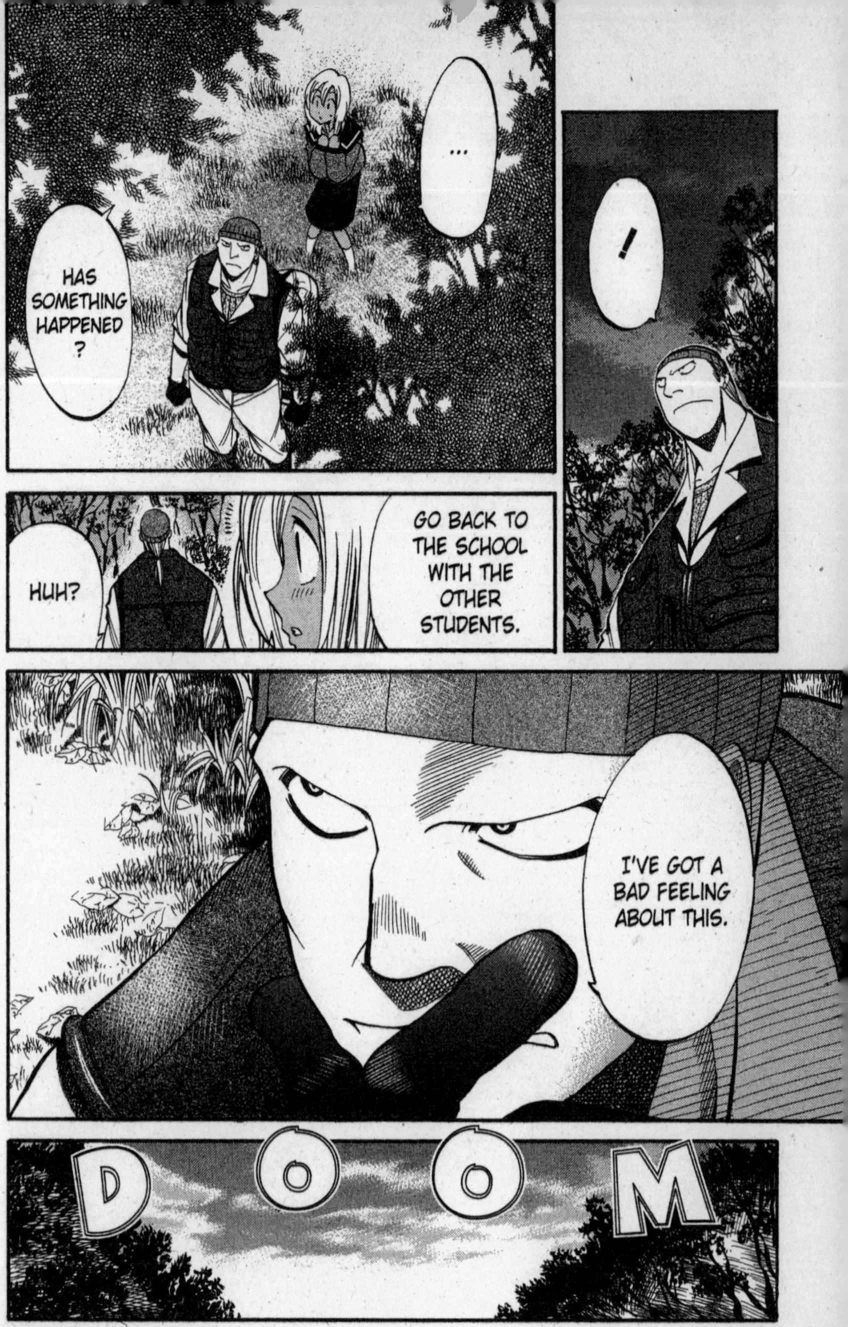
...
HAS SOMETHING HAPPENED?
!
GO BACK TO THE SCHOOL WITH THE OTHER STUDENTS.
HUH?
I'VE GOT A BAD FEELING ABOUT THIS.
DOOM

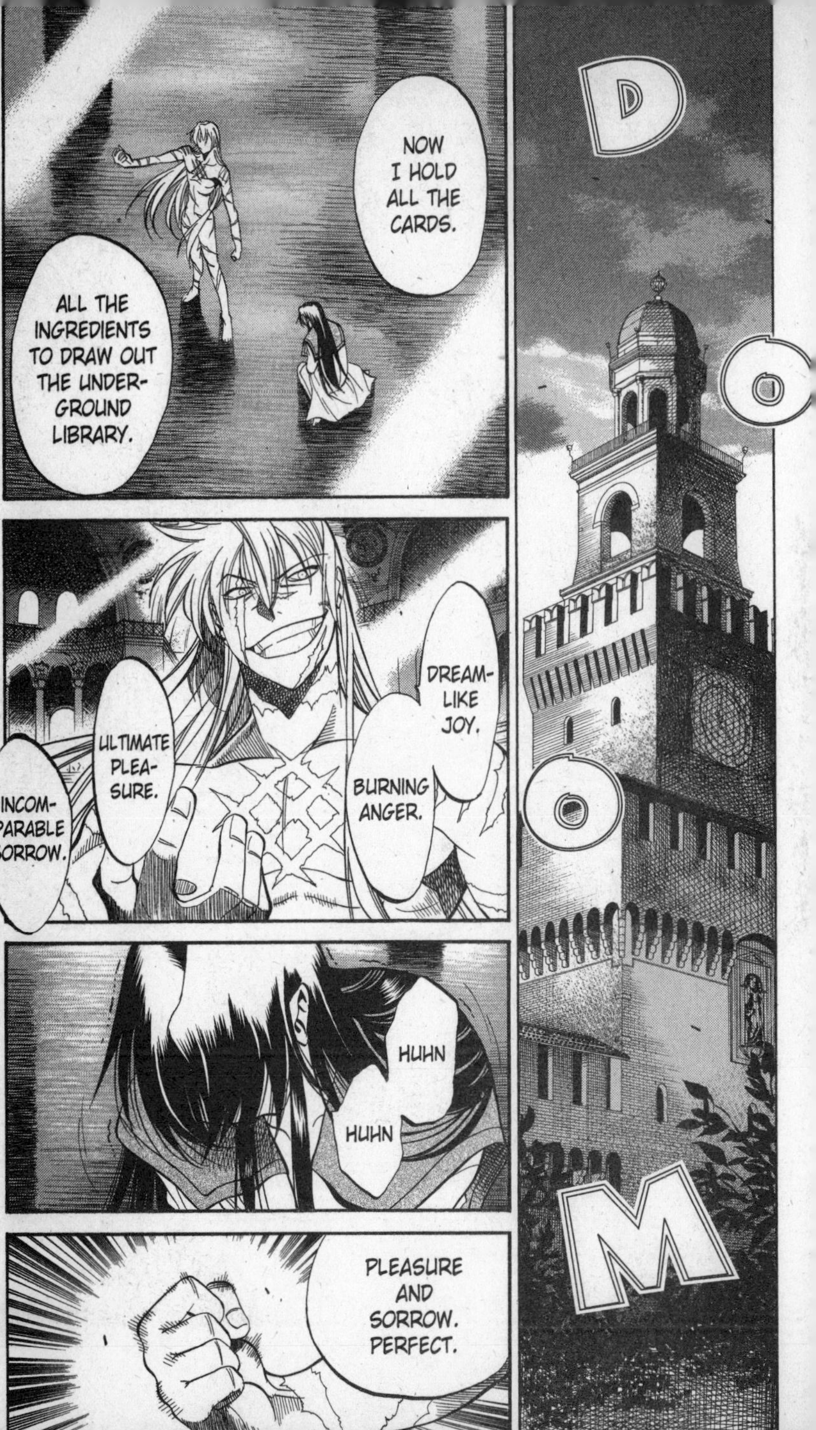
DOOM
NOW I HOLD ALL THE CARDS.
ALL THE INGREDIENTS TO DRAW OUT THE UNDER-GROUND LIBRARY.
DREAM-LIKE JOY.
BURNING ANGER.
ULTIMATE PLEA-SURE.
INCOM-PARABLE SORROW.
HUHN
HUHN
PLEASURE AND SORROW. PERFECT.

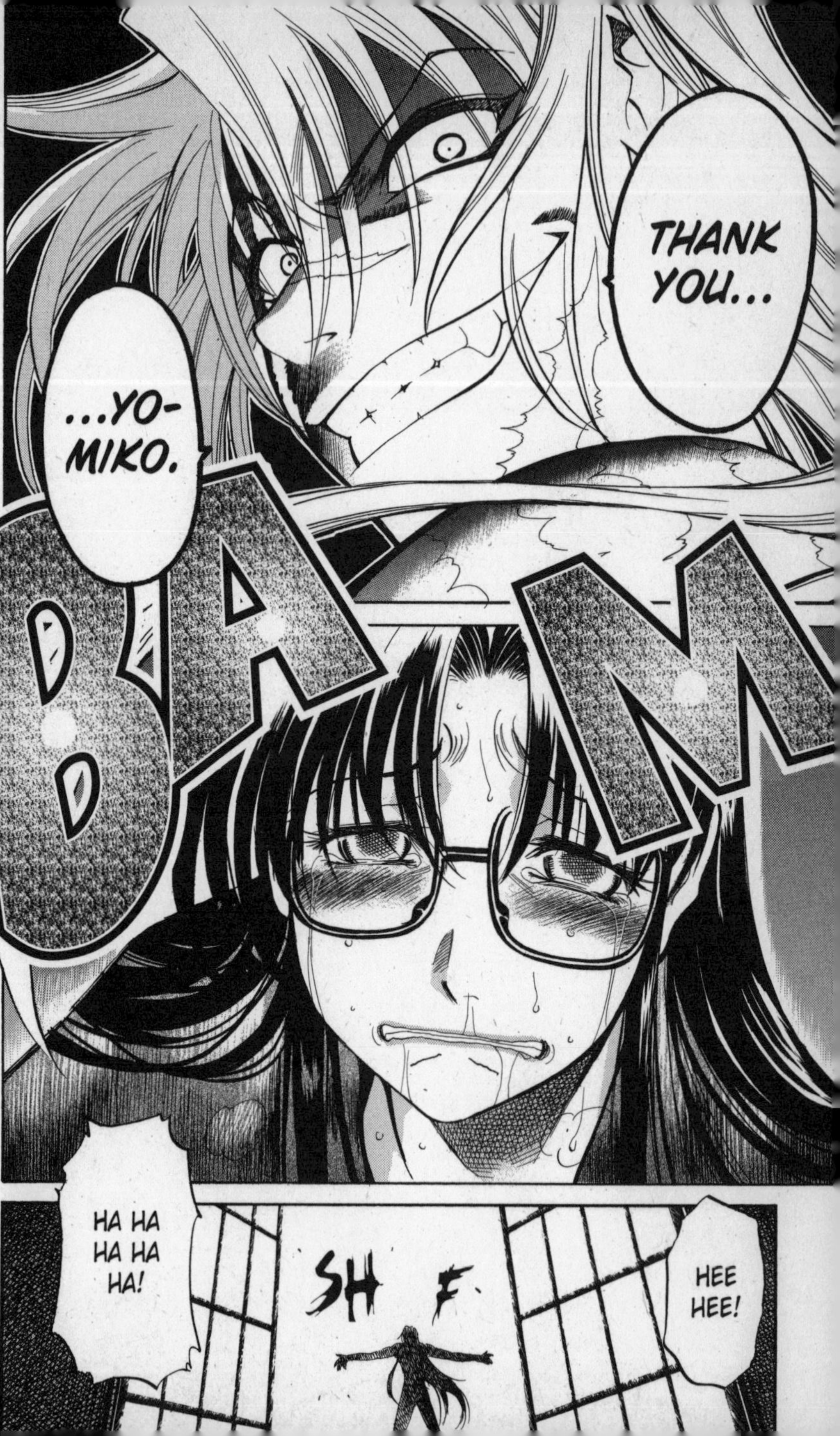
THANK YOU...
...YO-MIKO.
BAM
HEE HEE!
SH F
HA HA HA HA HA!

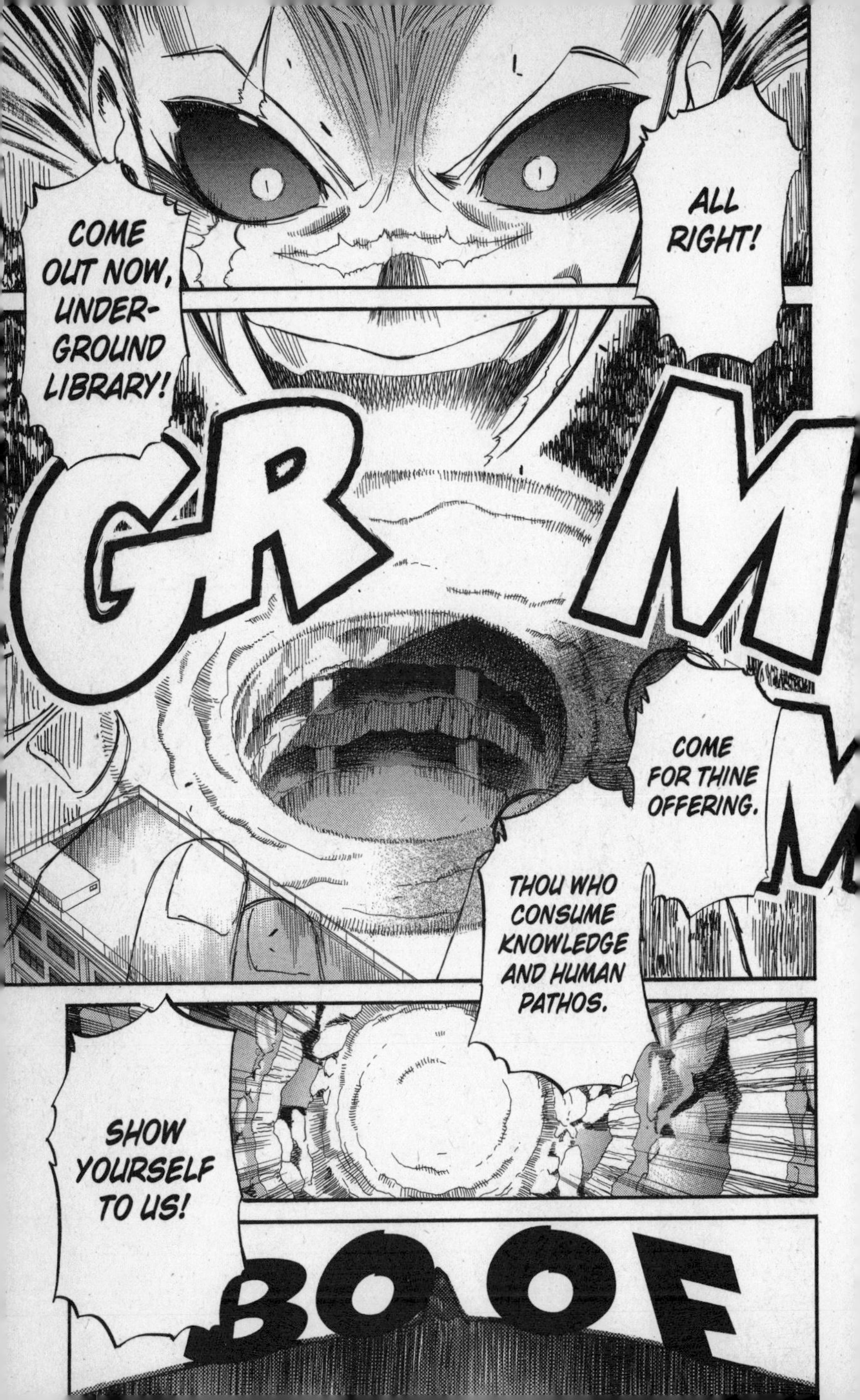
ALL RIGHT!
COME OUT NOW, UNDER-GROUND LIBRARY!
GRMM
COME FOR THINE OFFERING.
THOU WHO CONSUME KNOWLEDGE AND HUMAN PATHOS.
SHOW YOURSELF TO US!
BOOF

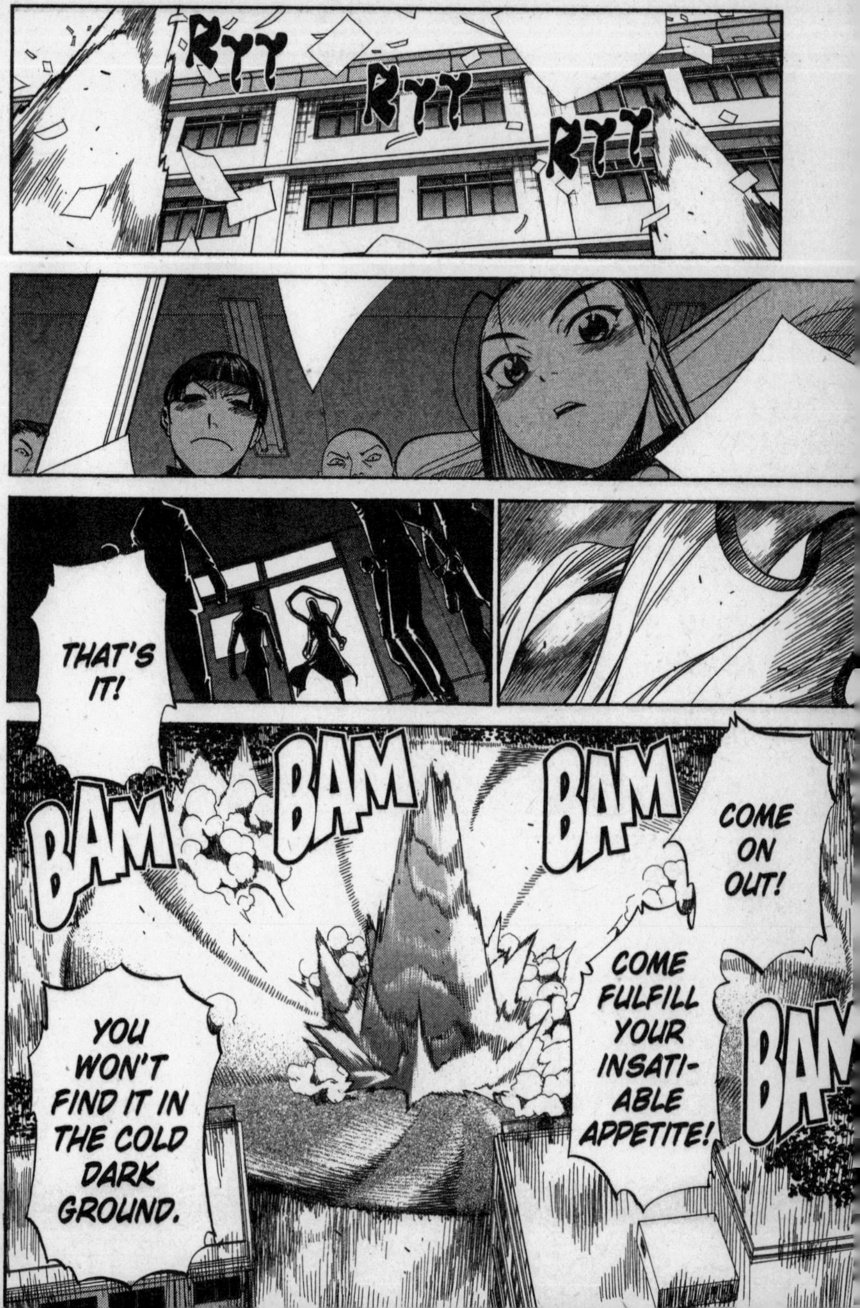
RYY
RYY
RYY
THAT'S IT!
COME ON OUT!
COME FULFILL YOUR INSATI-ABLE APPETITE!
BAM
BAM
BAM
YOU WON'T FIND IT IN THE COLD DARK GROUND.

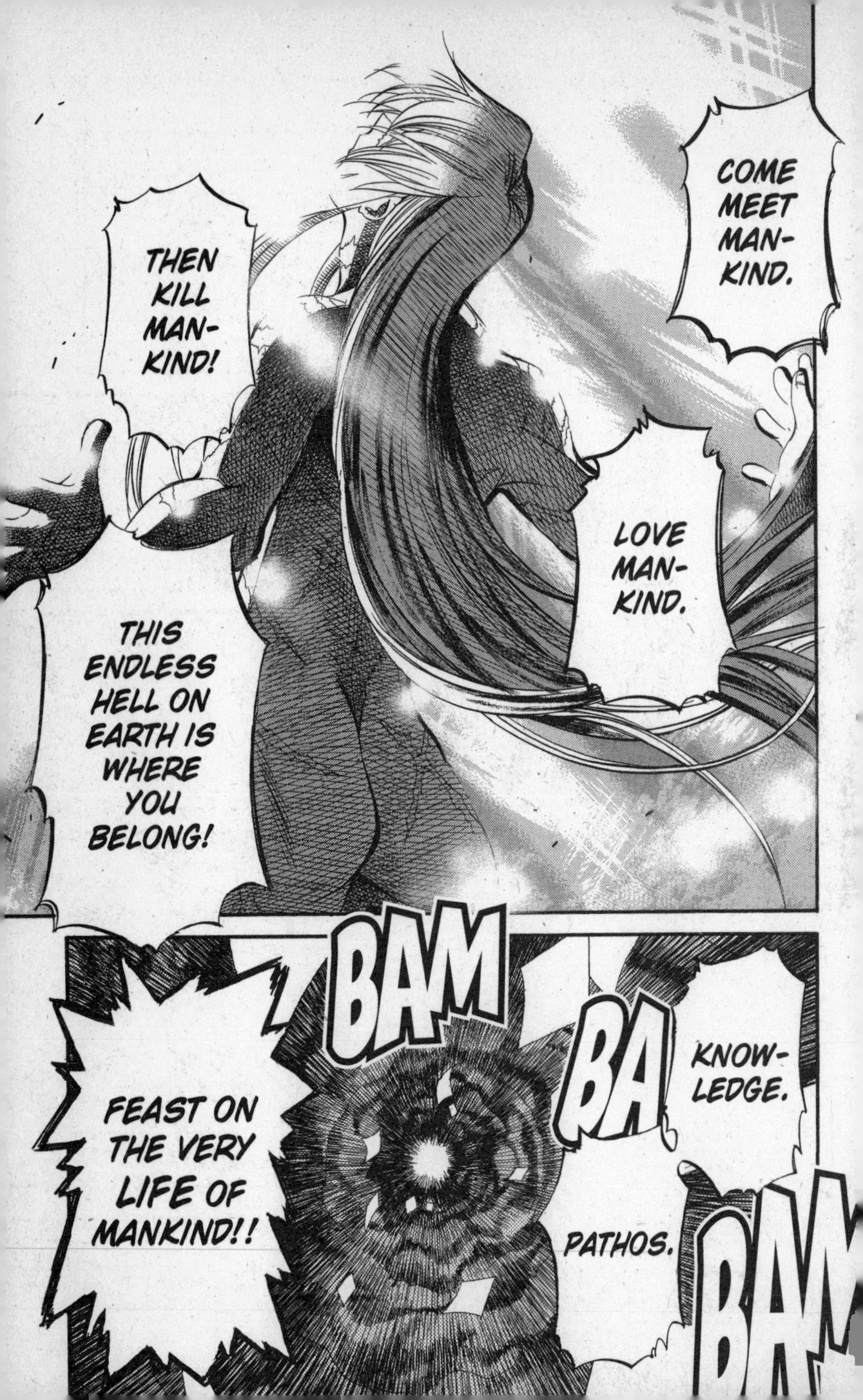

COME MEET MAN-KIND.
LOVE MAN-KIND.
THEN KILL MAN-KIND!
THIS ENDLESS HELL ON EARTH IS WHERE YOU BELONG!
KNOW-LEDGE.
BA
BAM
PATHOS.
BAM
FEAST ON THE VERY LIFE OF MANKIND!!

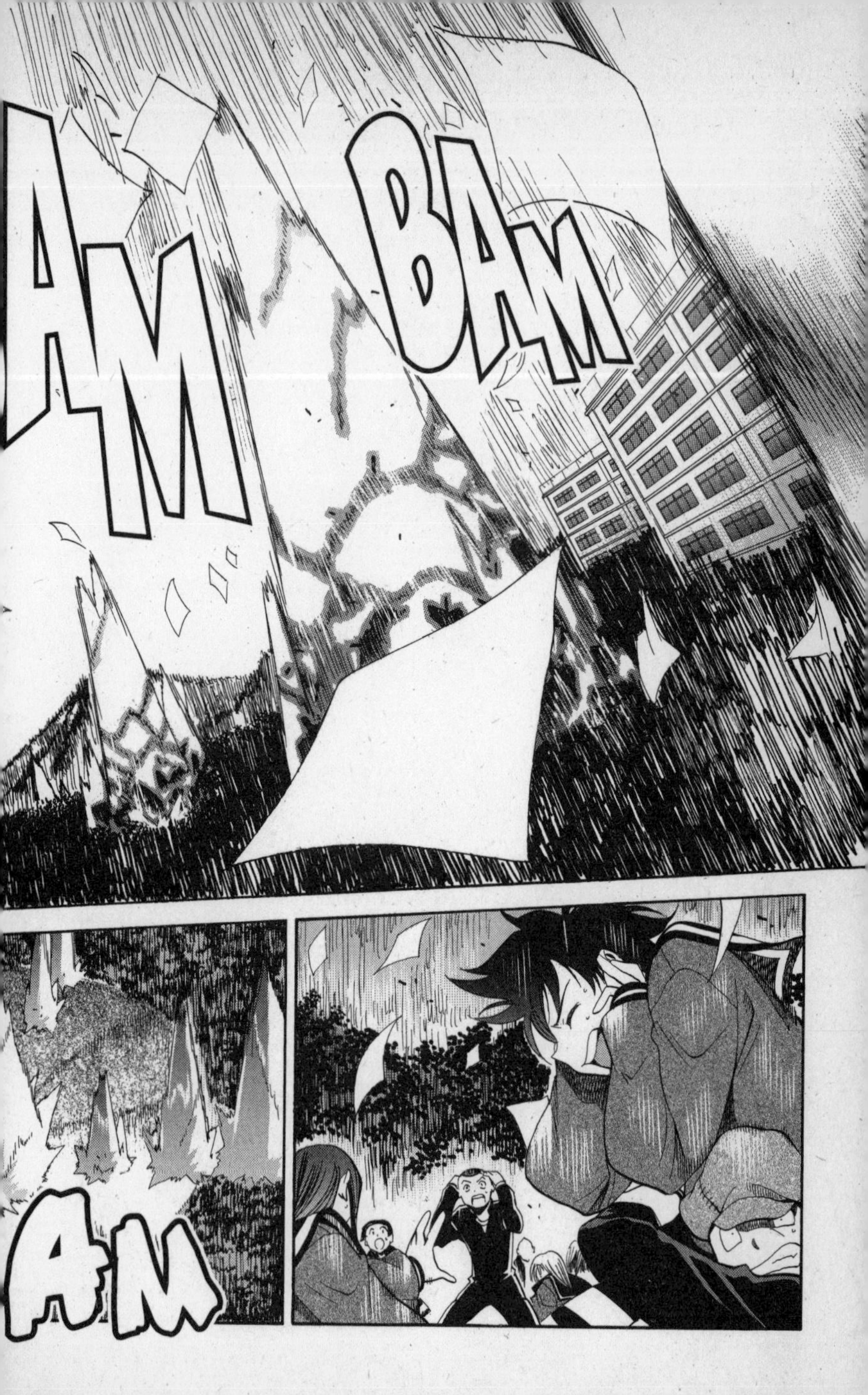
BAM
AM
AM

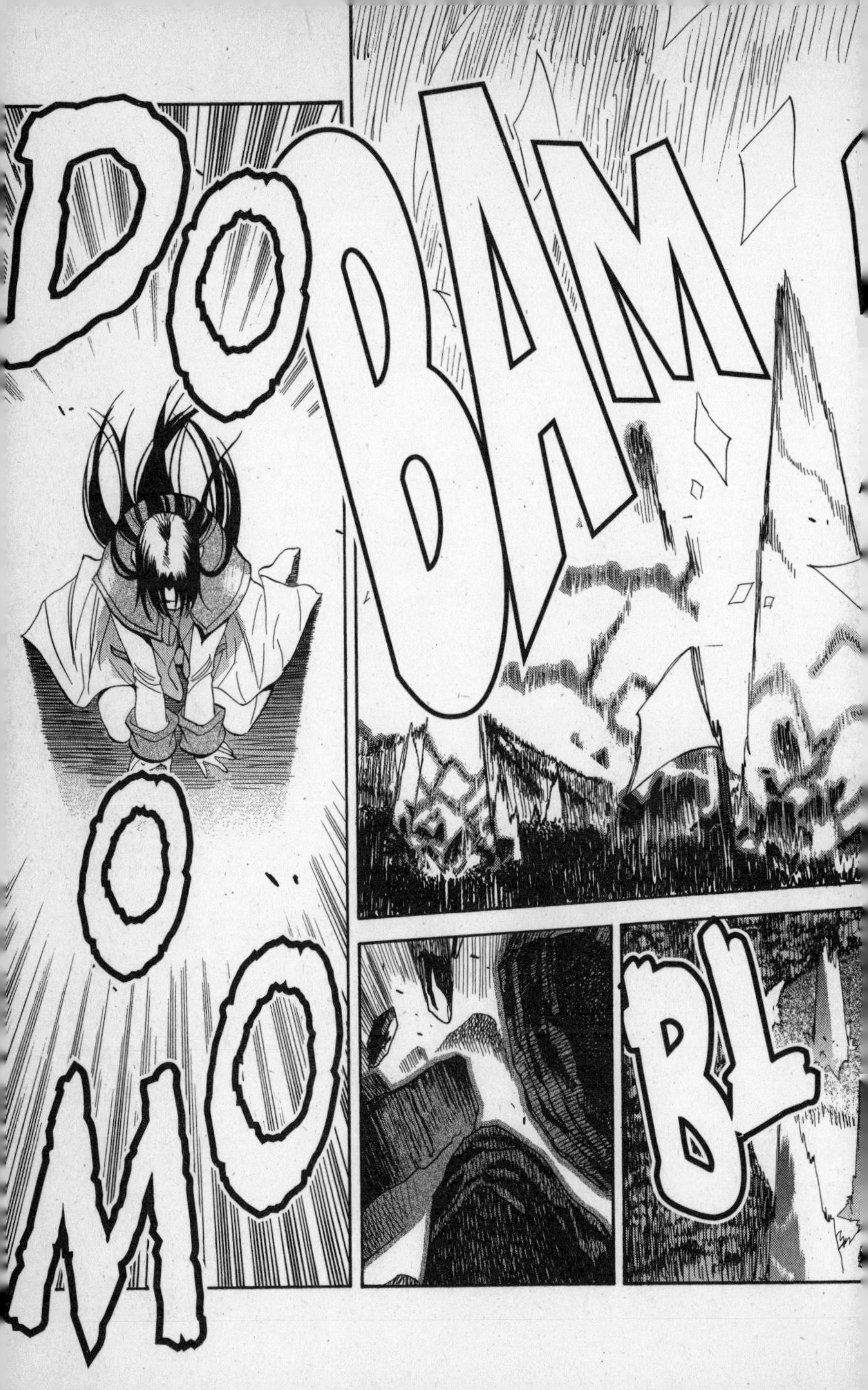
BAM
BL
DOOOM

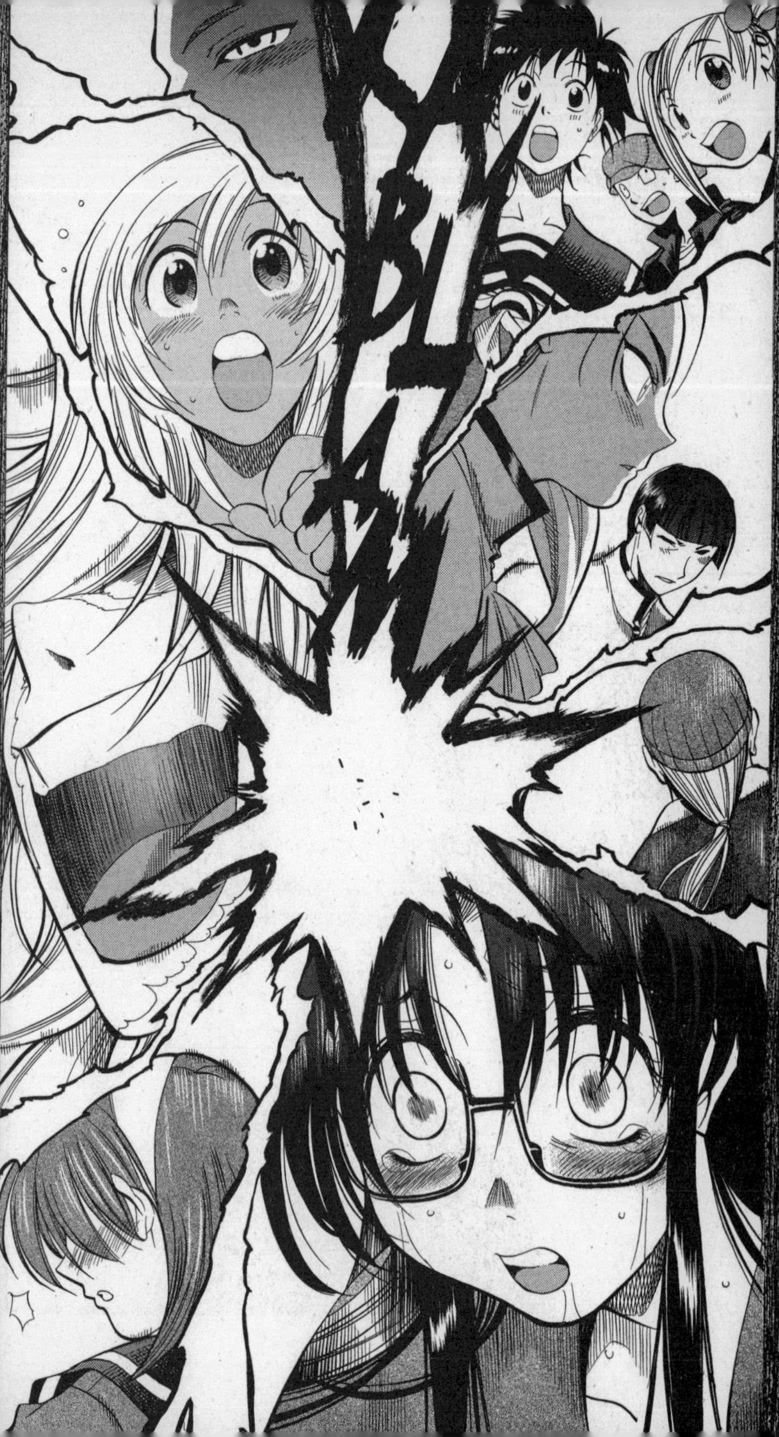
KBLAM

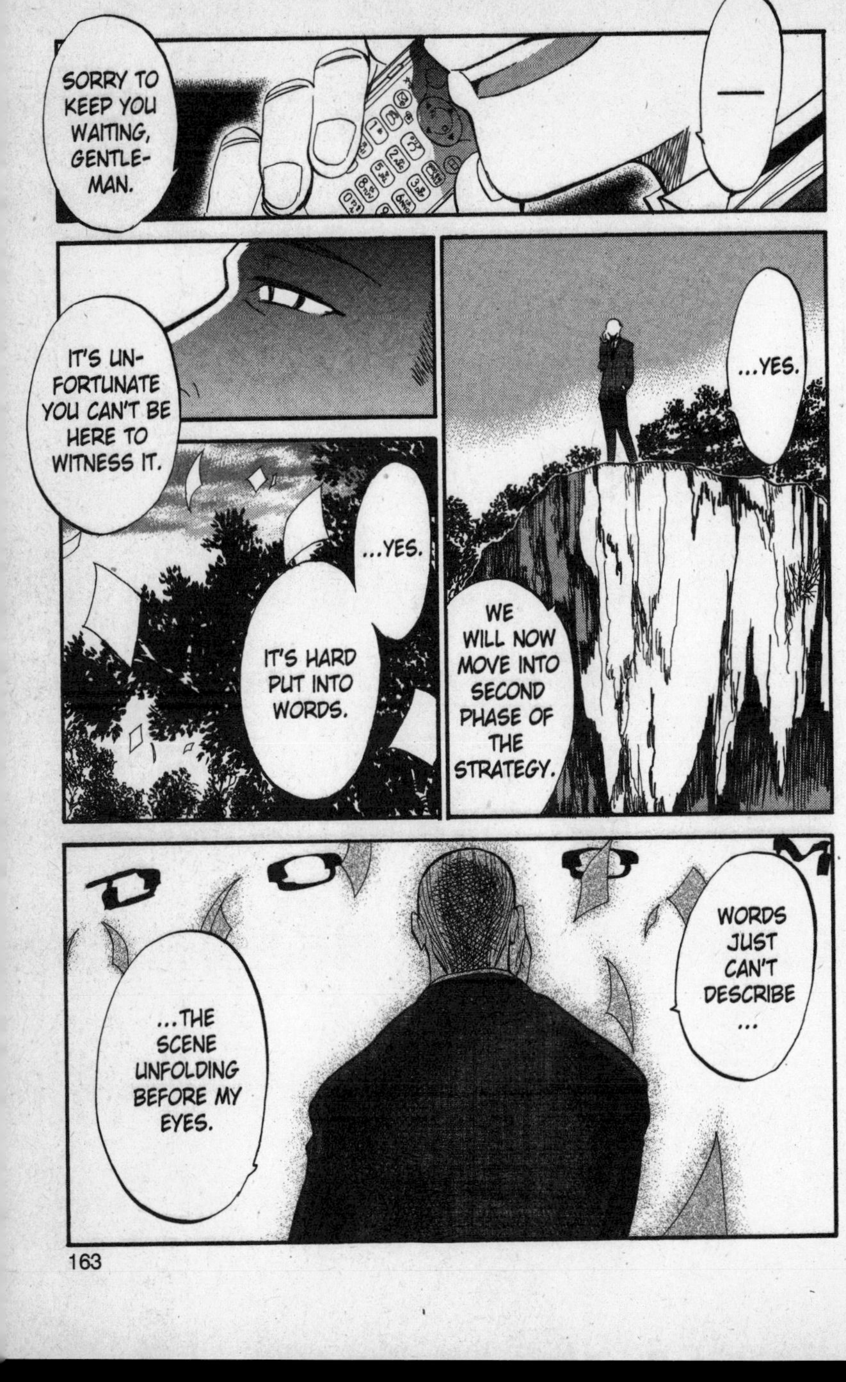
—
SORRY TO KEEP YOU WAITING, GENTLE-MAN.
...YES.
WE WILL NOW MOVE INTO SECOND PHASE OF THE STRATEGY.
IT'S UN-FORTUNATE YOU CAN'T BE HERE TO WITNESS IT.
...YES.
IT'S HARD PUT INTO WORDS.
WORDS JUST CAN'T DESCRIBE ...
...THE SCENE UNFOLDING BEFORE MY EYES.

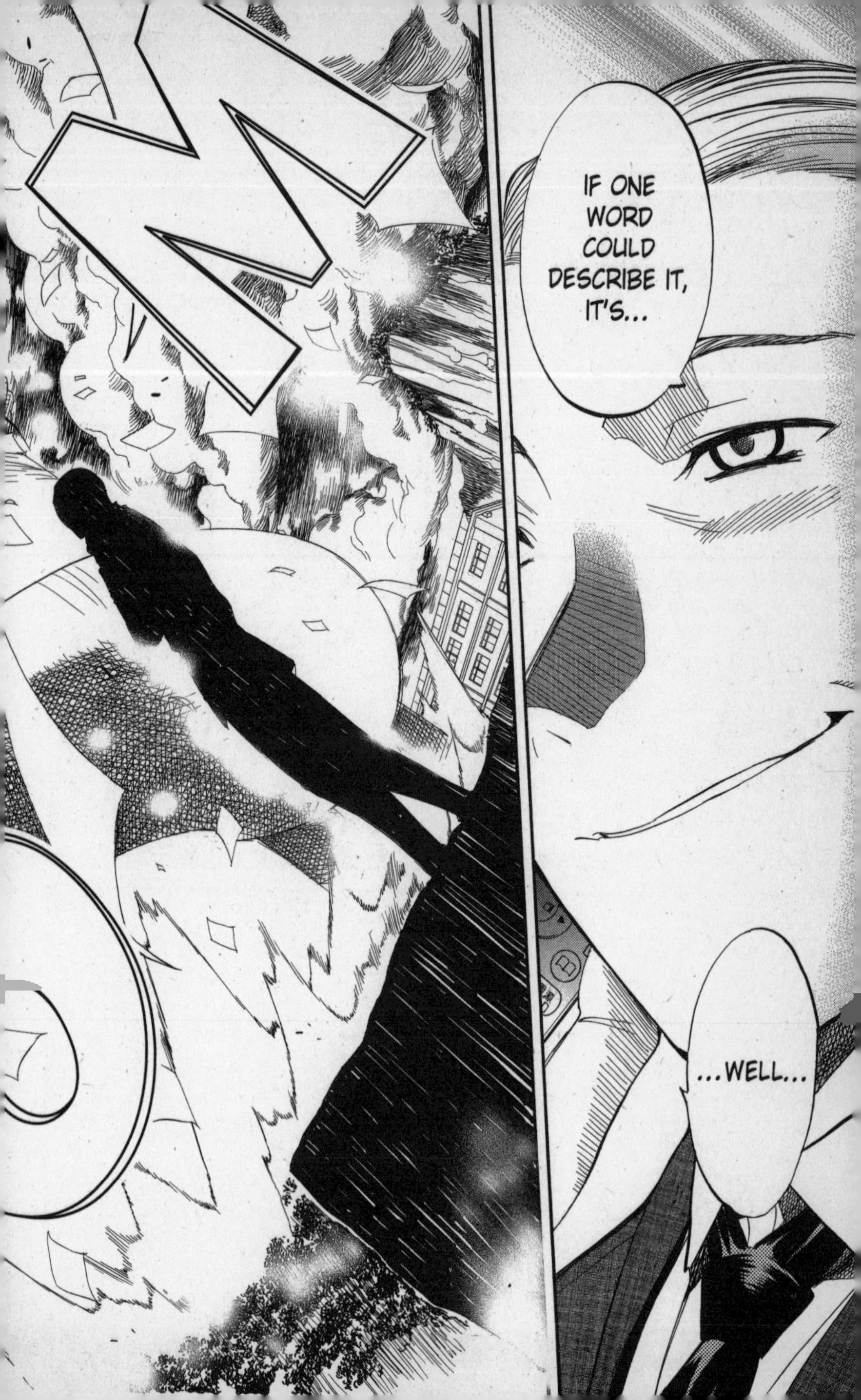
IF ONE WORD COULD DESCRIBE IT, IT'S...
...WELL...

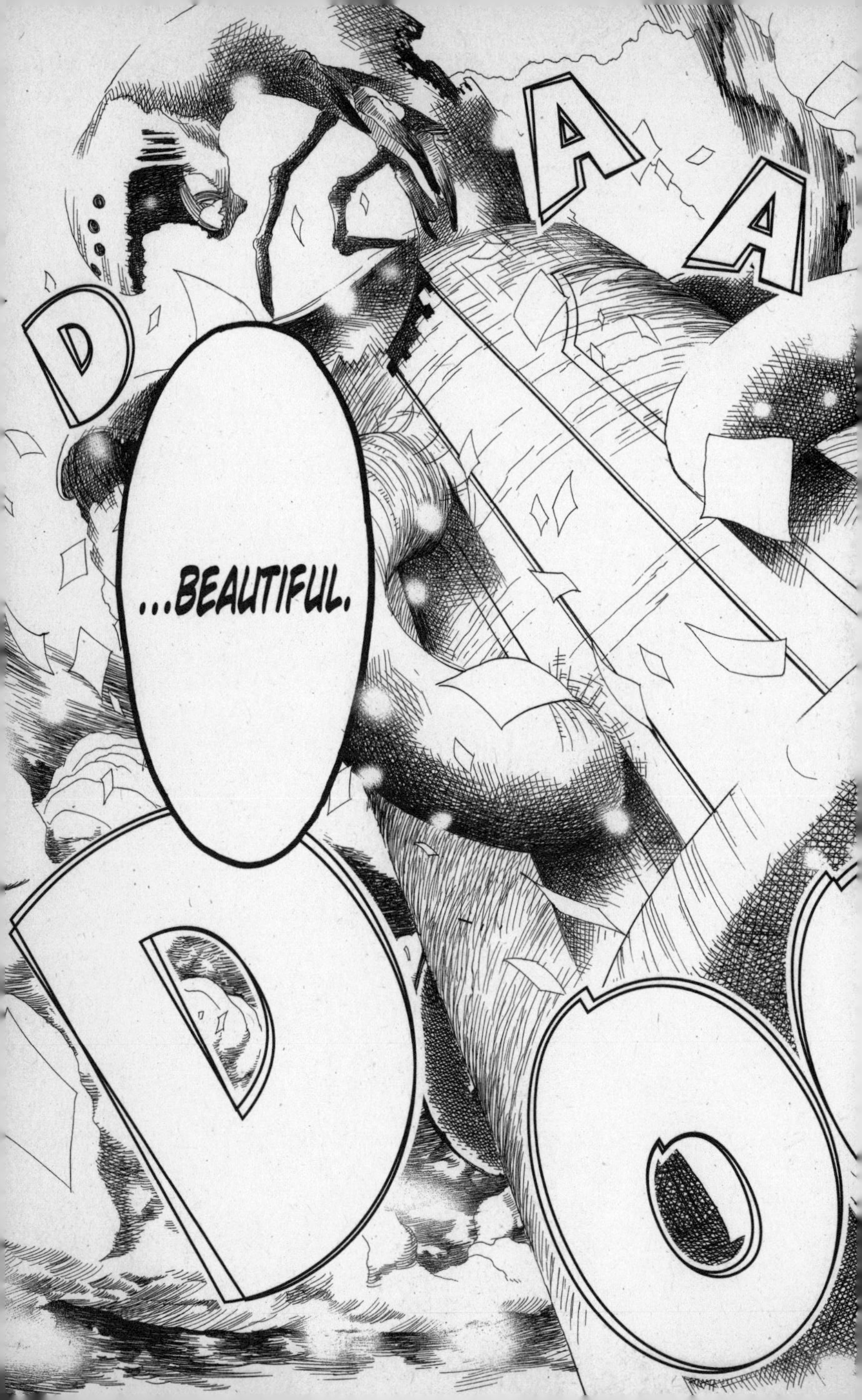
DAA
...BEAUTIFUL.
DO

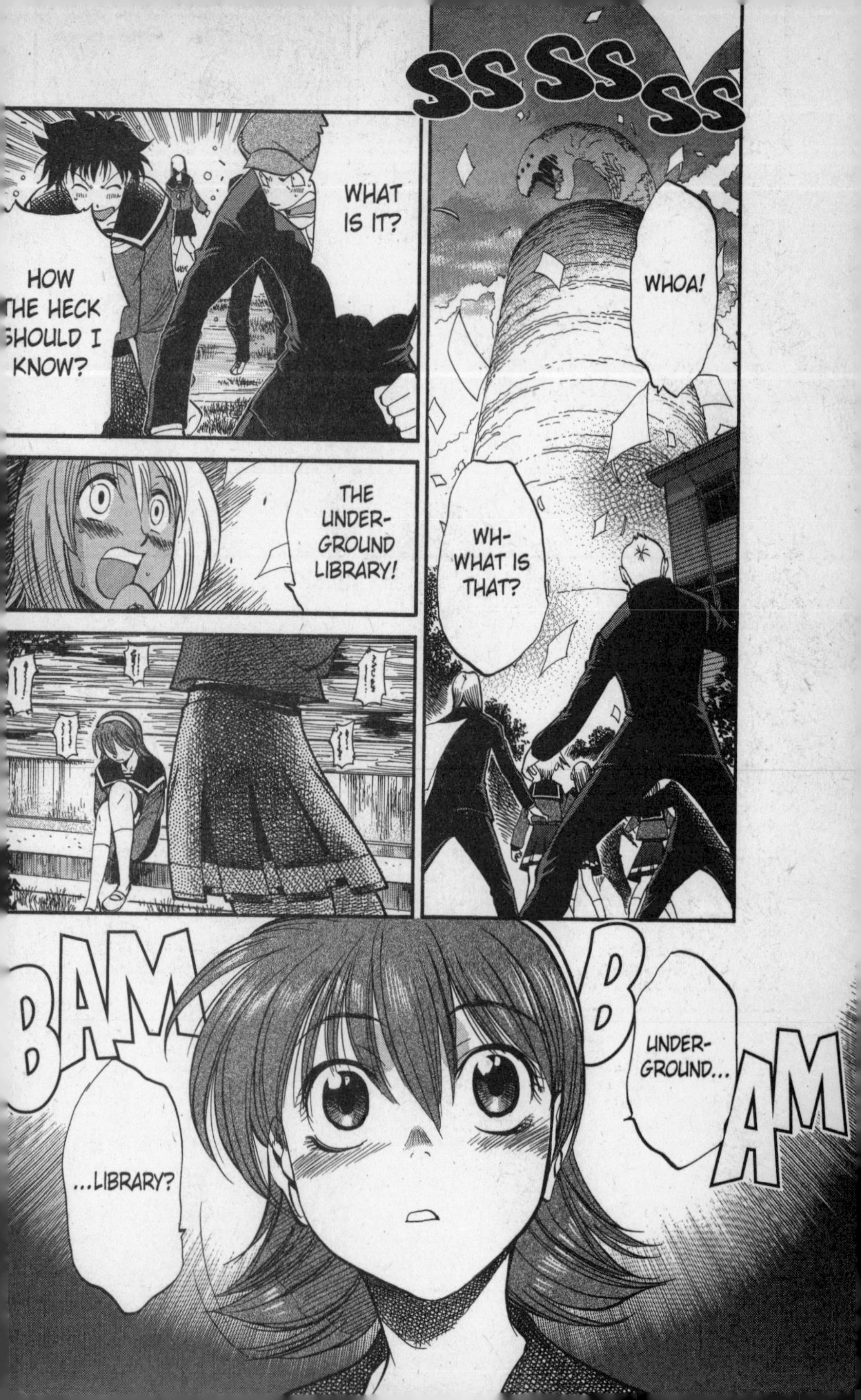
SSSSS
WHOA!
WH-WHAT IS THAT?
WHAT IS IT?
HOW THE HECK SHOULD I KNOW?
THE UNDERGROUND LIBRARY!
BAM
UNDERGROUND...
BAM
...LIBRARY?

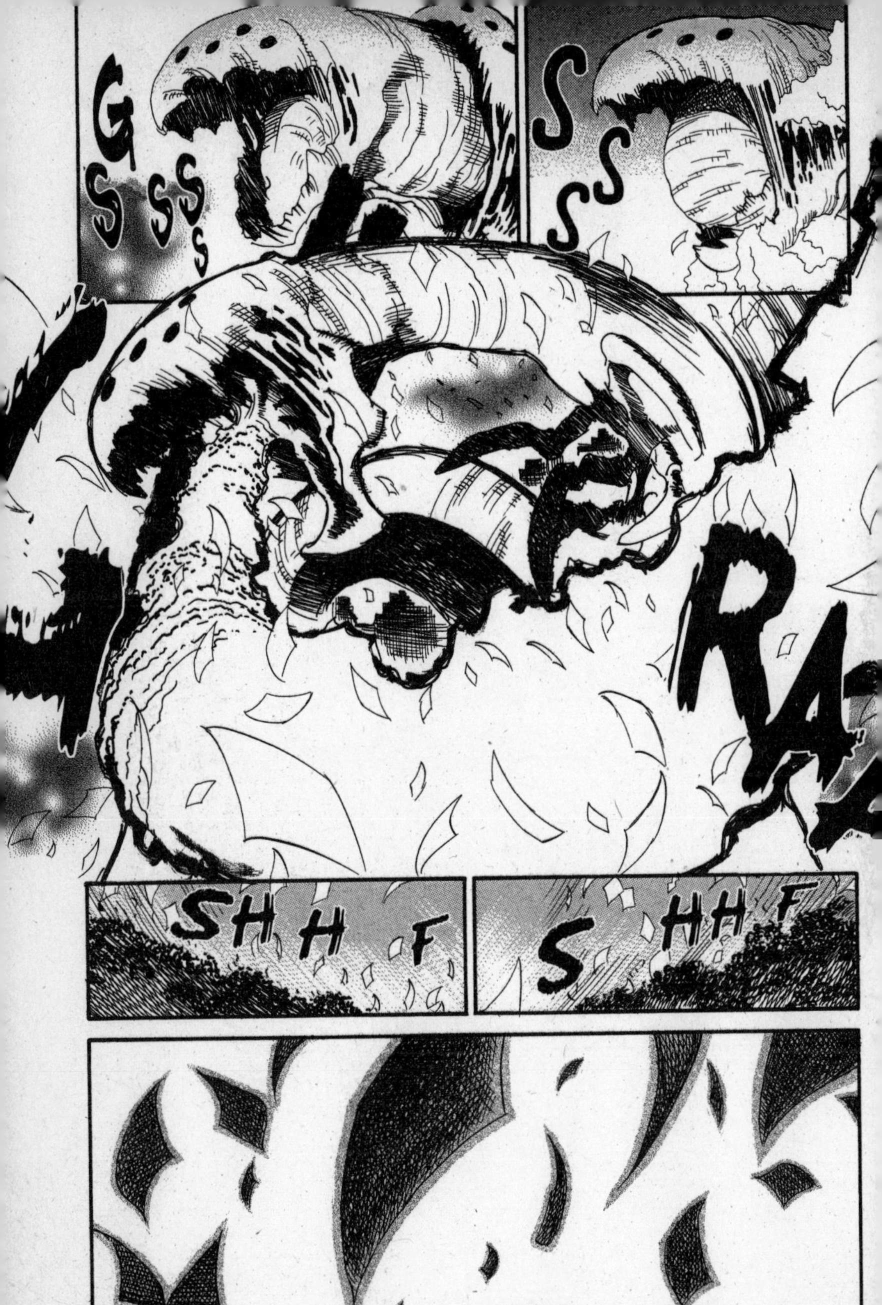
SSSS
GSSSS
RA
SHHF
SHHF

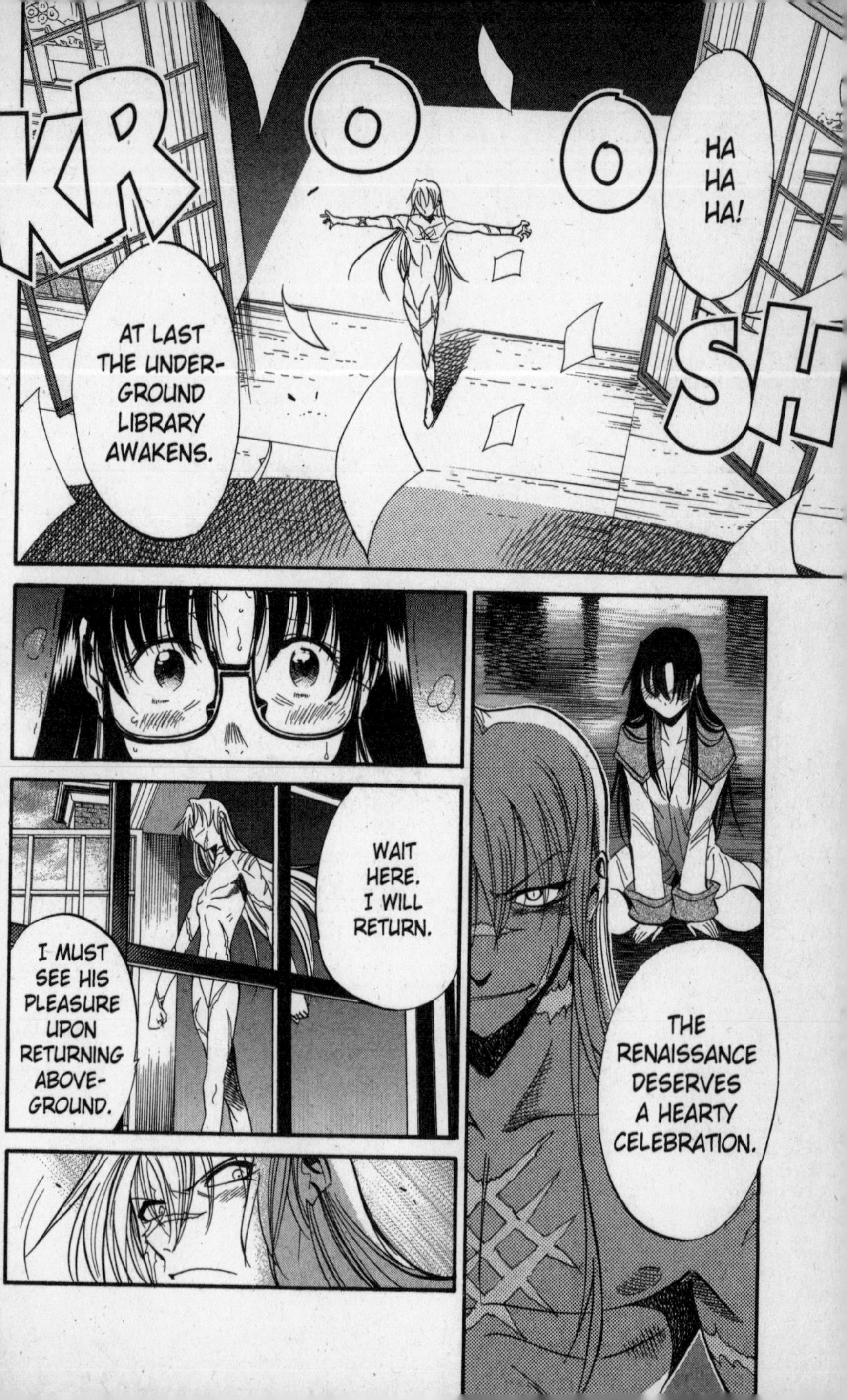
KROOOSH
HA HA HA!
AT LAST THE UNDER-GROUND LIBRARY AWAKENS.
THE RENAISSANCE DESERVES A HEARTY CELEBRATION.
WAIT HERE. I WILL RETURN.
I MUST SEE HIS PLEASURE UPON RETURNING ABOVE-GROUND.

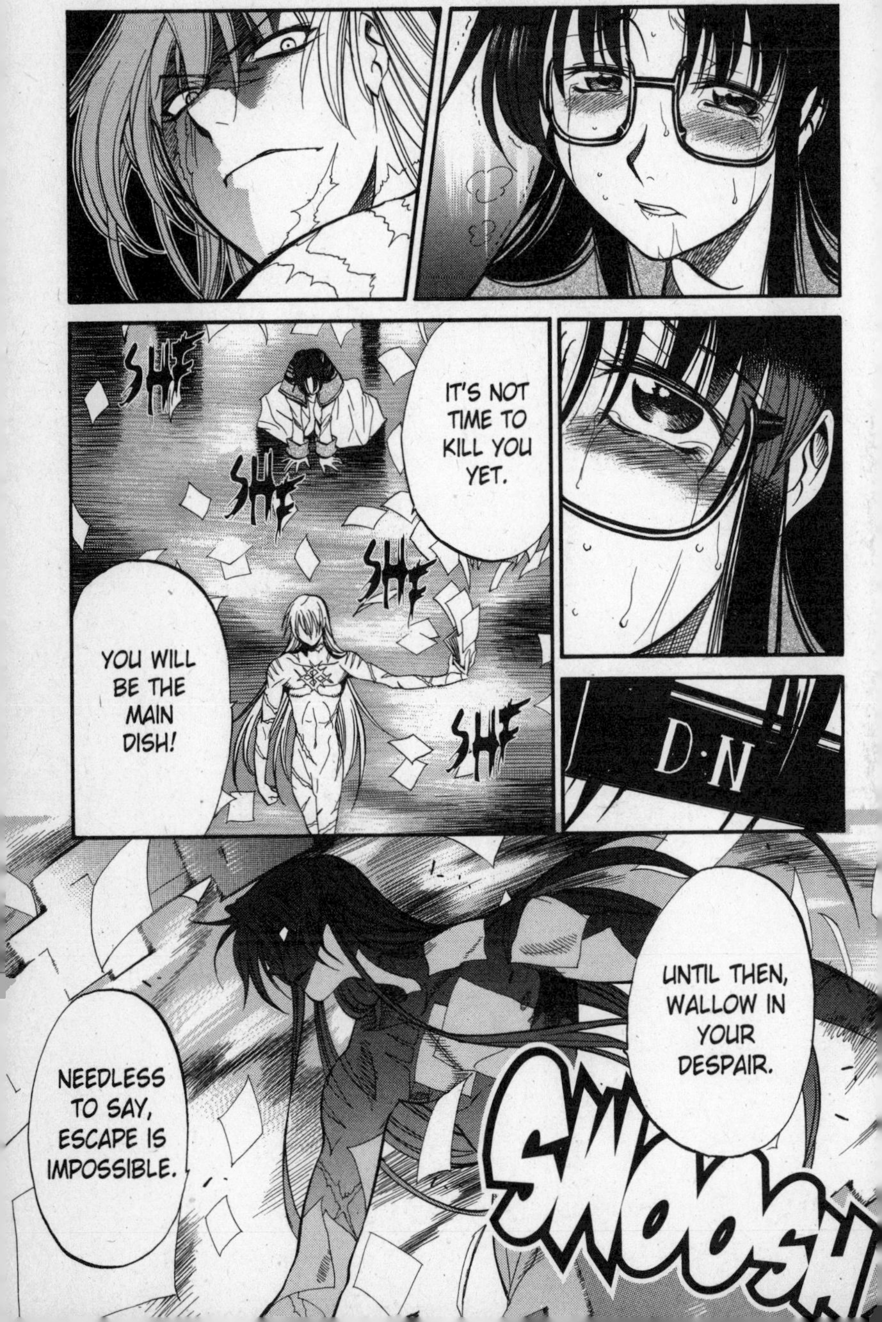
D·N
IT'S NOT TIME TO KILL YOU YET.
SHF
SHF
SHF
SHF
YOU WILL BE THE MAIN DISH!
UNTIL THEN, WALLOW IN YOUR DESPAIR.
NEEDLESS TO SAY, ESCAPE IS IMPOSSIBLE.
SHOOSH

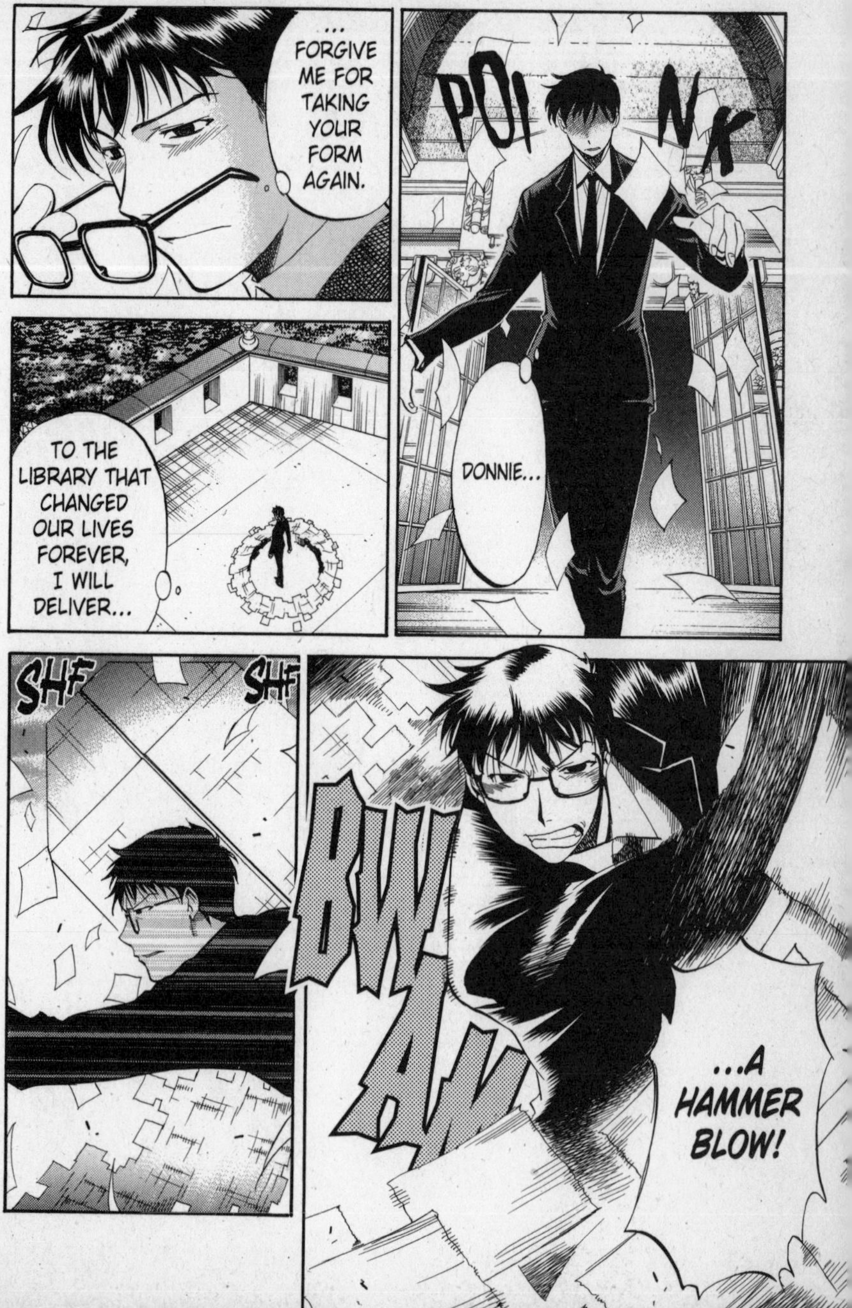
POINK
DONNIE...
... FORGIVE ME FOR TAKING YOUR FORM AGAIN.
TO THE LIBRARY THAT CHANGED OUR LIVES FOREVER, I WILL DELIVER...
BWAAM
...A HAMMER BLOW!
SHF
SHF

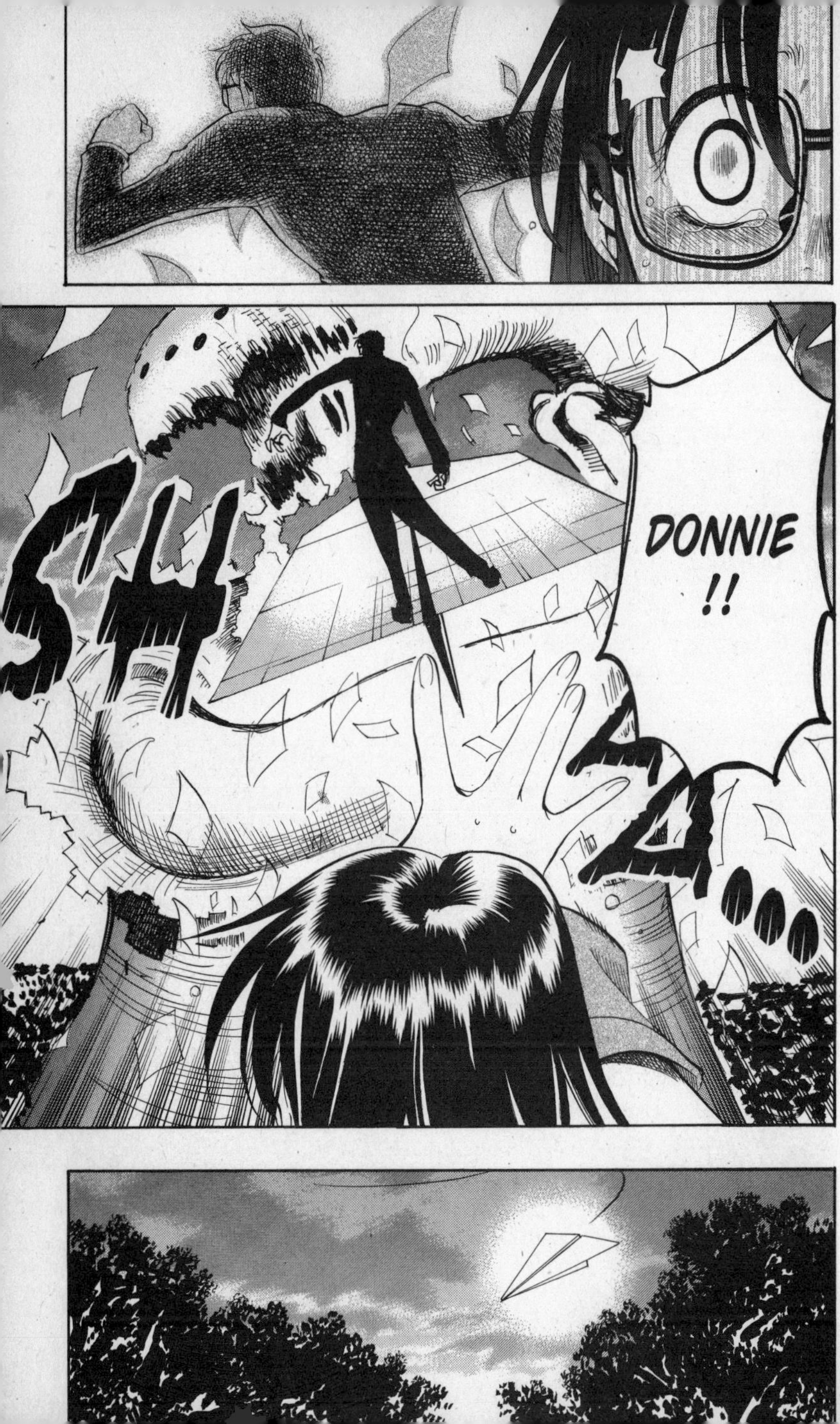
DONNIE !!

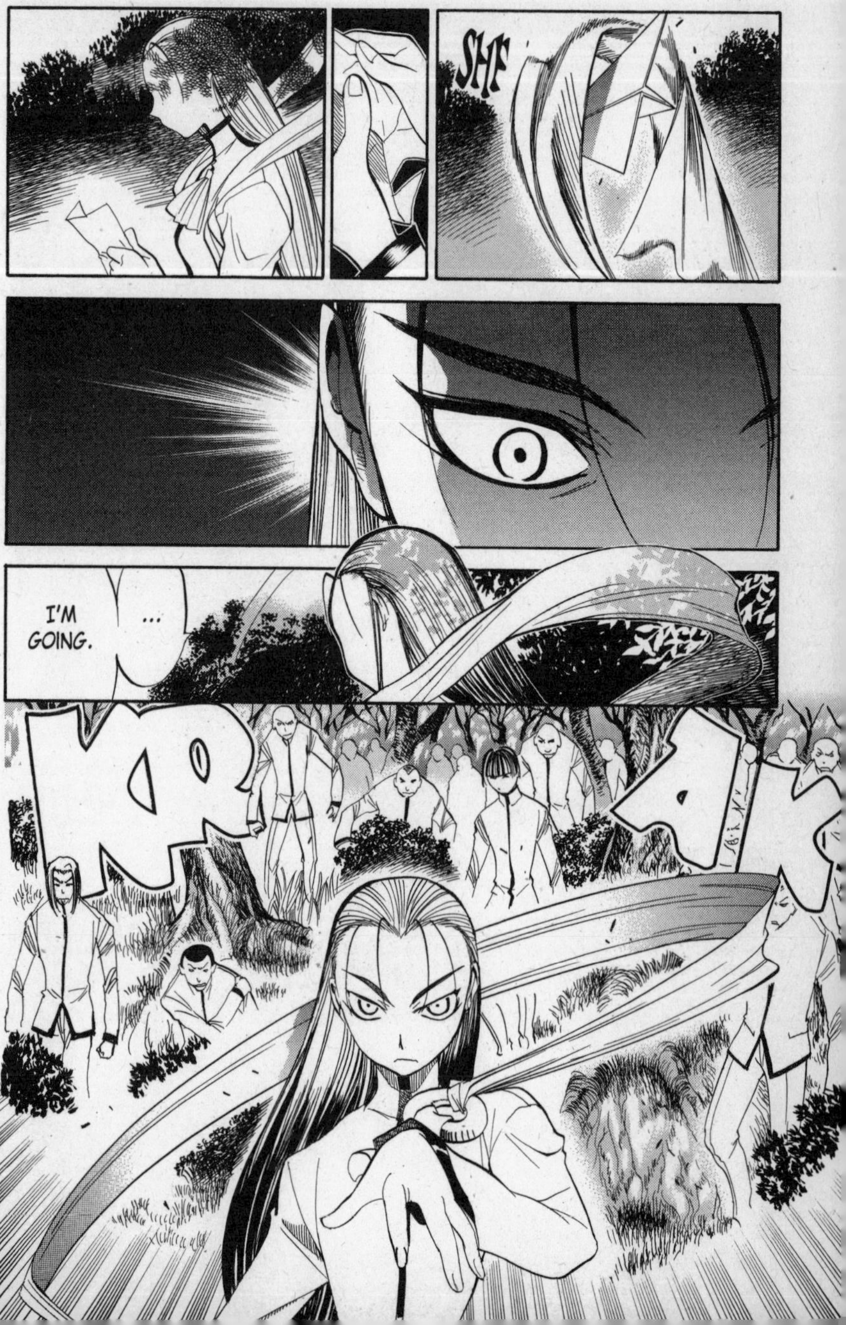
SHF
...
I'M GOING.

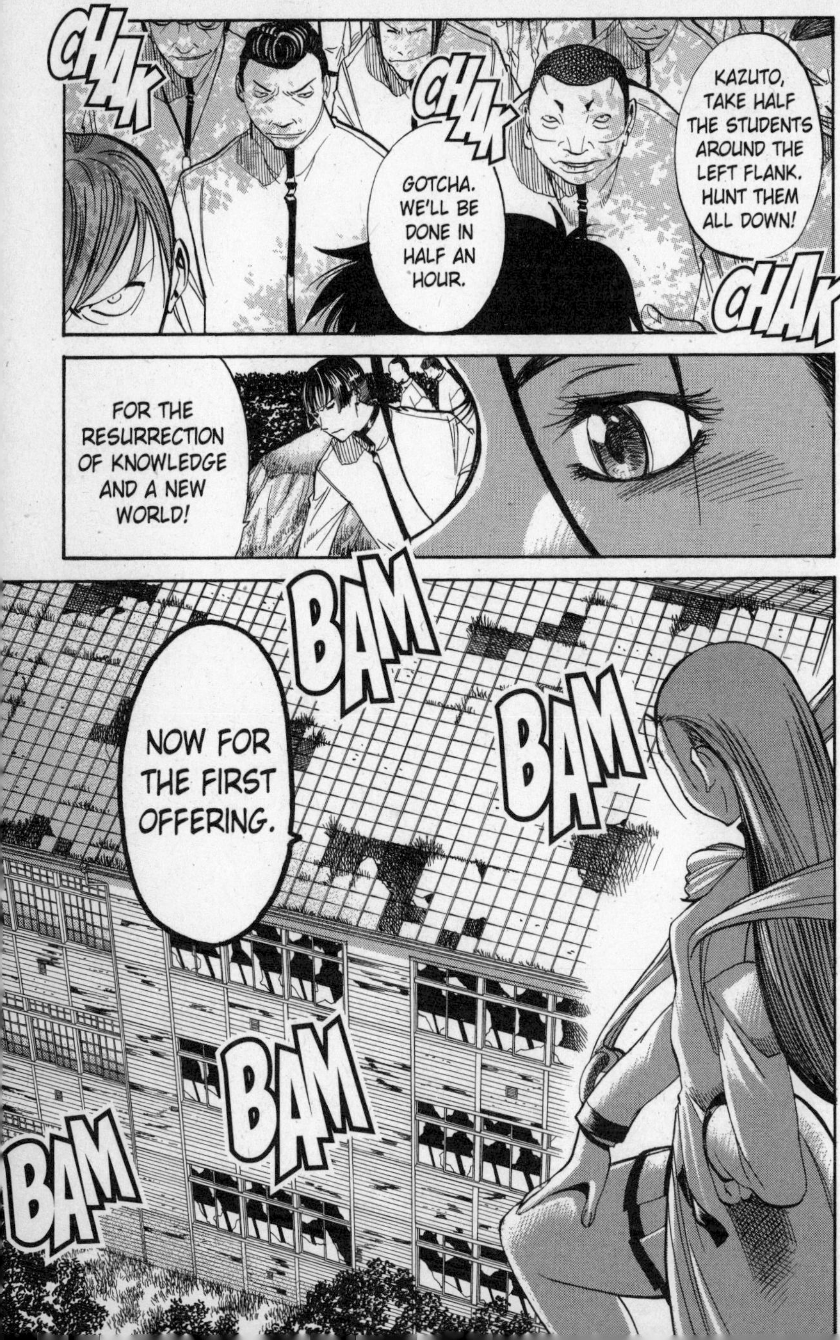
KAZUTO, TAKE HALF THE STUDENTS AROUND THE LEFT FLANK. HUNT THEM ALL DOWN!
CHAK
CHAK
GOTCHA. WE'LL BE DONE IN HALF AN HOUR.
CHAK
FOR THE RESURRECTION OF KNOWLEDGE AND A NEW WORLD!
BAM
BAM
NOW FOR THE FIRST OFFERING.
BAM
BAM

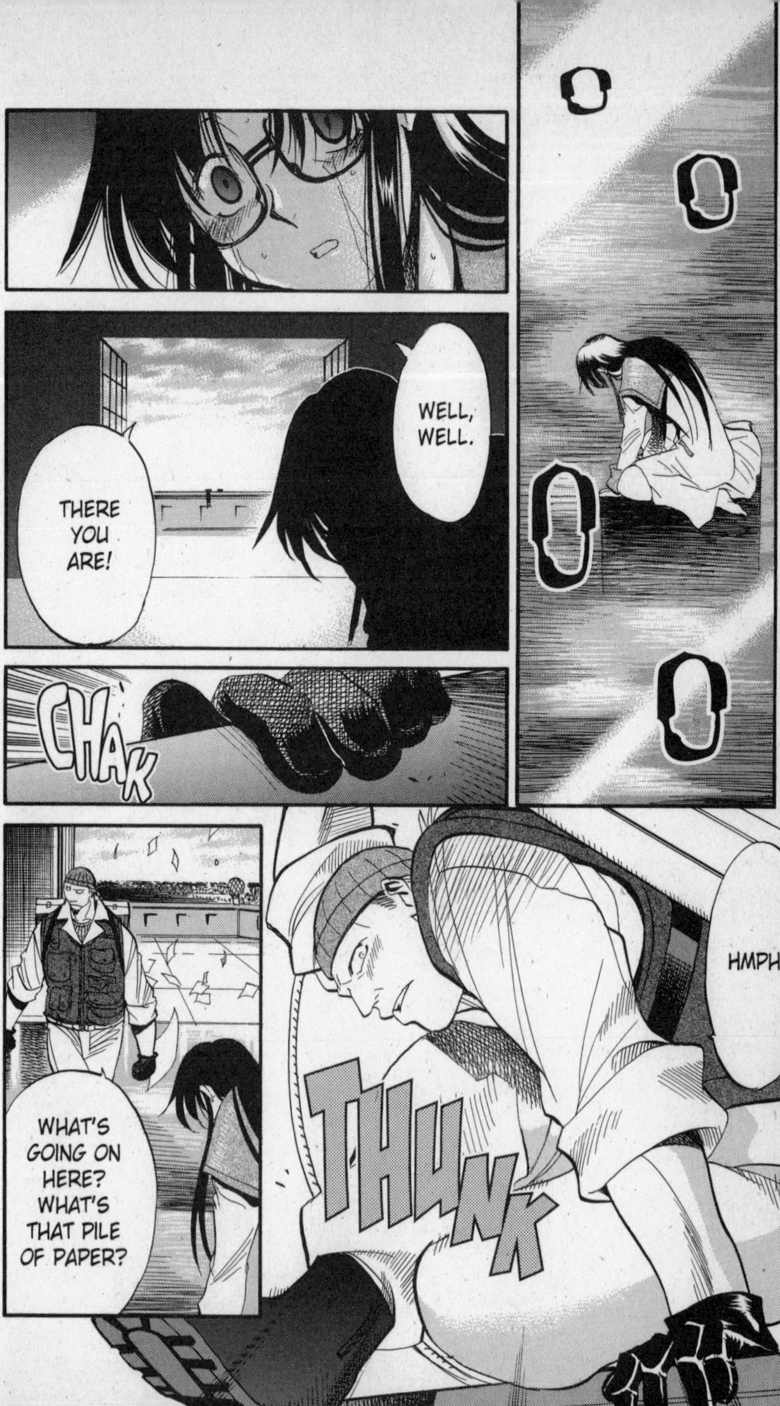
OOOO
WELL, WELL.
THERE YOU ARE!
CHAK
HMPH.
THUNK
WHAT'S GOING ON HERE? WHAT'S THAT PILE OF PAPER?

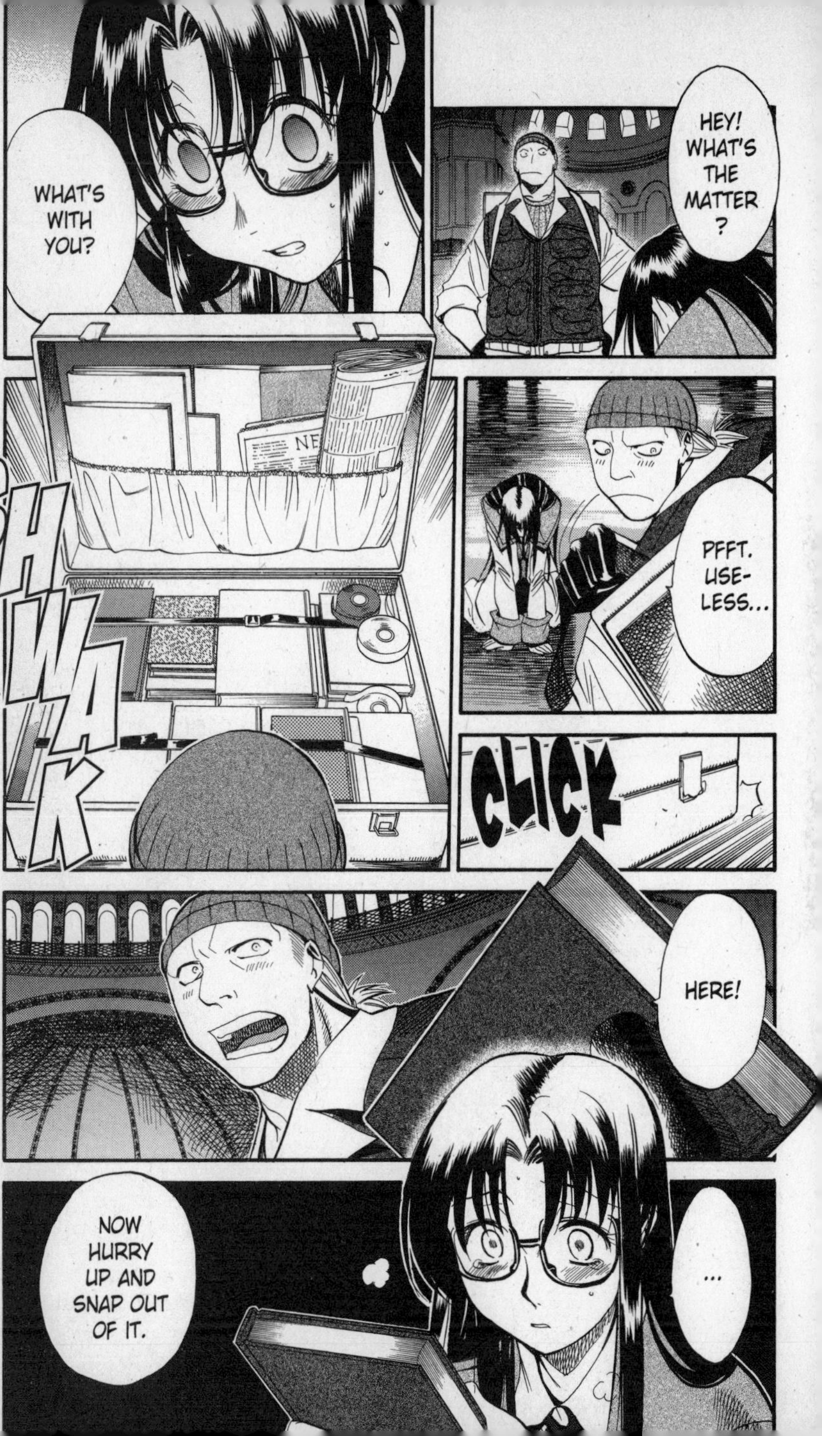
HEY! WHAT'S THE MATTER?
WHAT'S WITH YOU?
PFFT. USE-LESS...
CLICK
SHWAK
HERE!
...
NOW HURRY UP AND SNAP OUT OF IT.

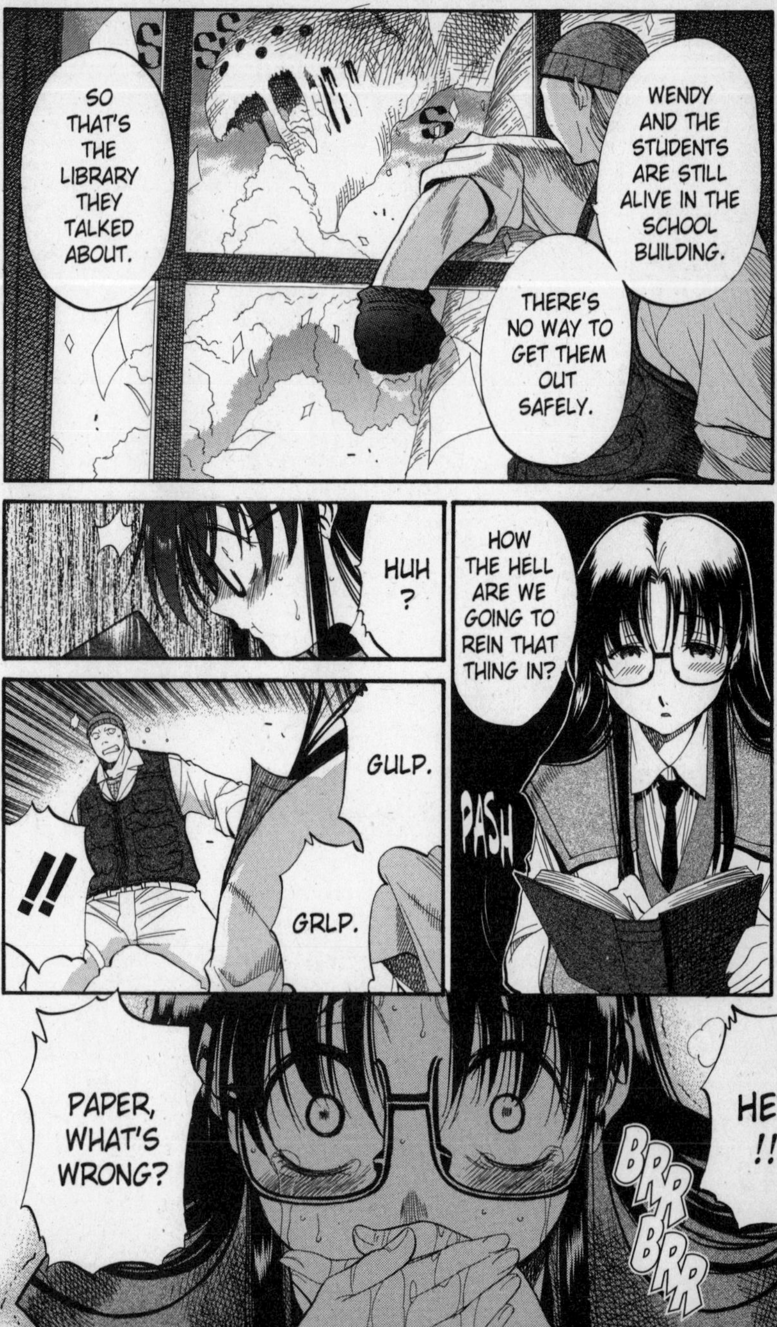
WENDY AND THE STUDENTS ARE STILL ALIVE IN THE SCHOOL BUILDING.
THERE'S NO WAY TO GET THEM OUT SAFELY.
SO THAT'S THE LIBRARY THEY TALKED ABOUT.
HOW THE HELL ARE WE GOING TO REIN THAT THING IN?
PASH
HUH?
GULP.
GRLP.
!!
HEY!!
BRRR BRRR
PAPER, WHAT'S WRONG?

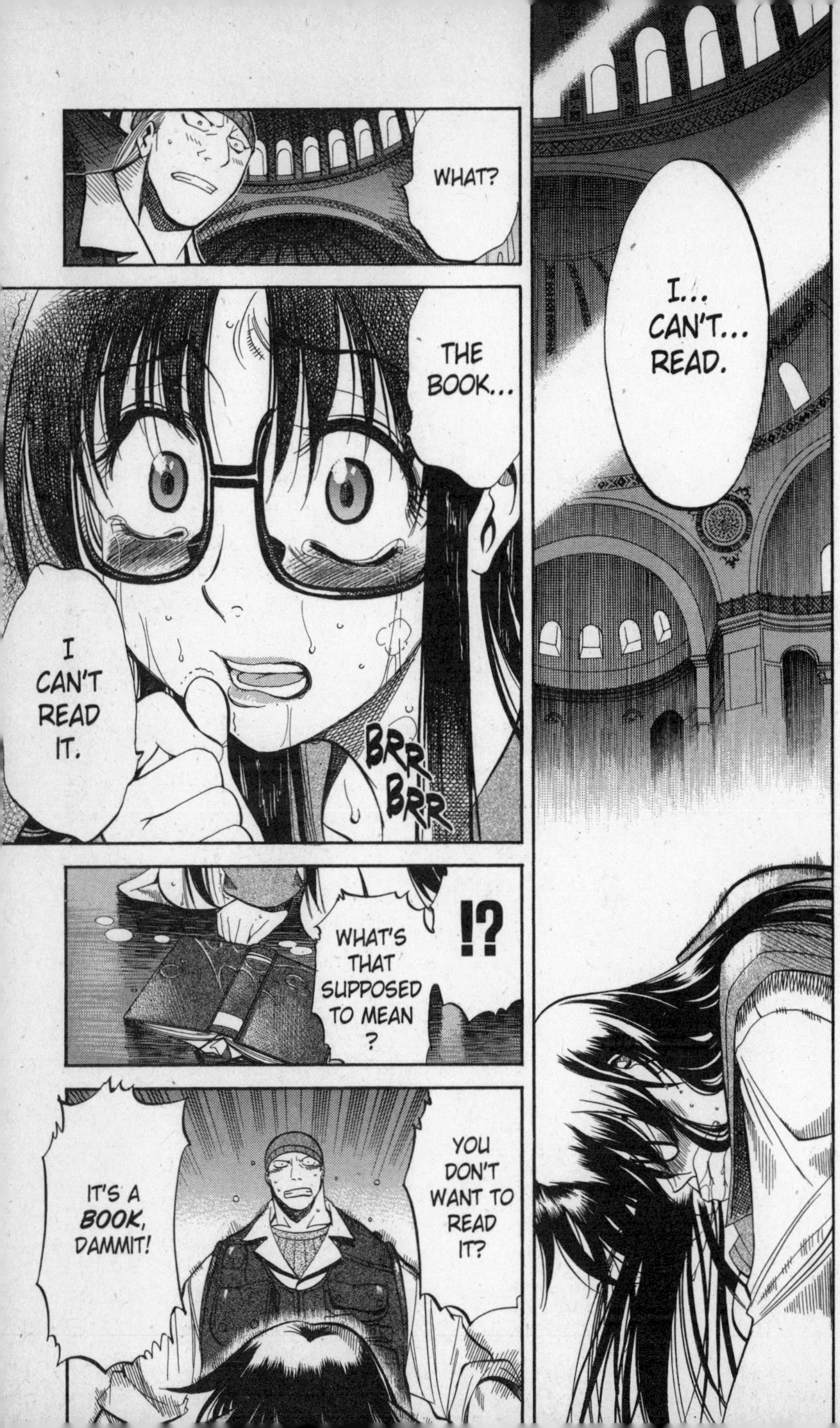
I... CAN'T... READ.
WHAT?
THE BOOK...
I CAN'T READ IT.
BRR BRR
!?
WHAT'S THAT SUPPOSED TO MEAN?
YOU DON'T WANT TO READ IT?
IT'S A *BOOK*, DAMMIT!

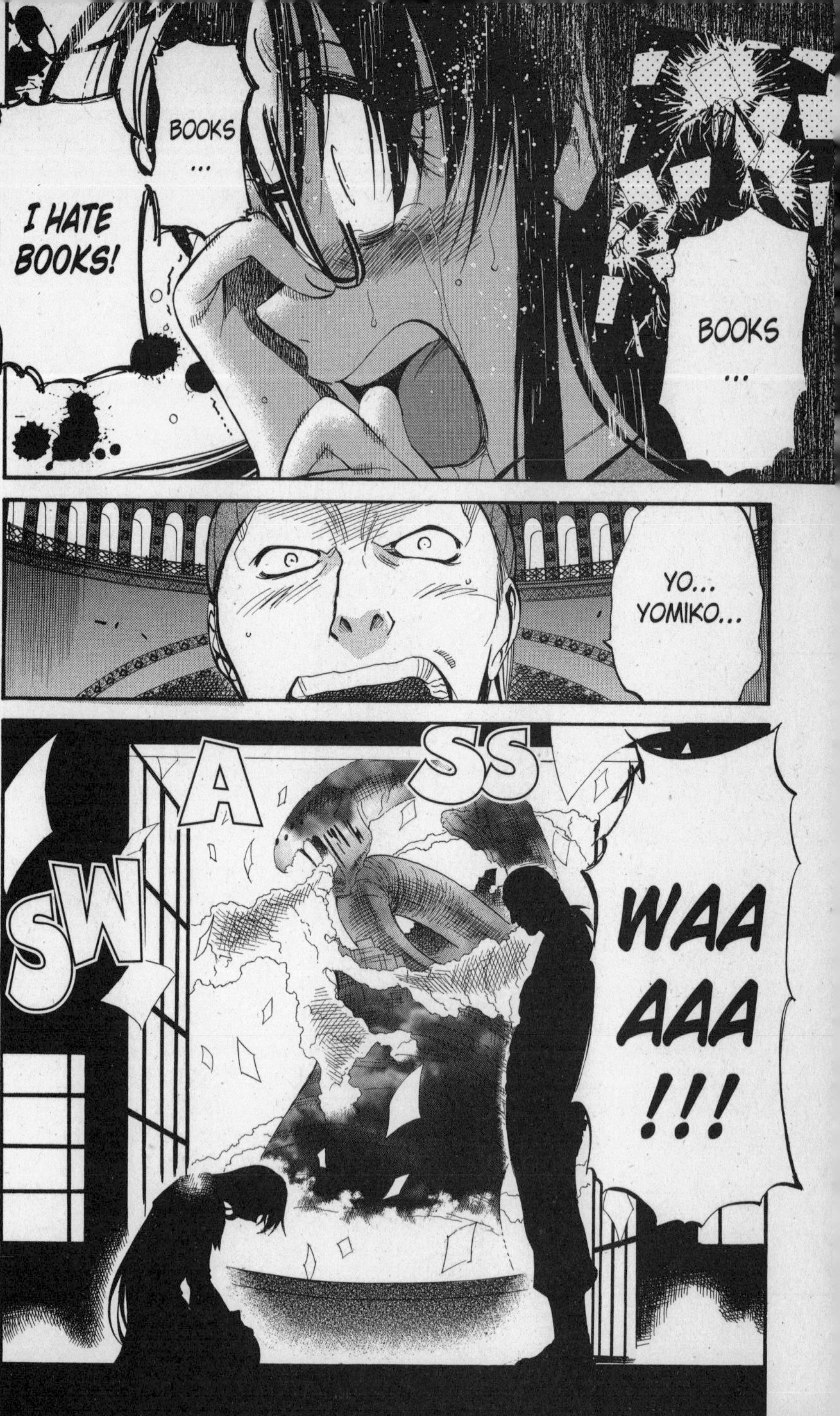
BOOKS ...
BOOKS ...
I HATE BOOKS!
YO... YOMIKO...
WAAAAAA!!!
SWASS

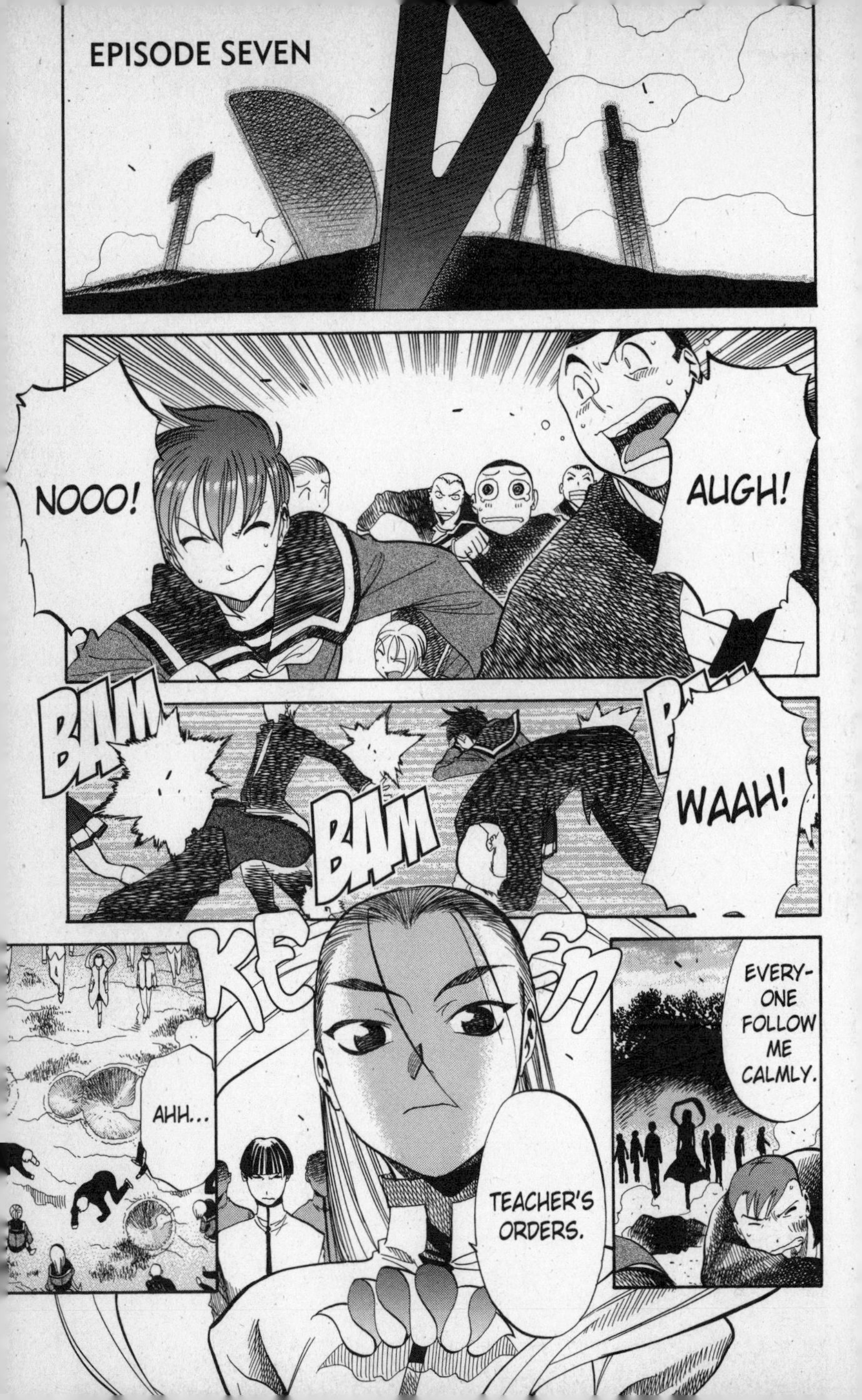
EPISODE SEVEN
AUGH!
NOOO!
WAAH!
BAM
BAM
EVERY-ONE FOLLOW ME CALMLY.
TEACHER'S ORDERS.
AHH...

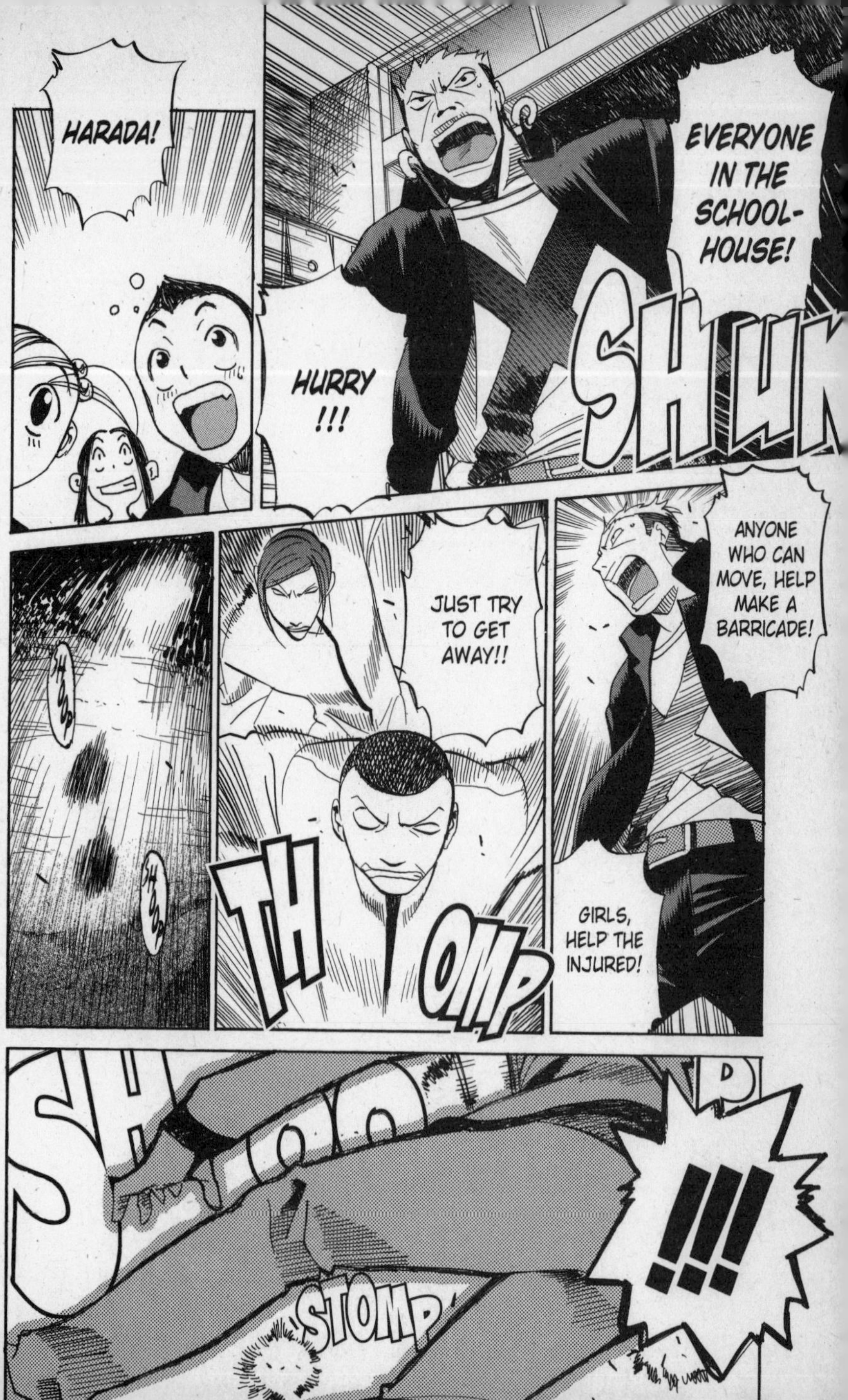
EVERYONE IN THE SCHOOL-HOUSE!
SHUNK
HURRY!!!
HARADA!
ANYONE WHO CAN MOVE, HELP MAKE A BARRICADE!
GIRLS, HELP THE INJURED!
JUST TRY TO GET AWAY!!
THOMP
SHOOP
SHOOP
!!!
STOMP

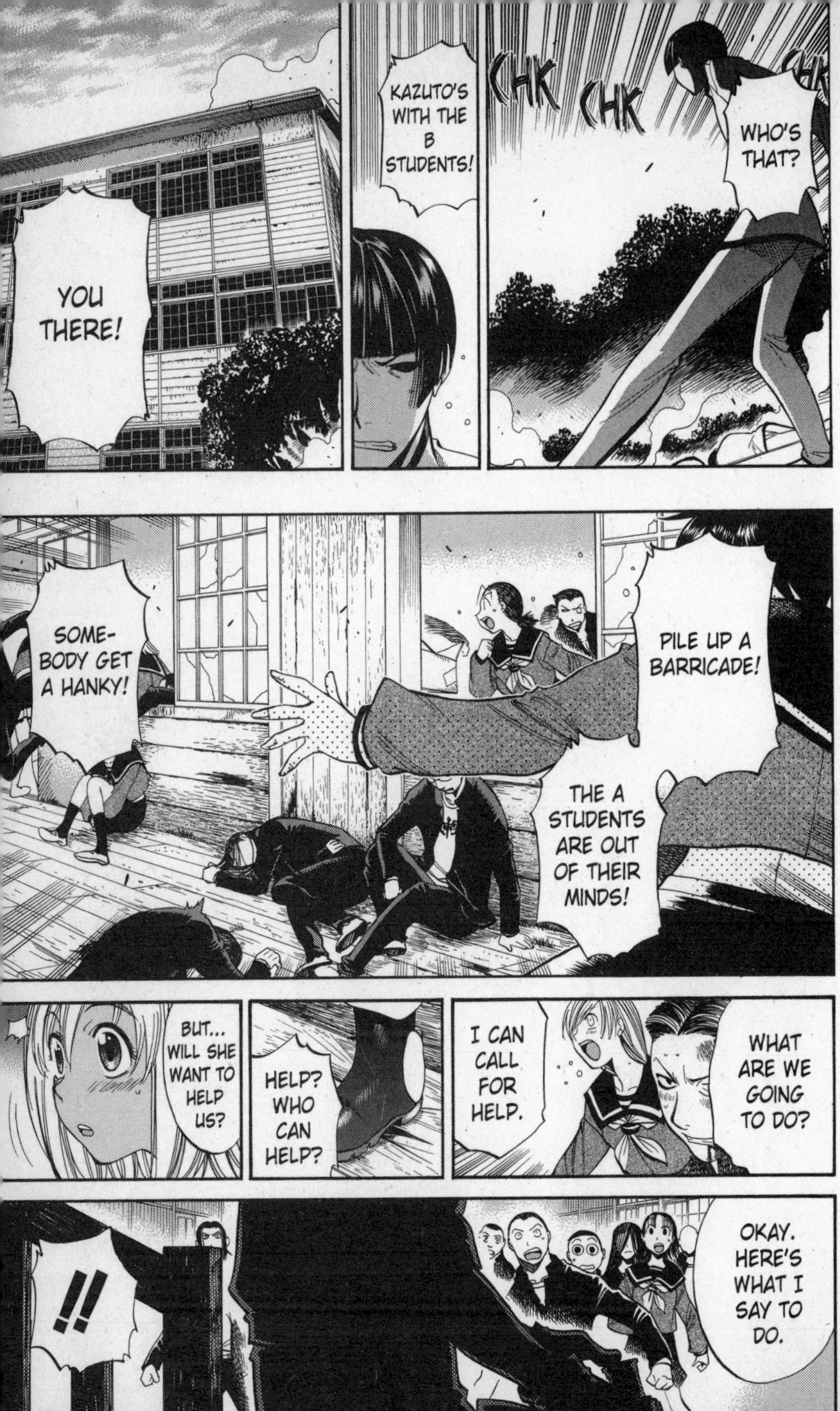
CHK CHK CHK
WHO'S THAT?
KAZUTO'S WITH THE B STUDENTS!
YOU THERE!
PILE UP A BARRICADE!
THE A STUDENTS ARE OUT OF THEIR MINDS!
SOME-BODY GET A HANKY!
WHAT ARE WE GOING TO DO?
I CAN CALL FOR HELP.
HELP? WHO CAN HELP?
BUT... WILL SHE WANT TO HELP US?
OKAY. HERE'S WHAT I SAY TO DO.
!!

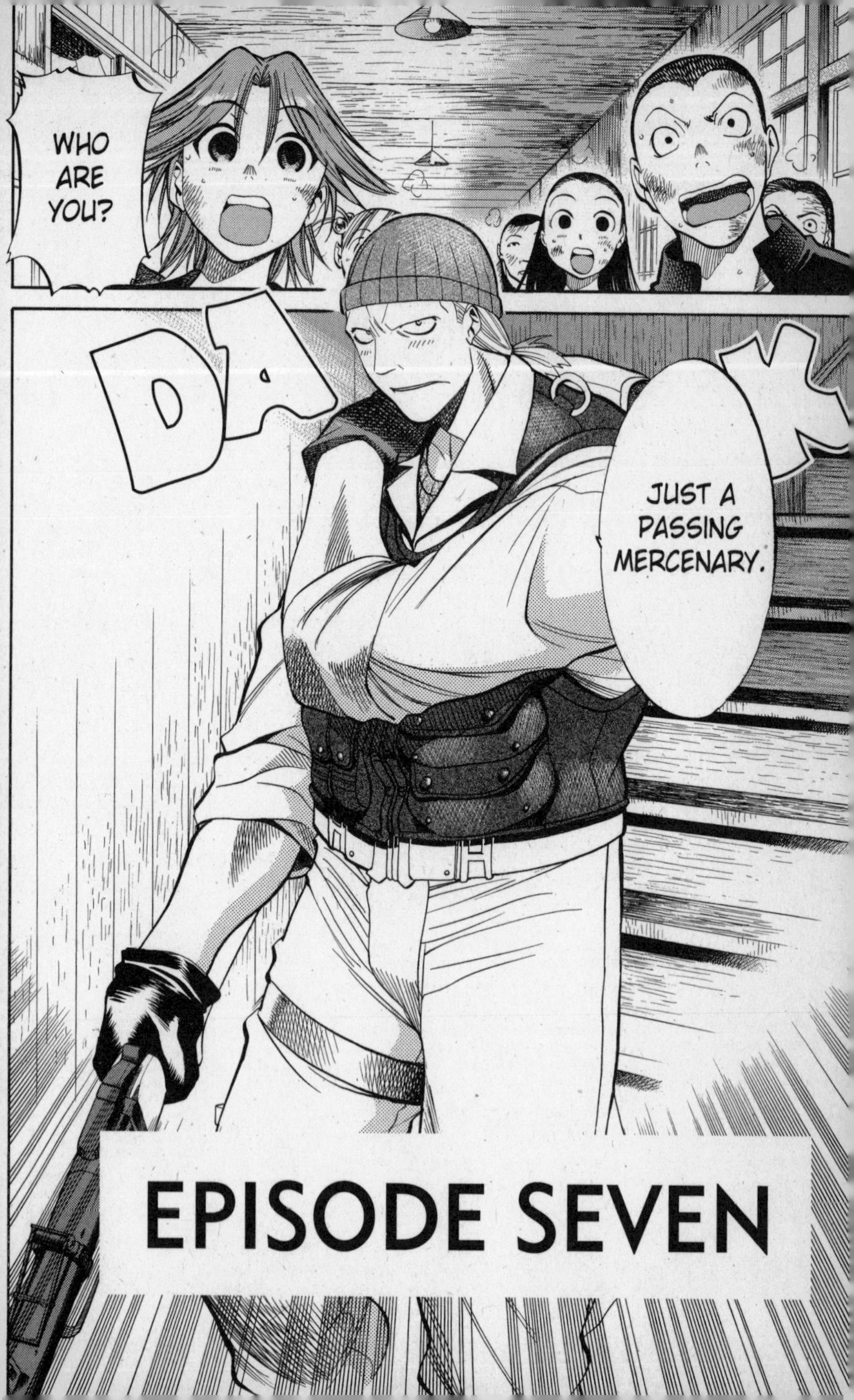
WHO ARE YOU?
DAK
JUST A PASSING MERCENARY.
EPISODE SEVEN

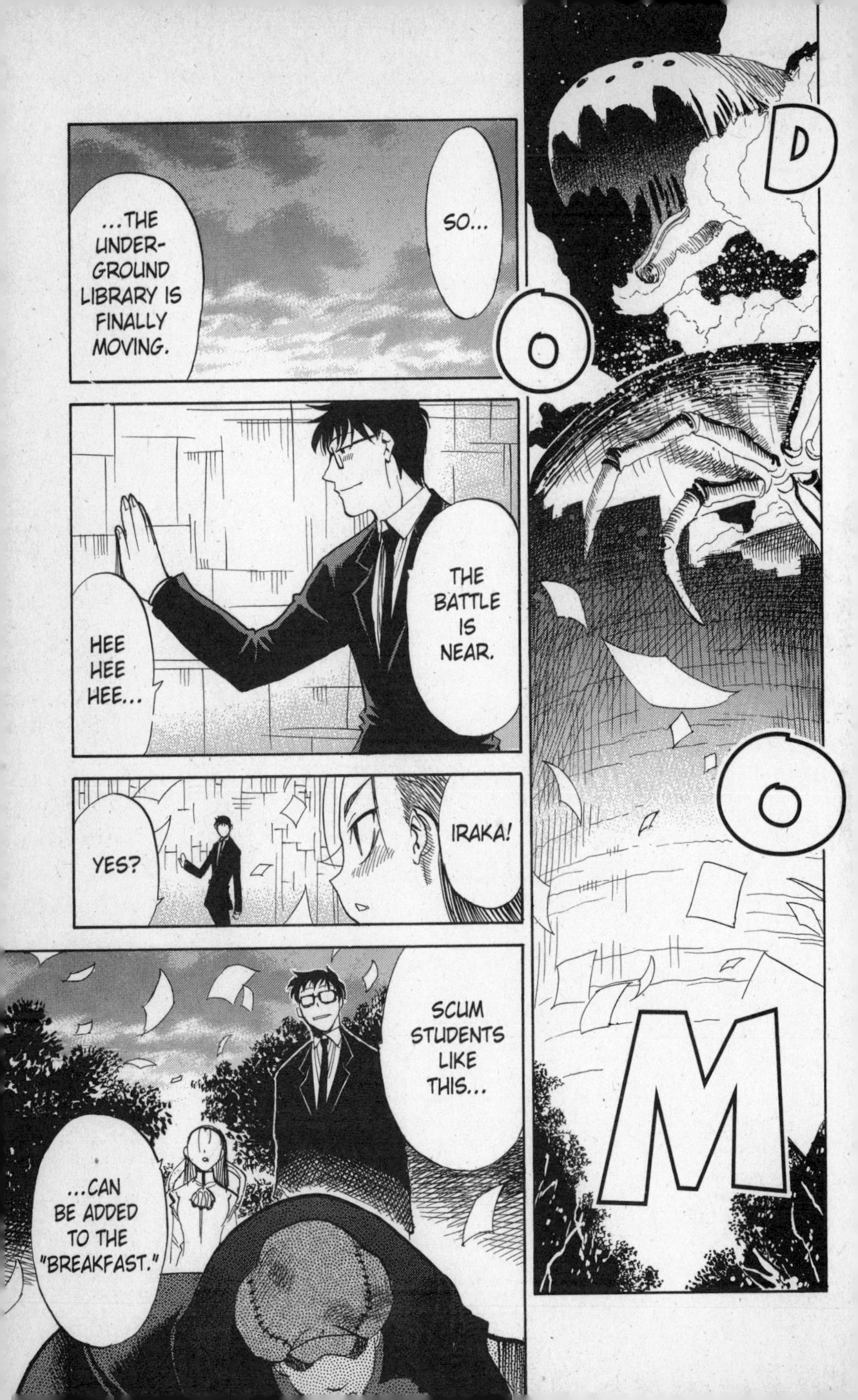
D
O
O
M
SO...
...THE UNDER-GROUND LIBRARY IS FINALLY MOVING.
THE BATTLE IS NEAR.
HEE HEE HEE...
IRAKA!
YES?
SCUM STUDENTS LIKE THIS...
...CAN BE ADDED TO THE "BREAKFAST."

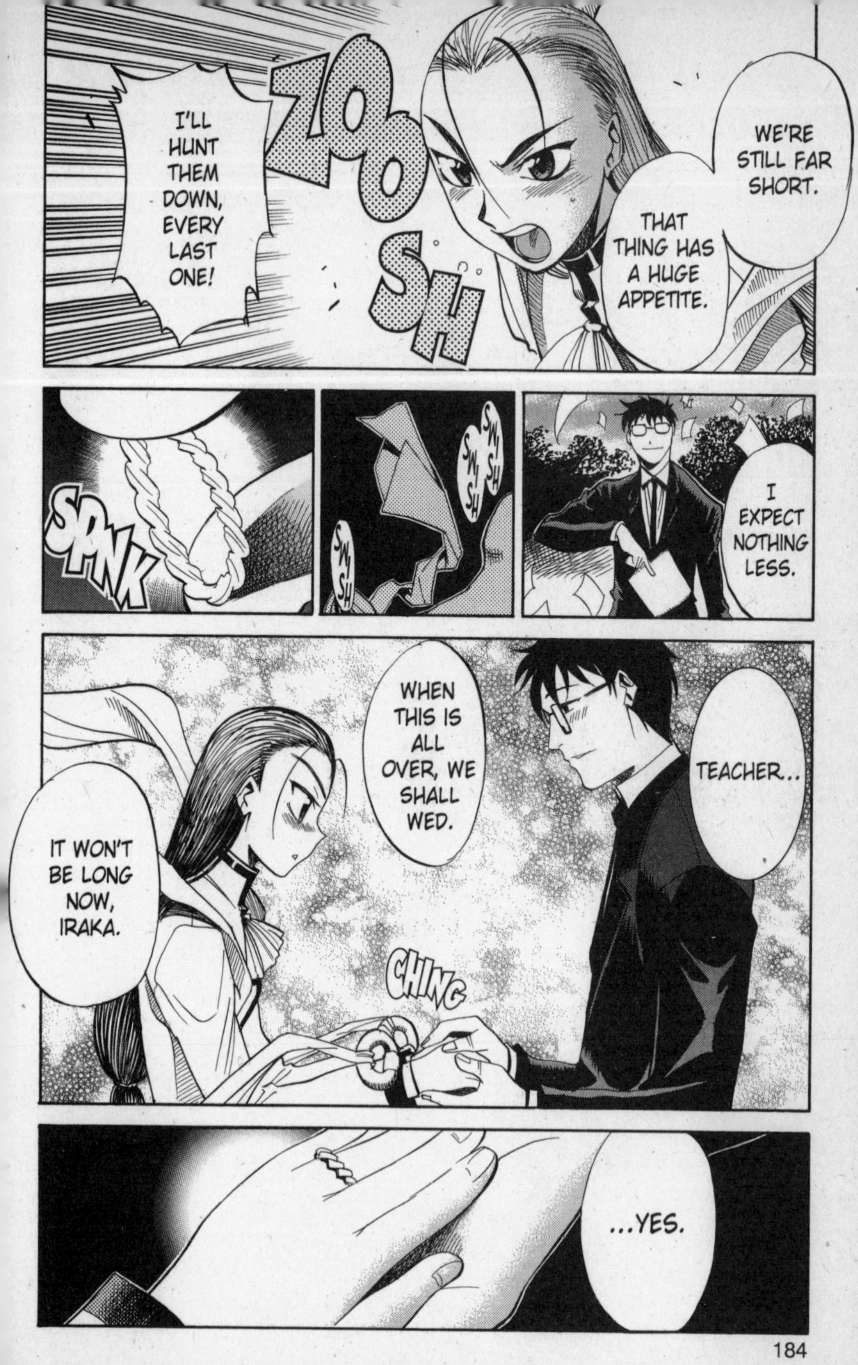
WE'RE STILL FAR SHORT.
THAT THING HAS A HUGE APPETITE.
ZOOSH
I'LL HUNT THEM DOWN, EVERY LAST ONE!
I EXPECT NOTHING LESS.
SWISH SWISH
SWISH
SPNK
TEACHER...
WHEN THIS IS ALL OVER, WE SHALL WED.
IT WON'T BE LONG NOW, IRAKA.
CHING
...YES.

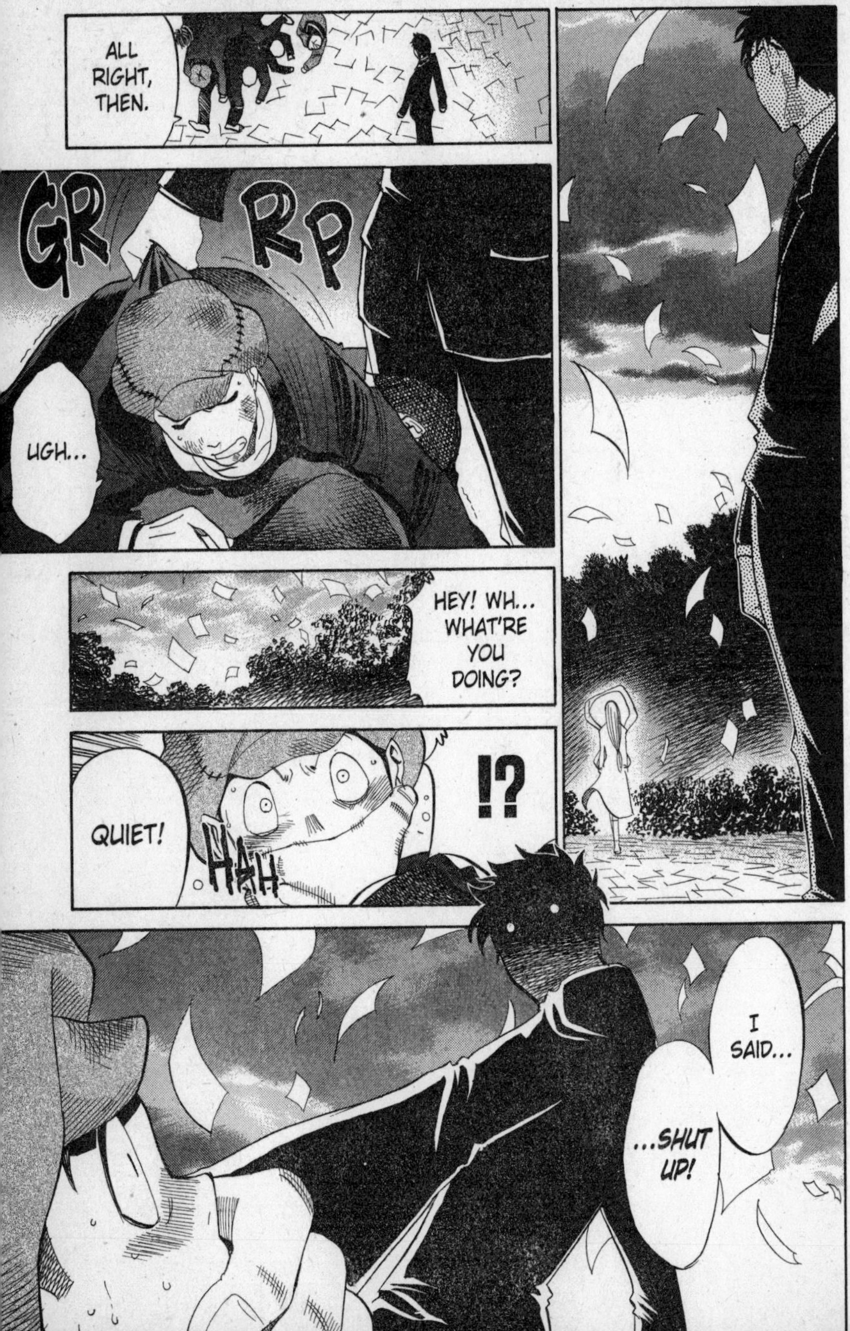
ALL RIGHT, THEN.
GRRP
UGH...
HEY! WH... WHAT'RE YOU DOING?
!?
QUIET!
HAH
I SAID...
...SHUT UP!

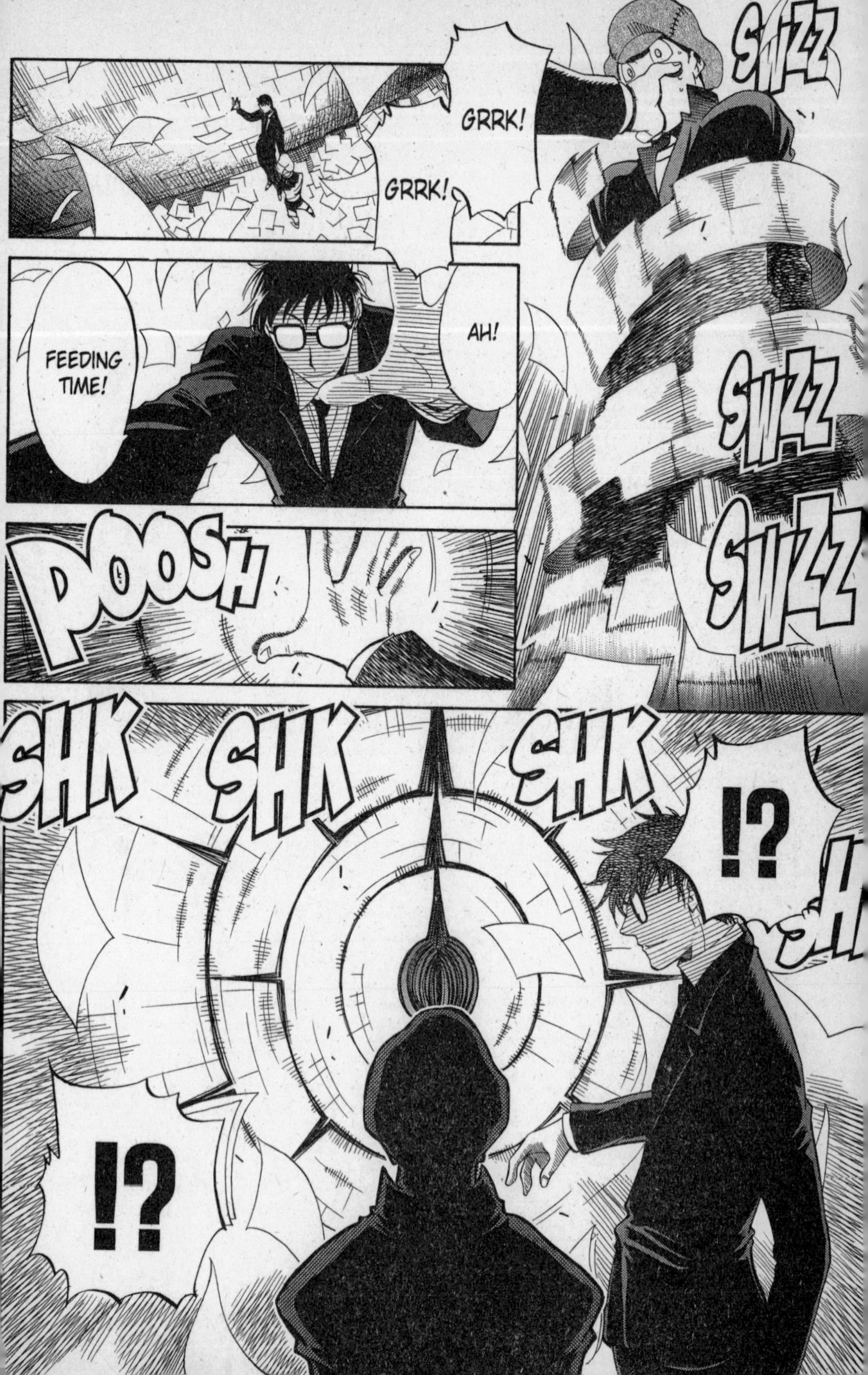
SWZZ
SWZZ
SWZZ
GRRK!
GRRK!
AH!
FEEDING TIME!
POOSH
!?
SHK
SHK
SHK
!?

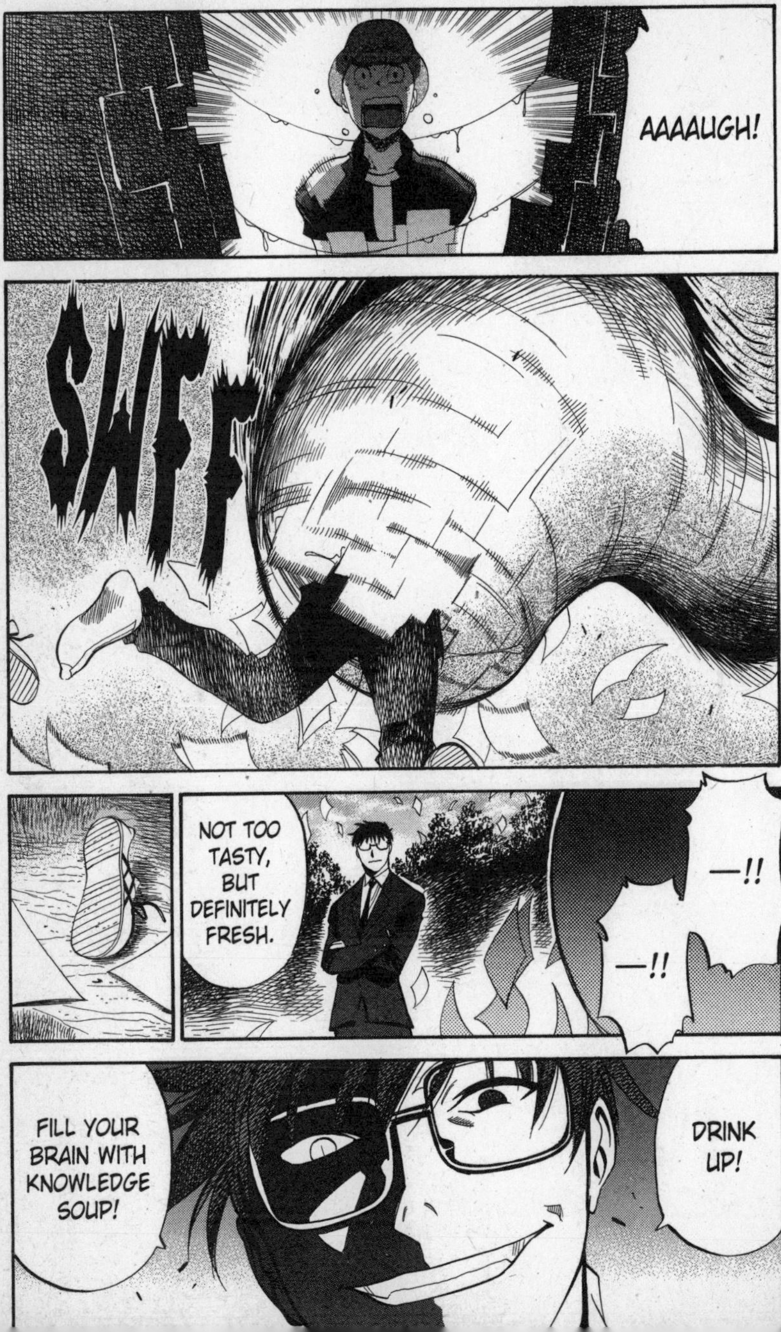
AAAAUGH!
SHF
—!!
—!!
NOT TOO TASTY, BUT DEFINITELY FRESH.
DRINK UP!
FILL YOUR BRAIN WITH KNOWLEDGE SOUP!

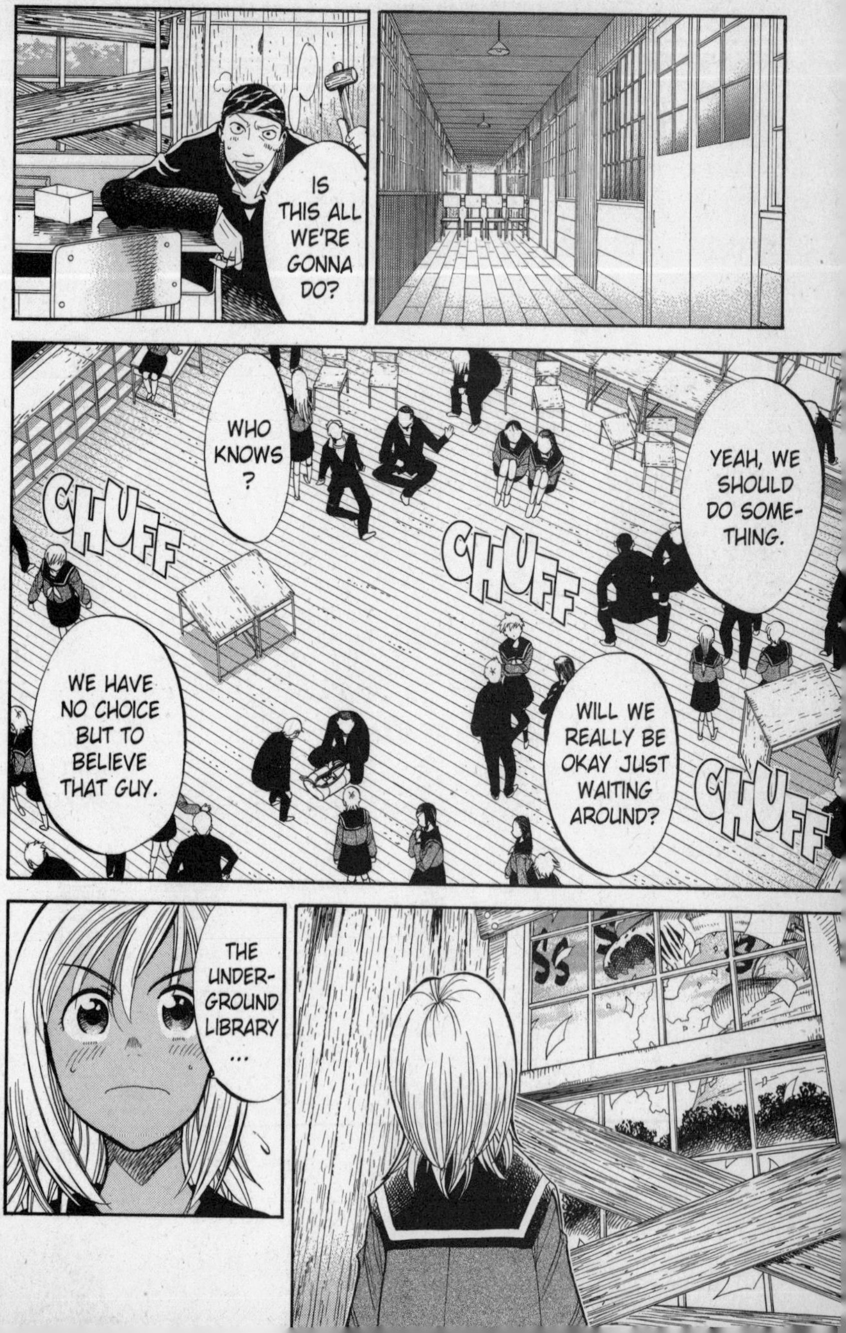
IS THIS ALL WE'RE GONNA DO?
YEAH, WE SHOULD DO SOME-THING.
WHO KNOWS?
CHUFF
CHUFF
CHUFF
WILL WE REALLY BE OKAY JUST WAITING AROUND?
WE HAVE NO CHOICE BUT TO BELIEVE THAT GUY.
THE UNDER-GROUND LIBRARY ...

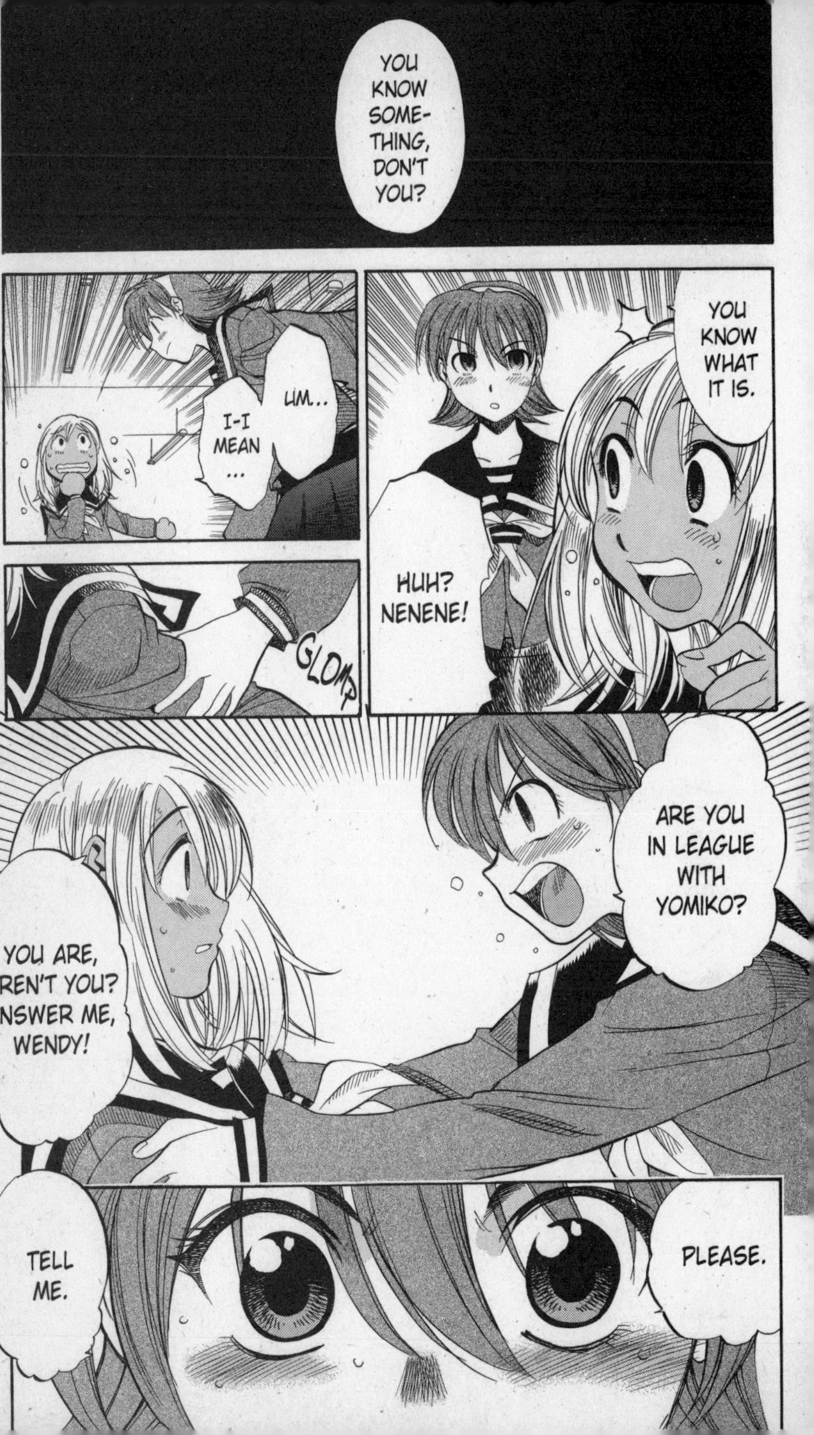
YOU KNOW SOME-THING, DON'T YOU?
YOU KNOW WHAT IT IS.
HUH? NENENE!
UM...
I-I MEAN ...
GLOMP
ARE YOU IN LEAGUE WITH YOMIKO?
YOU ARE, AREN'T YOU? ANSWER ME, WENDY!
PLEASE.
TELL ME.

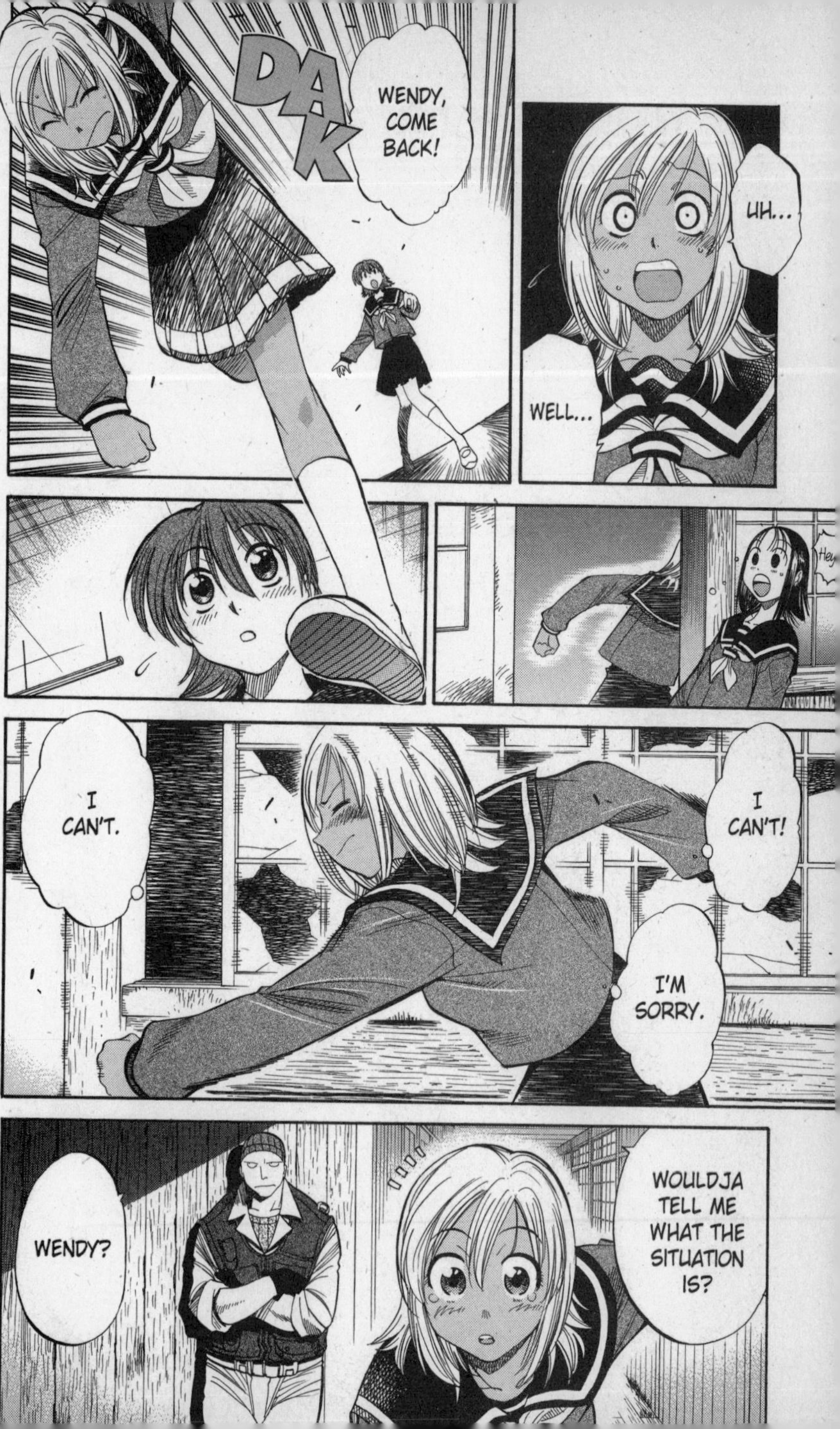
UH...
WELL...
WENDY, COME BACK!
DAK
Hey
I CAN'T!
I'M SORRY.
I CAN'T.
WOULDJA TELL ME WHAT THE SITUATION IS?
WENDY?

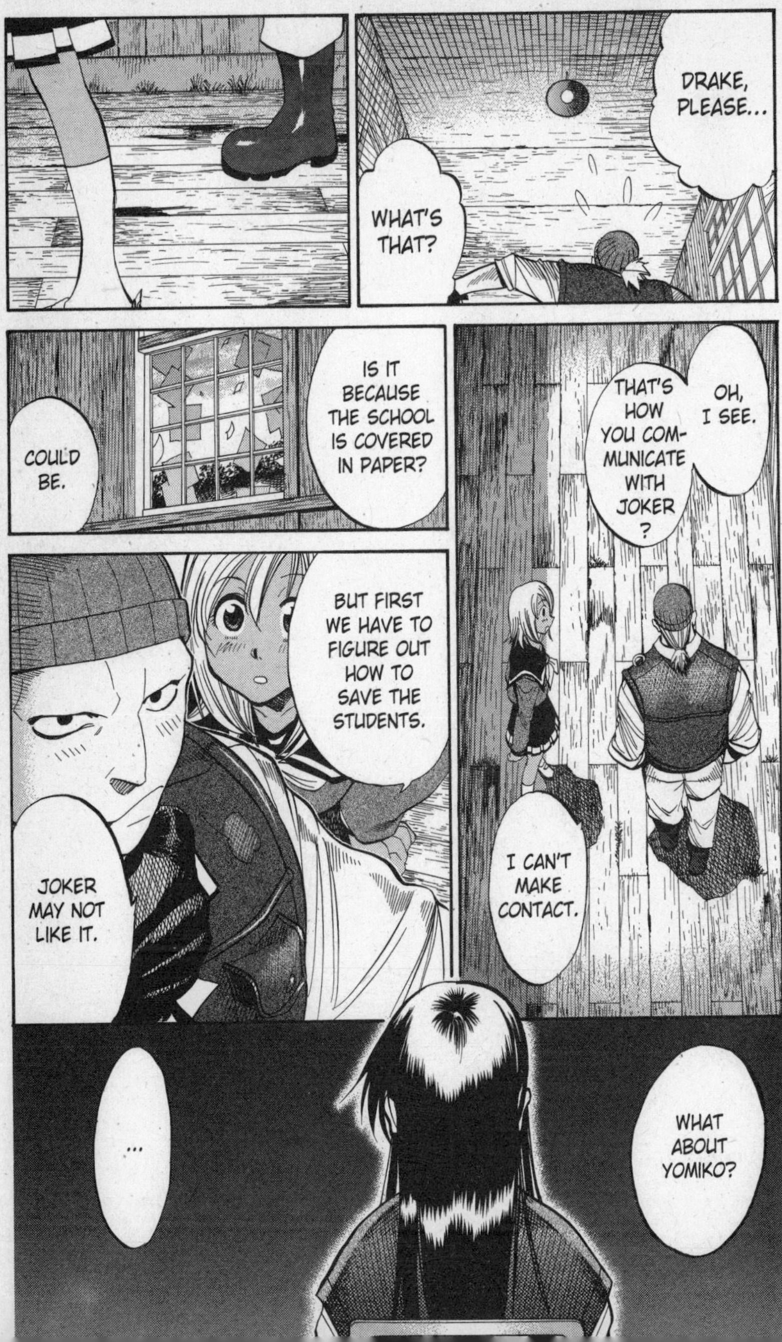
DRAKE, PLEASE...
WHAT'S THAT?
OH, I SEE.
THAT'S HOW YOU COMMUNICATE WITH JOKER?
I CAN'T MAKE CONTACT.
IS IT BECAUSE THE SCHOOL IS COVERED IN PAPER?
COULD BE.
BUT FIRST WE HAVE TO FIGURE OUT HOW TO SAVE THE STUDENTS.
JOKER MAY NOT LIKE IT.
WHAT ABOUT YOMIKO?
...

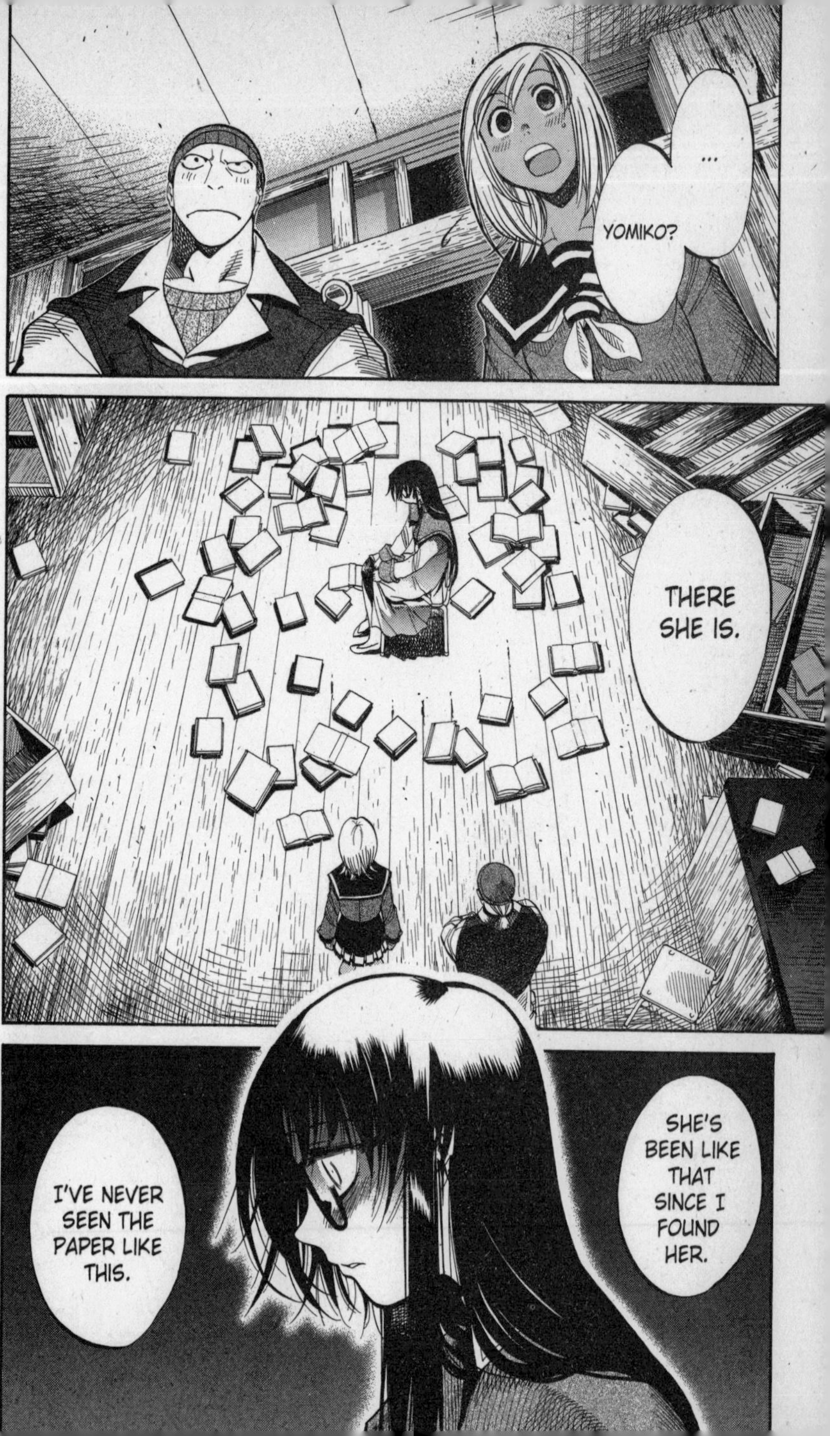
...
YOMIKO?
THERE SHE IS.
SHE'S BEEN LIKE THAT SINCE I FOUND HER.
I'VE NEVER SEEN THE PAPER LIKE THIS.

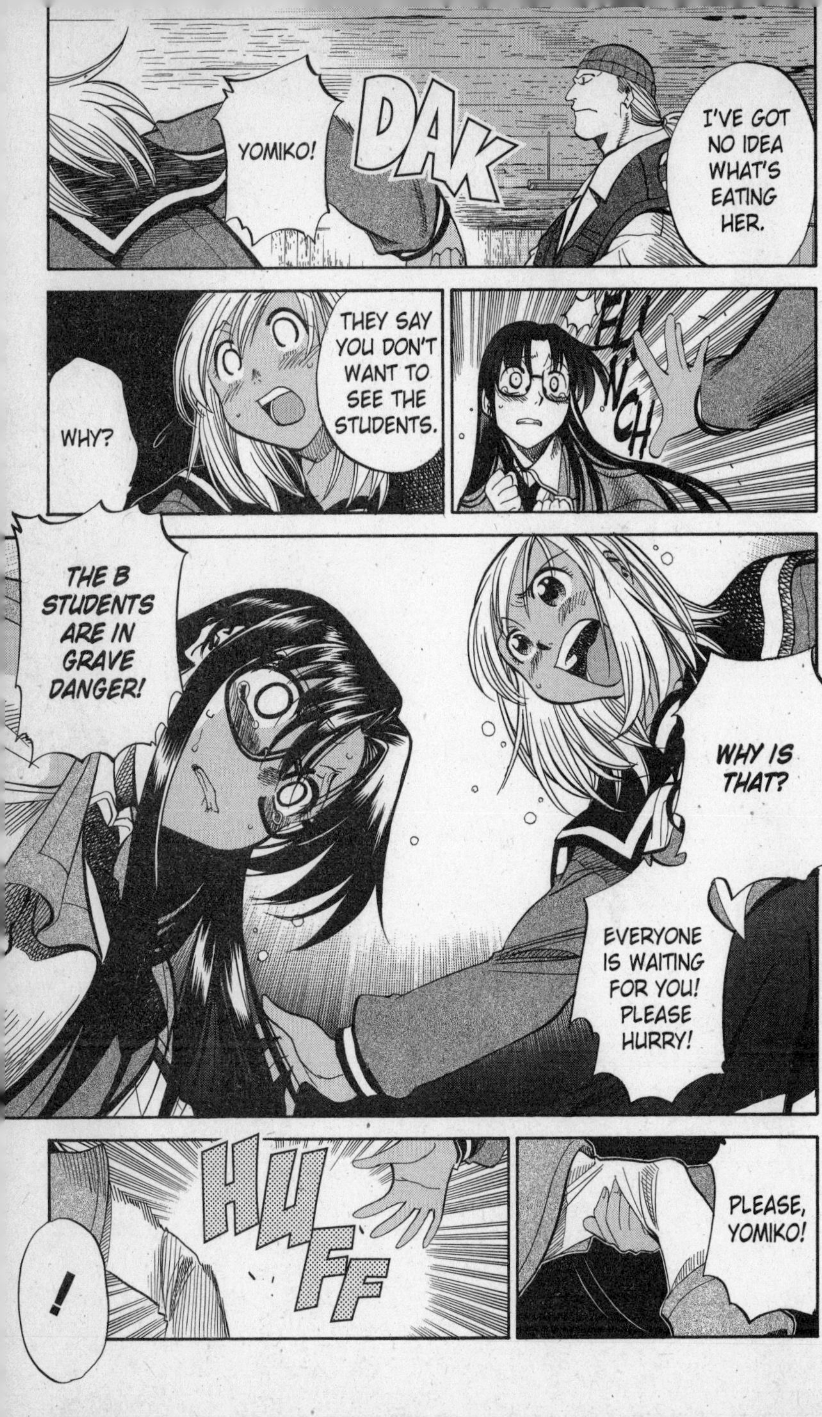
I'VE GOT NO IDEA WHAT'S EATING HER.
DAK
YOMIKO!
FLINCH
THEY SAY YOU DON'T WANT TO SEE THE STUDENTS.
WHY?
WHY IS THAT?
THE B STUDENTS ARE IN GRAVE DANGER!
EVERYONE IS WAITING FOR YOU! PLEASE HURRY!
PLEASE, YOMIKO!
HUFF
!

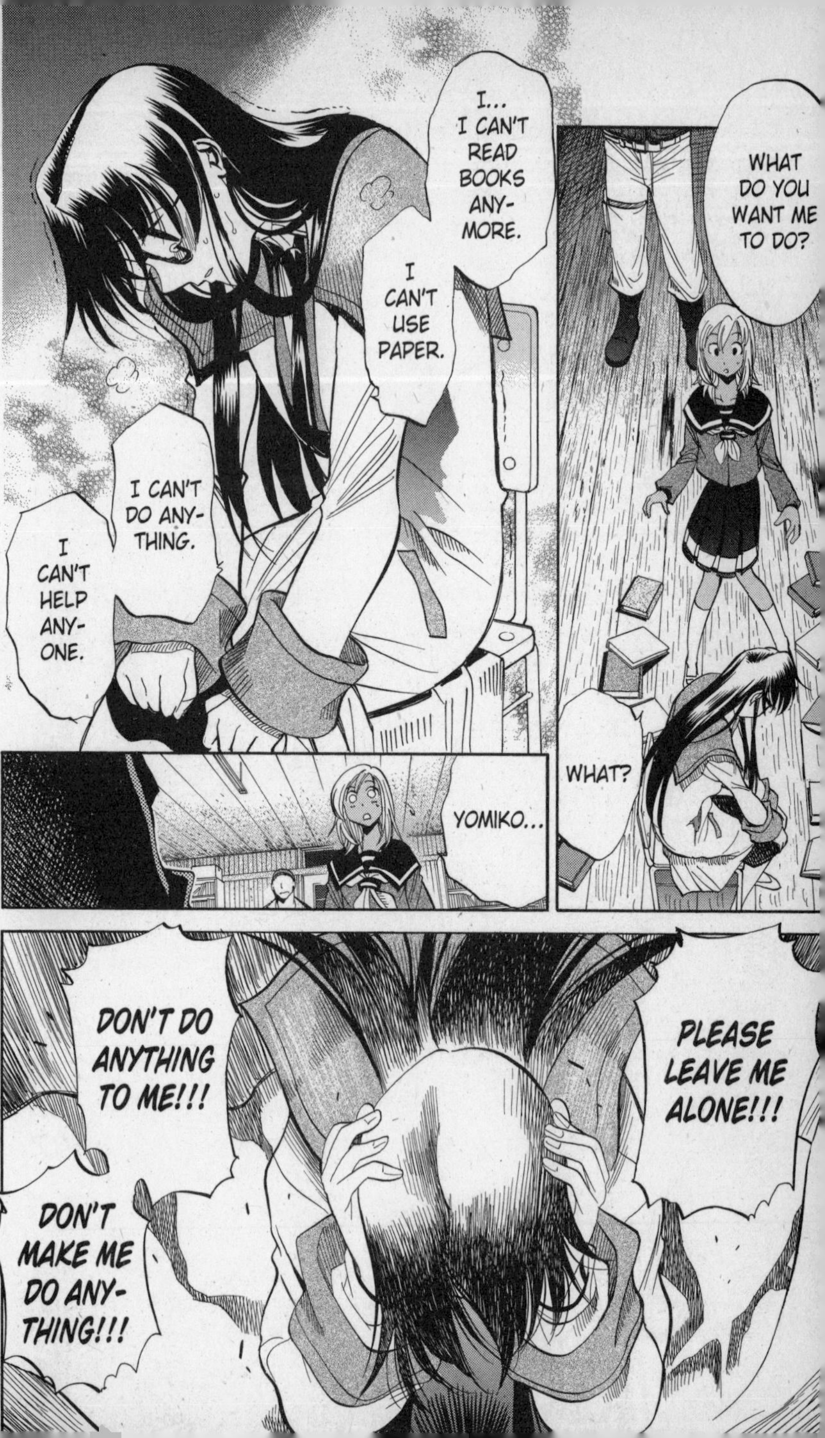
WHAT DO YOU WANT ME TO DO?
WHAT?
I... I CAN'T READ BOOKS ANY-MORE.
I CAN'T USE PAPER.
I CAN'T DO ANY-THING.
I CAN'T HELP ANY-ONE.
YOMIKO...
PLEASE LEAVE ME ALONE!!!
DON'T DO ANYTHING TO ME!!!
DON'T MAKE ME DO ANY-THING!!!

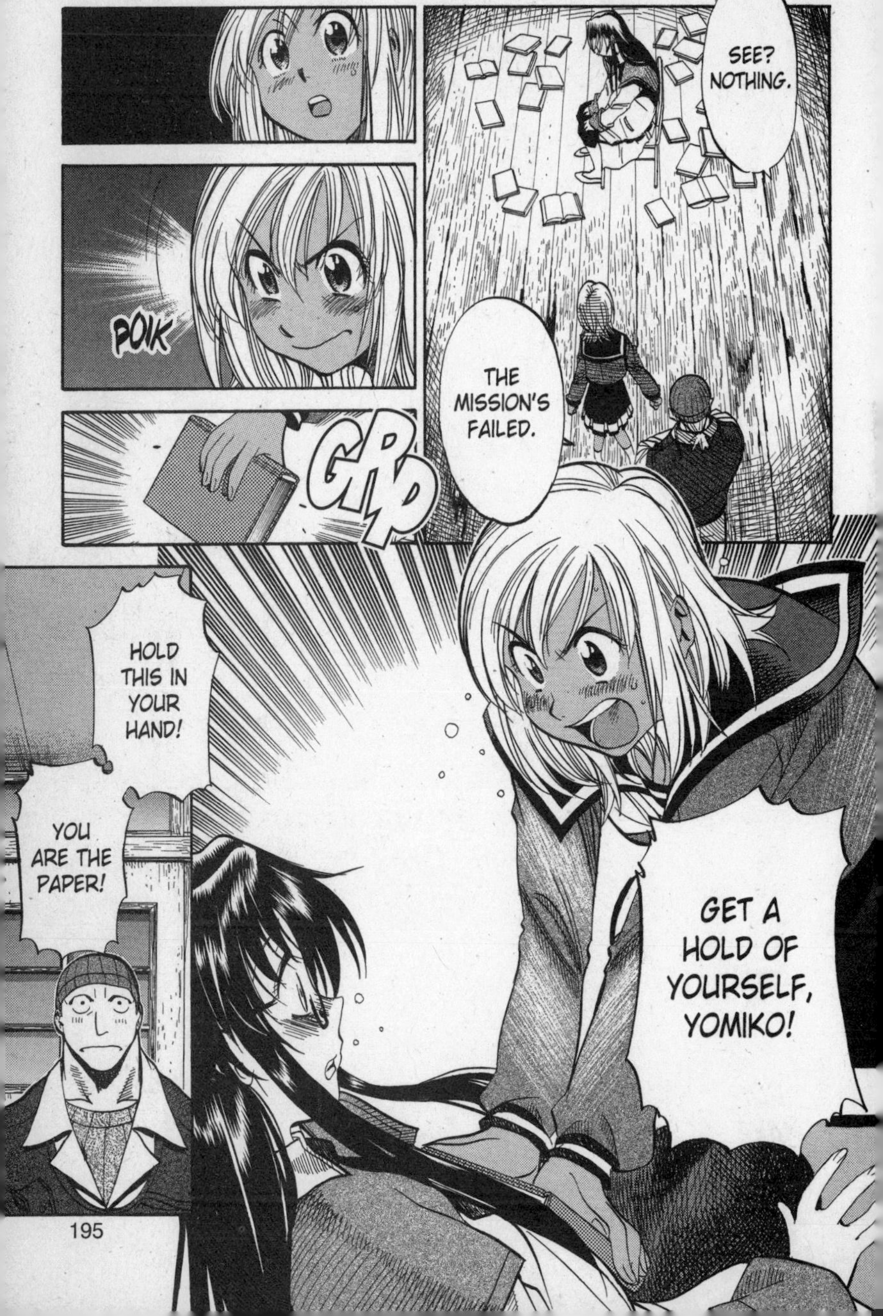
SEE? NOTHING.
THE MISSION'S FAILED.
POIK
GRP
GET A HOLD OF YOURSELF, YOMIKO!
HOLD THIS IN YOUR HAND!
YOU ARE THE PAPER!

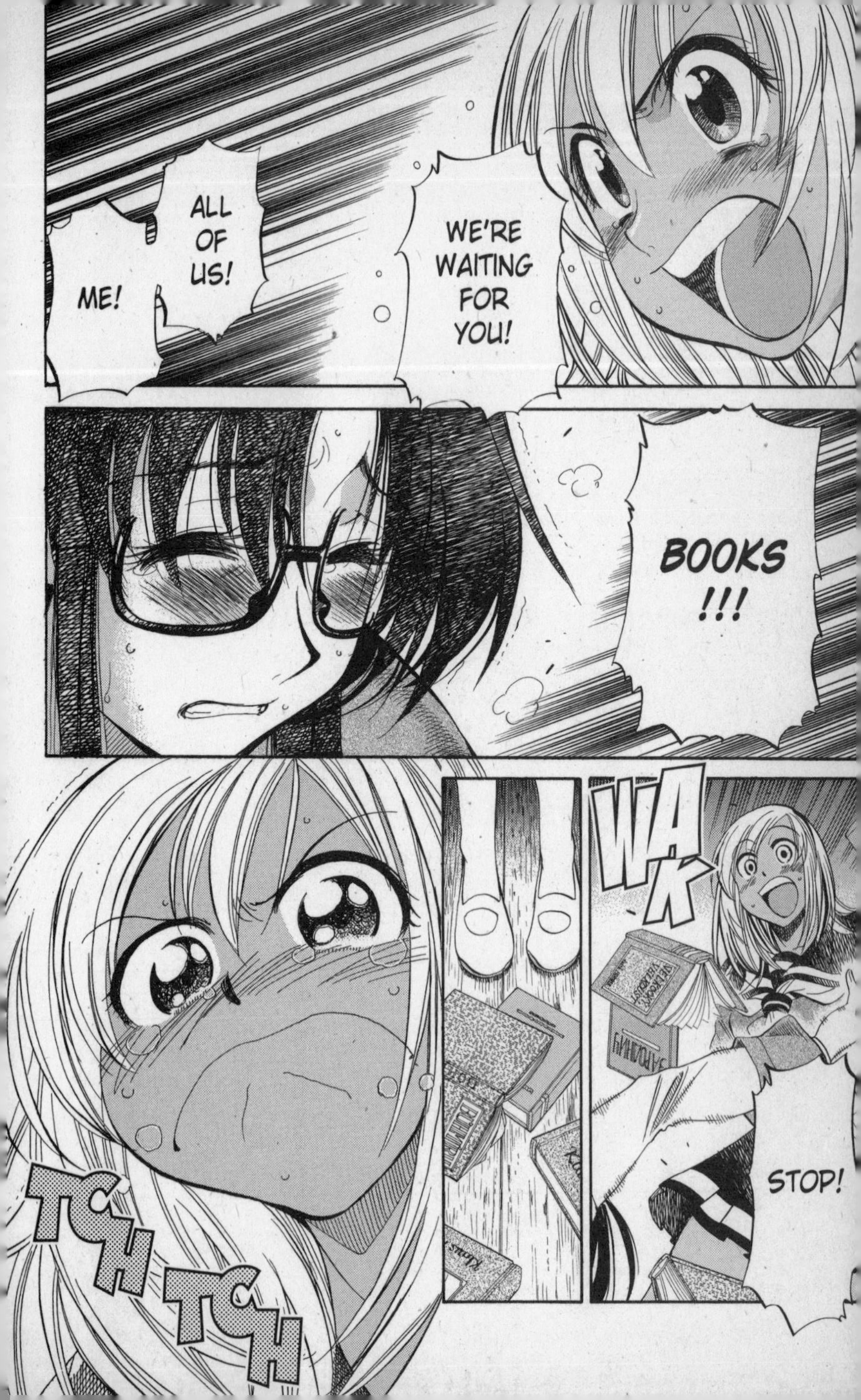
WE'RE WAITING FOR YOU!
ALL OF US!
ME!
BOOKS !!!
WAK
STOP!
TCH TCH

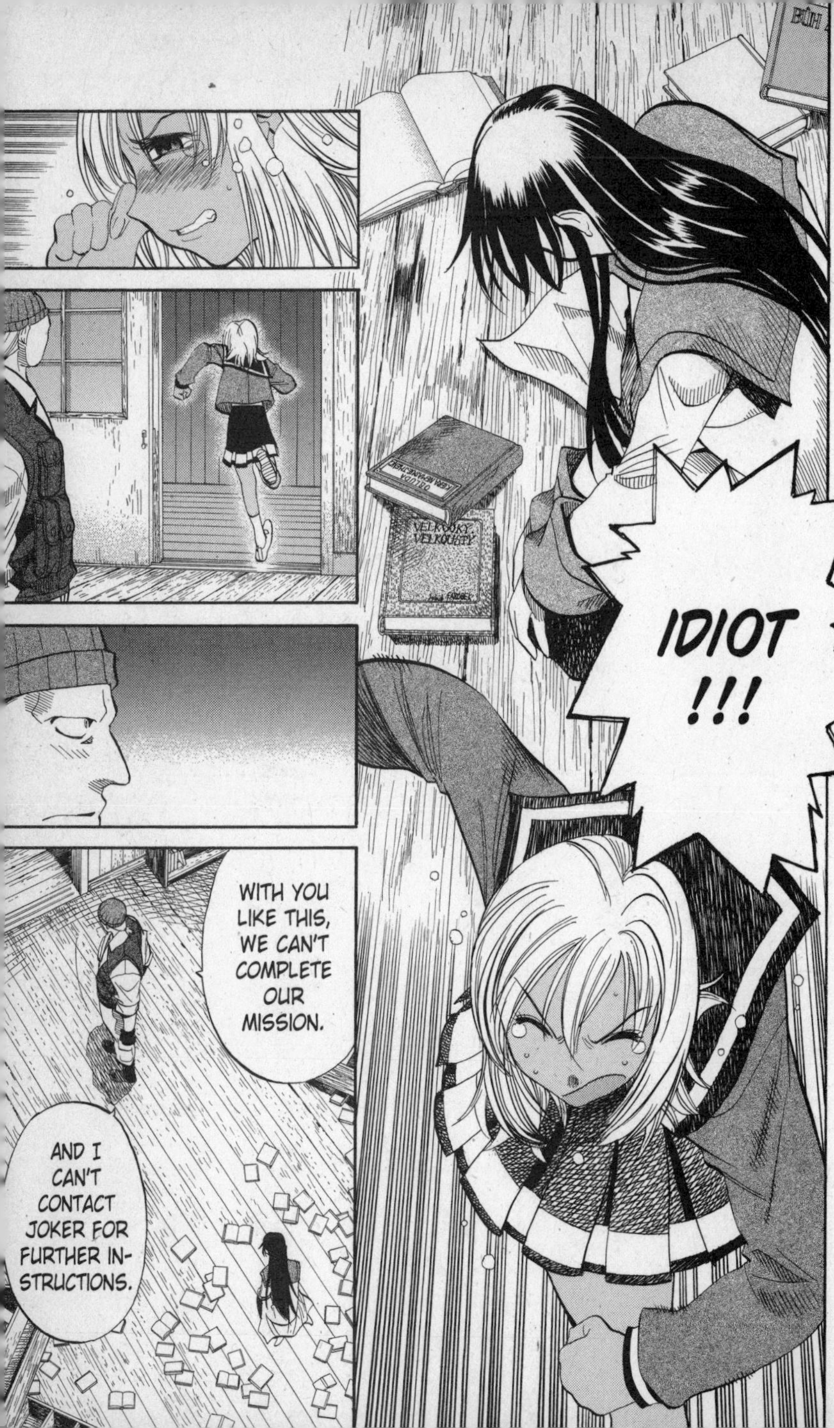
IDIOT !!!
WITH YOU LIKE THIS, WE CAN'T COMPLETE OUR MISSION.
AND I CAN'T CONTACT JOKER FOR FURTHER IN-STRUCTIONS.

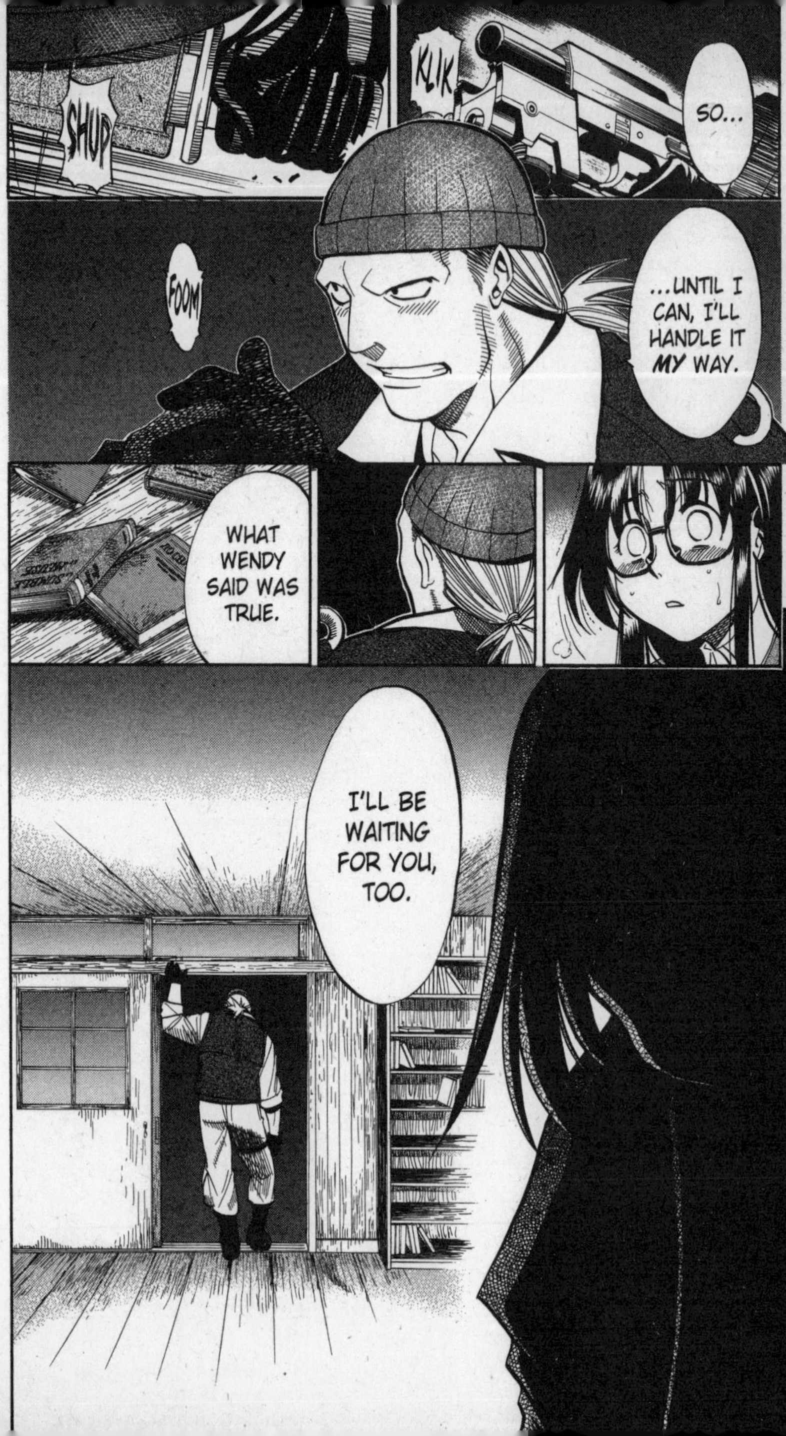
SO...
KLIK
SHUP
...UNTIL I CAN, I'LL HANDLE IT *MY* WAY.
FOOM
WHAT WENDY SAID WAS TRUE.
I'LL BE WAITING FOR YOU, TOO.

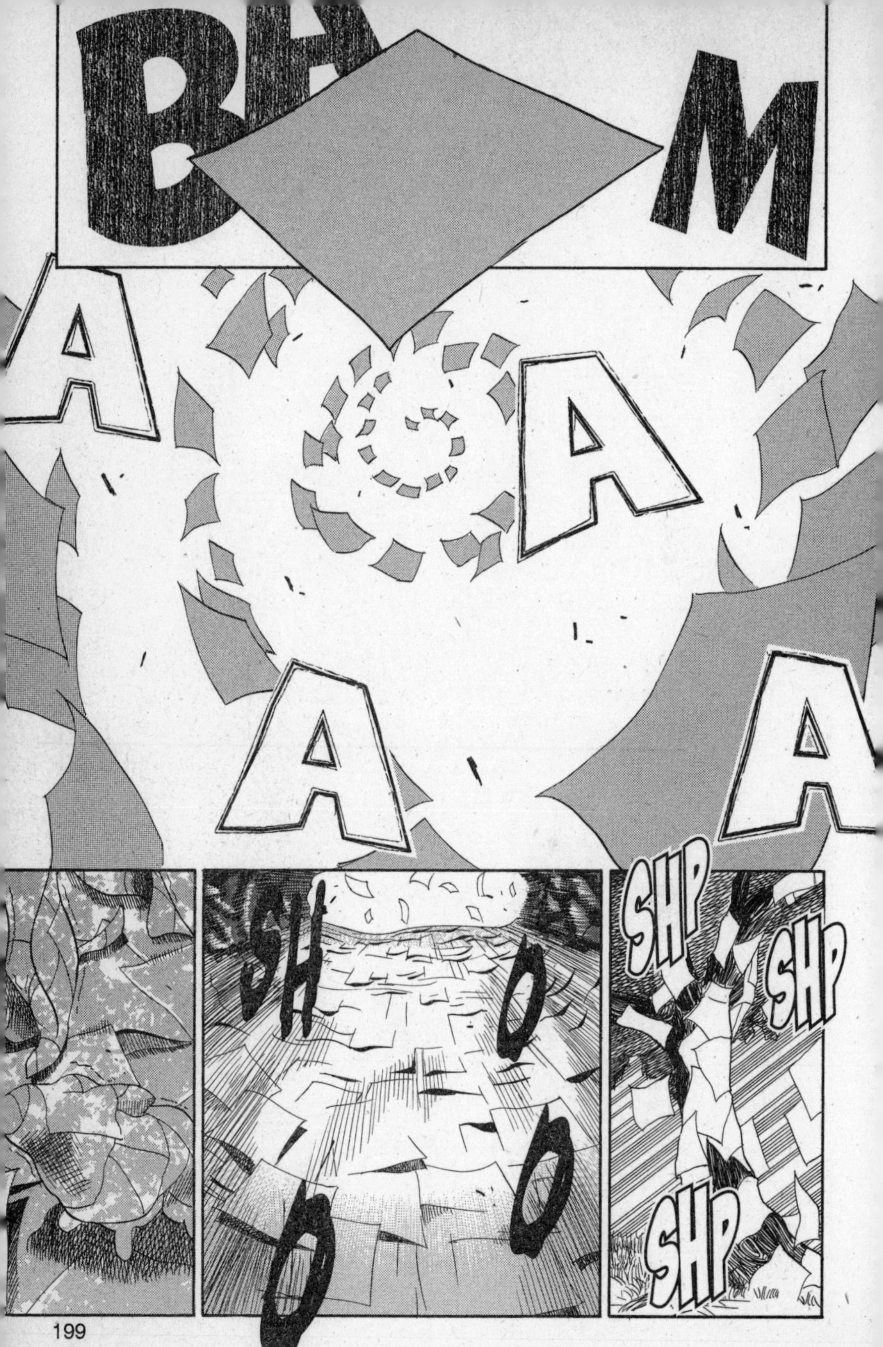
AAAA
SHP
SHP
SHP
SHOOO

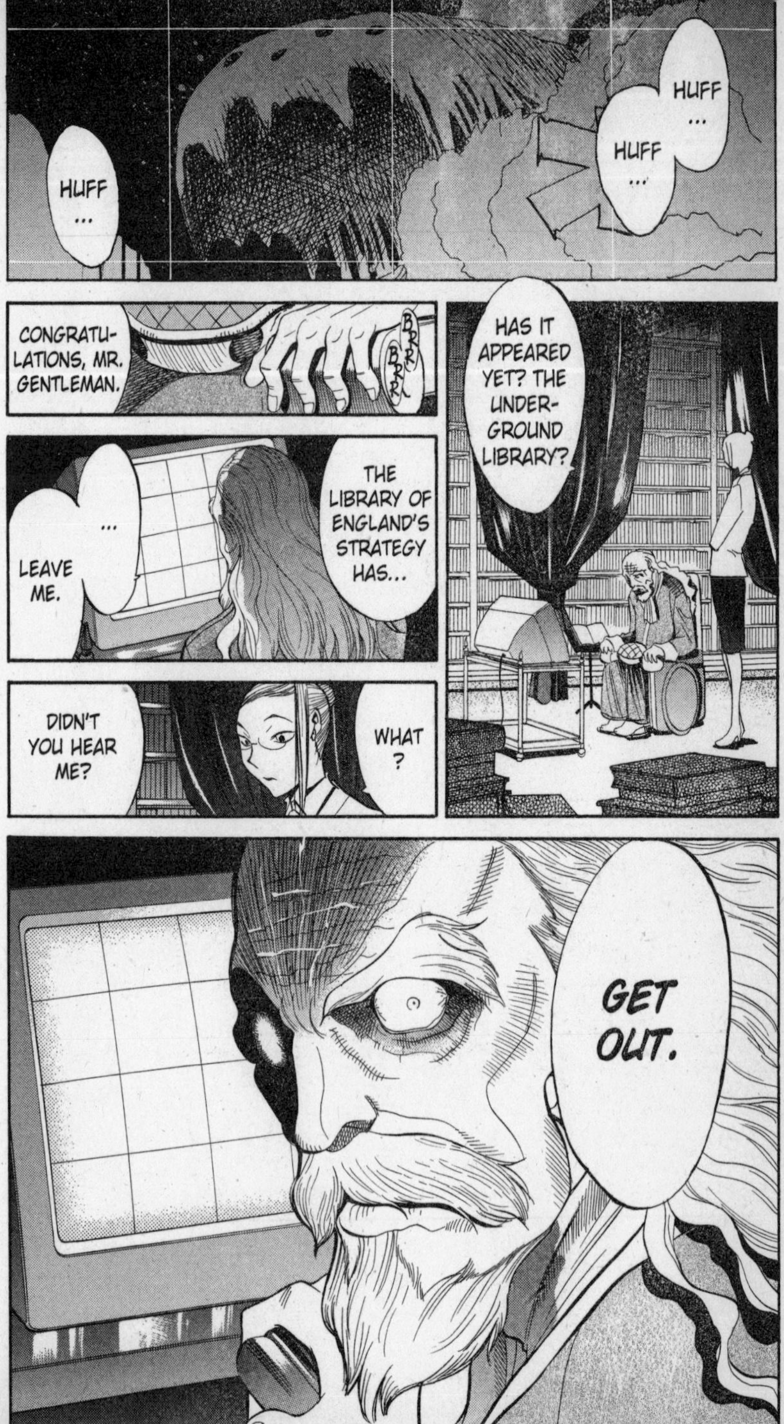
HUFF ...
HUFF ...
HUFF ...
HAS IT APPEARED YET? THE UNDER-GROUND LIBRARY?
BRR BRR
CONGRATU-LATIONS, MR. GENTLEMAN.
THE LIBRARY OF ENGLAND'S STRATEGY HAS...
... LEAVE ME.
WHAT?
DIDN'T YOU HEAR ME?
GET OUT.

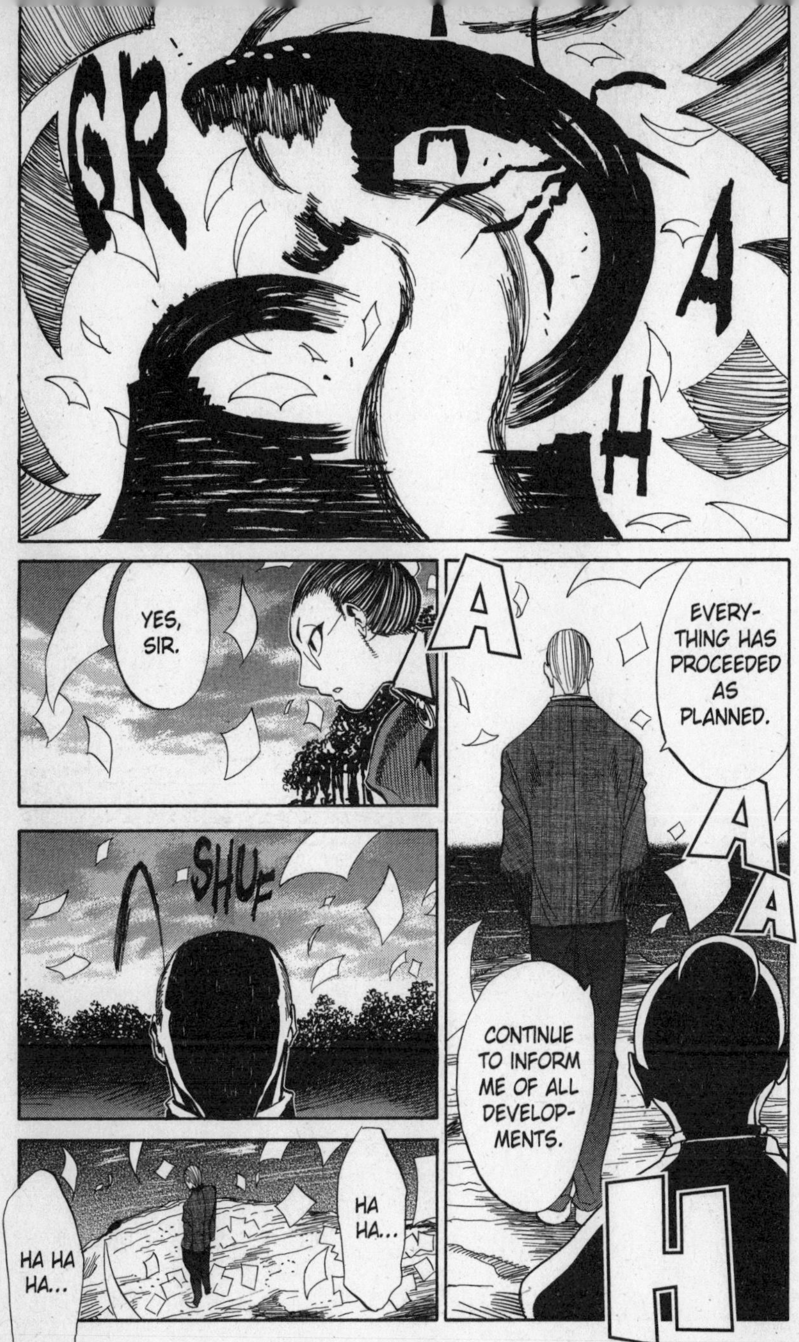
GR
A
H
EVERY-THING HAS PROCEEDED AS PLANNED.
A
A
A
CONTINUE TO INFORM ME OF ALL DEVELOP-MENTS.
H
YES, SIR.
SHUF
HA HA...
HA HA HA...

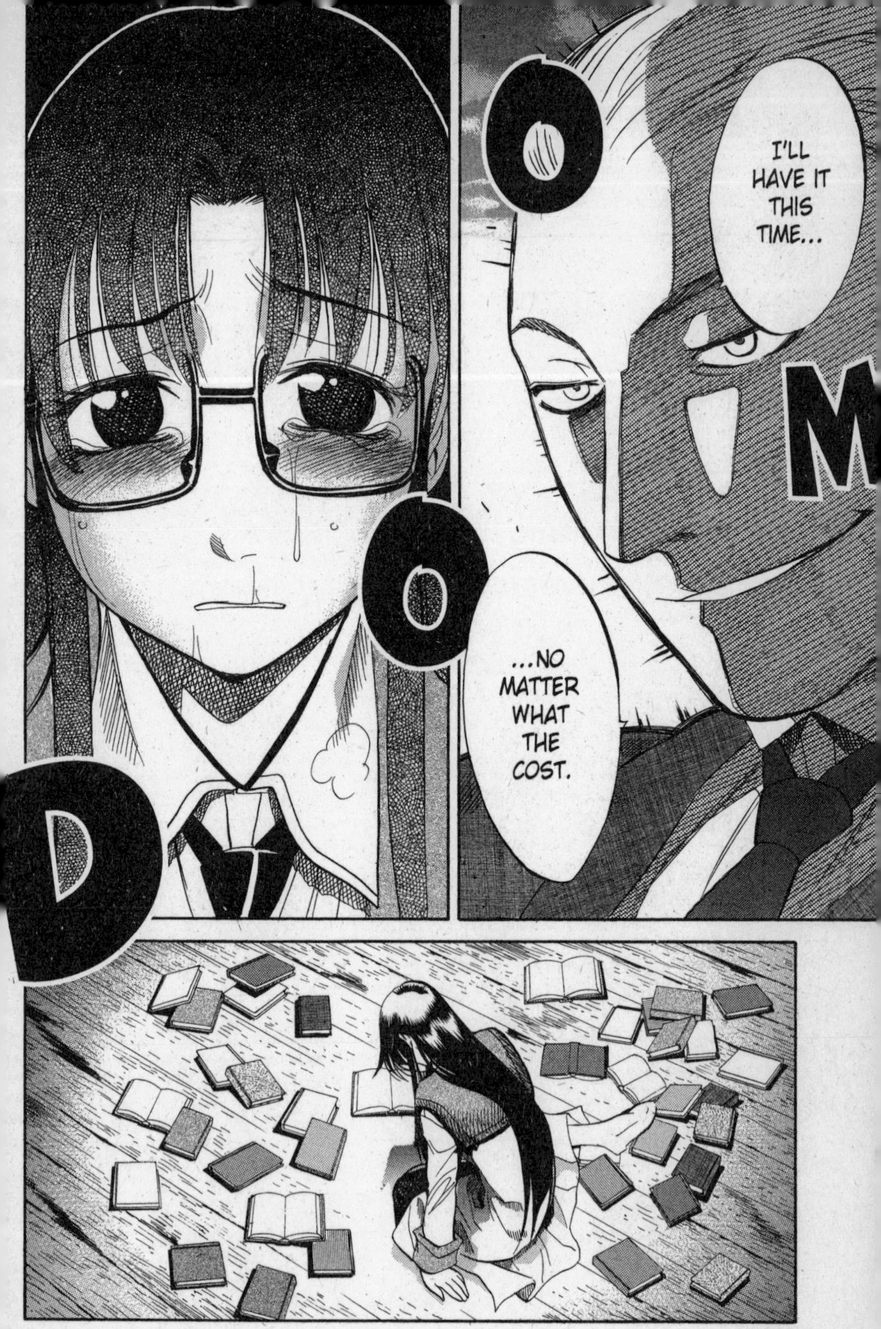
I'LL HAVE IT THIS TIME...
...NO MATTER WHAT THE COST.
DOOM

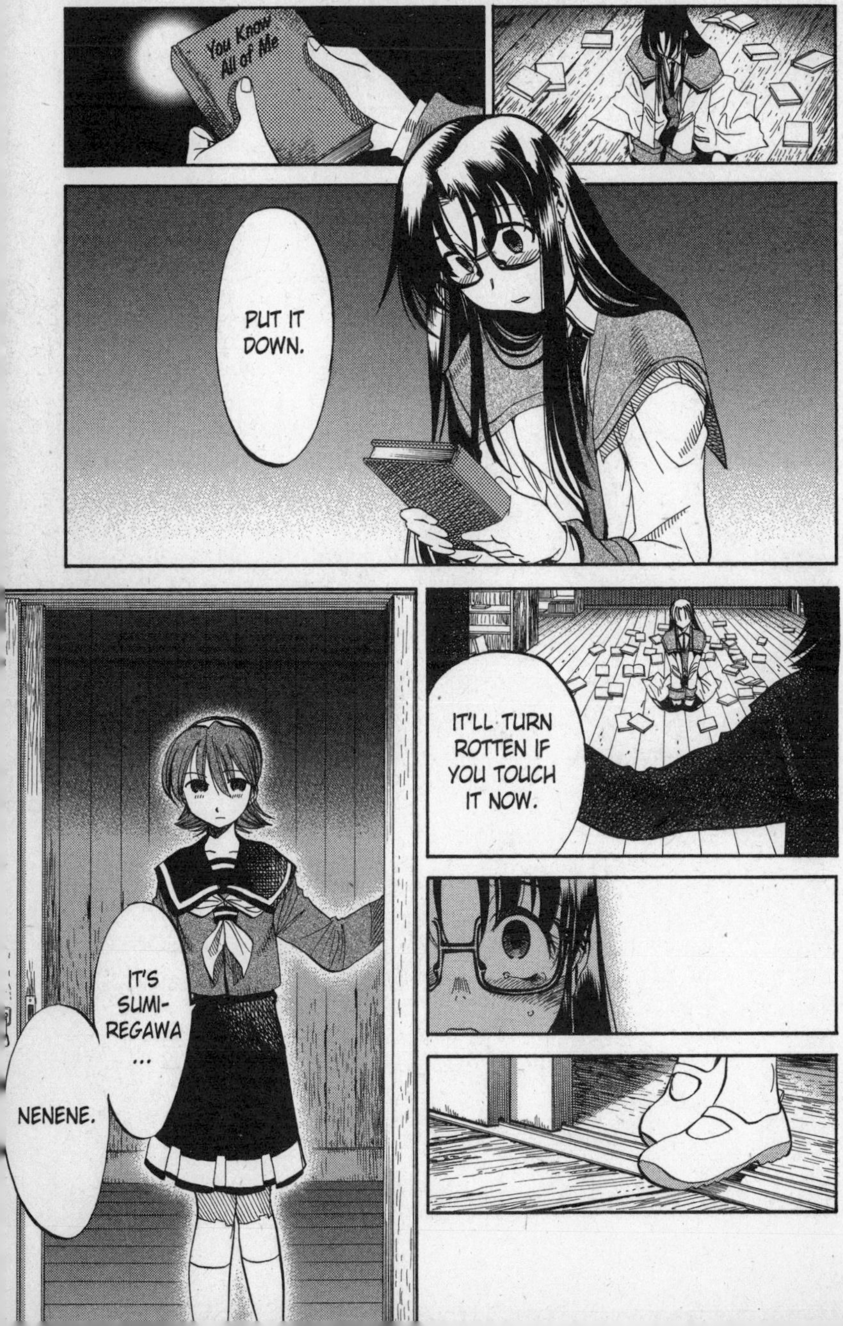
You Know All of Me
PUT IT DOWN.
IT'LL TURN ROTTEN IF YOU TOUCH IT NOW.
IT'S SUMI-REGAWA...
NENENE.

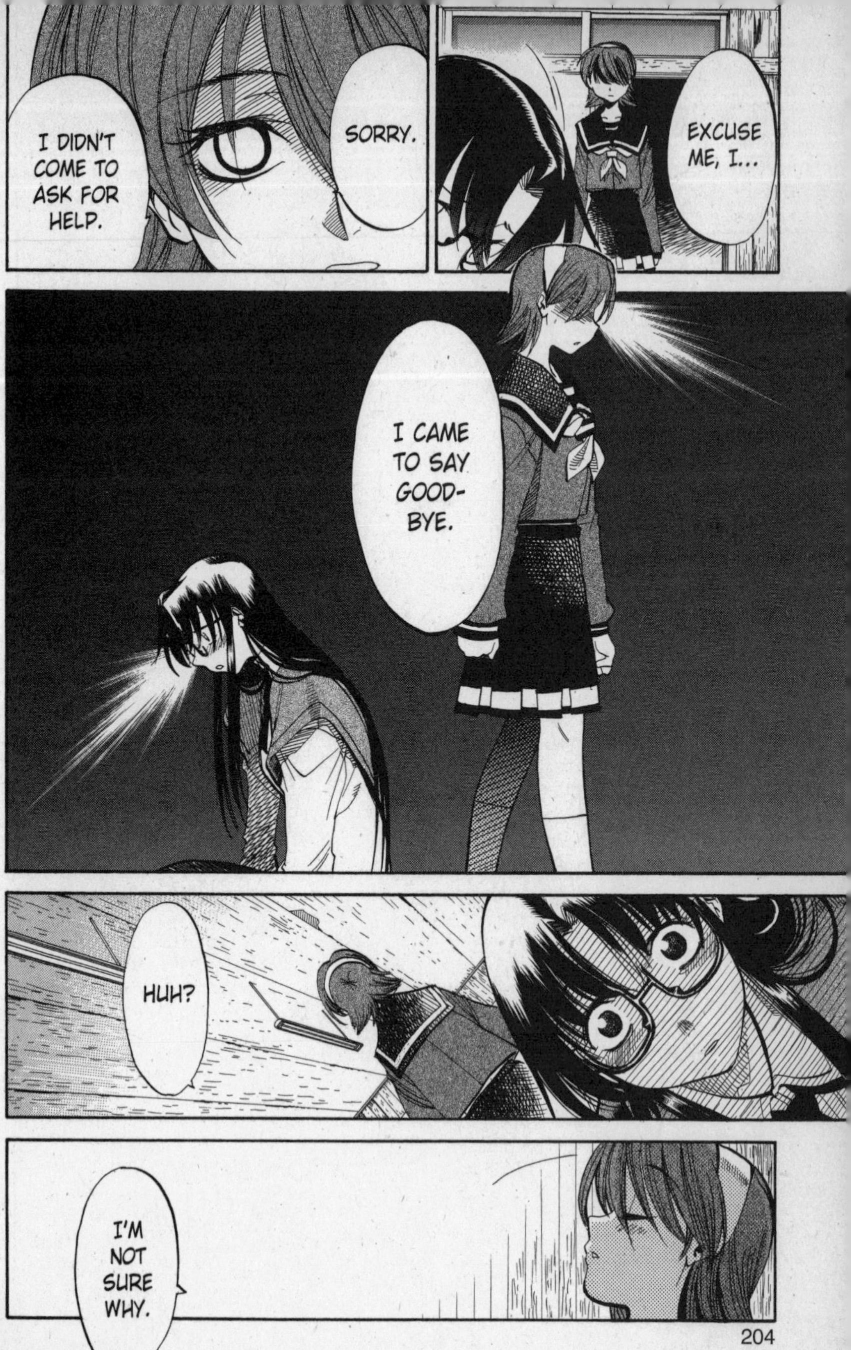
EXCUSE ME, I...
SORRY.
I DIDN'T COME TO ASK FOR HELP.
I CAME TO SAY GOOD-BYE.
HUH?
I'M NOT SURE WHY.

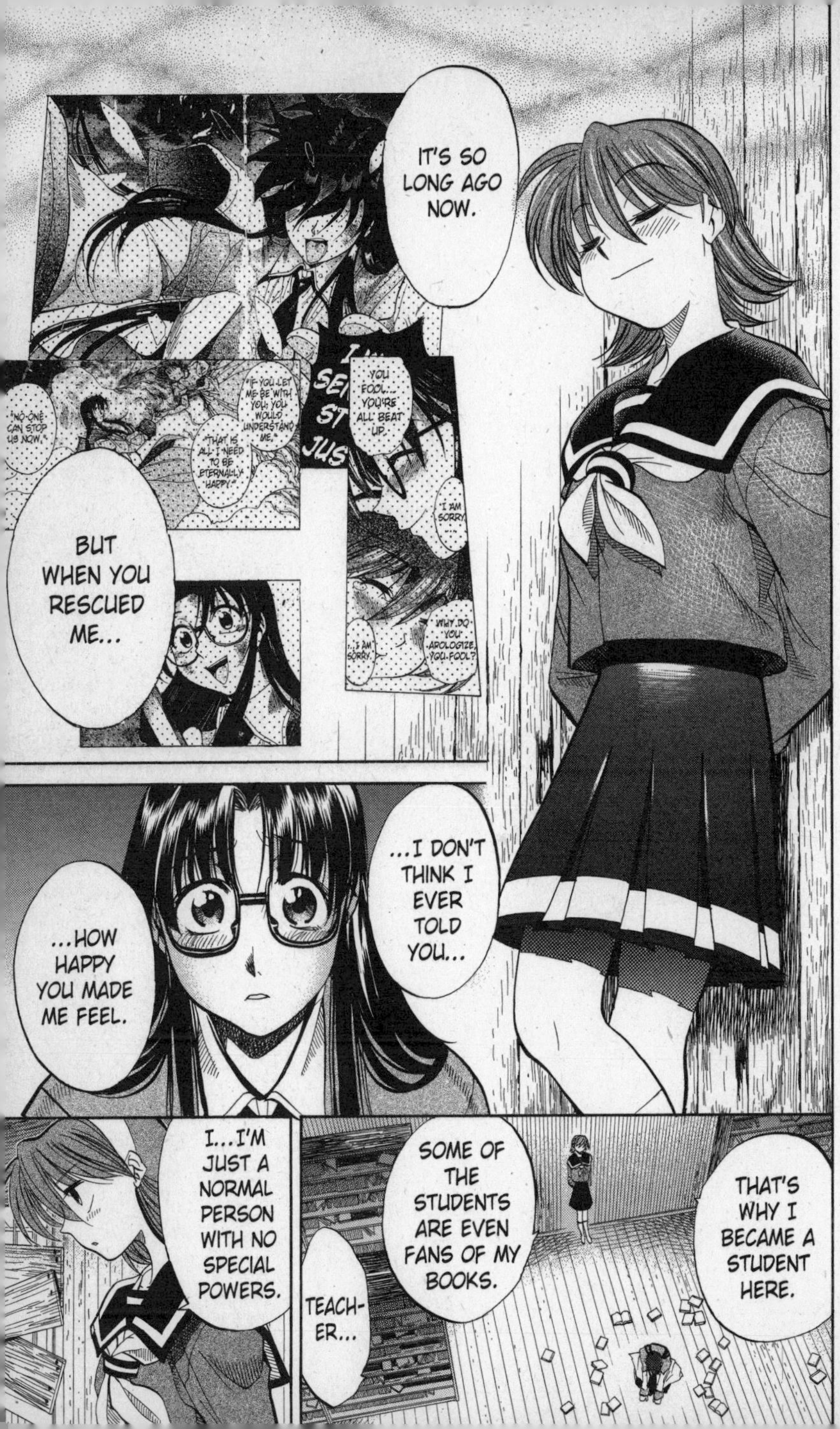
IT'S SO LONG AGO NOW.
YOU FOOL... YOU'RE ALL BEAT UP.
"I AM SORRY..."
WHY DO YOU APOLOGIZE, YOU FOOL?
...I AM SORRY.
"IF YOU LET ME BE WITH YOU, YOU WOULD UNDERSTAND ME."
"THAT IS ALL I NEED TO BE ETERNALLY HAPPY."
"NO ONE CAN STOP US NOW."
BUT WHEN YOU RESCUED ME...
...I DON'T THINK I EVER TOLD YOU...
...HOW HAPPY YOU MADE ME FEEL.
THAT'S WHY I BECAME A STUDENT HERE.
SOME OF THE STUDENTS ARE EVEN FANS OF MY BOOKS.
TEACHER...
I...I'M JUST A NORMAL PERSON WITH NO SPECIAL POWERS.

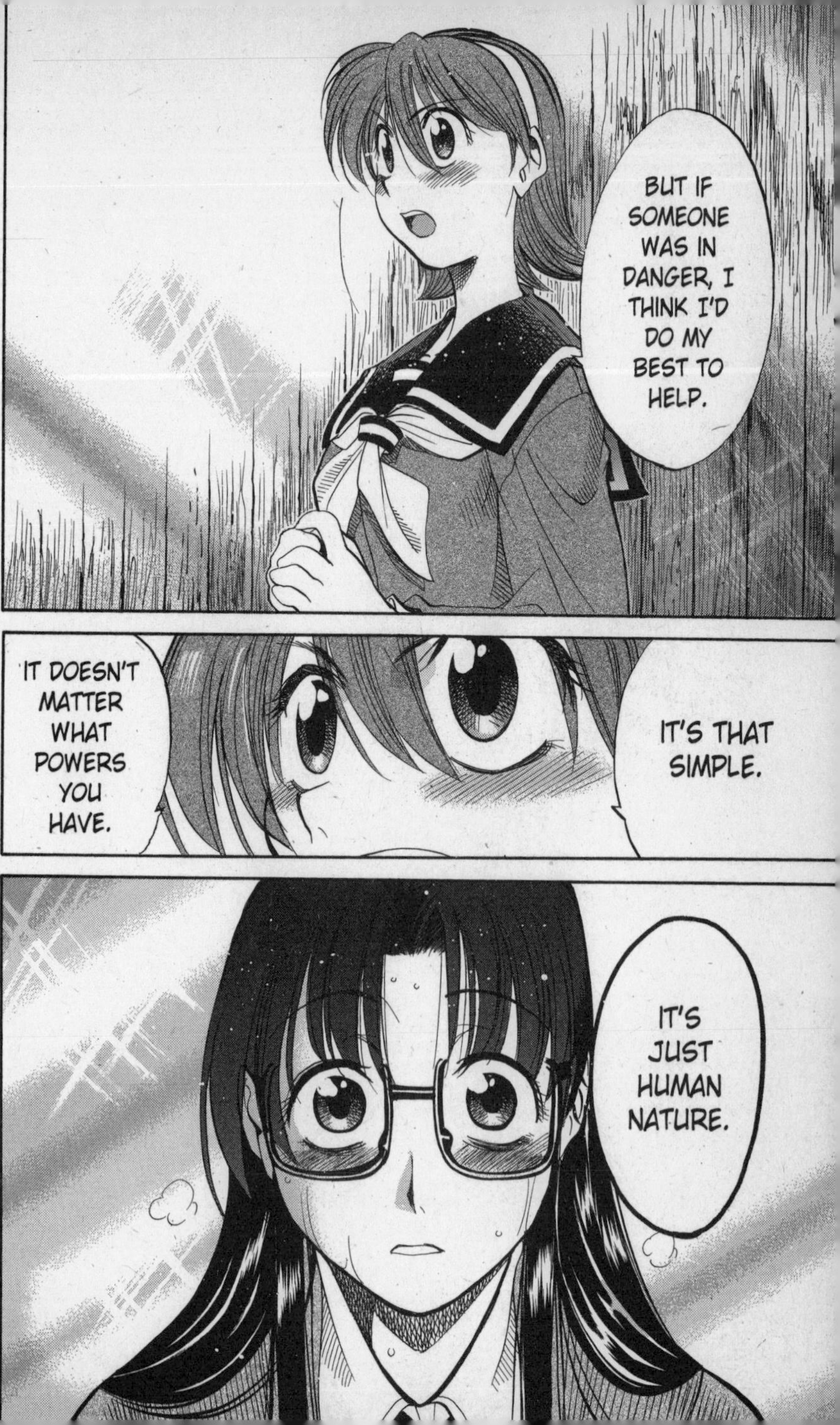
BUT IF SOMEONE WAS IN DANGER, I THINK I'D DO MY BEST TO HELP.
IT'S THAT SIMPLE.
IT DOESN'T MATTER WHAT POWERS YOU HAVE.
IT'S JUST HUMAN NATURE.

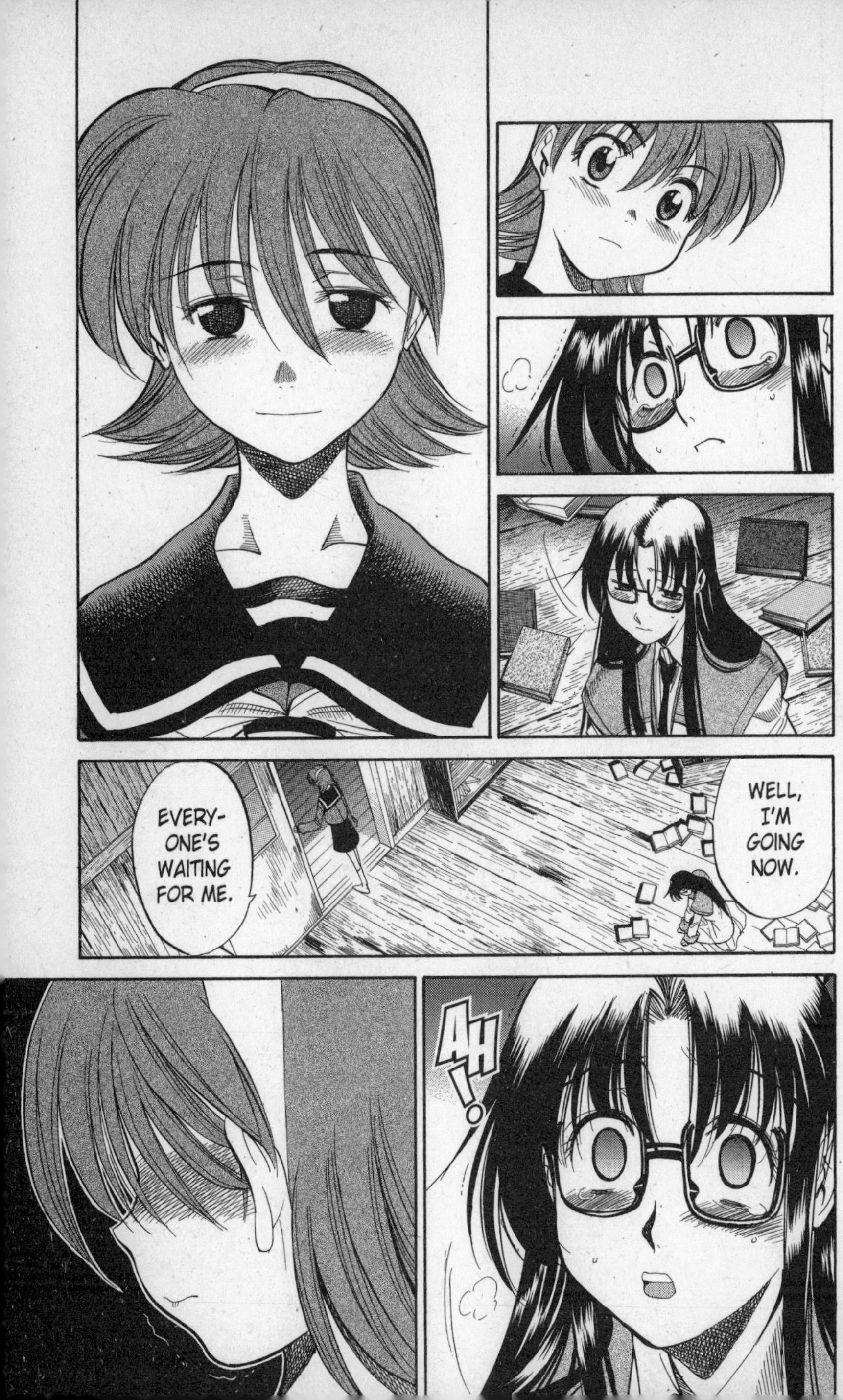
WELL, I'M GOING NOW.
EVERY-ONE'S WAITING FOR ME.
AH!

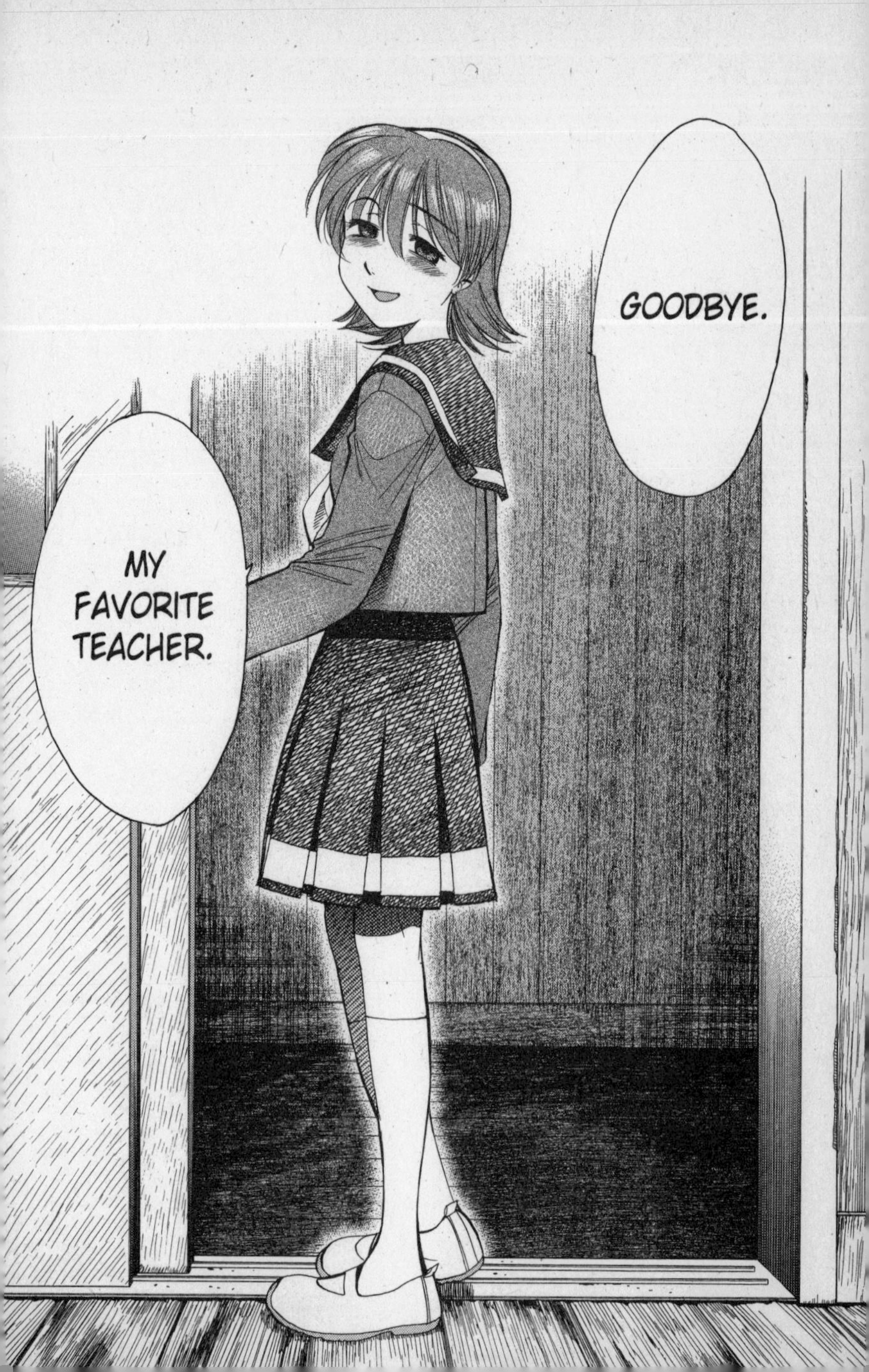
GOODBYE.
MY FAVORITE TEACHER.

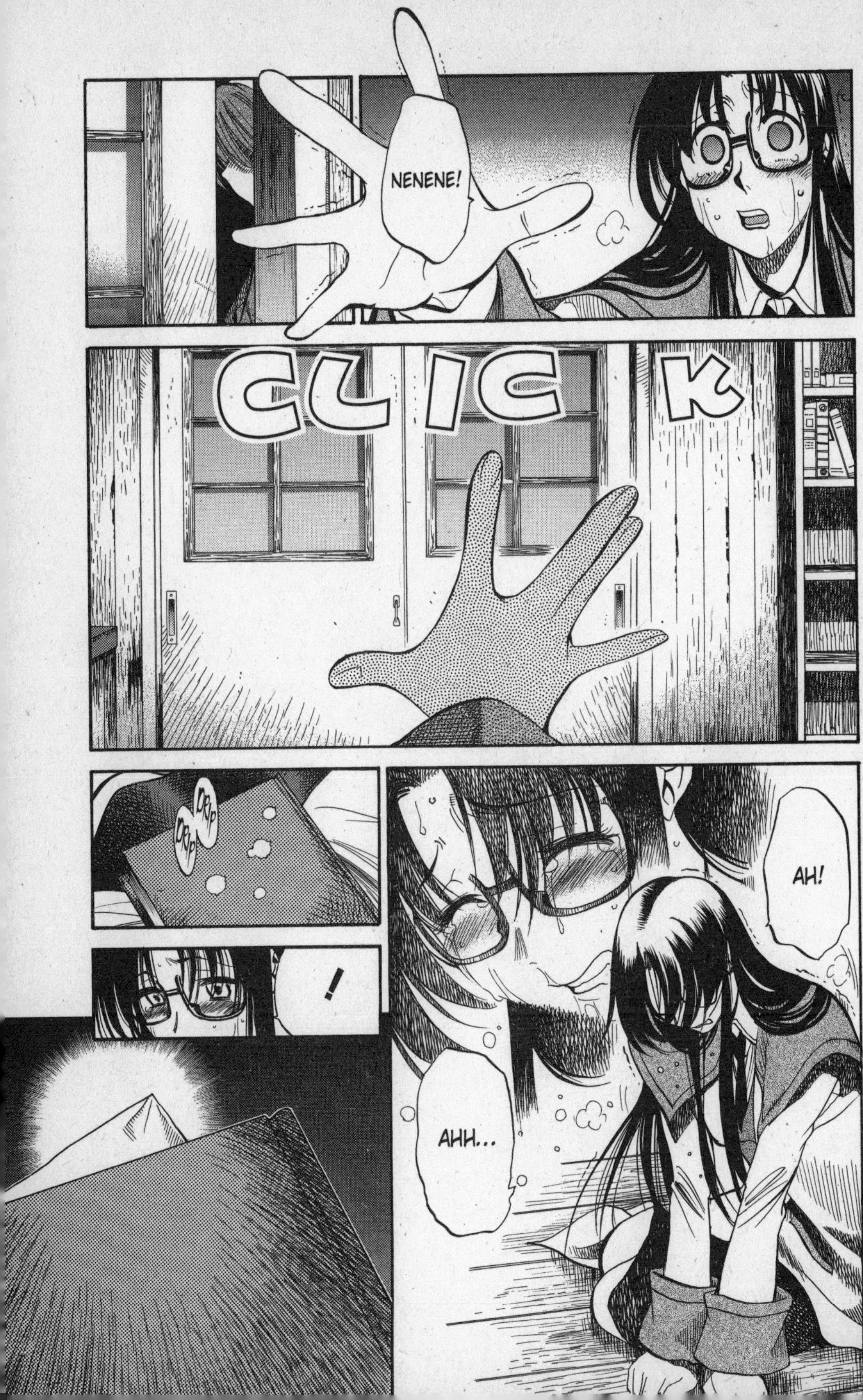
NENENE!
CLICK
AH!
AHH...
DRIP DRIP
!

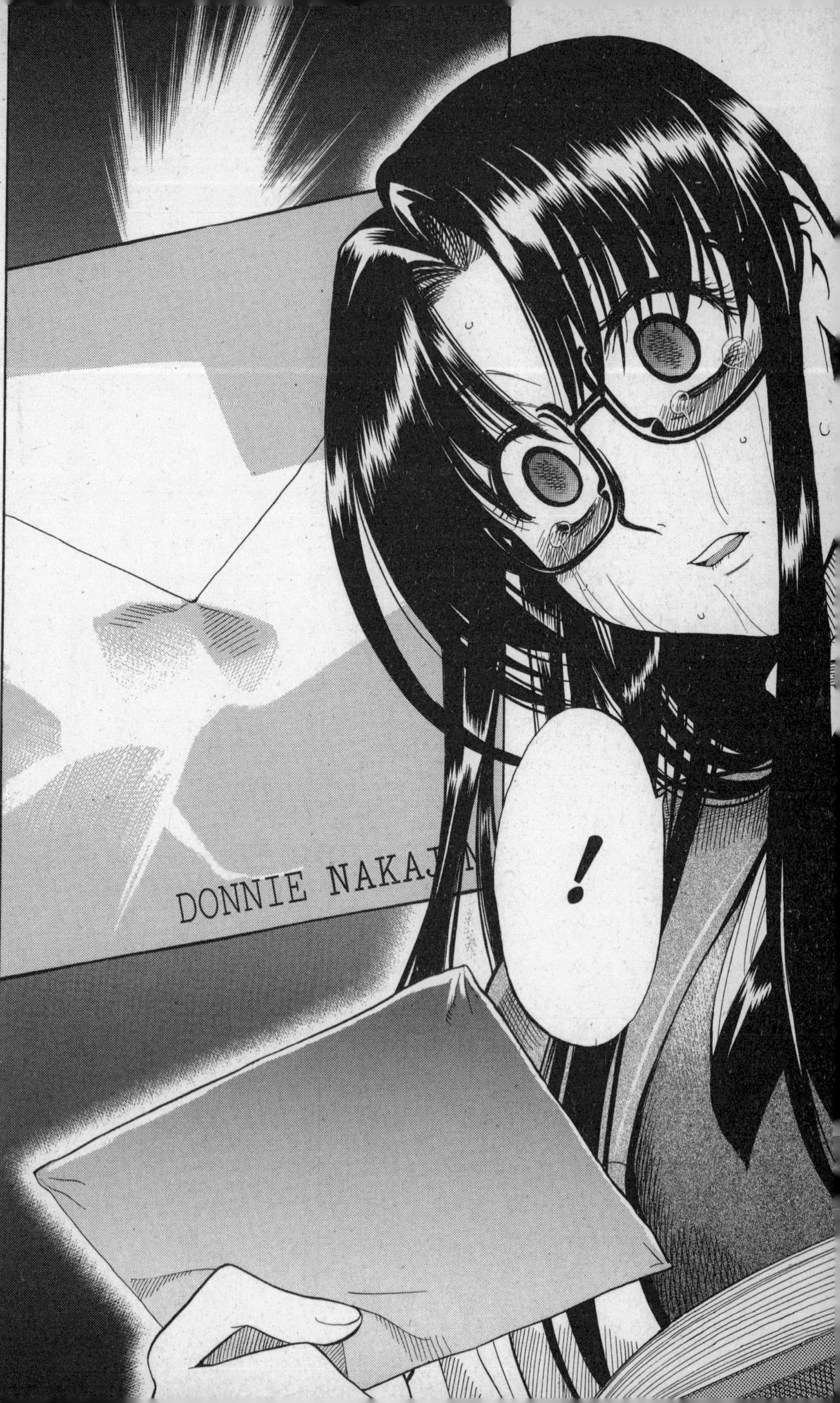
DONNIE NAKAJI
!

ULTRA ULTRA READER KING YOMIOH

SPECIAL STREAM-OF-CONSCIOUSNESS RAMBLINGS UPON THE RELEASE OF VOLUME THREE.

By Kurata Hideyuki

Whoa! *Back again already?* Hey, check out this awesome layout. This is Kurata Hideyuki, who, for the first time since this feature started, is feeling cold shivers, bafflement, excitement and tenderness like *half a Bufferin,* all at the same time. Just kidding! I'm as relaxed as when I handed in the original manuscript. *Where's my medicine?*

Wouldn't you know it? Just when the serial version of *R.O.D.* in *Ultra Jump* magazine comes to an end, the anime OVA[1] goes on sale and you know you gotta have it! This column is like *Terry Funk Jr.* coming back for one last bout[2] and is packed with more text than ever. Like Hasshoo, the Sneeze Genie.[3] Call him and he jumps out! This may be as far as you read when you find out the truth: I'm not revealing any new stuff. But there's still two and a half hours 'til deadline. I'm trying not to panic! I gotta just let the words spill out to fill up all this space. *Sachiyo, arrested!*[4]

This feels like a live report, though you probably won't be reading it 'til much later. It is now March 6, 2001, at 2:30 and 25 seconds, exactly! Hey, I gotta run out and get the *Detective Story* DVD box set that goes on sale today![5] I think I'll *somehow* be able to push myself to watch the whole series.

I thought, in a sort of '80s style way, *Hey yeah, it'd be cool to write like this.* Hey, beloved reader, you should've been writing this from the start. What were you thinking? You should apologize, do some serious soul-searching, and for your crime commit *suicide in heaven!* For which I say thank you, thank you. Now I'm really feeling the pressure.

Okay, everyone, slip off the dust jacket of this book and take a look at the cover.[6] Yep, there she is, the idol and heroine in glasses making her mark on manga history! *A cheap imitation!* If you leave this volume on the curb, some kid walking by is sure to shout, *"Arale-chan!"* and pick it up. Okay, all right, *all right!*

I am sure many of you noticed that each ***R.O.D.*** cover features some ***fun artwork***. Hey, did you notice?

This volume's drawing is a play on Akira Toriyama's ***Dr. Slump***, the second volume was Bronson and Hara Tetsuo's ***Fist of the North Star***, and the first volume was Akimoto Osamu's ***Kochikame!***[7] Yes, 33-year-old me and 28-year-old Yamaaki spent our childhoods poring over books, laughing, crying, and having our very beings rocked by the ***golden writers*** of ***Shonen Jump***. Frightening, isn't it? But we really wanted to do this since ***R.O.D.*** is bigger than pocketbook size. The new publication size begged for a new type of cover. When schoolboys pass the book around, the dust jacket will no doubt get lost and the pages of the book become ***completely ragged***, but the covers will survive! Among the several thousand copies piled up at used bookstores and book fairs, those covers will remain, ripped and covered with dirt like a ***warrior bent on fulfilling a mission***. That's right: we did it out of love for those great covers of the past! Please forgive our perverse adoration.

I also want to take this opportunity to express my gratitude to everyone who helped with these volumes, the managing editors, and Yamaaki and designer Jinguji.

Uh oh...still more space to fill. Oh, yeah, I recently saw the dubbing for the anime of Volume Three. My jaw hangs wider each time I see the ***mind-numbingly*** high-quality artwork, and this time it flopped open and wobbled around like it was going to swallow my body like a ***vanilla ice cream cone***. Those guys are merciless! Just when I was thinking I couldn't wait to see the final product, someone from Sony came up to me and said they wanted me to come upstairs for a secret meeting.

To be continued...

1. OVA: Original Video Adaptation, or direct-to-video anime.

2. American pro wrestler Terry Funk Jr. was very popular in Japan during the 1980s.

3. ***Hakushon Daimao*** (Giant Sneeze Demon) was a TV anime in the 1960s. In the American version, the sneeze demon was named Hasshoo.

4. This is a reference to Sachiyo Nomura, the much-disliked wife of baseball manager Katsuya Nomura. She was arrested in 2001 for tax evasion.

5. ***Tantei Monogatari*** (Detective Story) was a Japanese TV series that ran from 1979-80.

6. Hideyuki is referring to the Japanese edition of ***R.O.D.*** Volume Three, which included an illustration of Yomiko as Arale, the heroine of Akira Toriyama's manga ***Dr. Slump*** (now available from VIZ Media!).

7. All of these titles are well-loved manga from the 1980s. ***Fist of the North Star*** is an ultra-violent martial-arts series. ***Kochikame*** (a nickname for the full title, which translates as ***This Is the Police Station in Front of Kameari Park in Katsushika***) is a police comedy that has been running in ***Shonen Jump*** magazine since 1976.

Read or Die
Vol. 3

STORY BY **HIDEYUKI KURATA**
ART BY **SHUTARO YAMADA**

English Translation and Adaptation/Steve Ballati
Touch-up Art & Lettering/Mark McMurray
Cover & Graphic Design/Izumi Hirayama
Editors/Shaenon K. Garrity and Urian Brown

Managing Editor/Annette Roman
Editorial Director/Elizabeth Kawasaki
Editor in Chief/Alvin Lu
Sr. Director of Acquisitions/Rika Inouye
Sr. VP of Marketing/Liza Coppola
Exec. VP of Sales & Marketing/John Easum
Publisher/Hyoe Narita

Printed in the U.S.A.

Published by VIZ Media, LLC
P.O. Box 77010
San Francisco, CA 94107

10 9 8 7 6 5 4 3 2
First printing, July 2006
Second printing, September 2006

www.viz.com

PARENTAL ADVISORY
READ OR DIE is rated T+ for Older Teen
and is recommended for ages 16 and up.
This book contains violence.

store.viz.com

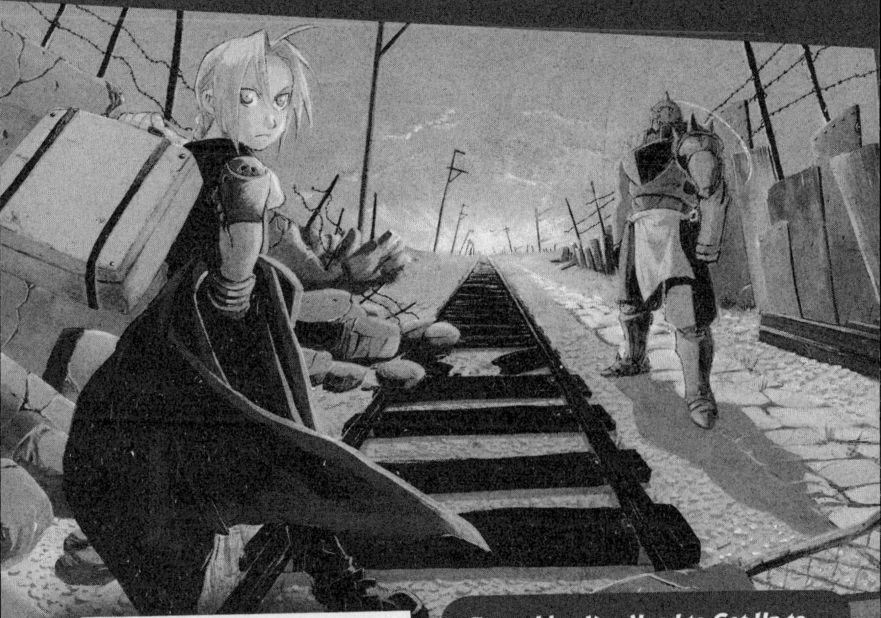

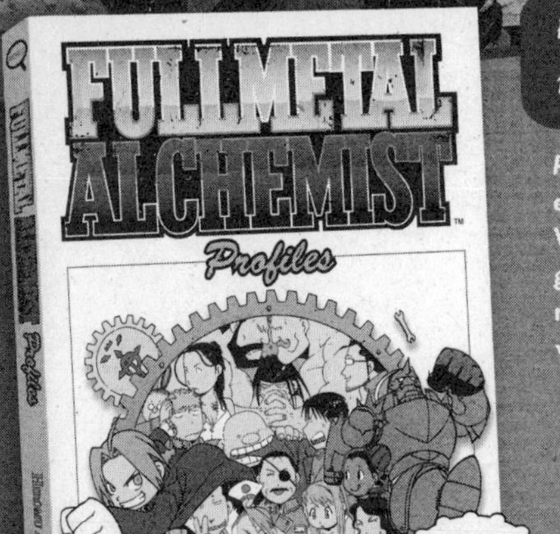
FULLMETAL ALCHEMIST
Profiles
Hiromu Arakawa
$14.99

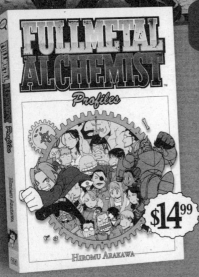

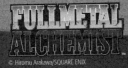

LOVE MANGA?
LET US KNOW WHAT YOU THINK!

HELP US MAKE THE MANGA
YOU LOVE BETTER!